THE
VON BÜLOW
AFFAIR

Books by William Wright
Ball
The Washington Game
Heiress
Rich Relations
Pavarotti: My Own Story
The Von Bülow Affair

THE
VON BÜLOW
AFFAIR

William Wright

Arlington Books
Clifford Street Mayfair
London

THE VON BÜLOW AFFAIR
First published 1983 by
Arlington Books (Publishers) Ltd
3 Clifford Street Mayfair
London W1

© *1983 William Wright*

Printed and bound by
The Pitman Press Ltd, Bath

British Library Cataloguing in Publication Data
Wright, William, 19 – –
The Von Bülow affair
1. Von Bülow, Martha Crawford
2. Von Bülow, Claus   3. Murder –
Rhode Island-Newport
I. Title
364.1'523'0924   HV6534.N54

ISBN 0 85140 626 2

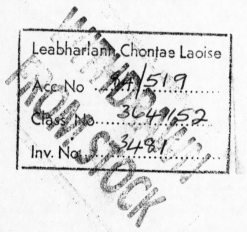

ACKNOWLEDGMENTS

The number of people who assisted me with their information are too numerous to thank individually, but I would like to single out for special thanks those many intimates of Sunny Von Bülow for their wisdom in acknowledging that a tragedy had stripped away her cherished privacy and that the most loyal action was to assure that the inevitable accounts were fair and accurate.

PREFACE

When I left Newport in March of 1982 and began to write up my four-hundred pages of notes from the Von Bülow trial, I was astonished at the broadened perspective given the story by the process of taking the six-week outpouring of testimony—and arranging chronologically the events leading up to and following the two murder attempts Von Bülow was accused of committing. The result was a full-blown drama, one that developed the inherent themes of treachery, betrayal, intrigue, and retribution.

All of the plot elements were present in the courtroom record. We had the Meek-Bring-Down-the-Mighty aspect of the maid's crucial role; the house of Atreus struggle of the children with the man who raised them; the vulnerability to those most trusted; the possibility that the rich enjoy a different brand of justice.

Testimony had also provided abundant background color: opulent settings, anachronistic privilege, impenetrable social bastions. I had no doubt the trial alone produced more than enough material for a gripping book.

As I began interviewing the principals in the case, however, I came to realize that the courtroom revelations represented only a portion of the story. Much of what occurred prior to the public airing of the scandal had not emerged. Also undisclosed were ramifications from witness-stand disclosures, ramifications that were devastating and, in some cases, permanent. I began to see the trial as an earth-mover dredging deep into a number of lives—leaving some aspects exposed but ravaging and burying others.

After spending considerable time with the major characters on both sides, I came to realize that I had been deeply affected by my year-long immersion in these intense feelings and outsized happenings. As a chronicler of the case I tried to keep my goal an evenhanded presentation of the story, one that would permit readers to make up their own minds. That is not to say I didn't form conclusions, but I struggled to put them off as long as possible.

I

ON a Saturday in March, 1982, in a small room behind the
courtroom of the Newport, Rhode Island, courthouse, Claus Von
Bülow called "gin" to John Sheehan, one of his lawyers, laid down
his cards, rose, and walked to the window. He glanced down to
the street below at the crowd that had grown each of the three
days since the jury had been out deciding if he had twice tried to
murder his wife, Sunny.

As the Newporters spotted Von Bülow at the window, they sent
up a cheer that evolved into a rhythmic "Free Claus, Free Claus!"
He smiled and waved, then returned to the table. His other lawyer,
Herald Fahringer, sat reading over the juror profiles they had
assembled at the start of the trial. The jury had been deliberating
for three days and the tension was beginning to show on the
defendant and his counsel. Prolonged deliberations were not a
good sign; uncertain jurors were being made certain, lessening the
chances of a hung jury.

In the nearby room that served as a similar retreat for the
prosecution team, Lieutenant John Reise, the Rhode Island state
trooper who conducted the investigation of Von Bülow, sat chatting with Susan McGuirl, the Deputy Attorney General of Rhode
Island. Both had been at the prosecution table throughout the
trial, backing up the prosecutor of the case, Stephen Famiglietti.
Reise was rehashing, perhaps for the fifth time, the significance of
the only development since the jury was sent out: their request for

a reading of portions of the testimony of Sunny's maid, Maria Schrallhammer.

"She was one of our best witnesses," Reise said. "If you believe her story, how could you think that guy was innocent? If you don't believe it, why would you want to hear it a second time?"

Famiglietti, who had just come in, threw his briefcase on the table and said, "They wanted her recipe for eggnog."

In his chambers behind the bench, Judge Thomas H. Needham sat mulling over a note he was planning to send into the jury, a water-testing ploy to learn if they were making progress, needed help, or were deadlocked. His wife, Ursula, who had come to the courthouse every day since the jury went out, sat reading near his desk. A sheriff entered to discuss arrangements for convoying the jury from the courthouse after the verdict.

In a far corner of the courthouse the jurors sat around a large table, two at each end and four down each side, thrashing over the six weeks of testimony. While they had not yet taken a formal vote, they knew how each felt. At the moment, four of them were not convinced that the prosecution's case removed all reasonable doubt of Von Bülow's guilt.

No one pressured the hold-outs. An unspoken strategy had sprung up among the eight who were convinced of his guilt; they feared that any attempt to lean on the others might drive them into a vote for acquittal. One of the four undecided jurors, a woman, spoke of her sleepless struggle with the evidence the previous night. With mounting emotion she said that she could no longer doubt his guilt. The other eleven jurors knew what the woman was suffering. Her announcement made, she suddenly blurted out, "How could he do that to his own daughter's mother?" and she burst into tears. Two of the other jurors cried as well.

Outside on the steps of the Colony House, the eighteenth-century statehouse that had been converted into a press headquarters, a reporter asked a woman who was wearing a T-shirt on which Von Bülow's photo was captioned with the one word Innocent, what made her so sure. She replied cheerfully, "He has the most beautiful eyes!" A man carrying a Free Claus placard said, "It's him against all of them; he's the underdog."

Inside the press headquarters, 140 media people—print and television journalists and cameramen—stepped around the snarl of cables, phone wires, and work tables, watched basketball on the TV monitors, typed filler stories on the Free Claus groundswell, and even interviewed each other to fill home office demands for something, anything, on the Von Bülow trial. From her table at the far end of the vast room, New York *Daily News* reporter Theo Wilson, who had covered every major American trial of the past quarter century, from Dr. Sam Shepherd to Jack Ruby to Patty Hearst to Mrs. Harris, looked around the room and told a kibitzer that she had never seen a trial receive so much press coverage.

Copies of the day's *New York Post* and *Daily News* strewn around the press tables carried stories of a Missouri woman who was indicted for murdering her seventh husband with insulin injection. This jolted the many who had been drawn to the Newport case by the all but unheard of method of murder Von Bülow was alleged to have attempted.

At the *Providence Journal* table, the four reporters who had worked on the trial since its beginning sat playing a variation of Scrabble they had invented and named Von Scrabble: every word formed had to relate to the case. Someone had laid down the word "Valium"; the next player was persuading the others that the word "money" he was hanging from the "m" of "Valium" was not too general and was certainly central to this case.

At one of the network tables circled around the courtroom monitor, CBS's Liz Trotta chatted with Richard Kuh, the lawyer hired by the victim's family to start the investigation of Von Bülow. When the CBS phone rang, Kuh slipped away and headed up Touro Street to visit the 1759 Touro Synagogue, the oldest synagogue in America.

Like many of those in town for the trial, he had been meaning to visit the lovely old building for two months but had been unable to move the short distance, not a hundred yards from the courthouse, into an area unrelated to Claus Von Bülow.

In bars along Thames Street and out on the recently fashioned tourist wharves, the mood was pro-Claus. The opinions were based on the he's-too-smart-to-have-bungled-so-badly defense, with overtones of the lone-individual-persecuted-by-powerful-interests theme. Occasionally someone would essay a more specific rationale, like a bartender at the White Horse Tavern who said, "It all boils down to greed; the kids want the money and he wants the money," oblivious to the trust officer's testimony two weeks earlier, which removed any financial motive on the part of the stepchildren.

Up on Bellevue Avenue one of the summer colony's reigning hostesses entertained eight for lunch in her epic mansion; from the first sip of sherry to the last demitasse, nothing was discussed but the Von Bülow affair. And the mood here was anti-Von Bülow to a near lynch-party degree. When someone said that all of Newport was convinced he was guilty, a young woman only recently returned from an unsuccessful European marriage said, "What about the Pells and the Winslows? I understand they think Claus is innocent."

"That's right," snapped the hostess, "they think so, as do about three others, but the other two hundred of us *know* he's guilty!"

Still farther down Bellevue Avenue sat Clarendon Court, the mansion whose rare majesty had made it very much a character in the Von Bülow drama. Little about the shuttered and gloomy house suggested its having been the setting, eighteen months earlier, of one of the most stunning parties in Newport's party-rich history; a lawn fête in which a hundred of Newport's most entrenched summer colonists, dressed by request all in white, strolled the magnificent lawn, sipping champagne, listening to an orchestra play Dixieland and musical comedy, and watching three croquet matches that had been set up more as tableaux than sport, while a fog rolled off the sea and gently brushed the refined panorama.

The house is all but concealed from the avenue by a high stone wall; it is one of the few mansions on the sea cliff completely invisible from the public Cliff Walk (which has at its entrance a bronze plaque expressing appreciation for the restoration efforts of Claus Von Bülow). The neighboring Astors and Vanderbilts felt no need for such obsessive and expensive privacy, which seems to have been created in anticipation of the kind of public scrutiny now focused on this house.

Down Bellevue Avenue a few hundred yards, Prince Alexander von Auersperg headed his blue Fiat Spider convertible though the gates of the exquisitely manicured estate of his grandmother, Annie Laurie Aitken, and drove the fifty minutes it takes to reach his apartment over a clothing store on the edge of the Brown

University campus in Providence where he was an undergraduate.

He was only in the apartment a few minutes when the phone rang. It was his sister Ala calling from Bermuda, where she had flown with her husband to shed a bad cold. No word yet, Alexander told her; he would phone as soon as he heard. Ala asked if anyone knew where she was; she was concerned that reporters could make her flying off to Bermuda sound extravagant and callous.

In Manhattan, the victim's personal maid, Maria Schrallhammer, whose suspicions initiated the effort against Von Bülow, sat writing a letter in Ala's East 77th Street apartment, where she was now employed—a letter to a friend in Germany whom she hoped to visit when the trial was over. Maria wrote of her role in bringing the authorities down on the man she was convinced had twice tried to murder her mistress.

A few blocks north on Fifth Avenue, across from the Metropolitan Museum, Annie Laurie Aitken, a handsome woman in her eighties, sat chatting with a friend in her vast apartment, which a prominent decorator had called "the most beautiful in the city." Housebound because of bad health, she had not testified at the trial or attended it—indeed, her friends wondered if she would live through it. Instead she followed the courtroom action on videotapes Richard Kuh obtained for her.

She had been talking to her visitor about her only child. "You know," she said, "I think Claus has tried putting all his failings on Sunny. He claims she was bored and depressed. The truth is she had many enthusiasms—her children, her homes, reading, travel, flowers, exercise. Claus wasn't interested in anything, except maybe parties. He never . . ." She stopped herself. "But I don't have to waste your time telling you what I think of him. You can imagine." She looked out the window at the gray sky, then said, "This never should have happened to Sunny."

Across Manhattan in the garbage-strewn streets of upper Broadway, Sunny Crawford Von Bülow, the subject of the Newport spectacular that had all but upstaged her, lay comatose in her private room on the tenth floor of the soot-darkened Harkness Pavilion, part of the Columbia Presbyterian medical complex. Curled in the fetal position, her skin was waxy and livid, the once blond hair now completely gray.

The heiress of a $75 million fortune made small, sucking noises and restlessly shifted her body while one leg twitched constantly. Despite the movement, a nurse sitting in the room rose to turn the patient as she did every two hours to prevent the formation of pressure sores. Later that day the nurse would give her a sponge bath, paying particular attention to the areas around the tube implanted in the throat, as well as the waste-removing catheter and the feeding tube in the mouth; all are prone to infection.

As the nurse rearranged the bedding and smoothed back Mrs. Von Bülow's hair, the patient's eyes opened suddenly and rotated wildly in their sockets, creating the impression she was reacting to a visual simulus. This was unlikely; doctors believed her to be blind. On a table next to her bed sat a vase of roses—Morris Gurley, Mrs. Von Bülow's bank officer, who arranged for daily flowers, had left instructions that they be highly scented, in case she had retained the sense of smell.

Next to the flowers three framed photographs faced the bed. One was of Sunny Von Bülow's son and daughter by her first marriage, Alexander and Ala von Auersperg; the second was of Claus Von Bülow and their daughter Cosima. The third picture was of Mrs. Von Bülow's favorite yellow labrador, Pan.

Outside the door to the room a guard sat reading a newspaper. Since a reporter slipped into the room and wrote about it two months earlier, the family had paid for round-the-clock guards in addition to full-time private nurses and daily visits from the family doctor. The cost for the room and all this attention was over a half million dollars a year.

Doctors believe Mrs. Von Bülow will never emerge from her condition. There is no reason to think she can smell the flowers or see the photograph of her husband or know that he is being prosecuted for attempting to murder her. Neither will she know that in three more days the twelve jurors will find him guilty of putting her into this irreversible state—the passage from life to death which for most people is a few moments, but for Sunny had already lasted two years and could last many more.

II

FOR a time the Von Bülow affair appeared to be a death struggle between two European factions—one Danish, the other Austrian —for an American fortune. Little was known about the fortune except that it was worth struggling over. Newspapers reported that Sunny was the only child of a utilities magnate named George Crawford, who spent most of his adult life around Pittsburgh. Crawford, it turns out, was very good at finding natural gas and getting it into people's homes.

He was born in 1861 in Emlenton, Pennsylvania, where he went to public school, then took a business course at the Eastman Business College in Poughkeepsie, New York. At the age of nineteen he went to work in the western Pennsylvania gas fields. For a time he joined his father and brother in an oil-hardware business, and subsequently, with his sister's husband, formed a company, Crawford and Treat, which was to thrive for years as a highly successful oil and gas operation.

Basically, the vast wealth that Crawford accumulated over his lifetime came from the ground. He was adept at every phase of the burgeoning gas business—from exploration and the most elementary operations to the future corporate complexities of the amalgamating independents.

Each time Crawford's firm merged with a rival firm he would emerge as the new company's board chairman and principal officer. He became head of the final result of the corporate mating, the Columbia Gas and Electric Company, which covered much of the Midwest and, at the time of Crawford's death in 1935, was valued at $700,000,000.

In addition to the corporation-building that was central to his life, Crawford also speculated with success in oil and gas exploration—first in Illinois, moving west to the Oklahoma Territory, then on to Texas, where in 1909 he joined a group to form the Lone Star Gas Company, for which he served as board chairman until his death. He was also involved in pioneer oil operations in Mexico and Colombia.

Crawford did not marry until he was sixty-six years old. His choice was an extremely pretty, vivacious twenty-eight-year-old, Annie Laurie Warmack, whose father, Robert Warmack, had been a wealthy St. Louis shoe manufacturer. Annie Laurie's mother, a widow of great style and personality, had no intention of hiding her beautiful daughter in suburban St. Louis and took her, Henry James style, to Europe and places of fashion in America.

On these travels, Annie Laurie noticed that the pleasant bachelor from Pittsburgh was turning up with remarkable frequency at places she and her mother were visiting. When the Warmack women, in order to visit Cairo, left a Mediterranean cruise Crawford happened to be on, he appeared there too. Annie Laurie found him attentive and considerate in a way her contemporary suitors were not, but was nonetheless stunned when he asked her to marry him.

She had not thought of him that way. He asked her to try thinking of him that way. She agreed to that effort. He followed her to Paris and inquired if she had reached a decision. She replied that her test of marriage was not if you thought you could get along with someone, but if you felt you couldn't get along *without* them. As he had never been away from her for an instant since making his suggestion, she had had no opportunity to make this test.

He returned to the States alone, but was waiting on the dock for her when she arrived. The experiment worked and they were married at White Sulphur Springs in 1927. They settled in Pittsburgh but kept a cottage at White Sulphur Springs and were visiting there four years later when Annie Laurie was 7½ months pregnant with Sunny. Signals indicated that the baby might not wait the full nine months, so Crawford, then seventy-one, rushed his wife onto a train to have delivery under the care of New York doctors.

They didn't make it. Their only daughter, whom they named Martha and who would later be nicknamed Sunny, was born in a Pullman car in Manassas, Virginia, with a porter acting as midwife. For years a family friend called the little girl "Choochoo," which she didn't like at all.

Annie Laurie and her mother remained close, but with the death of Mr. Warmack in the early thirties, Mrs. Warmack moved to New York City, where she had friends and where her daughter and son-in-law came almost monthly on business trips.

When George Crawford died in 1935, he left Annie Laurie an enormous fortune along with feelings of guilt that, by her marrying a much older man, she had left her four-year-old daughter fatherless. Annie Laurie resolved to make it up to Sunny as best she could, which may explain a protectiveness that went beyond the normal maternal concern.

Having no real ties to Pittsburgh, Annie Laurie took her infant daughter and moved east, buying an impressive estate, Tamerlane, in Greenwich, Connecticut. Mother, child, and grandmother spent summers together in Connecticut, then moved into Mrs. Warmack's apartment at 990 Fifth Avenue for winters so that Sunny could attend the Chapin School.

The two older women had strong personalities as well as brains, looks, and vast wealth. They were at once perfectionists and women with warm, loving natures—a personality mix that resulted in a concentration of energies on the pretty blond child. They lavished attention on her, exacting the same flawless deportment that a court chamberlain would demand from an heir apparent.

A contemporary of Sunny's who also lived at 990 Fifth Avenue can recall descending in the elevator in old clothes on her way to play in Central Park and encountering an eight-year-old Sunny immaculately dressed with white gloves and a handbag, each blond hair in place. Sunny was pleasant and friendly as always, but seemed of another species as she stepped into the waiting Rolls-Royce.

Later on, a Chapin classmate would tell a similar story of being in Paris in 1952, returning hot and steamy from a Versailles expedition and spotting Sunny on a corner of the Faubourg St. Honoré. While other young Americans in Bermuda shorts or jeans swarmed the intersection, Sunny in a couturier white-linen dress and hat looked stunning but so much in contrast with the scene that the friend avoided greeting her.

One summer Annie Laurie took Sunny on an exhaustive tour of Italy, missing very few towns of any historic importance. Afterwards she asked Sunny what part she had liked best, expecting her to name Rome or Venice.

"Assisi," Sunny replied to her mother's surprise.

"Why Assisi?" Annie Laurie asked, remembering only having stood for two fruitless hours watching a statue of the Virgin, who was said to smile from time to time.

"It had such an air of holiness about it," Sunny replied.

The shyness that would always afflict Sunny appeared early. A Chapin classmate, recalling Sunny, said, "She was absolutely gorgeous, but she didn't have a brain in her head." Those who knew her well, including Claus Von Bülow, insist this was untrue. But the strong negative recollection of the classmate suggests that Sunny suffered an emotional stunting that made her appear, to casual acquaintances, less than bright.

Even as a child, she seemed distracted, as though her mind were somewhere else. When she developed into a beautiful young woman, this quality took on for some a kind of unearthliness; people felt that the lovely apparition was hearing different music from that heard by ordinary mortals. There was a serious reflective side to her which young people around her, who didn't get to know her, found inappropriate and heavy. In social situations with large numbers of strangers, Sunny's nervous torment would sometimes reveal itself by her breaking out with red blotches on her neck.

Like many others blessed with looks, Sunny did not feel as enthusiastic about hers as other people did. Exasperated at this, a close girlfriend berated her: "Don't you know how beautiful you are, what an impression you make on people?"

Sunny frowned and said, "I know that when I get dressed up I can look pretty good."

From a young age Sunny, aware of how much better off she was than most of her friends, was extremely generous. She deliberately bought more clothes than she wanted in order to have items to give to friends whose wardrobes needed bolstering. For one friend of a different size, Sunny went so far as to buy clothes too big for her but right for her friend. Knowing the girl would accept a hand-me-down but not a gift, Sunny went through the pretense of "It no longer fits" or "I'm tired of it." The ploy was not only to avoid the friend's embarassment, but Sunny's at having so much money.

Annie Laurie and Mrs. Warmack carefully screened Sunny's friends and rarely let her spend a night away from home. The family chauffeur—a handsome, middle-aged Italian named Jimmy—was unofficial bodyguard to Sunny, his protective duties as important as his transportational ones. A much-loved governess, Nanna, stayed with Sunny until she married.

If all this surveillance from Sunny's mother and grandmother resulted in a fear of people and a bent for introspection, it seems a sad irony that the love-inspired attention of these two women should rob Sunny of the spontaneity and *joi de vivre* they both possessed in generous amounts.

It was not as though the older women forbade Sunny any good times. There were parties at 990 Fifth Avenue, Monday nights at the Metropolitan Opera—when Annie Laurie would turn her box over to Sunny and her friends—and summer swimming parties in Connecticut. But the older women, who loved the company of young people, were usually present at these events.

Despite her shyness, Sunny had a number of good friends. Ruth Dunbar, a Swift meat-packing heiress, who also lived at 990 Fifth Avenue, often played with Sunny in Central Park under the vigilance of Nanna and remained a lifelong friend. When Sunny left Chapin to finish her secondary education at St. Timothy's, a girl's boarding school in Maryland, she formed two friendships that would also endure: with Isabel Hinkley and Helen Wallace.

In Greenwich, Sunny's closest friend was Peggy Bedford, who threatened to be as rich from oil as Sunny would be from gas. Other natural resources the girls shared were blond good looks and amiable natures, although Peggy's was far more gregarious than Sunny's.

Of all the rich girls who became known to East Coast society in the early 1950s, Sunny and Peggy were generally acknowledged to be the most blessed. While their friends would have five evening dresses to get them through a party season, Sunny and Peggy would have thirty-five; while the other girls would take taxis to shop at Bergdorf's or lunch at Longchamps, Peggy and Sunny would be taken on their rounds by chauffeur-driven Rolls-Royces. As if all this wasn't enough to provoke envy, they were both turning out to be sensationally good-looking.

The similarity of their youth intensifies the irony of their fates. After marrying Tommy Bancroft, an heir to the banking Wood-wards, Peggy, like Sunny, indulged a taste for European aristo-crats by marrying first Prince Charles d'Arenberg and then the Duc d'Uzès. She went through most of her money making a name for herself as a hostess and was killed in an automobile accident returning from a party near her home in France in 1966.

Sunny's debut was a dinner dance held in 1949 at Tamerlane, her mother's Georgian manor filled with "F.F.F."—the ironic nickname Sunny and her friends had for "Fine French Furni-ture." For the party, the curtains throughout the ground floor had been replaced by ice-blue satin ones that matched the lining of the outdoor tents.

Passing through the house, guests emerged onto a terrace, now canopied in blue, where cocktails were served. A flight of some twenty steps led down to the principal marquee, where Lester Lanin's orchestra maintained the upbeat mood and where dinner tables awaited the guests. Another thirty steps led down to the swimming pool, part of which was also tented, and to the pool-house with its display of African game. Although Annie Laurie was a crack shot, (in 1959 she would take second place at the world championships at Seville) she limited her quarry to pigeons.

From the upper terrace, one could look down through the three tiers and through floodlit trees to the illuminated swimming pool. Even for that postwar time of lavish entertaining, the party was a landmark.

Sunny wore a strapless Dior ball gown with yards of white tulle and the two small Louis Seize diamond bows that she invariably wore for formal occasions—sometimes on her dress, sometimes in her hair, sometimes on a choker around her neck. With her tanned beauty, her blond hair, her white ball gown, her diamond ornaments, and in the opulent make-believe setting, she could have served as a symbol for the way the rest of humanity regarded Americans in those postwar years—healthy, good-looking, untouched by the world, and absurdly rich.

Sunny's debutante season had a number of legendary parties and she was invited to them all. For the parties on Long Island's North Shore, Sunny would stay in Manhattan. A frequent escort of those years, Alan Murphy, who remained a lifelong friend, remembers being picked up in the Rolls-Royce by Jimmy, who would return to collect Sunny on Fifth Avenue.

"I once sneaked in a bottle of champagne," Murphy says. "Sunny and I sat there, me in black tie, Sunny in a ball gown, our feet propped on the jump seat, sipping champagne as we headed over the Triboro Bridge in the early evening on our way to some incredible party."

Murphy also recalls Annie Laurie's protectiveness toward Sunny. Picking Sunny up for her first trip to a nightclub, Alan was greeted by Mrs. Crawford, who said she had seen his picture in the paper with a group at the Stork Club.

"If a photographer should ask if he can photograph you and Sunny, Alan, the answer is no."

According to her mother, it was Sunny's decision not to go to college. With this decision behind them, Annie Laurie was surprised when Sunny came to her to boast of high grades on the College Board exams.

"But I thought you weren't going to college?"

"I'm not," Sunny said. "I just wanted to show you I could if I wanted to."

Lacking a higher education when almost all her friends had one did not help Sunny's fragile self-esteem. The complex she later had about her truncated education launched her into reading programs in such academic preserves as anthropology and epistemology. Her reading habit—often a book a day—soon put her ahead of many matriculated friends. For Sunny, however, college graduates would always be privy to intellectual mysteries beyond her reach.

If she denied herself college courses, she allowed herself college weekends, with Princeton a frequent destination. Friends remember Sunny smartly turned out in a designer suit with a hat and handbag, arriving in the chauffeur-driven Rolls. She would show up in town the day of a football game, stay for the parties, then return to New York with Jimmy the same night. While the 1950s were far dressier than the next two decades, Sunny's get-up seemed excessively formal to her contemporaries. ("It all made her seem so much *older!*") While many of the other girls came from families with chauffeurs, none went off to college weekends with one.

Friends from this period, hinting at amorous escapades, refuse to elaborate, but leave a definite impression that Sunny was no prude, and that Annie Laurie's surveillance was not completely foolproof.

Her indecision about what to do with her life is apparent in her enrolling herself in a secretarial school, Miss Moon's Classes. The attempt at self-sufficiency was not a success; she hated the school and dropped out after only a few weeks.

She took a job with a prominent decorating firm and proved to have considerable talent for the work, but the lure of a few months in Europe and of sleeping till noon proved too strong for a long-range dedication.

Sunny's first serious romance was with a bearlike translator at the U.N. from a noble Russian family. Georgi Wasilichicoff was deemed inappropriate for Sunny by her two overseers. While they permitted Sunny to see Georgi occasionally, it was not nearly as often as Sunny wanted, so she would have her friend Alan take her to a party, then drop her somewhere else to meet Georgi.

When the romance with Wasilichicoff looked serious, Annie Laurie spirited Sunny off to Europe. Accompanying them was Russell Aitken, a longtime beau of Annie Laurie's, whom she would soon marry. The group landed at the Schloss Mittersell, a resort that specialized in shooting; both Russell and Annie Laurie were gun enthusiasts and crack shots.

Since there has never been an establishment quite like the Schloss Mittersell and it became the incubator in which Sunny's Austrian life developed, it requires a few words of description.

The castle was built in the Alps in the fifteenth century as a summer palace for the bishops of Salzburg. In the 1930s it had been converted, under the direction of a dashing young Austrian, the Baron Hubert von Pantz, into a resort for paying guests. Because of von Pantz's aristocratic connections and the glamorous friends he made during an affair with Coco Chanel, the Schloss Mittersell became to resorts what Elsa Maxwell was to hostessing—a mixer of titles, celebrities, and U.S. millionaires. In the short period of its operation before World War II, Mittersell attracted such international trend-setters as Lady Mendl and Cole Porter, the Duke of Sutherland, and Princess (later Queen) Juliana of the Netherlands, who spent her honeymoon with Prince Bernard at Mittersell with old Queen Wilhelmina along as chaperon.

World War II intruded and so, after only eight months of operation, Mittersell closed down, but not before the Nazis had heard of it and decided what was good enough for Cole Porter and Lady Mendl was good enough for Himmler. They moved in and started "negotiating" with von Pantz for the takeover of his club. Hubert pleaded that, in order to make it all proper, he needed some documents that were with his directors in Vienna. Pushovers for proper forms, the Nazis waved him off only to hear that he had gone not to Vienna but to Paris, then on to America.

After the war, Hubert returned to see what was left of his Schloss. All in all, the Germans had left the place in better shape than they had found it, improving the water supply that had proved a headache to Queen Wilhelmina and the others.

Visiting von Pantz in those first days after the war was an old friend from the nearby village of Kitzbühel, Prince Alexander Hohenlohe and his American wife, a dynamic southerner who would become a close friend of Sunny's. As Honeychile Wilder, she had had a career in show business which reached its peak when she traded jokes with Bob Hope in his earliest radio days. Now, as Princess Honeychile Hohenlohe, she brought to international society blond good looks, energy to burn, brains—and a Georgia accent to conceal them.

Hubert von Pantz amused his guests by showing them the Schloss Mittersell's prewar membership list. Honey Hohenlohe, seeing that the illustrious names had if anything grown more illustrious, suggested they reopen the club with her in charge. The men were unenthusiastic; no one had money for that kind of thing anymore. Americans did, Honey persisted. In this way, the dynamic of the club took shape: European bluebloods to lend the tone that would attract the big-money Americans.

The formula succeeded brilliantly. Before you could say Baby Pignatari, Honeychile was booking rooms for the Duke and Duchess of Windsor, princelings of the subgenuses von Furstenberg and Lobkowitz, various legatees of William Randolph Hearst, Anheuser Busch, Henry Ford, and the like. Jessie Donahue came, as did Grace Moore. Honey got Bob Hope to bring his pal Bing Crosby.

Apart from the guest list, the principal lure of Mittersell was shooting—for deer and chamois high up on the alpine slopes. But there was also tennis and excellent trout fishing. The biggest sport of Mittersell, matchmaking, developed after Hubert went off to Paris and returned with a rich American wife, a divorcee named Terry McConnell, who had a seventeen-year-old son attending the ultra-exclusive Swiss boarding school Le Rosay.

When summer rolled around, the McConnell boy would bring his Rosay chums to Mittersell. Hubert von Pantz, tired of feeding and housing these healthy young men, put them to work around the club as shooting guides and sports instructors. These were not just ordinary lollabouts, but first-quality bluebloods—dukes' sons, maharajahs' sons, Hapsburg offshoots. When the von Pantzes or Honeychile could say to a guest, "This is your tennis instructor, Prince Kumar of Barota," it had an electrifying effect on the wary mothers of heiresses, who normally regarded a sleek young tennis pro as Enemy Number One.

One of the most beautiful of the aristocratic functionaries was Prince Alfie von Auersperg, a first cousin of Prince Hohenlohe. Alfie was nineteen, blond, and with good looks that almost parodied the Prince Charming ideal. He was also an avid sportsman, ladies' man, and man's man. Everyone liked him.

Like the Hohenlohes, Alfie's branch of the ancient von Auersperg clan had lost their money after World War II when their estates fell into the Communist's hands. But the Communists couldn't confiscate Alfie's genetic heritage. His mother was Countess Larisch, one of a famous trio of beautiful sisters whose family owned most of the Czechoslovakian coal mines. She had first married Prince Orsini-Rosenberg, by whom she had a number of children, then married Prince von Auersperg and gave birth to

Alfie and his sister Hetty. Countess Larisch also lost a substantial inheritance to the Communists.

Alfie and Hetty, who still had close relatives of vast wealth, themselves had nothing. They were given enough money by their more fortunate kin to keep toeholds in the world they were born to. For Alfie and a number of other moneyless bluebloods, the Schloss Mittersell was custom-made: the club may have done much to save some esoteric bloodlines from extinction.

The young men were given not only playgrounds to indulge in the fresh-air pursuits that were so much a part of their heritage, but an audience of rich and impressionable young women to whom they could show off their athleticism for a more long-range evolutionary purpose.

Into this heiress trap walked Sunny Crawford. The presence of her mother did not prevent the inevitable from happening: at a dance in the castle's ballroom the day they arrived, Sunny met Alfie; the two fell instantly and resolutely in love. Everyone could see what had happened; those most concerned—the von Pantzes the Hohenlohes, and most particularly Sunny's mother and grandmother—were distressed about it. The reason for their disapproval was simple: Alfie von Auersperg was too young—twenty to Sunny's twenty-three—and too good-looking.

Press accounts of this liaison, a quarter of a century later, tried to fit Annie Laurie into the prince-hunting American mom category of European traveler. On the contrary, this American mother was dead set against Prince Alfie as a son-in-law, even though she knew his title to be Grade A and she liked him personally.

Annie Laurie was a staunch advocate of American men as husbands, believing that, above all alternatives, they were the most patient and all-suffering. She says her hope for Sunny was "the boy next door," which in her neighborhood meant a clean-edged Princeton or Yale type with a niche on Wall Street. In addition, Annie Laurie was very much against her daughter living so far from her and so "close by the Iron Curtain."

People in those circles had, by the 1950s, considerable reason to be pessimistic about marriages between American heiresses and titled paupers. The high failure rate of these alliances usually stemmed from the same problem: rich, beautiful American girls would not tolerate their husbands' infidelities. Titled European males, on the other hand, saw their amatory digressions as irrelevant to their marriages, and any constraint as a slur on their manhood. It was a fundamental difference in conjugal ideology and expectations. All the warning signs of this pitfall were evident in Sunny and Alfie.

Sunny was indeed beautiful, rich, and of a strongly romantic, monogamous nature. Alfie was just as beautiful, not rich, and flirtatious to an alarming degree. Sunny was young enough to expect a faithful husband; Alfie, being three and a half years younger, was still at an age when sexual constancy was almost an unreasonable demand. He was also Catholic. Those with experience in these matters foresaw nothing but disaster.

What made this romance a crisis was the fondness all who knew them had for both young people. And they were aware of how vulnerable and sensitive Sunny was. She was not the kind of hard-nosed heiress who could blithely discard a malfunctioning prince and get a new one. She could be badly damaged.

So upset were the von Pantzes by the mismatch launched on their premises that they arranged to take Alfie to New York, where they trotted before him a number of heiresses, various comely Whitneys and Phippses (in case Sunny's wealth was part of her allure) and saw to it the girls were closer to his age and tougher than Sunny. Alfie was polite to the decoys but immovable. Sunny was the only girl for him.

None of the stratagems or warnings had any effect. On July 20, 1957, Sunny became Princess von Auersperg.

III

A woman who had known Sunny Crawford slightly was taken to her house in Kitzbühel by a mutual friend for an informal afternoon visit one summer early in the 1960s. The woman, a wealthy Texan, was no stranger to prettified existences, but was overwhelmed by the perfection of the starched and polished life of the Princess von Auersperg.

The house Sunny built was in the style of the local chalets—broad, sloping roofs, wood-carved balconies for gazing at the alpine scenery, flower boxes full of geraniums, handpainted murals on the white plaster sections of the exterior. Inside, the tyrolean rusticity gave way to moneyed luxury; interesting antiques of the region were mingled with contemporary, deep-pile comfort and the high gloss that requires many unobtrusive hands.

Sunny herself, the visitor thought, had never looked more lovely —tanned from golf and swimming, dressed in a Pucci blouse and white linen slacks—her radiant good health an endorsement of the crystalline mountain air. A governess presented the two infants, the Prince and Princess von Auersperg, two imperial dolls in tyrolean dirndls and lederhosen, who bowed and curtsied and were led off so the women could chat. The visit was capped by the arrival, after tea, of the husband—dashing, amiable, solicitous of his wife and her friends.

To the Texas lady, it all seemed a story-book fantasy too good to be true. For the first few years of Sunny's marriage, it had been.

For Sunny, although the woman had no inkling of this, it was no longer.

When Alfie and Sunny first married, they settled in Munich in a large apartment overlooking the Englischer Garten in the city's fanciest section. Although the von Auerspergs were Austrian rather than German, both Alfie and his sister had strong ties in Munich and Alfie was involved in a publishing venture there with his father.

The young von Auerspergs' Munich apartment occupied the first two floors of an old town house; the upper two floors were the home of the Baroness Analiese Krupp, the wife of munitions czar Alfred Krupp, who had been convicted at the Nuremburg trials.

Perhaps at Sunny's request, Alfie launched an effort to find his wife a personal maid. He mentioned his need to the building superintendant, who told the Prince he knew an outstanding young woman who would be ideal for the job: the Baroness von Krupp's maid, Maria Schrallhammer. Alfie sent word to Maria that he wanted to speak with her about coming to work for his family. Maria refused the interview, thinking the rich, young von Auerspergs too high-powered for her taste. The superintendant told Maria she could not refuse to speak with the Prince.

She went and was won over—first by Alfie's persuasiveness and his wife's charm, but also by the prospect of eventual travel to America, a long-standing dream of hers. She explained her decision to the Baroness, who was sorry to lose her; in their short association the Baroness had come to regard Maria highly, finding her to be a person of exceptional character. She understood, however, the young girl's decision and sent her off with the bitter observation that Maria was unlikely to get to America working for her.

Maria would remain with Sunny throughout her life—throughout the marriage to Alfie, the birth of her two children, the years in Kitzbühel, the return to America and the divorce, the marriage to Von Bülow, the birth of a third child, Cosima— and the final coma.

Of all the figures in Sunny's life—her two husbands, her children, her mother, her closest friends—no one was with her so constantly over so many years as Maria. Devoted as she was to her mistress, Maria always maintained a proper distance. A long time later, on the witness stand, when Maria was asked by Von Bülow's lawyer if they had indeed not become like sisters, Maria was firm in her rejection of the suggestion. "Like sisters?" she said. "No. We liked each other."

As the Princess von Auersperg's personal maid, Maria had to look after Sunny's wardrobe, her jewelry, her possessions, and keep her bedroom and bath orderly. Since it is difficult to keep secrets from one who arranges your handbag and, literally, washes your dirty linen, personal maids often become the confidantes of their mistresses. This was not Sunny's style; in twenty-three years she almost never discussed personal matters with Maria.

When the publishing venture of Alfie and his father floundered, Sunny and Alfie decided to move to Kitzbühel, about a two-hour's drive from Munich, which would give them the outdoor life they both loved, and which had more of an international flavor socially than Munich. Kitzbühel was within striking distance of Salzburg; the Schloss Mittersell, with its heady flow of luminaries, was fifteen minutes' drive. It seemed such an ideal place for them that Sunny decided to build a house.

She threw herself into the plans for the house, taking part in every decision. While it was going up, she and Alfie stayed often at the Tennerhof Hotel and socialized with Honey and Alexander Hohenlohe and the many friends Alfie already had there. They kept the Munich apartment as a city base and staging area for trips.

Sunny and Alfie moved into their exquisite house during the heyday of Americans in Europe. There was still an aura of liberator heroism and a fascination with the new culture's shattering of exhausted traditions. Far as the dollar went throughout Europe, in no country did it buy as much as in Austria.

While for most Americans Europe meant tours, grand or guided, or perhaps pack trips, for some like Sunny it meant important marriages, impressive households, and dazzling social lives. Sunny loved entertaining in her new house, her frequent parties quickly earning her a reputation as the number one hostess in the party-oriented resort.

Although Alfie was in love with Sunny and it was her money

that was financing their fairy-tale life (her gift to him of a million dollars at the time of their wedding was spoken of in reverential tones among Europe's dollar-hungry elite), he never for an instant saw either fact as affecting the structure of their marriage as he saw it: the husband was in charge. Such was the tradition in which he had been brought up. The young women in Alfie's aristocratic milieu, some as wealthy as Sunny, were reared to defer to their husbands. Their job was to please the men, give them children, run their homes, and make them envied by their peers. Decisions were the husband's province.

Alfie exercised this right with gusto. His greatest enthusiasm, game hunting, he could now pursue beyond the tame slopes of the Alps. He dragged Sunny off on African safaris—a rarefied pastime she quickly came to loathe. Sunny was willing to play the subservient wife role up to a point and in some ways she seemed content with it, but she drew the line at safaris.

Not surprisingly, given her upbringing, Sunny turned out to have no stomach for roughing it. The little girl in starched dress and white gloves had come to Austria to live the life of a princess, not to tramp through bug-infested jungles, sleep in tents, and be menaced by startled game.

Her determination on this point is revealing of a contradiction in her nature. Most of the time, Sunny was the most easy-going of people—extraordinarily so for one so wealthy. She was happy to defer to the wishes of her mother, her friends, her husband. Occasionally, however, she would rebel and her obstinacy was of a strength to suggest it carried with it resentment for all the many acquiescences.

The daily life of Kitzbühel was most pleasant. Sunny would play golf almost every day, then drive the fifteen minutes into the mountains for lunch with Alfie and friends at the Schloss Mittersell. Afternoons, Sunny would take her children for walks in the woods with Maria. For the Americans living there, cut off linguistically from their popular culture, reading was an important pastime and one that Sunny always relished.

Greatly enhancing Sunny's life in Kitzbühel was the friendship she formed with Honey Hohenlohe. The dynamic American princess had the kind of aggressive friendliness that battered down the most reserved nature. Such insistent charm could drive Sunny deeper into herself, but, happily, she took to Honey and the two women became close.

Honey had had a fascinating life and had lots of stories to regale Sunny with. She had been married many times, had run one of the most successful celebrity resorts ever, and had had enough lovers —from Bob Hope to King Farouk—to enliven any number of evenings by the fire at Sunny's when Alfie was off hunting.

Occasionally Sunny and Honey would hop the Arlsburg Express and run up to Paris for a few days of shopping and restauranting. Honey remembers once meeting Sunny for lunch at Maxim's when Sunny showed her a jeweled cigarette case she had bought as a wedding gift for Peggy Bancroft, who was marrying Prince Charles d'Arenberg. When Honey raved over the exquisite gift, Sunny scolded herself for never having bought Honey a wedding gift.

"That's silly, Sunshine," Honey said. "You didn't know me when I got married."

"What difference does that make?" Sunny replied and pulled off two emerald earrings and handed them to the stunned Honey saying, "I want you to have something to remind you of me."

Another person who became important to Sunny during her life in Kitzbühel was Alfie's sister, Hetty von Auersperg. Unmarried and with no money, Hetty came to live in a lovely apartment Sunny and Alfie built over their garage. She assisted the young couple in many ways, first doing secretarial chores such as paying the bills, but eventually acting as a sort of an overseer in running the household.

Sunny grew very fond of Hetty, who like Alfie was outgoing and fun-loving. Hetty was a help to Sunny in more ways than helping with domestic operations. She was always available to play golf or sit and talk. The two women became lifelong friends. Ironically, Hetty would marry, years later, Arndt Krupp, the son of Maria's former employer.

At that time in Europe, there was a series of parties of a staggering lavishness. Whether they were in Paris, Venice, London, or Vienna, Sunny rarely missed one. Honey Hohenlohe scoffs at reports of Sunny's being antisocial, insisting she loved nothing better than dressing (with Maria's help) in one of her Paris creations, adding her jewels, and sweeping into a convocation of international society.

With Sunny's green eyes, blond hair, upturned nose, superb figure and carriage, she was often the most striking in a field of some of the world's best-looking, best-turned-out women. Honey remembers that Sunny's entrance into a party or nightclub would stop the action while everyone gaped. Honey also recalls how popular Sunny was in Kitzbühel, where she was liked for her dignity, her manners, and her generosity.

But life in Kitzbühel for Sunny became the equivalent of a Viennese pastry: delectable but cloyingly rich. Sunny, who had a strong tolerance for self-indulgence, began to feel she was vegetating. More important for her discontent, she felt more and more the drawbacks of being a foreigner in her husband's land. Even in America, Sunny had only a few close friends, never wide circles. In Austria, many of those around her were foreigners and therefore less accessible. Even the countrymen who were fond of Sunny, like Terry von Pantz, always felt at a slight distance, that Sunny never felt at ease with them.

Alfie, on the other hand, had battalions of close friends—school friends, tennis friends, skiing friends, hunting friends, and eventually, flirting friends. More and more, Sunny found her beautiful Kitzbühel house a meeting place for Alfie's coterie. Sunny, who was quite fluent in French, never became as adept at German. For a woman who had trouble communicating in her own language, it was disconcerting to find her living room filled with strangers speaking rapid-fire German.

It was confusing in other ways as well. Alfie would present a pretty young woman saying, "Sunny, this is your cousin the Countess von so and so."

The world was sweet for Prince Alfred von Auersperg. Still in his early twenties, he had a stunning and wealthy wife, a showplace home over which he ruled, money for a sleek Mercedes, big-game expeditions, pleasure trips to Paris and New York, social entrée to the most dazzling events in Europe—and two children who were bright and well behaved and who promised to maintain their parents' standards of looks.

In addition to his relish of hunting, Alfie shared another trait with Siegfried of legend—an absence of fear or its latter-day refinement, caution. He never thought for a moment Sunny would quit him, so he pursued his pleasures with little thought about the effect on his wife.

As the years passed, there seemed to be increasing numbers of beautiful young women in Alfie's entourage. People who knew him well in those days deny knowledge of specific infidelities—certainly of a substantial affair—but many agreed with the Baroness von Pantz, who said, "Sunny got contact lenses and finally saw what was going on." For Alfie, flirting seems to have been a reflex, but more than that, his dashing looks, which improved with each year, brought out the reflex to a reckless degree in any number of young women. Alfie's main crime was doing nothing to discourage this. In fact he seemed to love it.

Sunny had never found it easy to relate to groups. Now she found herself surrounded by people, not only a different nationality but a different age. In her early thirties, she was made to feel middle-aged by Alfie's friends in their mid-twenties. Her trips to Paris became more frequent. The trips to New York to see her mother grew longer—and started occurring on sudden impulses.

On one of these trips, just three years after her marriage, she stopped off in London for a few days. At a dinner party she met an attractive bachelor named Claus Von Bülow. If he made any impression on her, she mentioned it to no one.

The unraveling of her marriage was a bitter jolt for Sunny, who shared her mother's belief in the permanence of the institution. Although some friends from Kitzbühel, like Honey Hohenlohe, insist it is not so, others claim this was the one period in her life when Sunny drank too much. There also seems to be evidence that the drinking continued through her brief single period and her early involvement with Von Bülow. Whether or not the drinking persisted that long, the talk about it did, giving Claus a platform of truth upon which he later built an imposing lie.

It was not a third party that caused the breakdown of Sunny and Alfie's marriage. Aside from specific irritations—strangers in the house, game hunting, the flirting—Sunny was growing bored in a more general way with Kitzbühel and wanted to return to New York. Alfie disliked New York. Alfie was the husband. Alfie was also twenty-nine—too young to read the warnings and too proud to act on them if he had.

Early in 1965, after seven and a half years of marriage, Sunny took her two children, now six and seven, and moved back to New York. She settled into a suite at the Stanhope Hotel, on Fifth Avenue close by the apartment of her mother, who had remarried (the same year Sunny married Alfie) and was now Mrs. Russell Aitken.

Alfie was incredulous. He told a friend he still loved Sunny and would have her back within a year. Sunny obtained a Nevada divorce, and thirteen months later, in June of 1966, she married Claus Von Bülow at a small, family ceremony in the chapel of New York's Brick Presbyterian Church.

IV

PEOPLE who believe Claus Von Bülow guilty of trying to murder his wife tend to make wholesale dismissals of every positive aspect of his earlier life. They say "he is not really a 'Von,' " "he is not really a Bülow," "he is probably not even Danish." He was not Paul Getty's right hand man, they go on, but his secretary, his gofer, his pimp.

The truth is, Von Bülow's background contains distinguished facets. He was born Claus Cecil Borberg in Copenhagen in 1926. His mother, Jonna, was the lovely blond daughter of a prominent and wealthy Dane, Frits Bülow. She married a playwright and drama critic, Svend Borberg, but divorced him in 1930 when their son Claus was four.

Claus's grandfather was the dominant male in Claus's early life. Frits Bülow had been Denmark's Minister of Justice for several years, and was highly successful in business, but was wiped out by a financial panic in 1924. He took an ocean voyage, then returned to start over again. He never regained his former affluence but achieved a substantial level of comfort. The respect he enjoyed in financial circles never diminished. For a term he was head of Denmark's equivalent of the Federal Reserve Bank and sat on the boards of directors of a number of corporations.

When Claus was seven, he was sent to a Swiss boarding school, the Bellmunt School in St. Moritz. Attending school in the fashionable ski resort gave him an early peek at the *haut monde* at play, in addition to throwing him in with the sons of prominent Europeans.

His mother, still young and beautiful, seems to have had an active romantic life and may well have had tactical reasons for shipping the product of her brief marriage off to the Alps. Even if this were the reason, the volatile state of Europe brought to an end the Swiss sojourn. In 1938 Claus returned to Denmark and was enrolled in Herlufsholm, Denmark's first-rank boarding school, the educational crucible for the sons of the country's diplomats and aristocrats.

Like most Scandanavians, Claus was already proficient in a number of languages. ("The Swiss educate everyone to be a head-waiter," he would later say.) The Swiss interlude and this elitist boy's school completed the internationalization of the bright young man.

The collapse of his mother's marriage did not completely cut off Claus from Svend Borberg. He would see his father once or twice a year for stiff lunches. Borberg had achieved a measure of success in Denmark as a playwright. It is ironic that although Claus's mother's family, the Bülows, were linked to the distinguished German Von Bülows, his maternal grandfather, Frits Bülow, vehemently disliked Germans, while Claus's father, Svend Borberg, was markedly partial to them.

Shortly after his grandfather's birth in 1862, the Danish Bülows had lost four kinsmen in a war with the Germans, so Frits had grown up steeped in this family hatred. Claus's father, on the other hand, had enjoyed some success with his plays in Berlin and Hamburg, which resulted in gratifying ties with German intellectual circles.

When the Nazis marched into Denmark in 1940, Svend Borberg did not denounce the takeover as did most of his countrymen, particularly countrymen as prominent as he was. Those who felt such open defiance too dangerous settled for a silent boycott of German inducements to cooperation. Borberg did neither. He had been head of a Copenhagen organization called the Danish-German Literary Society; his principal act of collaboration—for which he was tried and convicted after the war—was primarily his remaining as head of this group, rather than resigning.

Claus, even at thirteen, had no doubt that his father had done the wrong thing. Looking back from today, however, he is anxious to distinguish between his father's collaboration—which he likens to that of misguided intellectuals like Ezra Pound and P. G. Wodehouse—and the war-movie variety of informing on one's friends and neighbors.

When the Nazis took over Denmark, Jonna Bülow happened to be visiting friends in Paris; she seized the opportunity of not returning home. She went instead to London, where principal among several influential friends was Oliver Stanley, then Minister of War in Churchill's cabinet. Since her son was only thirteen and still in boarding school, she decided he would be safe remaining behind with her father. Once in England, Jonna was able to take sufficient money to live on from a drawing account her father had arranged for her abroad.

Claus remained in Denmark little more than one year under the Nazis. The entire period was a military occupation; the nightmarish excesses of the Gestapo erupted later under an attempted imposition of a puppet political regime. As Denmark is an agricultural country, there was always ample food; from the idyllic confines of a boy's boarding school, the war seemed safely distant. Young Claus, however, brooded about his father's Nazi leanings and joined his grandfather in strong disapproval, a disapproval Von Bülow recalls voicing to his father.

A happy consequence of Svend Borberg's friendly relations with the Nazis was his obtaining permission for Claus to visit his mother, who was to meet him in Sweden for five days at Christmas, 1941. Although the scheme was for him not to return, getting from Sweden to the Nazi-free world was not easy; many Norwegians slipped across the border into Sweden only to find no way on from there. The only means were the courier planes; to obtain a seat required enormous influence. Jonna Bülow had the necessary connections. To the anger of the Germans in Denmark, Claus was spirited aboard a converted Mosquito bomber and flown to London to start a new life.

When Claus arrived in England, his mother was forty-one years old, still beautiful and socially well connected in England. Looking back on those early years of World War II, Claus Von Bülow today recalls an extraordinary kindness to his mother from the management at Claridge's. Having stayed at this top hotel on trips to London with her father, Jonna Bülow "was living there when the Germans marched into Denmark in April 1940."

Knowing what the invasion meant to her, she phoned down to tell the manager she had been cut off from her income and would have to move out. After thinking it over, the management said she could continue in her suite, repaying the hotel at the war's end, or "move to a smaller room at the prewar rate."

With such an appealing story, it seems rude to point out that on other occasions Von Bülow has said that his mother was visiting friends in Paris when the war broke out, that instead of returning to Copenhagen as planned, she had fled to England. Also, she does not seem to have mentioned her drawing account to Claridge's manager.

In any case, by the time Claus joined his mother in London she had rented a small house on South Street. With two years left of high school, Claus went to a London "crammers" for six months, then passed the Cambridge entrance exams and was accepted at the young age of sixteen—being helped by his mother's influential friends and a shortage of students. At Cambridge he had an allowance of four hundred pounds a year, which afforded him the best rooms and plenty of pocket money. As always, he had no trouble making friends.

In those first months after the war, while Claus was preparing to graduate from Cambridge, word came from Denmark that his father was to be tried as a collaborator. There is no evidence this caused much grief to Claus and Jonna. Svend Borberg was sentenced to four years in prison. He was released after serving eighteen months, but according to Claus he was socially ostracized and in every way a finished man. He died a year later.

During Claus's trial, thirty-five years later, he saw a parallel between his life, his father's, and his grandfather's. Each of them, he said, had a major crisis in their middle years—his grandfather's being bankruptcy when he was fifty. There was a significant difference Von Bülow did not comment upon: his grandfather survived for many years of respect and productivity. His father was destroyed.

Claus graduated from Cambridge in 1946 with a law degree. The youngest ever to have done so, he was too young to enter the bar, so he had to fill two years. He spent the first in recently liberated Paris, a giddy place for a nineteen-year-old to try life alone.

The second year, he got a job at the prestigious Hambro's Bank, where he did little but draw a salary and go to lunch. Finally old enough, he passed the bar exams and went to work for six months at the Senior Treasury Counsel to the Central Criminal Court (the Old Bailey) to gain experience, not because of any interest in criminal law but because his youth put him at a disadvantage for the civil law he wanted: "People are unlikely to trust substantial money issues to an inexperienced young man."

After six months Claus joined the chambers of the distinguished barrister Lord Hailsham, where he says he remained for eight years. The British Law Directory tells a different story, no longer listing Claus with Hailsham or anyone else after *three* years. Further adding to the mystery of his means of support before joining Getty is the British practice of not paying young lawyers who sit in the chambers of eminent jurists.

Still, for refugees, Claus and his mother had not done badly. While he was at Cambridge, Jonna had moved to a flat at 41 Berkeley Square, then to another at 1 St. James Street. In 1950, the year he joined Hailsham, they bought the large flat on Belgrave Square in which he lived for the remaining sixteen years of his bachelorhood and which he kept for the first two years of his marriage to Sunny.

Jonna had come to England knowing a few of the right people and had since expanded her social operation—but not to the degree her son had, with an address book fattened at Cambridge, Paris, Hambro's bank, and now a distinguished law firm.

Equally important for advantageous contacts were Claus's finely honed social instincts. On the rare nights when he didn't have a party to attend, he could be seen hanging around the bar at Claridge's, the Dorchester, or some other promising spot for a chance encounter of the right sort.

His success in the drawing rooms of Mayfair would seem inevitable. He was tall, handsome, well mannered, well educated, and intelligent. He spoke all the important languages and had a survivor's reflex for instantly determining who was who.

Claus often gave large parties at the rangy but sparsely furnished flat he shared with his mother. The Duchess of Westminster, now Lady Linslay, remembers one of these affairs in which the guests tried to figure out where in the sparsely furnished rooms the mother and son slept.

Three years after arriving in England, Claus officially changed his name from Borberg to Bülow; he had unofficially used the name at the Swiss boarding school, where the name Bülow meant something and Borberg did not.

Claus Bülow seems always to have concentrated on the pastimes of the highest social echelons. After graduating from Cambridge, he took a two week's holiday at St. Moritz, staying at the renowned Palace Hotel in one of the converted maid's rooms the management sometimes rented to scene-enhancing young men; this started an annual tradition of holidays at St. Moritz, where he became a life member of the Cresta Run, the famous toboggan races. During these Swiss interludes, Claus formed friendships with a number of Europe's top families—the Bismarcks were one example.

Claus's choice of St. Moritz over a dozen other fancy alpine resorts was in all likelihood because of St. Moritz's uncontested supremacy as the most fashionable, the richest, the most be-titled winter resort in Europe. London has many addresses fashionable enough for viscounts and film stars, but one stands head and shoulders over the others: Belgravia. And it was to that neighborhood Claus moved as soon as he was established in a promising job. Members of royal families allow themselves more deviation from their prescribed courses than Claus Bülow did.

Despite his caution, much about Claus Bülow in those years of highly social bachelorhood is suggestive of the epithet International White Trash, used by entrenched natives to describe those people of no discernible background who frequent the most rarefied salons of New York, London, or Paris. For a socially ambitious unmarried male, relocating in a different country— whether as a Frenchman in New York or as a Dane in London —provides freedom from all manner of cumbersome social impedimentae that might exist in his background.

The polite questions to a new acquaintance that will quickly tell a countryman volumes about the newcomer's status—school, college, hometown, friends—will tell a foreigner nothing. Who knows what is the best boarding school in Spain or the best suburb of Brussels? If a factory worker's son from Bridgeport aspires to the social heights, he avoids New York, where factories in Bridgeport carry disagreeable connotations; he takes himself instead to London or Paris, where Bridgeport and Greenwich are all the same and where his hostess, desperate for single men to fill out her table, will thank him for sparing her tiresome explanations. Prime specimens of International White Trash are not just of murky background because they are foreigners; they have made themselves foreigners because of their backgrounds. This move has rendered not only the future a clean slate, but the past as well.

Of course these infiltrators must possess something in the way of manners, education, and savoir faire. Claus Bülow had far more claim to social distinction than many who have flourished in the drawing rooms of Belgravia and Park Avenue, but he aspired to and succeeded with a social level that did not come to him naturally.

In one sense Claus Bülow had good justification for social climbing. He was smarter, better looking, better educated, and better mannered than most of those whose world he craved. In those bachelor years in London, after he arrived where ambition had brought him, his personal attributes took over and secured his position. By the time he met Sunny, he was socially established—known and liked by large numbers of those he valued. Of course he had detractors—he would always be controversial—but their rejection of him was personal, rarely elitist.

Claus did not rely on his attributes alone to win the favor of the rich and powerful. He proved particularly adept at being "useful" in his circle's pursuit of their pleasures. He could be counted on to know unattached beauties to leaven gatherings or to be the first with logistical information about a new nightclub or any other sybaritic enthusiasm of the moment.

Becoming liked by, if not indispensible to, the mighty was not for Claus an end in itself but rather a means. The end appeared at dawn over scrambled eggs at a debut dance at Belvoir Castle. Seated at the same table was the legendary oil tycoon J. Paul Getty, who was then considering moving the headquarters of his Los Angeles-based company to London. This casual, perhaps chance, acquaintance was quickly consolidated when a French friend of Claus's who was a Getty stockholder came to London and gave a dinner at which both Getty and Claus were present. As the dinner was small—only four people—it appears to have been engineered to convert the new friendship into something more solid.

Claus accepted with alacrity Getty's invitation to work for him as his administrative assistant. (Claus would later say "executive assistant," but Getty in his autobiography refers to Claus and one Robina Lund as his administrative assistants.)

At the time, Getty was running his empire from a suite at the London Ritz. Reminiscing about the period, Von Bülow says, "The filing system was manila envelopes. We found oil with greater ease than we found a particular document."

From the start the association with Getty was a success, not only profesionally but personally as well. Claus took particular delight in Getty's wry sense of humor. Once Getty asked his new aide to look over a contract he was about to sign with a group to which Getty was subcontracting work for a one-year period. Because Getty had never dealt with the people before, Claus suggested they not commit themselves to a full year but instead offer a one-month contract with an option to renew.

Getty, who was then sixty-nine to his assistant's thirty-three, looked over the top of his glasses and said, "Claus, I think you are letting your private life influence your business judgment."

Getty hated to fly so would often make Claus his surrogate on distant errands. On one of these trips, returning from the Mideast, Claus encountered a fierce storm over the Alps. Back in London, he played on Getty's horror of flying, saying the plane had brushed within feet of Mont Blanc's peak. Getty, sensing that Claus was angling for danger pay, looked at him wryly and said, "Where I grew up in Oklahoma we had a saying: a man destined to stretch rope is not going to die another way." (Von Bülow told this story during his trial for attempted murder.)

According to some who worked for Getty Oil at the time, Claus would have eventually been a major officer in the company. Not only did he represent Getty for negotiations in distant places, he took charge of specific aspects of the business, such as overseeing the purchasing for a Mideast operation where everything—from oil drills to cigarettes—had to be purchased abroad and shipped to the site.

Twenty-five years of inflation have obliterated the significance of Von Bülow's actual income figure—some £2500 a year from

Getty, or roughly $12,000. Although this would be considered meager today, it was then, according to Claus, "three quarters the salary of England's Prime Minister and two thirds the salary of the president of British Petroleum."

In any case, it enabled Von Bülow to live well in the Belgrave Square apartment where he kept a butler, entertained frequently, and even more frequently was in debt. The butler recalls unruly fluctuations in his employer's affluence. Weeks of parties would be followed by dark stretches of austerity during which Von Bülow would instruct the butler to run the house on the mimimum amount until further notice. He once showed the butler, by way of underscoring the need for economy, some eighty thousand pounds' worth of IOUs, at the same time assuring the alarmed servant that the debts would be cleared away in short order.

Shortly after Claus went to work for him, Getty bought Sutton Place, the Surrey manor house that would become his headquarters. Claus would commute against traffic to spend the working day and often the night at the country house. One of his functions was to be present at group luncheons, which were usually business but sometimes social.

One such personal guest of Paul Getty describes arriving for lunch at Sutton Place, being greeted by Claus Bülow, and having a visceral dislike for the man on sight. The visitor was the Baron Arndt Krupp von Bohlen, heir to the German armaments conglomerate, who ironically enough would later be married to Alfred von Auersperg's sister Hetty.

Recalling the episode, Krupp says, "It was like an encounter in a child's story book with a witch or a demon. My feeling of evil was so strong, I did not want to touch him even long enough to shake hands."

Adding to his dislike, Krupp felt snubbed by Getty's assistant, who he said was haughty and condescending to him, unlike Getty himself, who was warm and genial. Krupp felt that Claus Bülow's snobbishness toward him was unwarranted. With succinct self-awareness he said, "After all, at the time there was some argument whether the richest man in the world was Paul Getty or my father."

Others have spoken of a strong revulsion at the mere physical presence of Claus Bülow. But just as many of those who met him, particularly women, had an equally strong favorable reaction. His impact, good or bad, is not surprising, as the adult Claus was a formidable physical presence. His height is his most striking feature—an erect six foot three—but the face is memorable: cold blue eyes, lash-framed, giving a dramatic look some find ghoulish, others sexy. Also noteworthy is the nose, which has an elongated, ski-jump elegance to it. Thinning hair from his late twenties on did little to diminish his arresting presence.

His social manner was also distinctive. He had adopted for his own use the aggressive rudeness so often the gambit of upper-class English women. Claus was quick to launch the insulting banter ("My dear, all that makeup gives you the look of a female impersonator") that signals wickedness, irreverence, and an aristocratic self-assurance. A titled European, active socially in New York and Europe, said of Von Bülow, "He's corrupt and evil, but always fun," then added, "He's a big orgy man."

With those he valued, he had a knack for establishing a quick intimacy that bordered on the conspiratorial, whispering wicked asides at parties that allied him with whomever he was addressing against all the fools in the room. The word "cozy" is often used by people trying to define his winning manner.

While some found him cold and aloof, others saw a kind side. He was prompt to notice someone's discomfort or to defend someone he felt was being treated unjustly. All in all, he was adept at winning friends, at making good first impressions when he so resolved, and at being reliably amusing on subsequent encounters. It is not surprising he flourished in the most exalted social milieus.

Because of his easy aplomb, it was startling to learn at the trial of his reliance on Valium. This was one of several hints that beneath the hard enamel exterior was a goading insecurity.

If xenophobia was the problem, it was certainly one he shared with his wife to be. While Sunny's solution was to avoid people as much as possible, his seems to have been to arm himself with ever more exhalted friends. If you are pals with Paul Getty, Edmund de Rothschild and Anna Marie Bismarck, what difference does it make if Sarah and Harry Nobody like you? Claus's snobbery approached that of Prince Metternich, who once said, "For me, mankind begins with barons."

His charm and affability were not always put to use. A woman who was Claus's dinner partner on two widely separated occasions said that on the first he was arrogant, disinterested, and antagonistic. On the second, when he did not remember her, he was the opposite—warm, amusing, and sympathetic. Even allowing for the mood of the moment, she felt a worrying Jekyll-and-Hyde duality. As with Dr. Jekyll, the phenomenon may have been rooted in a drug.

Today Von Bülow will say little about his romantic involvements in those bachelor years, which lasted throughout his twenties and thirties. He had a number of affairs and once fell resoundingly in love with the wife of Herbert von Karajan. And there were rumors. First the inevitable homosexual one. Because any unmarried man over the age of thirty is suspect, Claus, with his English schooling, was a target for this shopworn allegation. Although Claus had a number of homosexual friends, the evidence for involvements with people of his own sex is flimsy.

The rumors improve. He is also said to have a sadistic streak, the allegations going so far as to place a fully outfitted torture room in his London digs. He was said to have a set of whips and a collection of military artifacts with sadistic overtones. (He kept a spike-topped Prussian helmet in his study at Clarendon Court.) Perhaps the most pungent rumor was the one of necrophilia, which his friends say originated on Capri as a joke about his un-Capri-like pallor. This rumor showed a remarkable indelibility. Twenty-five years later it found its way into an American magazine article about his trial, as did another joke from his spirited friends: that he had killed his mother.

While Claus seemed to know all the most social people, he did know many of darker claims to the public's attention. He was a good friend of Stephen Ward, the West End osteopath who became a key figure in the Profumo Affair for running the call-girl ring that supplied Christine Keeler to John Profumo. Claus stood bail for Ward at his arrest.

It is doubtful if Claus availed himself of Ward's stable. According to his butler, Von Bülow was sexually highly active but usually with women of social prominence.

One of Claus's closest London friends, who was also a regular at the Clermont, then a highly fashionable London gambling club, was the notorious Lord Lucan who in 1974 attempted to murder his wife with a lead pipe and, on his way from the scene, succeeded in murdering their children's nanny with the same pipe.

It goes beyond irony that these two friends—both of them handsome and polished ladies' men, sportsmen, gamblers, who shared a nostalgia for a more rigidly stratified society and who were in the eyes of all who knew them men of great potential—should end their days best known for the same thing: attempting to murder their wives.

V

SOON after her divorce from von Auersperg, Sunny bought a vast apartment on Fifth Avenue at 77th Street and hired the firm of McMillen to decorate it. During her years in Europe she had developed a conviction that her children should be educated in the United States. The lavish apartment was a clear announcement that her international phase had ended, that she had come home for good.

People from McMillen who worked with her on the apartment came to admire Sunny's taste and ideas but remember her as making the necessary decisions more from a sense of duty than from enthusiasm for the new home.

Sunny began seeing old friends. Her first boyfriend, Alan Murphy, had also recently returned to New York, he from a stint in Los Angeles as a film-world columnist for the Los Angeles *Times*. Now a decorator, Murphy took Sunny to parties with film celebrities that dazzled her. He remembers with amusement that Sunny, whom he felt to be the epitome of glamour, was particularly thrilled by a dinner at "21" for Rosalind Russell.

On the other side of the Atlantic, Claus, who was doing well with Getty, was quick to hear about the breakdown of the von Auersperg marriage. He had seen Sunny on several occasions while she was still married to Alfie. They were at a London dinner party together in 1964—a year before her return to New York.

Maria recalls making a trip from Kitzbühel to London with Sunny during the marriage's final year when Claus saw them off at the airport. This would suggest more than a casual acquaintanceship. In her first year in New York as a single woman, Sunny told Alan Murphy she was in love with someone, but wouldn't tell him with whom.

In the mid-sixties Paul Getty had extensive dealings with the Japanese and sent his assistant on frequent expeditions to Tokyo. Claus used the opportunity to stop off in New York to pay court to the divorcee.

It must have been a heady time for Claus, flying across the globe for the richest man in the world and stopping off in Manhattan to wine and dine a woman who was perhaps the world's most beautiful heiress.

During his trial for trying to murder Sunny, Von Bülow said that when he met her she was the most beautiful girl he had ever seen. While this is undoubtedly sincere, good friends of his have said they always knew that if the forty-year-old Von Bülow ever married it would be to someone wealthy. The observation did not require penetrating insight: his salary was insufficient for the life he was leading and far from sufficient for the life he wanted to lead.

To Sunny, Von Bülow must have been a salubrious contrast to Alfie. Alfie's strengths were his looks, his youthful exuberance, his hearty athleticism. He was an ideal companion for an Austrian mountaintop. Von Bülow, on the other hand, was cerebral, cultivated, suave—the perfect companion for a Fifth Avenue drawing room.

Annie Laurie does not seem to have taken a strong stand either pro or con Von Bülow as a second husband for her daughter. Her first meeting with him had occurred in London when Sunny arranged a meeting in a restaurant. Claus, whose head was bandaged from a recent hair transplant operation, asked Sunny to tell her parents he had been in an automobile accident. Sunny forgot and the meeting went off with no mention of his white-gauze turban.

Afterwards, Russell Aitken said, "You didn't tell me we were going to meet young Doctor Kildare."

While it seems Sunny wanted to be dominated at least in part by her husband, there was an important difference in the way the two men went about doing this. Alfie's technique was the willful attempt to bend Sunny to the life he wanted; Von Bülow seemed to be telling Sunny how to achieve the life *she* wanted. They both told Sunny what to do, but Von Bülow's technique was far more palatable.

The decorators from McMillen's give an interesting glimpse of the ease with which Von Bülow took charge. At the time of their marriage, work had been completed on the apartment's "backgrounds"—the floors, ceilings, and walls. What remained were the cosmetic details, such as curtains and furnishings.

Immediately, Von Bülow's voice was heard. Rather than annoying Sunny, his takeover seemed to relieve her. Sometimes it was a matter of subtly steering her toward a new plan, other times he simply overruled her. As an example, Sunny had installed a sound system, tubular loudspeakers that nestled in the room's curtains. The speakers were not of high quality but were sufficient for what she wanted: soft background music.

Von Bülow pronounced the speakers inadequate and had the entire system taken out and replaced by elaborate stereo equipment. The decorators were impressed. One of them said, "Usually the new spouse of the one who has the money waits a year or two before throwing his weight around."

While work proceeded on the New York apartment, the Belgrave Square apartment, too, was completely redone. The plan was to spend summers in London and winters in New York. Heading to London shortly after the wedding, Sunny was swept into Von Bülow's supercharged social milieu.

A great many parties were given for the couple. It was as though the entire British upper class and café society wanted to meet Claus's lovely American heiress. If someone had wanted to design a program guaranteed to discomfit Sunny, this was it. She was made the center of attention at a series of parties filled with worldly, self-assured people who were unknown to her. It was a measure of her devotion to her new husband that she went through it all in good grace.

But Von Bülow quickly became aware of her difficulty with strangers. At a large outdoor dinner given for them at the country home of Claus's good friend John Aspinall, Sunny and Claus were seated at separate tables. Alone with two men she'd never met before, Sunny was having difficulty, it was apparent to others at the table, holding up her end of conversation.

As dessert and coffee were served, a young tiger from Aspinall's famous menagerie got loose and wandered among the guests. He was little more than a cub, but of sufficient size to send a number of guests into the house with their coffee. One of Sunny's dinner partners was the first to flee. The tiger, seeing an empty place at the table, climbed next to Sunny.

When Claus came looking for his wife, he found her feeding the beast bits of her dessert and conversing with far more animation —and less fear—than she had shown the English gentlemen.

Sunny and Claus threw an enormous party at Belgrave Square shortly after arriving. The butler recalls the abrupt change in his master's style. Von Bülow always did things well, but with an eye for bargains and economy. Now, instead of a marked-down champagne of an out-of-the-way vineyard, it was jeroboams of vintage Dom Perignon. Instead of lilies from the Isle of Wight, it was huge potted orchids. At last, Von Bülow could entertain his friends as he had long wished.

Since Sunny did not abandon her resolve to raise her children in the United States, Von Bülow tried to manage his Getty job from his Fifth Avenue base. This involved a great deal of travel, mostly to London or Los Angeles. It grew increasingly obvious that if he wanted to keep his job they would have to move to one of those two cities.

"Sunny refused to live in either place," Von Bülow said later, "so after two years of marriage I had no choice but to leave Getty."

All information on this impasse comes from Von Bülow. It is curious that he chose to present himself as a man who would throw up an important career to appease a willful and unreasonable wife. It also seems odd that the matter had not been worked out at the time they were contemplating marriage. It is possible, of course, that Sunny thought she could adjust to his traveling, then found she couldn't. Still, Von Bülow's complaisance is remarkable. With no other job prospects in the city she insisted upon, he was making a sacrifice few men were in a financial position to make.

Another change came at the time the couple moved to New York. Claus, who had been simply Mr. Bülow in London, formally added the "Von" to his name. This belated addition, with its vainglorious announcement of noble blood, later became for some journalists a symbol of Claus's phoniness.

When Sunny gave birth to a baby girl, they named her Cosima, which gave the "Von" an even greater significance. Cosima Von Bülow, as any music lover knows, was one of the most famous women of the nineteenth century. An illegitimate daughter of Franz Liszt, she married a conductor, Hans Von Bülow, who achieved his greatest fame conducting premieres of Wagner operas, among them *Tristan und Isolde*.

While Von Bülow was championing Wagner's music, his wife was having an affair with the composer. The Von Bülows and Wagner traveled together and, for a time, lived together in what everyone in Europe except Hans Von Bülow recognized as a ménage à trois. Because of the patronage of Wagner by King Ludwig II in marriage-honoring Bavaria, the affair became a major scandal. Hans Von Bülow could close his eyes to it no longer and finally in 1870 divorced his wife, who later married Wagner.

Since this lady, who had been born Liszt and died Wagner, had treated the Von Bülow family shabbily at best, it would seem natural for any member of the family to feel that the less said about her the better. Instead, for a Von Bülow to name his daughter after her could be taken as a somewhat strained reminder that she was of the illustrious German family.

When Sunny went to the hospital to deliver Cosima, Mrs. Aitken stayed with the children at 960 Fifth Avenue. Entering Alexander's room, she found her seven-year-old grandson sitting on the floor absorbed with a construction set.

"What are you making?" she asked.

Without looking up he replied, "An automobile for my little brother."

"Well, you know, dear, it might not be a brother."

He looked up at her as if slapped. To soften the dismay at the dreadful possibility she had raised, Mrs. Aitken pointed out positive aspects to baby girls.

"If it turns out to be a sister, Alexander, you will be her big brother. She will need you to look after her and take care of her."

Alexander nodded thoughtfully and appeared somewhat comforted. The matter was dropped.

A day or two after giving birth to Cosima, Sunny, still in the hospital, received a packet from Alexander. It contained about three dollars in coins and a note that said the money was for taking care of his sister and that he would send more when he could.

While this is the kind of story that keeps grandmothers in business, it presaged a brother-sister relationship stronger than the customary, one that would have sad and dramatic ramifications when the family was later torn apart by criminal litigation. From earliest childhood, the relationship that developed between Alexander and his younger sister—whether or not a result of his grandmother's suggestion—was marked by a high degree of older-brother protectiveness and solicitude.

Alexander became preoccupied with his younger sister's well-being. Whatever she wanted from him, she received—whether a possession, an errand, or a favor of any sort. Even as a teenager Alexander would drop anything he was doing—even if he was entertaining friends—if Cosima wanted him to see something she had done, fix her bike, or drive her to the beach.

For her part, Cosima did not demand these attentions as from an adoring lackey but more as recompense for her adoration of him. She doted on her brother. If he went on a trip, she measured the time until his return, her spirits rising visibly as the day approached.

This closeness would survive even the violence done by Alexander's and Ala's subsequent accusations against Cosima's father —which made all the more sad the bond's rupture some months after the trial.

From the time the Von Bülows had returned to New York, Sunny's old friends had found it harder and harder to reach her. They would phone the apartment and ask a maid for Mrs. Von Bülow. Sometimes after a wait the phone would be hung up; other times Claus would come on and ask who was calling, often in a sharp bark. When the caller had been identified, Claus would say, "Oh, hello. Sunny's exhausted." Or packing for a trip. Or out with the children. Whatever it was tended to preclude further communication.

One friend who got this runaround was Alan Murphy. He was man of the world enough—and susceptible enough to the usual paranoias—to fear either that Claus had a strong aversion to him or that Sunny had given him up in the natural evolution of some friendships.

Shortly after the Von Bülows returned from England, Sunny had invited Alan to a lunch party. She seated her old friend to her right and they spent the entire meal laughing and reminiscing. Von Bülow, on the other hand, given his first opportunity to become acquainted with one of his wife's oldest friends, addressed not one word to him during the entire lunch—though his role as host alone would have required more.

After the meal, Sunny took Alan into her bedroom to show him the baby Cosima. While they were there, a governess brought in Prince Alexander and Princess Annie Laurie, who bowed and curtsied. Knowing both parents, Murphy was not surprised at the beauty and manners of the two children. Knowing Sunny's taste, he was not surprised by the splendor of her apartment, which he dubbed "Buckingham Palace on Fifth Avenue." Sunny's life seemed so idyllic, Murphy felt he could forgive her if she chose to view their meeting as a sentimental reunion rather than a resumption of a friendship. When he found it hard to reach Sunny, he eventually stopped calling.

It wasn't until a long time later that Murphy learned he had not been singled out for such treatment, that several of Sunny's oldest and closest friends had experienced the same evasions. He happened to mention it to Sunny's friend from infancy, Ruth Dunbar, who said that not only had she found it impossible to get through to Sunny but that Peggy Bedford, now the Princess d'Arenberg, had as well.

Commiserating with each other one day, the three compared Von Bülow's haughtiness to them on the few occasions when they'd had social encounters. Murphy was the first to admit condescension from Claus. "He treats me like a dilettante," he said glumly.

Peggy, the Standard Oil heiress, could match that. "He treats me like a courtesan."

Ruth, the Swift heiress, was not to be outdone. "You're both lucky," she said. "He treats me like the maid."

The three were relieved to learn that their exclusion from the Von Bülow circle was shared by all of them, that they were probably not social enough for Claus. The idea fascinated the three friends, none of whom had ever before felt themselves on the losing end of a snub.

It wasn't just friends from Sunny's school days who were banished. Honey Hohenlohe said that when she was in New York during the period between Alfie and Claus she would see Sunny every day. After Claus, on her two or three visits a year she was unable to see her at all.

It was not that the Von Bülows did not socialize. There were frequent dinners at 960 Fifth Avenue, but the guests were Claus's friends. And on a number of occasions, he berated Sunny for not being sufficiently friendly to one or another of them.

Because of the international smart set he traveled with in London, Claus had many well-placed friends in Manhattan. In short order he became a member of the Knickerbocker Club and the Union Club. Not the best, perhaps, but not accessible to every foreigner moving to New York.

A good part of Sunny's and Claus's energies went toward family activities. Alexander and Ala were arriving at an age where they could benefit from travel. Sunny, who no longer wanted to live abroad, still enjoyed visiting foreign places; they went to Europe at least once a year and traveled the United States as well, once taking the famous *Delta Queen* on its cruise down the Mississippi.

One summer soon after their marriage, the family spent time on the Spanish island of Majorca. It was here that Alexander and Ala recall their stepfather, whom they called "Uncle Claus," giving them syringes to play with. The children quickly saw that they made fine water pistols. (A long time later, Sunny would giggle to her old friend Isabel Glover about the hard time Customs had given Claus about his syringes and needles when he was returning from a trip to Europe.)

Also, Alexander and Ala at eleven and twelve were at an age when they should not be forced to remain in the city during the summer. But Sunny was strongly in favor of family togetherness and against devisive institutions like summer camps. So she started thinking about a second residence, some place on the sea, perhaps, that had tennis and swimming.

When her mother bought a house in Newport, Rhode Island, Sunny decided that an ideal solution had been found.

VI

CLAUS Von Bülow once said that the typical Newport cottage, if in Europe, would sit in the middle of thirty thousand acres. The gigantic Newport piles sit on four or five acres, sufficient for lawn parties and croquet, but not fox hunting and agriculture. Von Bülow added that, while Europe's palace building went on for a thousand years, America's all occurred within thirty years, much of it in Newport.

Not only was the short duration of the building period remarkable, but so was the geographic crowding. Traditionally, a nation's rich come together in the capital city—Paris, London, St. Petersburg—for a winter "season," then disperse in the warm weather to the isolation of their private estates. In its concentration of great summer estates Newport is unique.

George Washington Vanderbilt II went off to the mountains of North Carolina to build his princely Biltmore; his fellow Vanderbilts were more typical of the Gilded Age's millionaires in swarming to Newport to build palaces right on Newport streets for all the world to admire. The phenomenon contained a hint of the middle-class, big-house-on-main-street vision, but the palace-crowding had the practical advantage of providing rich neighbors to play with.

Newport, like a number of well-preserved colonial towns—Williamsburg, New Castle, Annapolis, Nantucket—had been highly prosperous in the seventeenth and eighteenth centuries but lost the commercial action to more advantageous ports. The early wealth brought it fine architecture; subsequent obsolescence saved it. Even before the revolution Newport had been adopted as a summering place by southerners, particularly Charlestonians, and it was later put to the same use by Bostonians of an intellectual bent. By 1830 it had attracted wide notice as a summer resort.

Both these groups, southerners and New England intellectuals, were swept aside after the Civil War when the robber barons trooped into town and began erecting their palaces.

Much has been written about Newport's colonial heyday, but rich as this period is, it can be rivaled by other places and would be of little interest to anyone but history-keen Americans. It is the period of Newport's most vulgar excess, roughly 1895 to 1914, that made the town unique. In those two decades, Newport experienced an unprecedented frenzy of mansion building and lavish entertainment. The brief season, a mere six weeks, packed into it a wonderment of ostentation—and death struggles for hostess supremacy.

During this era a number of Newport households could stage dinners for a hundred without bringing in extra help and have a liveried footman for every two guests. Newporters would nod appreciatively at such wanton fancies as that of Mrs. Hermann Oelrichs, who to prettify a ball had a mock armada built and moored and illuminated in front of her mansion because she felt the unadorned Atlantic Ocean too empty and bleak. Or of William Fahnestock, who enlivened his trees with fourteen-carat gold fruit.

World War I put a halt to Newport's careening extravagance. The merriment fluttered back to life in the twenties, but rolled over, seemingly for good, with the Depression. Amazingly, it survived and limped along with many of the same families occupying the same houses, but with the glory days still sufficiently in mind to tell them the Newport of legend was gone forever. It may be a happy coincidence that the taste for the lavish displays of the 1890s died out with the capacity to indulge it.

The wartime shuttering of the largest and most conspicuous mansions gave Newport the look of an imperial ghost town, but the summer colony was not extinct; it had merely moved from houses requiring thirty servants to houses requiring four. While more trend-minded rich were discovering less formal resorts like Nantucket and Southampton, the progeny of Newport dynasties were carrying on their harmless recreations and exclusions at Bailey's Beach and the Reading Room. Even the monster houses were not completely defunct; a Vanderbilt, Countess Szápáry, lived on until the 1970s in the largest, the colossal Breakers, which cost Cornelius Vanderbilt II three million dollars in 1893.

One of the most remarkable changes in Newporters was the three-generation conversion from ostentation to a diffidence that bordered on secretiveness. The turn-of-the-century tycoons used Newport to proclaim their wealth; they seemed terrified the world might not find out how rich they were. Their grandchildren showed an equal terror the world *would* find out. Over the decades several phobias brought about this retreat into shyness: fear of the IRS, of kidnapers, and of a more widespread and vocal social conscience. The rich had learned that no good comes from flaunting your good fortune—and much bad. Happily, this perception arrived just as the showy houses were becoming a logistical if not a financial impossibility.

Of course the attractions that lured the millionaires to Newport in the first place—the climate, the dramatic cliffs, the open-water vistas—were still present, and the area's beauty was enhanced, and to a degree preserved, by the large parcels of key land held by families who cared what happened to Newport.

Many of these families remained. They had less grandiose quarters, perhaps, but they had their memories, and to reinforce those memories they had each other.

Occasionally the public would be made aware that Newport lived on—most resoundingly in 1953, when Senator John Kennedy married Jacqueline Bouvier from her mother's Newport home, Hammersmith Farm. And attention was drawn to Newport by public events: Tennis Week, the America's Cup and, also in the 1950s, the Newport Jazz Festival—although to the Old Guard this last was more a symptom of Newport's death than its life.

Whatever the prognosis of the fashion watchers, Newport continued to draw settlers with outsized bank accounts. For the rich, it had several lures beyond the topographical: the availability of large houses, a tradition of grandiose living, a high level of security from incursion either by humans or the seas. A number of Texans and other rich of no Newport family tradition came to town, were deemed "nice," and settled into the scene.

The same social dynamic that caused Newport's fin-de-siècle flowering was still operating. The ticket of admission was the time-honored one: a huge fortune. If the summer colony liked you, you were in and that was that—if they didn't, there was no appeal.

Even though Newport seems like an inevitable place for Sunny and Claus Von Bülow—with her wealth and his taste for opulence —it was Sunny's mother, Annie Laurie Aitken, who first drew Newport to their attention. Russell and Annie Laurie Aitken had visited friends who were entrenched summer colonists, the Norton Adamses. For two summers they rented Champs Soleil, the former home of Robert Goulet, then bought the Bellevue Avenue showplace.

Alluding to the speed with which the Aitkens were accepted by Newport, Mrs. John Nicholas Brown said, "They had first come here as guests of Peggy and Norton Adams. And Peggy was a Brokaw, so it was all right." Mrs. Brown would be quick to concede that acceptance was expedited by Annie Laurie's formidable charm, beauty, taste—and vast wealth.

The decision of a mother to summer in Newport would not necessarily dictate the daughter following suit, but it did in this case because, except for Sunny's eight years in Austria, mother and daughter had never lived more than a few blocks apart.

In one regard Newport was the ideal resort for Sunny and in other ways it was a disaster. On the plus side was the grandeur Sunny loved. Newport was one of the few remaining places where stately, well-staffed houses were the rule. Not only was Newport set up for ducal living, but such pomp would not raise eyebrows there as it would anywhere else. Sunny was living proof one could love grandeur without loving the conspicuousness that often accompanies it.

What made Newport a bad place for her was the hermetic insularity of Newport's relentless socializing. Sunny's tendency toward reclusiveness was unmanageable in a town where each night of the season had an "A" social event at which attendance, for a couple like the Von Bülows, was mandatory. You could not say you were busy. Busy with what? Illness or a sudden business trip were the only excuses. Even for those programmed with social chatter, the nightly exposure to the same people presented conversational problems; for Sunny, it became a nightmare.

The cabana at Bailey's Beach Sunny picked for herself symbolized her dilemma. Hoping to avoid socializing as much as possible, she asked for a cabana at the remote end of a row. The stratagem backfired when she found that to reach it she had to run a gamut of socially hungry Newporters sitting in front of their cabanas. They greeted her effusively and lamented how rarely they saw her at the beach. They soon saw her less.

Bemoaning this mistake to a friend, Sunny said, "Maybe I could climb over the fence down at the end and avoid them."

Other aspects of Newport were ideal. As a playground for growing children it could hardly be improved on. Bailey's Beach with its swimming and tennis was walking distance from Clarendon Court; even for a family with many cars and a chauffeur, this gave a welcome simplicity to logistics.

During his trial for attempting to murder Sunny, Claus Von Bülow remarked that moving to Newport had been the mistake that led to the tragedy. He meant that his wife's psychological problems, his explanation for her comatose condition, were aggravated by the pressures placed on her by Newport. In another context, he said that if, instead of buying a Bellevue Avenue manor, they had bought a farm in nearby Middletown (almost as costly, but far less showy), the press would not have played up the case.

After renting a house one summer and making frequent runs up to Newport to look at possibilities, Sunny and Claus settled on the imposing twenty-room Bellevue Avenue mansion named Clarendon Court. It had been built in 1904 by Edwin Knight, an executive of the Pennsylvania Railroad, who named it Claradon after his wife, Clara. The architect, Horace Trumbauer, also designed two of Newport's most majestic cottages, The Elms and Miramar. Trumbauer modeled the house after a Paladian manor of 1710 that sits in County Durham, England.

A later owner of the Newport edition, a flamboyant character named Maysie Hayward, renamed the house Clarendon Court. The house made its first appearance before the American public as the setting for the 1950 film *High Society,* a second Hollywood version of Philip Barry's *The Philadelphia Story,* reset in Newport and starring Grace Kelly, Frank Sinatra, and Bing Crosby, with a score by Cole Porter.

A witty and knowledgeable history of the house constitutes a chapter in an anthology of sketches on distinguished Newport mansions. The author is Claus Von Bülow. He concludes with a plea to future historians that has become highly ironic: "The author of this article has lived happily at Clarendon for the past four years. As a European he has found much to admire in Newport with its sense of history and its preservation of a unique architectural heritage. He hopes some future writer will cover the occupancy of his family at Clarendon with as much wistful charity as he has endeavored to extend to its previous owners."

The most extensive renovating Sunny and Claus did at Clarendon Court was to the grounds. They rebuilt the retaining sea wall and completed the house's privacy by paying the Army Corps of Engineers to build a tunnel for Cliff Walk to pass under their lawn. (To ensure that privacy, Claus, probably at Sunny's instigation, phoned the local tour-bus company to ask them to make no mention of Clarendon Court or its owner as they took tourists down Bellevue Avenue.) A seventeen-foot knoll was removed to open up the view of the sea. The gardens were replanted and relandscaped and a swimming pool was installed that many in Newport declared the most beautiful they had ever seen. The cost of the exterior work was in the neighborhood of one million dollars.

Inside, the only architectural change was to convert a ground-floor wing of several sitting rooms into a master-bedroom suite: a large bedroom, a hallway leading to a study for Von Bülow, and a bathroom for each.

Because of the architecture's derivation, and perhaps because her mother's furnishings were predominantly French, Sunny set out to furnish her house with British antiques and paintings. The dining room had a Waterford chandelier and Chippendale chairs; the large entrance hall with its sweeping marble staircase contained an armchair said to have been made for George III; the pièces de résistance in the treasure-filled living room were two large Gainsboroughs and a Romney.

The scale of everything was accomplished with a perfectionist's eye; no picture was too large or small for its spot, no piece of furniture of a bulk incongruous with the items around it. Removing the museum curse from these two stately rooms was an assertive use of color—particularly in the rose-dominated Aubusson and the blue fabrics of the living room and in vivid peach-colored walls in the dining room.

The two rooms most popular with Sunny and her children were the breakfast room and the library, both of which formed extensions to opposite ends of the house's ocean side and both of which had windows on three of their four walls giving a bright, indoor-outdoor feeling that was a welcome contrast to the ground floor's more formal rooms.

The breakfast room in particular had an airiness about it. White wooden lattice covered the walls between the French windows; a white-marble floor, many plants, and a long glass dining table added to the summer-house feeling.

Sunny decorated the master bedroom in the same English-manor style the fourteen-foot ceilings required, again achieving warmth with color: reds in the oriental carpet were echoed in pink hangings. Her bathroom, which would be a major setting for the drama to come, was a fantasy of pink marble and gold-plated hardware, all brightly illuminated with artificial light from concealed sources.

After seeing the results, one dowager said, "They took the most boring house in Newport and turned it into a masterpiece."

Even though they had the help of a local decorator, friends insist the house was mostly Sunny and Claus, in equal parts.

Von Bülow himself says that their tastes were parallel precisely up until the point of completion. Von Bülow liked to finish off, he said, with a touch of whimsy—some silly object he picked up somewhere, or some incongruous personal memento, but Sunny insisted, he said, on maintaining the purity of the concept, doggedly sticking to the adopted theme, no deviations.

With Mrs. Aitken already ensconced in town, Sunny and Claus's assimilation into Newport mainstream came quickly. The preservation-conscious town was delighted to have a local landmark resuscitated by a newcomer who, in addition to possessing the requisite fortune, happened to be beautiful and, by Newport standards, young.

Many in town were even more delighted by the arrival of Claus. He was urbane, charming, and—that all-important portmanteau quality—*amusing*. In addition, he brought an air of cultivation and brains to a colony often derided for its shortage of these qualities. When the legendary Newport social arbiter of the century's early days, Harry Lehr, suffered a nervous breakdown, his chum Mrs. Stuyvesant Fish urged him to return to Newport immediately. "You know quite well, sweet lamb," she wrote him, "that you won't need any mind to go with the people here."

Von Bülow had not negotiated the perilous social waters of London and New York only to make a faux pas in Newport. He charmed such key figures as Mrs. John Nicholas Brown, Oatsie Charles, and John Winslow, who relished his wit and style.

Not everyone was charmed. The head of the Reading Room, the popular and dynamic investment banker Barclay Douglas, received a note from Von Bülow shortly after meeting him. The note contained a check for a few thousand dollars. Von Bülow wondered if Douglas might be good enough to invest it for him? Von Bülow, who was already a member of the Reading Room, asked if Douglas would consider sponsoring him for the even more exclusive Brook Club in Manhattan.

Douglas, already offended by the transparency of the proffered check, indicated to Von Bülow that the Brook Club was a stuffy group of men who had known each other their entire lives. He saw no reason why Von Bülow would be interested in them or vice-versa.

"Here is where Von Bülow lacked style," Douglas said. "Instead of shrugging it off with a smile, not letting on that it mattered, he barely spoke to me from that point on. That was dumb."

While Sunny was throwing herself into the house, Claus was busy involving himself in the right Newport causes. He served on the board of the Casino, the Cliff Walk Association (which he headed), and the Preservation Society—whose president was the very social John Winslow. Within a remarkably short time the Von Bülows, particularly Claus, were deeply enmeshed in the fabric of Newport. If a hostess had guests in her house who required bright conversation, her immediate thought was to get Claus—and, of course, Sunny—to come for dinner. He soon became one of the resort's prime exhibits to prove Newporters weren't all mindless socialites.

* * *

Though pleased with her grand setting, Sunny was anything but grand in her habits. Even with a cook, butler, and various other servants, Sunny would often go to the kitchen to get a snack for herself. To the dismay of her French chef, she loved simple food —shepherd's pie was a favorite and she had an even greater fondness for Colonel Sanders's chicken legs, at odd times sending her chauffeur for an order. Often, if an item was needed at the store, Sunny would not send a servant but would run off alone to the shopping center. In the words of a friend, "She was not one to sweep up Bellevue Avenue in her chauffeur-driven limousine."

While Claus's Newport activities were the gregarious and social good works, Sunny's were, predictably, more private. She had always enjoyed sports, but now conscious of the assaults of age on her looks, she worked at keeping fit playing golf often and, each morning and afternoon, swimming laps in her pool. Ten years later, when Maria Schrallhammer testified at the trial, she mentioned watching through the library window, for long periods of time, her beautiful mistress slicing through the water in the magnificent setting.

Another of Sunny's pastimes was arranging flowers for the house. This was no casual amusement but a daily, hours-long operation, often performed with the help of Maria. Once the gardens were redesigned, Sunny kept on eleven gardeners for her eleven acres; much of the planting was done with an eye to cutting. Maria and Sunny would forage out, return to the house with baskets of blooms, and spend hours fashioning elaborate arrangements.

Existing vases of flowers, although still fresh, were removed and the new ones installed. This was done in every room that was so much as passed through, not just the ones that were actually used (Von Bülow later complained that they used only two rooms: their bedroom and the library). The house always looked as though eighty people were expected for dinner, but dinner parties were sporadic; the flowers were for Sunny and her family.

The floral displays were symbolic to Von Bülow of the waste he felt in the Clarendon Court spectacular. Having put so much energy and taste, if not money, into making Clarendon Court a showplace, he was keen to show off the results with a round of entertaining. This was not Sunny's style. The house was for her enjoyment and her family's; it was not to instill envy or respect in people she barely knew and cared nothing about.

This touches a fundamental difference between the husband and wife. Discreetly concealed under Von Bülow's Belgravia-nurtured restraint was an insecure urge to impress with wealth. Sunny, who could certainly match Claus insecurity for insecurity, had an opposite drive. She seemed embarrassed by her wealth and felt it made people like her less. Although she adored the luxury and beauty it could buy her and was determined to have these things, she feared showing them off.

When she did have dinner parties, they were often paybacks to people like Mrs. Brown. The older Newport matrons, always gimlet-eyed with any newcomer who dared to entertain them, sipped the Bordeaux, admired the Gainsboroughs, and dubbed Sunny an "adequate" but by no means brilliant hostess. It is a tribute to Sunny that they didn't see she was a suffering one.

A guest at one of these parties describes a scene that reveals the relationship between the Von Bülows. After dinner one night, Sunny was giving a tour of the house to a group of guests who had expressed an interest in the furnishings. Handed such a "script," Sunny could be outgoing and was enjoying pointing out the most interesting objects and giving their backgrounds.

Claus, who had been in the library with other guests, emerged into the living room and encountered Sunny's tour group. Without a word of apology, he interrupted her discourse and took over the explanations. Sunny stood quietly for a few minutes; then, when it became apparent she was not to be given back the floor, she wandered off to the other guests, not in pique but rather in an awkward attempt to mitigate the shock everyone present felt at Von Bülow's rudeness.

Although the family maintains they were not against Claus until the suspicions emerged, that is not to say they were unaware of character flaws. Frequently on these house tours he would point to something costly that Sunny had acquired before marrying him and say "I gave that to Sunny for her birthday three years ago."

Generally this was passed over in embarrassed silence by Sunny and her family until at a dinner party at Sunny's Fifth Avenue apartment a European guest was raving to Mrs. Aitken about the home's furnishings and said how lucky her daughter was to have a husband of Mr. Von Bülow's taste and generosity. Mrs. Aitken indicated her daughter was not lacking in taste and implied she was not in need of generosity by telling the woman that almost everything in the house was there before Sunny married Claus.

Groping for the origin of her impression, the woman said, "But that exquisite antique Limoges at the dinner table. He told me specifically that he gave that to Sunny."

"I fear you must have misheard him," Mrs. Aitken said sweetly, having overheard Von Bülow say precisely that. "I gave that china to Sunny myself."

From the start in Newport, as now in New York as well, Sunny gave only the minimum number of parties required of her. Eventually, accepting invitations became onerous to her. Attempting to avoid offense at Sunny's refusals, Claus told his good pal, Mrs. John Nicholas Brown, that Sunny only enjoyed dinners if she were seated next to someone intelligent. Perhaps with an I'll-fix-her malice, Mrs. Brown, at her next party, seated Sunny to the right of Sir Kenneth Clark.

"And do you know," said Mrs. Brown, "she still looked bored?"

Barclay Douglas, a long time veteran of leaden dinner partners, prides himself on being able to converse on a broad range of subjects, ranging from Elizabethan poetry to contemporary sex. Seated next to Sunny he exhausted his repertoire trying to ignite conversation. Douglas concluded she was a woman of unsurpassed dullness. It does not seem to have occurred to him that Sunny was intimidated, perhaps put off, by Douglas's aggressive charm.

Years later, when the press was foraging for details about Sunny and decided (with Claus's help) that she was reclusive, it annoyed an old friend in Manhattan: "Didn't anyone ever think that maybe she just didn't *like* all those dreary people in Newport?" This is a bright defense, but too much evidence exists that Sunny found most socializing painful, especially in Newport, where it was repeatedly with the same people.

Author Walter Hackett once rented a garage apartment from the Von Bülows. He stopped in at the main house on some small matter and was asked by Von Bülow to come in for a drink.

While they were chatting in the library, Sunny came in, greeted Hackett pleasantly, and sat down. She sat silently for about ten minutes without entering the conversation, then excused herself and left.

"He was always very friendly," said Hackett, "Sunny wasn't— but I sensed she wanted to be."

The vignette seems to typify Sunny's ambivalence about social intercourse. She made her decision for sociability, whether accepting an invitation or issuing one or joining her husband and a neighbor for a chat. When it became clear to her that whatever she had hoped would come from her effort—perhaps even a change in herself—was not going to come, she plotted her escape. As time went on, she made this pessimistic judgment, not at the party, but just before setting out.

But when parties were necessary, Sunny didn't stint. In June of 1976, just after Ala's graduation from St. Timothy's, Sunny gave her a debut ball at New York's Plaza Hotel, preceded by a dinner dance given by Mrs. Aitken.

Sunny's two older children were becoming involved in interesting activities. Through the efforts of Von Bülow's friend Senator Claiborne Pell, Alexander, after graduating from Deerfield, worked for a summer as a Senate page. Ala would use her fluency in German to get a job as an assistant to famed photographer Alfred Eisenstaedt while he filmed a documentary on Germany.

Both children would fly off at least once a year to visit their father—sometimes in Austria, sometimes at a house he had in Marbella, and sometimes to Africa, where he had established a career as a professional hunter and safari guide. Sunny was always highly cooperative in bringing about these reunions. Everyone was struck by what an amiable divorce it was—and had been since the beginning. The first year after the split Sunny sent Alfie a pup tent for Christmas, perhaps as symbolic endorsement of the outdoor life she wanted no part of. Hearing of this gift, a friend who knew of Alfie's infidelities said, "But, Sunny, I would think you'd hate Alfie."

"You can't hate Alfie," Sunny replied. "It would be like hating trees or grass."

VII

BY April of 1978, the month Claus met Alexandra Isles, he had been married to Sunny twelve years. The marriage had settled into a pattern that seemed to have been exactly what Sunny wanted—two beautiful homes and three splendid children, four frisky dogs and a husband in constant attendance. The children would later deny that Sunny had any objection to Claus's taking a job, as he claimed, but evidence is strong that, whether or not she insisted on it, she liked having him on call for a quick game of backgammon, to discuss plans for the houses or the children or merely to have company for watching television. But while Claus went along in his role of companion in Sunny's home-oriented existence, it clearly exasperated him. Nevertheless, he couldn't change her.

Sunny liked both her houses, but Clarendon Court was very special for her. In addition to being a spectacular house in a spectacular setting, it had two of her enthusiasms that New York lacked—her gardens and her dogs.

The four labradors occupied an important place in Sunny's affections. When she came up from New York she usually brought them gifts. The dogs came to expect this; when the family arrived from New York, they were frantic until the rubber bones or whatever were produced. Ala speaks of going into the master bedroom and finding her mother tugging on one end of a towel and a labrador tugging on the other. Sunny insisted on the dogs sleeping with her and Claus, but the togetherness presented a problem: the dogs snored. Sunny's solution was not banishment, but earplugs for herself and Claus.

Friends who knew Sunny well—and there were not many—insist she had a wonderful sense of humor and a great relish for the ridiculous, enjoying nothing better than sitting for hours talking and laughing. While such a session might seem a good occasion for drinking, one friend who sat often with Sunny, and who shared a weight problem with her, recalled Sunny inventing new "drinks" for them to try on the order of cranberry juice, soda, and a dash of lemon.

Sunny was particularly delighted by other people's foibles and pretensions. A newly rich manufacturer had bought a mansion several houses from Clarendon Court and, on his walks, had spotted Sunny strolling in her garden in the morning wearing a full-length peignoir. He assumed the beautiful mistress of the beautiful estate was so rich she wore evening clothes all day. When one morning he made a neighborly visit bearing a large basket of fruit and cheese, he presented himself at Clarendon Court wearing a dinner jacket and black tie. Sunny loved his visit, but laughed for weeks about his rig.

People who knew Sunny over a period of many years think she was at her most beautiful in the mid to late 1970s, when she entered her forties. Sunny's remarkable looks were of the bland, open variety that benefited from the character added by age. Nevertheless, Sunny was not satisfied with her looks.

In 1975 she went to a doctor on West 59th Street, the well-known Dr. Ju, and said she wanted to improve the appearance of her face and neck. After a careful examination Dr. Ju told her it was too early for surgery: her degree of aging did not warrant it. She should come back in two years. She returned in the summer of 1978 and Dr. Ju scheduled surgery for January, 1979. After operating on Sunny's face and neck, Dr. Ju had her moved into Essex House, a luxury hotel next door to Dr. Ju's office where she stayed for the ten days it took her scars to heal. She was determine to keep the surgery secret telling Claus and Maria but not her children; she would not be seen in public, not even at her exercise class, until Maria assured her the scars were no longer noticeable.

* * *

While the couple seemed compatible on the surface, Sunny and Claus had a fundamental difference in their outlook toward money that frustrated Claus increasingly as the years went by. To Von Bülow, great wealth was the key to happiness. All his life he had rubbed as close as he could to it, pitting his social and professional energies to remaining near it or possessing it. Sunny, who had never known anything else, held an opposing view. She knew that great wealth brought little in fulfillment or fundamental contentment.

There is, however, no evidence that Sunny disdained her husband's veneration of wealth; certainly he was not the only one in her world who espoused that faith. But there is considerable evidence that Von Bülow was maddened by his wife's nonuse of the limitless possibilities her money afforded them for pursuing a high-energy social life, flying off to the most luminous social events in Europe or California, drawing the world's most fascinating people to their homes, and filling seasonal gaps by leasing castles and yachts to sample high-life delights in unfamiliar locales. To possess two thrilling showplaces and not have them filled constantly with parties was, to Von Bülow, like owning a Masarati and keeping it in the garage.

But while Sunny never lost her enthusiasm for travel, her idea of a marvelous time remained dinner at home with her husband and family followed by a board game or television. It may say something about the times that Sunny's preference for family evenings at home as opposed to nightly parties was later portrayed as a symptom of mental illness.

Claus, on the other hand, was trained for the salon just as a Thoroughbred is trained for the track; his interests were the basic currency of drawing-room talk: money, art (a function of money), sex and sexual perversion (also a function of money), good food and wine (yet another), music and opera, literature, theater, scandals, eccentric dowagers, horses and pets, women's clothes and jewelry, history, and lineage.

He could engage in conversations on any of these topics in five languages and he could do it with a wit that, while less than dazzling, was depressingly rare in his rarefied circles. Whatever interested them, interested him, and his ability to hold forth with knowledge and humor on their subjects often won him quick and hearty approval. Von Bülow was an unusually social animal and an odd mate for his antisocial wife.

An extension of this mismatching was that Von Bülow's friends, of whom he had many, invariably were like him, people who felt alive only when eating and drinking in a room full of people known to each other more by their real estate holdings than by their characters. To such energized types, Sunny was not very interesting. Because Von Bülow saw to it that it was *his* friends they saw, she became a rather sad tagalong in her own life.

Von Bülow must have been aware of this stay-at-home side of Sunny when he married her, but the personality difference was less of a problem in the marriage's first years, when he had more functions. Decorating the two houses was no small undertaking —involving much planning, buying trips to Europe, art-hunting expeditions at home—and it was an enthusiasm they shared. The completion of the homes may have played an important part in Von Bülow's growing disquiet.

Also, he had acted as a father for Alexander and Ala, who were now grown. While the relationship had been a good one ("We loved and respected him," Ala said after the trial), they had less and less need of a father—and were more capable of making direct contact with their real one.

As for the physical relationship between him and Sunny, Von Bülow claimed that at the time of Cosima's birth thirteen years earlier Sunny had called an end to sex. A psychiatrist from Newport Hospital later testified that Sunny had told him they hadn't made love for five years, an amatory discrepancy of nine years. A good friend of Sunny from years back said that Sunny had a very healthy sexual appetite and adored men but was totally monogamous; had Claus not been performing as a husband, the friend said, Sunny would have gotten rid of him in short order.

It is difficult to uncover the truth about something known to a certainty only by the two people involved. But allowing for Sunny's reputation for outspokenness and candor, the five-year version is probably accurate.

Even in his attempts at community activities, Von Bülow found himself frustrated. He accepted a seat on the board of the Newport Casino—the tennis club that had lost much of its Gilded Age glory—but found the club to be the private fiefdom of Jimmy Van

Alen, who needed no help from Von Bülow or anyone else in making decisions. Von Bülow resigned in a huff.

There is no doubt that Von Bülow's life was at a crisis; he was feeling himself more and more a hired ornament in Sunny's uninteresting life and made self-pitying remarks along these lines to his stepchildren and others. His desperation produced two immediate results: first he fell in love, then he resolved to go back to work.

The order of these two occurrences is important. Sunny's pleased acquiescence to his taking a job casts doubt on his claim that she had forbidden him to work. It is more likely that, until he fell in love with a woman who wanted him to divorce Sunny —thereby for the first time needing money of his own—returning to work had not occurred to him as a cure for his boredom and frustration.

In April of 1978 a mutual friend introduced Claus to Alexandra Isles at the Knickerbocker Club. Much later, newspapers would refer to her as a "socialite" and a "television actress," but she was difficult to characterize so neatly. Alexandra was then thirty-two, fourteen years younger than Sunny.

She had a luxuriant mane of dark brown hair, trusting blue eyes, and a facial structure Hollywood agents refer to as "money bones." Her mother, Mab Moltke, came from a socially prominent San Francisco family and had married Count Bobby Moltke, a wealthy and aristocratic Dane with whom she had Alexandra and another daughter. Moltke was a popular figure on the international social scene—as well known in Long Island and in London as he was in Copenhagen, where he lived.

Alexandra, like Sunny, attended Chapin and later St. Timothy's. She married Philip Henry Isles, a Wall Street financier who had shortened his name from Ikleheimer and whose mother had been a Lehman, of the prominent and enormously rich New York banking Lehmans. With Isles, Alexandra had a son, Adam, whose custody she retained when she was divorced.

With a comfortable income from both her own family and her ex-husband, she settled into an apartment at 91st Street and Park Avenue and pursued an acting career. Through contacts she won a plum job on the popular afternoon television series *Dark Shadows;* she played Victoria, an ingenue who had little to do, as

Alexandra complained, but wander through the vampire-plagued sets saying "What's going on around here?"

Off camera she maintained some of the wide-eyed wonderment that made her so perfect a foil for the television sit-ghouls and perhaps an accompanying ingenuousness that made her an easy mark for a suave European.

Apart from her youth, she had other qualities that compared favorably to Sunny's. She had shown a marked amount of independence in her single-handed raising of a son, her pursuit of a career, and her active social life in Manhattan.

An odd coincidence helped draw these two transplanted Danes together: Von Bülow knew Alexandra's father, although it is said that Count Moltke never had any use for Claus. (Honey Hohenlohe said that Moltke phoned her in alarm when he heard that Von Bülow was marrying Sunny, whom he barely knew.) If Von Bülow knew of Moltke's disdain, it is unlikely he mentioned it to Alexandra.

Claus began his campaign by inviting her to lunch parties at top restaurants like Caravelle. On these occasions Alexandra quickly sensed that she was the event's *raison d'être,* the other guests merely tactful hedges against the embarrassment she might feel at being courted by a married man.

The discreet campaign continued for nine months. Then, in January of 1979, Von Bülow took Alexandra to a dinner alone, again at Caravelle. He told her that he loved her. While she made no counter declaration, she did not—as she would testify later—"do anything to discourage him." They started an affair. After another two months he told her he wanted to marry her, but such a step would require the time and careful handling necessary to extricate himself from his marriage to Sunny.

Alexandra made it clear she was not interested in a back-street situation, no matter how permissive the wife might be. She was seeking not just a lover for herself but a father for her son. Work in the theater and play with fast society had not corrupted her middle-class values. She wanted a husband—Von Bülow, if that proved possible; if not, then she would keep looking.

When Claus asked what amount of time she would allow him to straighten out things with Sunny, Alexandra replied that she would like the whole matter settled and them all together as a family by Christmas—a highly significant calendar marking in light of subsequent events. Making mental calculations to allow time for the necessary steps, she told Von Bülow she thought he should have his side arranged by October, or in about six months.

Early in 1979, just as Von Bülow won Alexandra, he had mutual friends introduce him to Mark Millard, a Wall Street titan who had for years been a power at the investment firm of Kuhn Loeb, specializing in oil deals. A series of mergers brought him under the corporate blanket of Shearson–American Express, where he ran a $300 million investment operation.

Von Bülow told Millard he wanted to go to work for him. Millard at first dismissed him as a rich dabbler who was not serious about hard work. The financier was impressed, however, by Von Bülow's persistence.

When they finally sat down to talk seriously, Von Bülow said he was not so much interested in salary at the moment as in working into a position of usefulness that would reestablish him in the world of big business, where within a reasonable period he could earn substantial money. In exchange for asking little in the way of remuneration, Von Bülow requested a loose schedule. He had "domestic obligations" that necessitated shorter hours—off by 4 P.M., half day on Fridays, entire weeks off here and there. Since Von Bülow would be working on a fee basis, Millard found the propositions reasonable; he gave Von Bülow a try.

Millard was struck by Von Bülow's diligence. "He packed a forty-hour week into thirty hours," he said. Millard was also impressed by Von Bülow's ability, his analytical skill, his negotiating acumen, and, perhaps most surprising, his willingness to attack with energy the most menial tasks.

When Millard had occasion to travel to Los Angeles to talk with the Getty organization, he took Von Bülow along and was happy to see his new lieutenant greeted by the Getty people as a member of the family. Warm greetings were given in other cities as well: Von Bülow seemed to have a highly useful address book.

Millard was delighted with his protégé; Von Bülow seemed intent on proving something to himself. His financial arrangement with Millard evolved into a fee of three hundred dollars a day plus expenses. This arrangement didn't get under way until 1980, when he earned from Millard a yearly total of $25,250.

Although his toehold with Millard was encouraging, even with his salary expectations he would suffer a sharp drop in affluence if he divorced Sunny. And though he would not have to give up his social position—he had devoted friends in the inner circles of Newport, New York, and London—he was not willing to settle in one of those small, third-rate apartments in first-rate addresses from which he could emerge twice a day to dine with the truly rich. He had been one of them too long.

But neither was it Alexandra's style to be a mistress to a man in a highly visible marriage. If Von Bülow's self-view as a grandee locked him into his marriage with Sunny, Alexandra's self-view as a respectable mother locked her into her insistence on his getting a divorce.

In 1979, with Alexandra fixed in his life, he talked frequently to friends about his wife's drinking and her depression. He told each one as though it was in strictest confidence, thereby lowering the risk of anyone's questioning why the hurtful gossip about Sunny was coming from her own husband, who should be honor-bound to cover up her weaknesses, not broadcast them.

As for the manifest disloyalty, it served to make people think the problem must be *worse* than Von Bülow indicated. He was, as everyone knew, a gentleman of honor. No one questioned the validity of this information, yet no one, including Sunny's children and servants, who were around her constantly, saw the slightest evidence of either drinking or depression. Von Bülow never mentioned these failings at home, so those in a position to, never challenged his stories until Ala one day confronted him.

She had heard, she told him, that he had been telling people her mother had a liquor problem.

"How could you think such a thing of me?" he replied. "Especially when you and I both know it's not true."

Von Bülow did not limit his whispers to the Upper East Side dinner-party circuit. He told their family doctor Richard Stock that Sunny was having a problem with the bottle. Without a pause, into her permanent records went this important medical "fact," coming as it did from an unimpeachable source.

Many months later, at the trial, it was alarming to trace the path of this alcoholic stigma as it became fixed on Sunny's medical records, first with Dr. Stock, then with Newport Hospital, then a Boston hospital, moving with her to the Columbia Presbyterian

Hospital in Manhattan, and when the story broke in the newspapers, ending up as common knowledge to the American public.

At the time of the trial the victim's "drinking problem" was tossed about so frequently in the press that old ladies in Palo Alto and teenagers in Tampa knew Sunny Von Bülow was a drunk. Later it was shown there had been but one source for this charge: her husband. It was a frightening lesson in the contagion of harmful rumors.

Friends of Sunny's say that the earliest instance of Claus telling anyone Sunny had a drinking problem was in July of 1978, three months after he met Alexandra Isles and a year and a half before her first coma. It occurred during a visit to Clarendon Court of a school friend of Sunny's and had consequences that were baffling at the time.

After dinner one evening Sunny had two drinks that hit her so visibly that she excused herself and went to bed early. For the remainder of the evening Claus poured out to the guest his anguish about Sunny's drinking, which, he said, was chronic and serious.

The friend was so alarmed she phoned a mutual friend, even closer to Sunny, who had herself overcome a drinking problem. Would she come to Newport and talk to Sunny? Or just observe the situation? The second friend called Sunny and, on the pretext of investigating the St. George's School for her son, said she was coming to Newport. Sunny invited her to lunch.

When the two old friends had a chance to talk alone the woman told Sunny of her struggle with alcoholism. Sunny was sympathetic about the ordeal her friend had gone through and upset that her friend had not confided in her during the difficult period.

The woman offered Sunny every opportunity to confess a similar problem but nothing was said and not so much as a missed beat suggested that Sunny might be holding back. The friend, like most people who have experienced alcoholism, was alert to signs. She could see none.

Wine had been served at lunch, but Sunny had passed it up for a glass of milk. (Others in the household said this was typical of her at dinner, when Claus would invariably drink wine.) The friend left Newport convinced that Sunny had no problem and was perplexed by Claus's alarm-sounding.

In addition to telling people Sunny was incapacitated by an

addiction to liquor, Claus became increasingly watchful of her at public appearances—perhaps to heighten the suspicion that she needed watching. In Newport, Sunny and her mother would frequently be at the same party. Annie Laurie, who would have been quick to notice if her daughter had had too much to drink, became aware of a new pattern: Claus would whisk Sunny from a party early, particularly if she seemed to be enjoying herself.

At the time Annie Laurie thought he was concerned for Sunny's health, although Sunny had no health problems whatever. Von Bülow now says he had to get Sunny home before she disgraced herself with her drunkenness. Another construction of his behavior might be his fear that Sunny, by staying late at parties, would prove that she drank next to nothing.

When at the trial the question of whether or not Sunny had a drinking problem became so important, no one could be brought forward to substantiate Von Bülow's claim that she drank excessively during their marriage. Seven witnesses who lived in the same house—Alexander, Ala, and five servants—testified that Sunny drank far less than the average person.

Von Bülow's accusation, however, was not a complete fiction. Evidence emerged that during the unhappy last years of her marriage to von Auersperg, Sunny was seen on numerous occasions under the influence of alcohol. The doggedly loyal Maria, who insisted Sunny had no drinking problem when Von Bülow claimed she did, was asked in an interview after the trial if it was true Sunny drank too much in this period some eighteen years earlier.

"Yes, it is," Maria said, but added, "but she needed very little. She would take two drinks and appear to have had too much."

Since the von Auerspergs led a highly conspicuous social life in a fluid international group, Von Bülow had surely heard such gossip about Sunny. As the problem appears to have persisted for a short time after her return to New York, he may have witnessed it himself. If so, it throws a curious light on something Maria added to her remarks: "When we were living at the Stanhope Hotel and Mr. Von Bülow was courting Princess von Auersperg, he would bring her gifts of bottles of whiskey."

In the late 1970s Alan Murphy planned a dinner for a South American couple popular on the international circuit who were coming to New York. The guest of honor told Murphy he would like to see the Von Bülows.

Calling their apartment, Murphy as usual got Claus, who said Sunny was unable to come to the phone. Murphy explained that the couple would be visiting New York only briefly and hoped to see the Von Bülows at Murphy's dinner, which was scheduled for a Wednesday night.

"Oh, yes, we know they are coming," Von Bülow replied coolly. "We will be seeing them; they are coming to the apartment. Besides, Sunny and I never go out during the week."

Arriving at the dinner, the South Americans asked if the Von Bülows were coming. Murphy repeated his conversation with Claus.

The husband looked at Murphy fixedly. "We are not going to their apartment. We are not seeing them at all."

Another odd change came over Von Bülow in the late seventies. Having taken charge of the operation of the households, he suddenly became aggressively economy-minded. At one point he called together the Clarendon Court staff and gave a speech on the need for cutting back expenses. They were no longer to shop for groceries at the expensive Brick Market, but at Almac's; each week he wanted to go over the checkout receipts.

Shortly later he asked a maid if she would accompany him through the house. Pointing out lighting fixtures, he said he wanted all bulbs replaced with 25-watt bulbs, to reduce the electric bills. At a cost of several hundred dollars he had timers installed that automatically turned off the lights in Alexander's and Ala's closets. "They never turn them off," he complained.

Von Bülow had told the head gardener to reduce the spring planting of flowers to the minimum; they had been spending far too much on this. A bit later in the spring, Sunny was by the pool and asked the gardener why the planting was so skimpy. With Von Bülow standing nearby, he replied that Mr. Von Bülow had so instructed him. Sunny immediately turned to Claus and began berating him as the gardener edged away. The heated discussion went on for some time, ending with Von Bülow storming off into the house.

When he was gone, Sunny went over to the gardener and told

him in detail what she wanted done. By the time she had finished, she had ordered twelve thousand dollars' worth of planting.

Another oddity occurred at Clarendon Court during this economy push of Von Bülow's. The maid he had instructed about the light bulbs was the wife of a retired police officer who also worked in the house. Sunny once told the man that because of his police background she felt more secure having him around.

One day Von Bülow called the man and his wife into the kitchen and told them they were fired and should leave the house immediately. No reason was given. At home later the same day, the couple received a call from a highly agitated Sunny. Why weren't they at work? They said what had happened.

"I want you right back," she said angrily. "Please come immediately."

They drove up to Clarendon Court and were met at the gate by Von Bülow, who refused to let them in. By now the couple had had enough. They are convinced Sunny never knew that they had tried to come back.

As for Von Bülow's economies, it is difficult to know what exactly he had in mind. Sunny's trust officers are firm in stating there was never the slightest need for economizing, certainly not for replacing 60-watt with 25-watt bulbs. They add, however, that Von Bülow was given a drawing account with which to pay household bills.

Toward the end of 1979 Sunny signed a will that superseded one that had been in effect since 1969. The juxtaposition of dates —the new will with the first assault—alerted the investigators once Claus was under suspicion. It turned out, however, that the new will had been in the making for a considerable time; the main change in it was the disposition of Clarendon Court and its possessions, which Sunny did not own at the time of the first will.

Although Clarendon Court and its contents were left outright to Von Bülow, his net benefit from the will—sizable as it was—was little different from the earlier one.

Although Alexandra Isles thought herself in love with Claus, she began to doubt his ability to break with Sunny. By the summer of 1979, well before her October deadline, she decided it was hopeless. She didn't doubt his sincerity so much as his willingness to confront the emotional wrenches of a divorce.

One of the things that made her doubt that Von Bülow would keep his promise was his concern over Sunny's "problems" with alcohol and pills, problems he discussed with Alexandra enough for her to know they worried him considerably. Alexandra began to see this concern as an obstacle to his initiating a divorce. If Sunny's problems were his inventions for other reasons, as was later brought out, they also served the purpose of stalling his marriage-bent lover.

When Alexandra went to Ireland in July to visit her mother, she decided to phase out the affair with Von Bülow. She returned to New York in August. When he came back to Manhattan from Newport in the fall, she saw little of him. Each for his or her own reason was unhappy about the impasse and this created a tension between them.

Toward the end of 1979, Sunny dropped by her son's bedroom on Fifth Avenue for a chat. She told Alexander she would get a divorce; her marriage with Von Bülow was not working out. His new position was developing into the kind of work he had done before, work that would keep him away much of the time. She didn't want this. She felt she was holding him back from the life he now wanted to lead.

Alexander listened with sympathy but did not view this opening on his mother's part as an opportunity for him to lobby against Von Bülow. Like his sister, who would later have a similar tête-à-tête, Alexander felt that Von Bülow, in his dutiful attentiveness, was good for his mother. The conversation was marked by the absence of any hostility toward Von Bülow or any anguish about the divorce prospect on either Sunny's part or her son's. It appears the only person who viewed divorce with distress was Von Bülow himself.

VIII

SUNNY Crawford Von Bülow loved Christmas, particularly at Clarendon Court. Her family was the most important thing in Sunny's life; Christmas was the time when her preoccupation was not just acceptable but the order of the day.

Ala had been with her mother until Christmas day when she had flown to Austria to spend the remainder of the holidays with her fiancé's family. Sunny was wistful about this gap in the family unity but knew she would be seeing Ala again in a few weeks.

On the evening of December 26, 1979, after their usual early dinner, Alexander now a handsome twenty-year-old, was talking in the library with his mother, who was sipping a glass of eggnog. A family tradition was to mix up a batch of eggnog each Christmas from Sunny's own recipe—a dozen eggs, a quart of bourbon, and a quart of heavy cream, blended with sugar and nutmeg. The rich concoction was set out in a bowl in the breakfast room during the afternoon and evening, available to anyone who wanted it. At night it was refrigerated, then put out again the next day.

As he spoke with his mother, Alexander noticed that her speech had become slurred and her voice so weak that, at times, although he was sitting next to her, he could barely hear her. He had seen his mother react to alcohol: she would become talkative and a bit silly. Never before had he known her to slur her speech and lose audibility. Yet she seemed in good spirits when he escorted her into her bedroom.

When Von Bülow entered the room, Alexander told him his mother seemed weak, and left. Maria came in to say good night to her mistress and saw that she was already asleep with Von Bülow lying fully dressed on the bed beside her. This was just after 8 P.M.

The next morning Maria came down from her third-floor room at eight o'clock and had her usual breakfast in the kitchen. She then went back to the third floor to busy herself ironing Mrs. Von Bülow's things while waiting for the intercom call from the maid, Mrs. Sullivan, telling her that Mrs. Von Bülow was awake. When by 9:30 Mrs. Sullivan hadn't called, Maria went back downstairs. She had almost reached the bottom of the main staircase when Von Bülow came into the entrance hall from the living room. (To reach Sunny's ground-floor bedroom, you had to pass through the living room.) Von Bülow stopped Maria on the stairs and said her mistress was not well, she had a sore throat; it was not necessary for Maria to do her usual work.

According to Maria, Von Bülow then went back into the living room, closing behind him the double doors from the hall. These were ten-foot-high ornamental doors and never closed. (Von Bülow's lawyers later denied that he had closed these doors. While most of the crucial discrepancies between his version of the day's events and Maria's could be considered differences of interpretation and perception, this was one detail on which they were firm and in direct contradiction.)

Maria then went into the pantry to ask the other servants why the living room doors were closed. No one knew.

Maria returned to the hall, opened the living room doors, and passed through to the door of Mrs. Von Bülow's bedroom. Listening at the door, she heard her mistress moaning. She knocked. Getting no response, she opened the door and went in.

As part of Sunny's decor, twin beds had been placed together and then canopied in champagne-colored silk hangings so that they appeared to be one large bed. On one of the beds Sunny Von Bülow lay asleep or unconscious. On the bed next to her Von Bülow lay reading the paper. As she approached the bed, Maria, who had often seen her mistress asleep, sensed something was wrong. Mrs. Von Bülow was usually a light sleeper who woke the minute Maria opened the door. Now she lay immobile with one arm hanging from the bed.

Maria called her name, first in a normal voice, then louder. She took her mistress's arm, which was limp and cold, and shook it lightly. There was no response. Maria carefully placed the arm on the bed and pulled covers over her mistress. Now very agitated, Maria told Von Bülow that she felt Mrs. Von Bülow was seriously ill and that a doctor should be called. Von Bülow said Mrs. Von Bülow was simply asleep and that Maria should leave her alone.

Maria said, "She's not asleep, she's unconscious." In twenty-three years with Mrs. Von Bülow, Maria had never seen her in this condition.

"No, Maria," he said. "Mrs. Von Bülow has not slept much the last two nights and she's finally fallen into a deep sleep. She needs it badly."

Maria was beside herself. She did not want a confrontation with her master and knew that any action on her part—phoning Mrs. Aitken, for example—would mean all-out war with Von Bülow. Maria returned upstairs to her ironing but within thirty minutes came back to her mistress's bedroom.

She found Mrs. Von Bülow in the exact position in which she had left her, her husband still lying on the bed beside her. Once again Maria tried rousing her but could get no response. Again she expressed alarm to Mr. Von Bülow and said he should call a doctor. He replied that they had no doctor in Newport. Maria reminded him of Dr. Gailitis at the Newport Hospital, whom they had telephoned the previous summer when Mrs. Von Bülow had had stomach pains. (Gailitis, suspecting ulcers, ordered tests, which Von Bülow later canceled on the grounds that his wife didn't want them; in the summer of 1978, Dr. Gailitis had been called to Clarendon Court to treat Sunny for a bad cold.)

Now Von Bülow once again brushed aside the need for a doctor; his wife, he told Maria, had been drinking the night before and was sleeping it off. Maria doubted this was true but asked the servants if Mrs. Von Bülow had had an unusual amount of eggnog. None of them knew of her drinking more than a moderate two or three glasses. (Also, Maria felt—as jurors did later—that the drinking story did not fit with the no-sleep story. Had she been drinking excessively, she probably would have had no trouble falling into a deep sleep.)

At about ten thirty Alexander woke up and left for an indoor-tennis date without encountering Maria, so he knew nothing of her concern. One of the other servants told him his mother had a sore throat and was not to be disturbed. Everyone else in the house was more aware of Maria's alarm. They saw her make repeated trips into the bedroom, where she continued to find her mistress in the same condition and Von Bülow stretched out beside her. On one of the occasions she noticed he had changed from pajamas into daytime clothes but remained prone on the bed.

Of the many bizarre aspects to this tableau, one of the strangest was never under dispute by Von Bülow and his lawyers: that he lay awake on the bed beside his not-conscious wife while Maria —and it appears anyone else who chose—passed in and out of the room. Quite apart from considerations of whether or not he was waiting for her to die, as was later alleged, the picture of Von Bülow stretched out beside his sleeping wife leads to the question of whether he had injected himself with something to fortify himself for what could only be a trying day.

Dr. Stock would later testify that Von Bülow had told him of having had an addiction to Valium—and that jarring fact was one of several unexplored aspects of the case. Under our criminal justice system, of course, nothing can be introduced in court about the defendant unless it relates directly to the commission of the crime; with the victim, on the other hand, any hint, slur, or innuendo is admitted for airing, examining, and amplifying. Every cocktail Sunny Von Bülow had had in the last four years was served up again in court, while the defendant's addiction to a drug was touched on only fleetingly. Maria's famous remark "What for insulin?" might be joined when contemplating Von Bülow, by "What for Valium?"

In considering the events leading up to the first coma, Von Bülow's tranquilized befuddlement is only a free-wheeling supposition. He had only, however, to bar Maria from the room and he would have eliminated any witness to a scene that harmed him greatly in court. Forbidding the maid entrance would not have been an untoward action on the part of a husband with a sleeping or perhaps indisposed wife, but instead he let Maria wander freely in and out gathering, as it turned out, the most damning evidence.

The possibility of his being "on" something has even greater relevance as a response to the best argument in Von Bülow's defense: how could such an intelligent man make such a mess of a job? The answer might be that his competence was chemically dulled.

Another occurrence on that fateful December day strengthens the possibility that Von Bülow was not functioning normally. On about the third visit to the bedroom Maria, in perhaps her most assertive thrust of the crisis, said to Von Bülow, "If you don't call the doctor, I will."

His response was a non sequitur of almost insane proportions. "You know, Maria," he said, "it is not that easy being married to Mrs. Von Bülow."

Finally, Von Bülow took some action. Just after two o'clock he phoned Dr. Gailitis, who was not in his office; Von Bülow left a message on the doctor's answering machine.

Around three o'clock Von Bülow got Dr. Gailitis on the phone and told him his wife was not waking up, should he be alarmed? Von Bülow had asked Maria to be present for the call. She heard him say that yes, his wife had been up once or twice to go to the bathroom and at one point he had fixed her a ginger ale. Mrs. Von Bülow, he told the doctor, had an alcohol problem, and the previous evening had been "one of those nights."

Maria left the room. When asked on the witness stand why she had done this, she said, "Because it was not true." To others she was even more explicit. "I left," she said, "because he was telling the doctor a bunch of lies."

Von Bülow told Dr. Gailitis that he needed his advice. His wife was an alcoholic, a fact he was ashamed to admit, and it embarrassed him to discuss it with anyone. His wife had abused drugs as well as alcohol. Now she was under an added emotional strain because her daughter, Ala, was planning to marry an Austrian and live abroad. Having had a bad experience married to an Austrian herself, Mrs. Von Bülow was very upset about the development and had not slept for two nights, even though, Von Bülow said, she had taken something to make her sleep when she had gone to bed the previous night.

Von Bülow said this was not the first time he had had to deal with such a problem, but his "wife had always slept these things out before." Gailitis told Von Bülow to keep a careful eye on his wife and to look for any change in her breathing pattern. If any new symptoms appeared, Von Bülow was to call Gailitis immediately.

A few hours later, around 6 P.M., Sunny Von Bülow's breathing became irregular and rasping. She was also making a chest sound that Maria later described as a "rattling." Maria was convinced her mistress was dying.

Maria rushed to the bed and tried lifting her to a sitting position but was unable to move her. She asked Von Bülow for help; he shook his head no. The change in his wife's condition, however, was so apparent, she could no longer be dismissed as a sleeping-it-off drunk. Von Bülow phoned Dr. Gailitis and told him to come as quickly as possible. He would pay him anything, Von Bülow said, now highly agitated, if he would come at once. Von Bülow also called Mrs. Aitken to tell her of Sunny's crisis.

Alexander returned from his tennis date and stopped by the ground-floor bedroom to see how his mother's throat was feeling. He walked into a scene of complete panic. Von Bülow was pacing up and down, Maria was sitting on the bed cradling in her arms the gasping Sunny. Alexander was dumbfounded. "Good God! What's happening?" he said. His eyes met Maria's.

"Alexander," Maria said bleakly, "I don't understand anything."

Dr. Gailitis arrived a few moments later. Entering the room, he could see Sunny turning blue in a losing struggle for breath. As he listened to her chest with a stethoscope, he barked at Von Bülow to phone the fire department, his wife had to be gotten to the hospital immediately.

Gailitis was at Sunny's side no more than two minutes when she vomited, then stopped breathing. There was no pulse; her heart had stopped. With his finger, the doctor cleared her throat of kyme. He punched her chest to start her breathing, then pressed her chest again and again.

Roughly, as though handling a rag doll, Gailitis wrenched Sunny's head downward to drain additional fluids, then gave her mouth-to-mouth resuscitation. As Dr. Gailitis worked frantically to prevent Sunny from dying, the commotion drew the other servants into the bedroom.

Gailitis ordered the butler, Robert Biastre, to help him lift Mrs.

Von Bülow to the floor, where the doctor could apply greater pressure for artificial respiration. After about fifteen minutes of strenuous effort, her pulse returned. The fire department rescue crew arrived and applied an oxygen mask to the woman on the floor. Within another ten minutes her breathing was normal enough, Gailitis decided, to move her to the hospital. In the frenzy of getting Sunny into the ambulance, Maria pulled Alexander aside and said, "Later, I must talk with you."

Still with the oxygen mask over her face, and with Von Bülow sitting beside her stretcher, Sunny was rushed through the now-dark winter streets of Newport to the hospital about ten minutes away. Dr. Gailitis drove his own car. When he arrived, he found the emergency room in full action over Mrs. Von Bülow. Alexander drove in his car, but when he arrived at Newport Hospital, he was denied entrance to the emergency room.

When inexplicably unconscious people are rushed to hospital emergency rooms, they are routinely tested for the most common causes: drug overdose, too many sleeping pills, alcoholism. It is common practice that blood for these tests be drawn before any treatment is administered—on the sound theory that you don't treat a condition until you have some notion what it might be. An important reason for this procedure is to assure drawing blood that reflects only the condition and not the hospital's treatment. That is, for tests to tell doctors anything useful, they must be performed on virgin, unadulterated blood.

When Sunny Von Bülow arrived at the Newport Hospital around 7:30 the evening of December 27, 1979, these procedures were followed. Blood samples were immediately taken and sent to the lab to be tested for blood gases, blood count, blood sugar, alcohol, electrolytes, toxicology.

When the results came back, Gailitis found her blood sugar very low, 41 milligrams per 100 milliliters. One hundred milligrams is considered normal. Also low was her potassium level (3 mg) and her phosphorous level. Perhaps most significant, in light of Von Bülow's remarks to Gailitis, was that no traces of alcohol or barbiturate were found in her blood and only a negligible amount of aspirin.

Of all the tests, however, the most alarming was to come. After being in the hospital three and a half hours and receiving sugar in the form of glucose injections, her blood sugar level was measured again and found to be even *lower;* it had dropped from 41 mg to an astonishing 20 mg. This was all but impossible for the doctors to explain except for the presence in her system of a high level of insulin, insulin that was "eating" her blood sugar—the effect insulin has on all blood sugar.

At midnight a blood sample was drawn to be tested for insulin level. This test had to be performed outside the hospital; it turned out to be 72 mg per 100 ml, indeed a high level. Another sample drawn the next morning at 7 A.M. was a more normal 54 mg.

The glucose injections Sunny Von Bülow had been receiving since arriving at the hospital three hours earlier would have had the effect of reducing her insulin level; it was safe to assume that the insulin level had been higher, perhaps considerably higher, on admission than it was when first tested at midnight. The constant administration of glucose finally had its effect. By midmorning the next day, December 28, her blood sugar level was up to 154; although high, a far more normal level.

The previous night, once it had been determined that Sunny was going to pull through, Alexander had returned to Clarendon Court to find Maria waiting for him in the kitchen. Joining her at the table, he listened with increasing bewilderment to her account of the bizarre day and her belief that Von Bülow did not want Sunny to survive whatever it was that was happening to her.

Alexander had trouble taking in the extent of Maria's suspicions, but agreed his stepfather's behavior was extremely odd and they should keep their eyes on him. Alexander felt they should tell his grandmother; they both agreed that they could say nothing to Sunny until they had something substantial to back up the incredible possibility that Von Bülow wanted her dead. Later, explaining to a friend this fear of saying anything to her mistress, Maria said, "If we had, the roof would have fallen in."

Shortly after Maria's and Alexander's dark talk, Von Bülow returned to the house and asked Alexander to join him for a drink in the library. With Maria's accusations still churning in his head, Alexander barely heard as his stepfather ruminated about his general discontent. He was not comfortable in his life, he told his stepson; he wanted to pursue a career—not halfheartedly, but fully—to realize the capabilities that had gotten off to such an auspicious start with Paul Getty. Sunny, however, was against his working. Von Bülow knew how people in Newport talked. He was made to feel like a kept man, a gigolo, someone content to live off his wife's money. He was not.

Despite his talk with Maria, Alexander was too shaken by the day's events to seek out a connection between his mother's struggle with death and his stepfather's unhappiness with his life situation. Neither did Alexander know that this was the second time since the crisis began some twelve hours earlier that his stepfather had digressed from his wife's frightening condition to an unsolicited soliloquy on his own lack of fulfillment.

It says a good deal about Von Bülow's forlorn situation that he had to make his lament to the maid and to his stepson. Having been shut off by Sunny into a world of family and servants, he was in need of a confidant. Of course he had his circle of friends in Newport and New York, but even though a case could be made that more of these liked Von Bülow than Sunny ("We hardly knew her," they would say, "but Claus was a lamb"), still, regardless of his success in her world, it was *her* world.

If Alexander proved unsatisfactory as a confidant, Von Bülow had one person at least whom he regarded as totally his: Alexandra Isles. After his stepson excused himself and left the library, Von Bülow picked up the phone and called Alexandra in Ireland.

Like most "other women," Alexandra felt she knew her lover's wife; unlike many, she had no bad feelings toward her—indeed she felt a good bit of sympathy for her. The news of Sunny's hospitalization upset Alexandra considerably.

Her upset, however, was triggered by more than mere compassion for a woman she wished no harm. Having heard from Von Bülow about Sunny's depression and her suicidal tendencies, Alexandra feared that her romance with Claus might have been the cause. She thought immediately of emotional distress coupled with drugs and alcohol. She didn't necessarily feel that Sunny had made an active suicide attempt, but perhaps, to use Alexandra's phrase, it had been a "passive" one.

On the transatlantic call, Alexandra tried to give Von Bülow what comfort she could, but the call had the opposite result than the one Von Bülow had hoped for: it caused Alexandra to view her romance as more problem-riddled than she had realized. She resolved to put more than geographic distance between herself and it.

Although Sunny's blood sugar rose throughout the night in Newport Hospital, she remained unconscious until the following afternoon. As soon as she awoke, her family, including Von Bülow, arrived. They brought with them food, satin pillows, and framed photographs of themselves for her bedside table. Everyone was baffled about what had happened to her but agreed that that question could await the hospital's reports. For now it was enough that she would recover; it never occurred to any of them that the hospital would not reach a conclusion on exactly what happened.

In addition to private nurses, a number of hospital personnel passed in and out of Sunny's room, the various technicians and nurse's aides who perform tests, draw blood, and generally monitor patients recently discharged from intensive care.

Among them was a young, darkly handsome technician named Robert Huggins, who drew some blood samples. If Sunny had passed Huggins on the street two weeks later, it was unlikely she would have recognized him as someone she had ever seen. But Huggins was to play a prominent role in the attempted-murder trial of Claus Von Bülow.

By the second morning, the pampered rich woman in Sunny had returned. She refused her breakfast. When the nurse admonished her, saying she had to eat something, Sunny replied, "They'll probably bring me something from home. If not, I'll go hungry."

Going over Sunny's test results, Dr. Gailitis found himself perplexed at the cause of her bizarre seizure. Her blood sugar had been abnormally low when she arrived at the hospital, her insulin level high; three hours after admission and after receiving glucose pushes, her sugar level had dropped *even lower*. It made no sense.

As often when Gailitis was confronted with a peculiar set of circumstances, particularly circumstances involving a patient he did not treat regularly, he sought background from a family member. With Von Bülow's confidences about Sunny's drinking still much in his thoughts, Gailitis called Von Bülow and asked him to drop by his office on New Year's Eve—December 31, 1979.

Von Bülow responded with alacrity. Sunny's problems, he told

Dr. Gailitis, were the result of an upbringing by two domineering women—a mother and grandmother of enormous wealth and energy and no one to focus these assets on except Sunny. They had been particularly overbearing in the matter of Sunny's friendships with the opposite sex, having watched her every contact like priestesses supervising vestal virgins.

Naturally, this vigilance developed strong sexual inhibitions in Sunny. When she struggled through this libidinal blockage to fall in love with Georgi Wasilichicoff, the older women found him unacceptable. The relationship was squelched and Sunny whisked off to Europe, to make her forget him.

It was while abroad on this recuperative mission, Von Bülow went on, that Sunny met and fell in love with Prince Alfie von Auersperg. Although he was poor, his ancient lineage made him acceptable to Mrs. Aitken, so they married. When Sunny's first major action on her own turned out so badly—and here Von Bülow threw in a number of highly disparaging remarks about his predecessor—it was a devastating blow to Sunny's fragile self-esteem. It launched her on the path of liquor and pill-reliance from which Von Bülow had tried in vain to rescue her. Since he had known her, Von Bülow told the doctor, Sunny had been plagued by fits of depression, pathological shyness, periods of withdrawal. While her drinking had improved somewhat through Von Bülow's efforts, it was still a problem. In addition, she relied heavily on tranquilizers.

Their sexual relationship, at his wife's request, had been terminated after the birth of their daughter Cosima eleven years earlier. For three years Sunny had insisted on separate bedrooms. As far as Von Bülow knew, she had found or sought no replacement for him in this department. If she had, he hoped he would be enough of a man of the world to understand.

It is not surprising that Dr. Gailitis came away from this interview convinced that Mrs. Von Bülow needed psychiatric help. He went directly to his patient and was aghast to find her smoking. She had just come off a respirator, she had had a touch of pneumonia, and here she was with a full ashtray and a cigarette burning in her hand. With all his medical sensibilities offended, Gailitis was convinced that the portrait Von Bülow had painted of a deeply neurotic woman was an accurate one.

Gailitis told Sunny she must give up smoking, then sat down

to relate her husband's catalogue of weaknesses. Sunny, who was never enthusiastic about heart-to-heart talks, was even less so with people she hardly knew. She sat stony-faced and silent through Gailitis's recitation of the failings he had just heard from Von Bülow. When he got to the drinking allegation, she said angrily, "I am not an alcoholic."

Gailitis said he wanted Sunny to talk with a psychiatrist. She said she would do so only if he felt it absolutely necessary. He did.

The next day Dr. John Carr, the chief of psychiatry at Newport Hospital, presented himself at Sunny's bedside and told her he was a psychiatrist. Sunny was not happy about the visit, again asking if it was necessary. He persuaded her to talk with him. Despite his psychiatrist's trick of starting off with anxiety-reducing questions, Sunny on three occasions asked him to leave—once when he asked her about being an alcoholic. He insisted he had to stay just a little bit longer.

He asked if she had been happy. Almost never. Ever bored? Frequently. What do you project for your future? She hoped it would be more fulfilling than her past. Had she tried to kill herself? No, but she had often wished herself dead. Carr concluded that the woman in front of him was very neurotic and desperately in need of psychiatric help.

When he recommended psychiatric counseling, she said she would be willing to try it. He didn't believe her, knowing that patients often make this promise if they fear being institutionalized. After twenty minutes with her, he left.

Later that day, January 2, Sunny told her nurse she was eager to be with her family. She dressed and left the hospital, although Dr. Gailitis had wanted her to remain a few more days. Her body had successfully combatted whatever it was that was trying to kill her. With no recollection of what brought her to the hospital and little idea of how to find out, Sunny returned to Clarendon Court, to Von Bülow and one more year of life.

IX

SINCE Sunny's coma, her New York doctor, Richard Stock, had been in daily contact with Von Bülow or members of the family. Up until her collapse he had had no reason to suspect a blood sugar problem. As part of routine checkups he had run blood sugar tests on Sunny in 1965 and twice in 1977; *the results were normal.* When the Von Bülows were back in Manhattan, Stock asked Sunny to come to his office for a checkup.

On the day of the appointment, January 21, 1980, Von Bülow accompanied his wife to Stock's office. While Sunny undressed, Stock questioned Von Bülow about Sunny. Von Bülow obliged by repeating much of what he had told Gailitis; that Sunny was alcoholic, depressive, pill-dependent. Von Bülow's briefing on this occasion had a difference: Stock had treated Sunny for twenty-six years while Gailitis had treated her only twice before.

Despite his long association with Sunny, Stock knew that he saw her only on an average of two or three times a year; he could be unaware of problems, possibly even a major problem like alcoholism. Still, he doubted the allegation; drinkers show symptoms —shaky hands, flushed faces, alcohol breath—Sunny showed none of these.

In addition, he had always known Sunny to be forthright, never devious or—when it concerned facts relating to her health —self-protective. Even though he suspected Von Bülow of lying, Stock said nothing to Sunny about Von Bülow's allegation. He later explained that he did not feel it his place to interfere in a marriage.

It is doubtful that anyone—even Maria Schrallhammer—had a clear suspicion that Von Bülow at that point was trying to murder Sunny. A number of those involved, however, felt that his behavior on the day of the coma had been shockingly negligent. Maria was beating the drum on this issue. She already had an ally in Alexander, and she had another when Ala returned from Europe late in January.

After conversations with Maria and Alexander, Mrs. Aitken confronted Von Bülow about the inexplicable delay in getting her daughter help. Never implying more than carelessness or ineptitude, she made it clear that she felt he had been extremely remiss. Her daughter had serious health problems; it fell to Von Bülow, before anyone else, to look after her.

Von Bülow's response to Mrs. Aitken's reprimand was curious. On January 22, the day after taking Sunny to see Dr. Stock, Von Bülow left Sunny watching television and went into his study to write Dr. Gailitis the following letter:

22 January 1980

Dear Dr. Gailitis,

My wife is making excellent progress and has really fully recovered her physical strength. We are both most grateful to you. Now I need your professional opinion, preferably in writing.

My mother-in-law feels that I was remiss in not getting medical aid earlier in the day. On hindsight it is naturally a question I asked myself repeatedly in the days following the crisis. The facts, as I have given them to you, can be recapitulated as follows:

(1) I have witnessed a great many "out for a count" over the last 14 years. None of them, at the time or in retrospect, required a doctor. When my wife broke her hip two years ago, I naturally blamed myself that I had not stayed with her when she went to the bathroom. I did not make that mistake this time.

(2) My wife hardly slept the night of Tuesday 25th. Her voice was very hoarse, and her throat sore the morning of the 26th. She did not sleep at all the night of Wednesday 26th, and I stayed awake with her then, and throughout the day of the 27th. The only times I left her were when I went to get her ginger ales, or portions of tapioca pudding, which she wanted. When she finally fell asleep the morning of the 27th I felt she needed it. Our perfectly healthy teenagers often sleep through lunch, when we allow it. Anyway her breathing was perfectly regular, and she would get up from time to time to go to the bathroom. I tried to reach you around 2.30 P.M., and reached you on the telephone about an hour later when I gave you a resume of the above facts. Shortly after 6 P.M. my wife's breathing suddenly changed to a rattle and I called you immediately. You came very quickly, as did the ambulance, and you saved the day. It was my impression that the actual crisis came very quickly, and quite unexpectedly. Earlier there had been nothing to distinguish this occasion from many previous vigils I have held. Indeed, if there had been no aspiration, there would have been no crisis on this occasion either. If I were to make a guess I would say that the violent flu my wife had some ten days earlier had not completely left her system, and had left a residue in her lungs. Combined with the depressants this nearly proved fatal. Dr. Stock and you are still mystified about the low blood count factor.

Have I stated everything fairly? Was I to blame? By lunchtime on the 27th I had myself gone without sleep for over 50 hours, and my judgment may have been poor. I already have cause to be grateful to you, and I now need your opinion on this question, even if it turns out to be frank and unpalatable.

> Sincerely yours,
> Claus Bülow

Von Bülow's request for a written response from Gailitis is more suggestive of one wanting tangible evidence, should it be needed, than of one seeking only ammunition to refute a mother-in-law's carping. Why could he not phone Mrs. Aitken and say "I spoke with Dr. Gailitis today and he assures me I did everything possible to help Sunny"? Relations had not gotten so bad in the early part of 1980 that Von Bülow and his mother-in-law had to document their communications.

The letter to Dr. Gailitis, which would play a major role at the trial, is significant in several ways. If read carefully against the version of the events of that day of others present at the time— Maria, Alexander, Mrs. Sullivan, Robert Biastre—it is highly revealing of Von Bülow's confidence in his own ability to manipulate the truth—to color, bend, and refashion events as he chose until his behavior emerged as responsible and dutiful.

If he were only contradicting Maria, his insistence on his version might be considered an aristocrat's shrugging off of a servant's clamor. But that he would try to reconstruct events in a way that did violence to the recollections of a number of others suggests he had worked himself into an odd feeling of omnipotence. As far as facts relating to his wife and household were concerned, he considered himself the sole custodian of the truth. If he dubbed Sunny an alcoholic, then she *was* an alcoholic. If he described himself as a concerned, vigilant husband, that then was what he was.

The letter also shows another snobbery-based delusion. His seeking of a doctor's endorsement of his behavior indicates his lawyer's belief in the sovereignty of a professional man's opinion when pitted against the yammerings of servants and children; never mind that the professional man was not present during the hours in question, that the servants and children were.

Von Bülow's ploy produced the exact response he wanted. Dr. Gailitis was somewhat perplexed over Von Bülow's letter but gave him the assurances Von Bülow requested because, he later testified, "That was what he seemed to want."

He wrote:

February 8, 1980

Dear Mr. Von Bülow,

I am glad to hear that Mrs. Von Bülow is improving. It would be helpful for me to get a report from her consulting endocrinologist regarding low blood sugar levels observed at Newport Hospital.

The events leading to the catastrophic deterioration of Mrs. Von Bülow's condition—vomiting, aspiration of gastric contents and cardio-respiratory arrest—were unpredictable.

There is no doubt in my mind that by recognizing the change in Mrs. Von Bülow's condition and by alarming me you saved her life.

Sincerely,
Janis Gailitis, M.D.

Von Bülow now had his talisman—not only against Mrs. Aitken but against who-knew-what future vicissitudes. The letter from Sunny's doctor vouchsafing what an alert and dutiful guardian Von Bülow had been of his difficult wife was like a letter of credit to be used in the event that his luck, not his money, ran out.

Considering his confidence in his exonerating letter, it is ironic that the exchange with Dr. Gailitis was eventually more hurtful than any other item.

One morning in February of 1980, Maria took her mistress her usual breakfast tray of tea and toast and found her feeling sick, with slurred speech and, most alarming to Maria, without the strength to sit up. Maria had to help Sunny upright enough to eat her breakfast. She had never seen her in this condition and said so to Von Bülow. He dismissed it airily; a greasy hamburger Sunny had eaten the night before had brought on the morning's reaction. In a few hours Sunny felt herself, but Maria remained worried. Von Bülow's glib explanation did not satisfy Maria, who took it as further evidence something sinister was going on.

Maria was haunted by Von Bülow's obstinate resistance to summoning medical help for his wife. Whenever Maria complained of feeling unwell, Von Bülow would always call a doctor instantly. With little idea of what exactly she hoped to find, Maria resolved to keep her eyes open.

One day she was tidying up a closet off Von Bülow's study in the Fifth Avenue apartment. The closet was Von Bülow's, but her mistress kept ball gowns and other rarely used items in it. As Maria was checking dresses for repairs, she noticed an open-topped canvas satchel with loop handles, rather like a beach bag. Maria had seen Von Bülow carry this bag when traveling. In plain view inside the satchel was a black leather bag, about four by seven inches with a zipper that ran around three sides. It looked like a case for an electric razor.

Maria unzipped the bag and found inside a number of prescription-drug vials, the plastic kind with twist tops. All the typed labels were made out to C. Von Bülow except one, which was made out to Leslie Baxter, a name which meant nothing to Maria. Inside one of the vials was a white powder; there was a butter-colored paste in another. The substances did not look professionally concocted to her.

At first Maria tried to memorize what was on the labels, but unable to keep the words in her head she returned to the closet later when Von Bülow was not home and copied down the label inscriptions. When Alexander came down to New York from Brown one weekend, Maria showed him the bag and its contents. He agreed it was suspicious, but he had little idea of what to make of it—or indeed what to do about it.

Maria phoned Ala and asked her to come to the apartment to see something she had found, something that might be important. When Ala examined the black bag and its puzzling substances, she told Maria to bring it to her apartment, which was in the same building. Safe in Ala's, the two women removed small quantities from each vial, later taking them to Dr. Stock for analysis. This was March 4.

A pivotal aspect of the story came into play. Although Ala, Maria, and Alexander were sufficiently suspicious at this point to engage in such surreptitious sleuthing, they felt constrained to conceal their suspicions, not just from Von Bülow but from Sunny as well. Ala and Alexander were convinced that their mother, once aware of their hostile and, at this point, unsubstantiated suppositions about her husband, would have "thrown them out of the house."

There is no doubt Ala and Alexander loved their mother, and being as family-oriented as she was, would have dreaded such a break. There is a suggestion here, however, that Von Bülow may not have been the only one reluctant to jeopardize the hefty benefits of being a member in good standing of Sunny's beloved family.

Sunny's childhood friend, Ruth Dunbar Flood, later offered a plausible explanation for the trepidation those close to Sunny felt about going to her with negative suggestions about Claus.

"Sunny felt very deeply that she had failed with her first marriage," Ruth said. "She hated the idea that she might have failed a second time."

Whether or not this was the only reason the family felt they could not speak openly to Sunny against Von Bülow, much of the ensuing tragedy hinges on this reluctance to confront Sunny, not so much with their suspicions of Claus's homicidal intentions, which they had good reason to consider explosive, but *any* of his questionable actions regarding her.

The only one who dared criticize Von Bülow to Sunny was her mother; as the others predicted, Mrs. Aitken's forthrightness proved more of a threat to her relationship with her daughter than to the relationship between husband and wife.

For an altogether different reason, the dread of scandal, Sunny's family were equally determined not to utter a word about their suspicions to anyone outside the family. It would come out at the trial that others at this time or shortly later, by no means family intimates, had thoughts about what might be going on that, if coupled with Alexander, Ala, and Maria's meager file of evidence, might have prevented the outcome.

At the end of the first week in March, Dr. Stock received the results of the analysis of the black-bag substances. The yellow paste turned out to be Valium—but in a form never sold commercially—and the white powder was secobarbital, a barbiturate.

Although everyone was relieved the substances were not more sinister, the forms they were in was worrying. Why a paste and a powder? Weren't barbiturates and tranquilizers always taken in pill form? The innocuous drugs may have reduced fears that Sunny was in immediate danger, but the strange forms only strengthened their belief that Von Bülow was up to something underhanded.

At this point—early in 1980—one of the most remarkable developments in the entire story occurred, one that shows how the strategies of great wealth release those possessing it—or managing it—from the confines of normal logic. Claus sent a letter to those handling Sunny's affairs saying that Sunny was insisting on setting him up with money of his own. He asked that the matter be put into motion.

It is not unusual for wealthy women to establish some sort of financial independence for their husbands; Sunny had offered several times over the years to do this for Claus, but he had always declined. Not only was he now acquiescing—he appeared to be instigating the gift. The amount mentioned was in the area of one or two million dollars.

Previous attempts to transfer a substantial amount of money had been abandoned when it was realized that, in order to give Claus a million dollars, the gift tax would cost close to an additional million. Morris Gurley, the Chemical Bank trust officer for Sunny and Mrs. Aitken, had been working on a plan to avoid this IRS bite by setting up a residual trust, with a charity as the ultimate beneficiary and with Claus receiving the income for his lifetime.

Claus's letter brushed aside this scheme and insisted Sunny wanted the gift to be outright; the tax bill could be worried about later. Claus was overruled, and a two-million dollar irrevocable trust was set up for the Metropolitan Opera; a guaranteed one hundred and twenty thousand dollars of the income went to Claus. This stipulation was also irrevocable.

The three parties to this agreement had widely different motives for wanting the trust fund for Claus. First, Von Bülow himself now needed money of his own.

For her part, Sunny knew that Claus was becoming a problem to her. He was moody, on edge and, she feared, close to a nervous breakdown. She believed the problem to be his frustration about not having a successful career and his financial dependence on her —the aspects of his restlessness he was willing to discuss with her.

When Claus shortly before joining Mark Millard had expressed an interest in working on Wall Street, she had made available to him the half-million dollars needed to buy into Hentz and Company, but the firm had gone out of business before the deal was consummated. She was delighted when he wanted to invest in a Broadway play, *Deathtrap,* and happily gave him the money ($44,000). She had read with relish the thriller about a man who ingeniously plots to kill his rich wife and thought the play terrific.

She felt sure it would make Claus a lot of money, which it did.

Still the problems persisted. Sunny came to the conclusion that the only remedy for this recurring sore in her husband was substantial money of his own.

In the trial, Sunny was quoted as saying she was considering divorce because she felt she was "restraining Claus." This was taken to mean that, in wanting him with her much of the time, she was keeping him from dedicating himself to a career. As presented in court, the interpretation is baffling. For one thing, Claus was already working for Mark Millard. But if she was truly concerned about restraining Claus from an all-out career effort, she had but to stop constricting him in this area and encourage him to work full-time like other husbands.

Her concept of restraint was far more insightful. Sunny believed, according to her children, that not she but *her money* was restraining him, that he wanted his freedom for reasons she didn't know, but was held back by the comfort of his position as her husband.

Her idea in setting him up with his own money was to test her theory. She wanted to eliminate money as a consideration in the resolution of their marital problems—handicapping him, in effect, so they could work things out on a more equal footing. And even if it all ended in divorce, she told Gurley, she did not begrudge Claus the money; he had been a good husband, a good father to her children—he had "earned his keep."

Strange as it may seem for a woman who knew her marriage was in trouble to settle a substantial income on the husband, Morris Gurley's motivation in expediting the gift is even more unusual. He had, he later admitted, "heard the rumors"; that is, he knew the family thought the possibility existed that Claus was trying to kill Sunny.

Ordinarily, he said, he would have tried dissuading Sunny from setting Claus up with an income. Because of the suspicions, however, he agreed to it—as did Sunny's lawyer Sims Farr for the same reason—in the hope that giving Claus money would eliminate the grotesque possibility.

A year later, Gurley related all this to Stephen Famiglietti at the time the prosecutor was preparing his case against Von Bülow. Famiglietti, no stranger to unlikely plots, couldn't believe what he was hearing. It sounded to him as though Sunny's trust officer and lawyer, hearing that Claus was trying to kill her, responded by settling two million dollars on him.

Gurley corrected this misapprehension on Famiglietti's part by stating that they had nothing to go on but vague suspicions based upon little more than Von Bülow's obstructive behavior the day Sunny went into her coma and his overwrought condition ever since. He stressed that the money-for-Claus notion had been revived, not by him, but at 960 Fifth Avenue. Gurley and Sims Farr had merely endorsed the idea because they felt if Claus represented a danger, the money might nullify him as one. They, like Sunny, saw it as a device for "relieving whatever pressures Von Bülow was under."

When the above story was learned through other sources, Gurley acknowledged it and said, "In my work I become involved in the most intimate details of some flamboyant and dramatic lives. You can't imagine the kind of things I get into. But I had never before encountered the possibility of murder."

On a Sunday in the middle of April, Sunny again woke up in a strange condition. As in February, her speech was slurred, she was extremely weak, and she was so uncoordinated she had trouble finding her mouth with her teacup. She stayed in bed. The next morning she told Maria she felt better, but when she started out of bed to dress for an appointment, she found herself too weak to stand. She asked Maria to cancel the appointment. Maria did more than that. She phoned Mrs. Aitken and told her about her daughter's worrying condition. Mrs. Aitken immediately called Dr. Stock, who went directly to 960 Fifth Avenue.

Stock found Sunny as Maria had described her to Mrs. Aitken —extremely weak and uncoordinated. He checked but found no indication of alcohol—breath, bloodshot eyes. Stock was sufficiently worried to insist that Sunny go to Columbia Presbyterian Hospital for ten days of tests; he booked her in for a week later, April 21.

Returning to the apartment and learning of Dr. Stock's visit, Von Bülow was furious. He went into his wife's bedroom and closed the door. For half an hour a heated discussion could be heard. When Von Bülow emerged, he told Maria her mistress wanted to speak with her.

In a voice Maria described as sad and tired, Sunny told her maid she was never again to phone Mrs. Aitken or the doctor without consulting first with Mr. Von Bülow. Hearing of this, Mrs. Aitken wrote an irate letter to Von Bülow telling him as forcibly as she could that she considered him responsible for her daughter's health, that his behavior in this regard up until now had been appalling, and that he was immediately to call a doctor if Sunny "had so much as a hangnail."

Relations between Mrs. Aitken and her son-in-law were further damaged about this time by Mrs. Aitken's hearing that Von Bülow was spreading stories around New York and Newport that Sunny was an alcoholic. In a rage at such calumny, she phoned Sunny and told her. Von Bülow was sitting nearby when Sunny got the call. Without hanging up, she turned to him and asked if he were telling people she was a drinker. He replied that the idea was absurd. Sunny reported this back to her mother.

Sunny seems to have been more easily reassured about her husband's odd behavior than the rest of the family was. They could perceive so little logic or purpose in his actions, however, that they found it easier (and more palatable) to believe that he was losing his mind than that he was pursuing an integrated plot.

In spite of the domestic battle caused by Maria's calling Dr. Stock, Sunny was delighted about his decision for tests. Since her December coma she had been worried about her health and was relieved that concrete action was finally being taken.

In retrospect it is unfortunate that Stock waited a week before running tests. A week is ample time for an adulterated system to return to normal. Had Stock gotten her to the hospital the day he was called, he might have discovered an altogether different internal chemistry.

With Sunny in the hospital, Stock brought in three specialists as consultants. One was a neurological expert, another a blood sugar expert, the third a specialist in metabolic disorders. Their conclusions were that Sunny's insulin dynamics were normal; that is to say, when deprived of sugar, her blood sugar dropped and her insulin did as well. Since insulin is only produced by the pancreas as it is needed to lower excessive blood sugar levels, it was to be expected that the insulin would drop as the sugar level did.

The four doctors had been looking for an islet-cell tumor in the pancreas. This is the most common of several conditions which can throw the insulin regulator out of kilter, causing it to produce more insulin than the body needs. Because her insulin level went down along with the blood sugar level as it should (and because of the results of eleven other tests), the doctors eliminated the possibility of a tumor.

The ten days of tests produced one startling result; when given a large amount of sugar—100 units of glucose—Sunny's blood sugar dropped to an extremely low 23 milligrams per 100 milliliters. This is a very abnormal reaction, but one consistent with hypoglycemia. Perhaps the oddest part about her reaction was that—despite a blood sugar level low enough to cause other people considerable distress, perhaps even to render them unconscious—Sunny showed no symptoms whatsoever. She was fine.

The doctors concluded not only that the Newport Hospital had been right—she was hypoglycemic—but she may have suffered from the condition for years. Producing no symptoms, the condition could have existed in her undetected. On a handful of occasions over the many years Dr. Stock had treated Sunny, he had taken blood sugar levels; all were normal. This proved little except to make the doctors add to the hypoglycemia diagnosis the terms "spontaneous" and "reactive": reactive because it occurred in reaction to an abundance of sugar and spontaneous because it didn't always happen.

The whole nomenclature is rather whimsical. Hypoglycemia—referred to by some as "this year's disease"—is less a disease than a condition, in the way rashes and fevers are not diseases but conditions. Since the human body is beset by many more problems than it has conditions to respond with, the conditions must do double duty and are shared by a number of different causes.

Although the April tests convinced the doctors something was wrong with Sunny's blood sugar metabolism, the rush to affix the condition upon her seems to have been done in the hopes that a twelve-letter word would discharge some of the mystery. (And how fast the press later picked up on her "hypoglycemia" as though it was as precise and immutable as blue eyes.)

However arbitrary the diagnosis, it didn't prevent the doctors from telling Sunny she had to eliminate sweets from her diet: a

standard admonition for hypoglycemics. It is a confusing direc-
tive, since the condition is described as *low* blood sugar. Why then
are sweets forbidden? The answer is that a sudden intake of sugar
will start the pancreas pumping out insulin, and an overabundance
of insulin will gobble up the new sugar as well as some of that
already there. The net result is a lowering of blood sugar.

When it was later suggested that Sunny's continuing to eat
sweets indicates she didn't believe the hypoglycemia diagnosis, her
two older children replied, "None of us did."

One reason Sunny may have given little credence to the diagnosis was a campaign on Von Bülow's part, immediately after the
tests' conclusion, to discredit them. "You go and let them treat
you like a guinea pig for ten days," he sneered, "and what is the
result? Absolutely zero!"

Looking back after the tragedy unfolded, those who believed
Von Bülow the cause of her first coma think he was at first against
the medical poking about but came to see an advantage to his plot
in the doctors' hypoglycemia diagnosis. This would be an answer
to the question, Why would Von Bülow, having failed once, try
the same method a second time? Perhaps because with the April
tests the Columbia Presbyterian Hospital had provided him with
an alibi.

Many months later Maria wrote a friend that she and Von
Bülow were "at daggers' points," but it appears that even in the
spring of 1980 the hostility between the maid and her mistress's
husband was out in the open. An episode shortly after the mid-
April crisis bears this out. Cleaning Von Bülow's study, Maria
noticed three woman's wristwatches. She opened the safe and
checked Sunny's jewelry case. Three watches were missing.

Maria reported this to Sunny, reminding her that she and Von
Bülow were the only others who knew the safe's combination.
"And," Maria added, "*I* did not take the watches."

In Maria's presence, Sunny asked Von Bülow if he had them.
At first he was speechless and sputtered "What! . . . What!"
Recovering, he said that he had them in order to take their meas-
urements for an anniversary gift he was buying Sunny.

The effect of this scene on any civility remaining between Maria
and Claus can be imagined; more significant is what the story says

about Sunny's relationship with her husband. Suggestions were later made that she feared Claus or was under his domination like some bill-paying Trilby. People who saw them together in public said that up until the end Sunny doted on Claus and would follow him fondly with her eyes throughout an evening. That she did not hesitate to accuse him of stealing three watches shows that, at least as far as material items were involved, she was not afraid to slap his wrists.

What with his mother-in-law, his wife's maid, and now his wife gunning for him, it was not a good period for Claus. But not everything in his life was going so badly that spring. Alexandra Isles agreed to see him again. With the Columbia Presbyterian tests, Von Bülow could cheerfully report to Alexandra that Sunny's collapse was unrelated to suicidal tendencies, but resulted from a bona fide medical condition, hypoglycemia—a malady that had nothing whatever to do with shattered marriages, wandering husbands, and other women but pertained solely to such guilt-free matters as metabolism, insulin secretion, and blood sugar levels.

With that weight lifted from her conscience, Alexandra resumed her affair with Von Bülow, seeing him about twice a week. The discussion of marriage was also resumed with enthusiasm.

Ala's marriage to Franz Kneissl was set for May 31. Because of the prominence of the groom's family and because of her own gilt-edged Austrian name, Ala's wedding was to be an important one with most of Austria's nobility as well as its financial leaders in attendance. The wedding would take place with great pomp and splendor in Salzburg.

Weeks before the wedding date the Austrian papers were preoccupied with the coming event. "Poor Princess Marries Rich Ski Czar" said one headline, nearly getting the financial picture backward: the Kneissl ski firm was in trouble. If that bad news reached anyone, it did nothing to dampen the festive mood. Both Ala and Franz were good-looking and there seemed to be money somewhere. What difference did it make where?

Von Bülow later claimed that Sunny, because of her own unhappy marriage to an Austrian, was distressed about Ala's choice of husband. The Kneissl family's financial problems was one of Claus's favorite conversational topics. Ala was under the contrary impression: she felt her mother was delighted about the marriage and liked Franz very much. If Von Bülow's version was correct, Sunny had an odd way of showing her disapproval. She gave Ala one of the most lavish weddings Austria had seen in fifty years.

For an event of such pomp, one that would include a number of formal events, Sunny had brought with her much of her jewelry, which she carried with her on the plane in a small locked case. When she unpacked in her Salzburg hotel room, several of the most costly pieces of jewelry were missing, including a diamond necklace worth in the neighborhood of $100,000. She phoned Maria in New York to ask her if she had forgotten to pack the items in the carrying case. Maria was certain she had put them in.

The authorities called in immediately noticed two aspects to the jewelry's disappearance that set it apart from a normal theft: the case showed no sign of forcible entry, and not all of the jewelry was taken. Detectives reasoned that even a knowledgeable thief would not trust his eye to make an evaluation but would take every piece and figure out at his leisure which were truly valuable; the risk was the same. The theft was never explained.

The night before the wedding Sunny threw a ball in the historic Archibishop's Palace. Because Ala was of royal Austrian blood, they were permitted to hold the party in the private apartments of the palace, which were an eighteenth-century fantasy of opulence. The dance itself took place in the vast and glittering Hall of Four Hundred.

As guests entered the palace, they were ushered up a grand staircase along which, at intervals, footmen in green velvet and gold-braided livery held lit candelabra. As hostess, Sunny was at the head of the receiving line—smiling, gracious, at ease, breathtaking in a ball gown that modulated from pale lavender to purple. Next to her was Prince Alfie, then Ala, Franz, and a pride of titled von Auerspergs. Ala wore a full-skirted black strapless dress with two green velvet streamers down the back, a gift from Mrs. Aitken.

The next morning was rainy, but the sun came out around eleven, in time for the noon wedding in the seventeenth-century

St. Peter's Church. Ala and Franz arrived in a royal carriage pulled by six white stallions. Throughout the ceremony and lunch afterwards, Sunny was radiant and thoroughly enjoyed herself.

Von Bülow, on the other hand, had been in a particularly grumpy mood ever since he arrived in Austria. He missed no opportunity to throw cold water on the high spirits and made one or two scenes; the most awkward was when he insisted it was improper for Sunny to go with her former husband to visit Franz's parents—Ala's in-laws to be—in the nearby countryside. Ala was eager for her mother to make the visit in order to see where the couple would be living, but the trip was canceled.

Von Bülow was not the only second husband to be upset by his predecessor, but his jealousy of Prince Alfie von Auersperg seems to have been particularly virulent. Through the years, Sunny and Alfie had remained friends, having lunch when Alfie visited New York and communicating frequently about their children. They had remained fond of each other and now their happiness at Ala's marriage was heightened by their joy at seeing each other.

Even though Sunny and Alfie were visibly enjoying being together again, some have suggested that Von Bülow's unease was based on something altogether different. Ala's wedding occurred in the midst of his campaign about Sunny's drinking and depression. Von Bülow may have been unnerved to have so many people see an altogether different Sunny—cheerful, outgoing, calm. (Ala complained that it was unfair that she should be nervous with all these people, many of whom she had come to know, while her mother, who knew none of them, remained unruffled.) As for drinking, Sunny would make a glass of wine last an entire evening.

It is possible, then, that Von Bülow was upset by such forceful refutation of his portrayal of Sunny, but he could have claimed she had pulled herself together for this important occasion. It is more likely that Von Bülow, in the midst of this display of his wife's wealth (the wedding cost Sunny $150,000) and an equally impressive display of her first husband's blue blood (at least a dozen princes attended the wedding), had not for years been made to feel so much like Claus Cecil Borberg, a frequently unemployed man from Copenhagen.

* * *

After a few weeks in Europe, Sunny and Claus returned to America and settled down for the rest of the summer in Clarendon Court. The first thing Sunny did was to arrange a large party to celebrate Alexander's coming of age. The invitations went out to some seventy of Newport's most popular and well-entrenched summer colonists for a "croquet with music" party. Someone asked Alexander what that meant and he replied, "It's a cocktail party," focusing on the most relevant fact: no dinner.

Even without the tragedy that came so soon afterwards, the party would have long been remembered in Newport, a town accustomed to memorable social gatherings. Sunny's party represented a bench mark for full use of magnificent settings with imagination and style.

Guests were asked to wear all white. Since it was a lawn party, this meant that most women wore long dresses and garden hats. Men wore white jackets and slacks and were given white plastic bowlers on entering. The result was a tableau of white figures gliding around the sweeping lawns with the sea beyond. The effect was pure Fellini.

Most of the Cliff Walk mansions sit rather close to the sea. Clarendon Court sits back toward Bellevue Avenue the maximum distance the plot allows. Because the coastline juts out at this point, it allows an uncommonly long stretch of lawn from the house to the ocean. The sides of this broad strip of green are flanked with rows of trees. For the party, three croquet courts had been set up end to end along the allée.

An orchestra played while white figures clunked wooden balls around and other figures—some with parasols, some with canes—strolled the paths on either side of the croquet fields and sipped champagne. As the daylight faded, a mist rolled in from the ocean, causing spectacular haloes to form around the flares that were lit for illumination.

Her magnificent entertainment typified the pretty settings Sunny had created for her own habitation. It also typified her fondness for social events as tableaus rather than as vehicles for verbal communication.

As she wandered among her guests, blond and willowy, as lovely as ever, her face registered happiness for her son's coming of age, and a party's ability to induce people, for an afternoon at least, to behave with kindness and grace. As seen at this moment, her party emerges as a tragic final signature, a statement of her vision of beauty, of how she felt life might have been.

Regardless of whether Sunny thought so consciously or not, she was, with her party, paying honor and saying good-bye to a world of taste, sensitivity, and graciousness—a world she loved but in which she had never felt comfortable.

For there was an ominous valedictory quality about this enchanting party. Since her coma the previous Christmas, Sunny had sunk deeper into reclusiveness. She lived in dread of doing something to cause another coma. As a result she accepted fewer and fewer invitations, saw fewer people. She was already flirting with the nether world of nonlife that, within six months, would claim her permanently.

While Claus Von Bülow was enjoying his summer in Newport, Alexandra Isles was in New York, happy in the knowledge that her lover was working matters out with Sunny so that divorce was not far off. Early in August Alexandra flew to Ireland to stay with her mother, keeping in touch with Von Bülow by phone. To have these conversations in private, Von Bülow would use a separate telephone line he had installed in Clarendon Court's garage.

In one of these calls, Von Bülow happily told Alexandra he had taken an apartment in Manhattan. Alexandra was ecstatic about this hard evidence of progress toward their goal. Alexandra asked how Sunny felt about this, still worried about causing distress to this vulnerable woman she didn't know. He had not yet told her, Von Bülow said.

All of Alexandra's back-street fears were rekindled: she was furious. Rather than presenting her with their first step toward a legitimate union, he was instead holding out something that looked very much like a sex pad. The trans-Atlantic phone calls ceased.

When she returned to New York in September, Alexandra did not see Von Bülow, despite efforts on his part. Her suspicions that he was not serious about divorcing Sunny were confirmed. She had to show him she was serious in her resolve not to be a married man's mistress.

One reason Sunny may not have noticed this romantic games-playing going on under her nose was that she had problems of her own. Word came that Ala, only six months into her fairy-tale marriage, had suffered a miscarriage in Munich. Sunny wanted to fly to Munich to be with her daughter. Ala discouraged her, but was not unappreciative of her mother's concern and the transatlantic pep talks assuring Ala she was young enough to have many children still.

Sunny came to learn about her husband's apartment in a strange way. Her close friend Isabel Glover received a phone call from a carpet company saying that she had been overcharged for her recent carpet purchase and had a credit. Isabel, who was registered as a decorator, said she knew nothing about any purchase with the company. Investigation showed that Claus, perhaps to get a carpet at wholesale price, had given Isabel's name and had neglected to tell her. Thinking the carpet was probably for Claus's office, Isabel mentioned it to Sunny in a telephone conversation. Sunny said she knew nothing about a carpet; Claus's office didn't need one. She asked the address. Isabel, who hadn't noticed the address, read it with dismay as she realized what she probably had done. The matter was dropped. Sunny was clearly upset, although according to Isabel, Sunny almost never revealed it when something bothered her.

Isabel does not know if Sunny knew then or later about Alexandra Isles; she is certain, however, her friend could have taken the news in stride. Talking about Sunny after she went into a permanent coma, Isabel said, "People kept trying to make Sunny out to be a fairy-tale princess, but more than most people I've met, Sunny knew it was not a fairy-tale world. She knew that women got older and lost their looks, that they lost their husbands, that people get sick and die. She was very realistic—and she was not judgmental. If Claus had wanted to go off with another woman—or a man, for that matter—Sunny would have understood."

In November, Claus phoned Alexandra Isles to say he had at last taken the crucial step: he had moved out of 960 Fifth Avenue. Since this is what Alexandra had long wanted, he said, no further reason existed for her to avoid him. She was pleased but cautious; she had been buffeted enough by this on-and-off maneuvering to tell him she needed a few days to think things over. She was beginning not to trust Von Bülow and devised a plan to test him.

In a few days she telephoned the Fifth Avenue apartment. A maid answered. Without identifying herself, Alexandra asked for Mr. Von Bülow. The maid responded that he was not in at the moment but would be returning for supper that evening.

That was enough. She felt totally deceived by Von Bülow and told him so when he called. He had lied to her; she had caught him outright.

Unperturbed, Von Bülow smoothly responded in a way to make Alexandra feel guilty. He *had* moved out from the Fifth Avenue apartment when he spoke with Alexandra a few days earlier, but receiving nothing from Alexandra but coldness, he had returned to the home where he at least had a daughter who loved him.

Like a virtuoso, he played on Alexandra's charitable instincts: it was *her* mistreatment of him, *her* lack of trust that was causing problems; he concluded this lament by raising a flag sure to evoke a salute from Alexandra, the flag of parenthood. His ploy succeeded in confusing her but not in winning her back. She went off to Washington to work and resolved to have nothing further to do with him.

Von Bülow was frantic at the thought of having finally pushed Alexandra too far and lost her for good. He made feverish efforts to reach her in Washington. Anticipating this, she had taken pains to avoid his finding her. She took refuge in the apartment of a friend, a shabby place that had the advantage of no telephone. When Von Bülow found out where she was staying she moved to another place, this one with a phone. Almost immediately Von Bülow was on it. He had to speak with her. She refused.

One day, working in Kennedy Center, she was called into the office of her boss and found Von Bülow sitting there. He had come to Washington to talk with her and had not hesitated to use professional leverage for a purely personal matter. Not wanting to create a scene in front of her employer, she agreed to a private conversation. They went across the street to the Watergate Hotel and sat at a table in the coffee shop.

Von Bülow proclaimed his love and said he wanted to marry her right away. To prove his sincerity, he would go directly to the pay phone and call his lawyer. He would also phone Sunny and tell her of his intention. Alexandra could stand beside him and hear every word. She refused to let him do this.

"You shouldn't say anything like that to anyone unless you look them in the eye," she said. Once again she had given him a lesson in morality and form.

The phone offer succeeded in convincing her that Von Bülow loved her. Alexandra responded that she loved him as well; she regretted behaving as she had, but she had been confused and angry. Von Bülow returned to New York confident he could still have Alexandra.

Thanksgiving, 1980, the Von Bülow family had dinner together at 960 Fifth Avenue. Cosima was there and Alexander had come down from Providence. Sometime during the weekend Sunny came by Alexander's bedroom for a chat. As she had the previous Christmas, she brought up the subject of divorcing Von Bülow. This time, however, she was not deliberating the move but had definitely decided to go ahead with it.

What made her so determined, her son asked? It was something, Sunny replied, "too horrible to tell."

Later, when Alexander testified to this conversation in court, he said that he repeatedly asked his mother to tell him what she had learned that was so horrible but that with a slight shudder she had refused to tell him.

No one knows what it was that Sunny learned about her husband that was too horrible to tell her son. It is certain that a woman of Sunny's frankness and sophistication would not consider her husband's philandering "too horrible to tell." (Indeed, Alexander later recalled her discussing with nonchalance an infidelity of his father's.) Von Bülow was a man about whom the most shocking gossip swirled—not, as some people think, since the accusation of attempted murder, but all his adult life. It is possible that Sunny heard one of these stories or—more likely, since she surely had heard the gossip before—learned that one of them was no joke.

Von Bülow's life had reached an impasse; he seemed caught in an implacable grip. He was miserable with his marriage and was in love with another woman, a woman who loved him and wanted him as her husband. His wife talked to him and to others of wanting a divorce. His new career looked promising, the woman he wanted to marry had money, and he had lifetime interest on two million dollars.

For all this, Von Bülow was unable to make the simple move of asking Sunny to end their marriage. Whatever it was that was preventing him from taking this commonplace step must have been powerful indeed.

When Alexander was home for Thanksgiving, Maria waited until her employers were out of the apartment, then got him to join her in a search for the black bag. When they found it in one of Von Bülow's closets, Maria noticed among the contents something she had not seen before: a small glass vial with a metal top filled with a clear liquid. It was labeled INSULIN.

Maria knew that insulin was a substance taken by diabetics. She also knew that no one in the household was diabetic. She showed it to Alexander and said, "Insulin. What for insulin?"

Alexander, intent on discovering more sinister drugs, was uninterested in Maria's finding what to him was an innocuous medicine.

About a week later, a mere two weeks after Von Bülow's Watergate love scene, Alexandra received a note from him saying that Sunny had had another mishap and had been rushed to the hospital.

X

ON December 1, Sunny awoke feeling miserable—her sinuses had tormented her for days, causing constant headaches. Now alarmed by any fluctuations in her health, she decided to stay in bed. As Claus had left for his Shearson–American Express office, Maria looked after Sunny until he got home that evening. After Maria had retired for the night around 10:30, Von Bülow came to the maid's room.

"I'm afraid something has happened," he told Maria. "It's not bad, so don't get excited. Still, you'd better come."

Maria rushed to the bedroom and found her mistress lying in bed, her hair and the pillow beneath it soaked with blood from a wound on the back of her head. An area of the carpet some distance from the bed was also covered with blood. Not seeing anything near this spot on which her mistress could have hit her head, Maria was baffled how the wound occurred.

Von Bülow phoned the emergency number, 911. In short order an ambulance arrived and rushed Sunny to the nearest hospital, Lenox Hill, at Park Avenue and 77th Street. She was treated for aspirin toxicity, and stitches were taken in her head wound. She was also given several units of plasma for her loss of blood and treated for hemoturia (blood in the urine), a common result of aspirin toxicity.

When Dr. Stock learned that Sunny had been hospitalized without his knowledge, he was incensed. Von Bülow, he argued, should have called him, not 911, whose rescue squads cart you to the anonymous mercies of the nearest hospital. What made Von Bülow's reaction to the crisis perplexing to the doctor was that he lived so close to the Von Bülows—less than five blocks away—that he could have reached Sunny faster than the ambulance. Also, he was not affiliated at Lenox Hill and so was prevented from treating his patient of twenty-six years.

As soon as he could, Stock had Sunny transferred to his hospital, Columbia Presbyterian Medical Center. When she arrived in intensive care there, she was delirious. "I will never see my children again; I will never see my husband again," she moaned, in almost unintelligibly slurred speech. Stock had her blood sugar level tested and found it normal.

When she returned to herself the next day, Sunny remembered having taken considerable aspirin for the sinus headaches over the two or three days preceding her collapse, but she could remember nothing else that happened before losing consciousness. (Excess aspirin damages memory centers.) The wound on the back of the head was a mystery. On the assumption she had fallen, nothing more was said about the odd injury.

From the high salicilate levels in her blood, Stock concluded that aspirin toxicity was the cause of the crisis, which in his judgment had never been life-threatening. Had he been called, he said, he probably would have treated her at home instead of rushing her across Manhattan in an ambulance. But he wasn't called.

For several days Sunny remained in the hospital. On one of his visits to her, Dr. Stock encountered Von Bülow, who followed him to the elevators and asked if they might talk. Finding a place to sit in the hospital lobby, they briefly discussed Sunny's condition but passed quickly into more general matters. Sunny had been upset, Von Bülow told the doctor, over her daughter's recent miscarriage. He said this in such a way to suggest that his wife's immediate crisis might not have been accidental, as everyone believed, but rooted in emotional distress.

Von Bülow broached his main concern. He was contemplating ending his marriage to Sunny, but hesitated because of Sunny's health and emotional state. Did Dr. Stock think she was strong enough to undergo the upheaval of divorce? His reason for wanting a divorce, he told Stock, was that his new job required considerable travel, while Sunny wanted a husband who remained with her constantly.

According to his testimony at the trial, Stock by this time did not trust Von Bülow. He was convinced that the concern for Sunny now being expressed was not sincere. The doctor was baffled, however, over what prompted it; but then so much happening in Sunny's household was baffling. Stock told Von Bülow that he definitely believed Sunny was strong enough to endure a divorce from him.

Von Bülow was showing a marked inconsistency in his confidential talks about Sunny. Earlier that year he had told Dr. Stock and Dr. Gailitis about Sunny's chronic alcoholism, as he had a number of acquaintances. Yet Isabel Glover, perhaps the only one of Sunny's old friends who had a good relationship with Claus, remembers distinctly Claus telling her at this time—December, 1980—that Sunny had not had a drink in two years.

One evening later in December, Alexander was speaking with his mother on the phone from Providence. He noticed that her speech was becoming thick and weak—just as it had the previous Christmas before she went into the coma. He asked if she had taken a sleeping pill. She said no. As the speech distortion grew more pronounced, Alexander asked several more times if she was sure she hadn't taken something. Each time he got a firm denial.

Alexander was perplexed. Again he ruled out liquor, since she rarely drank, and on the few occasions when she did, she showed other signs, but not this odd speech. What made it particularly worrying to Alexander was that on several occasions since the previous Christmas he had noticed the strange difficulty in speaking, but never in all the years before.

But if Alexander was concerned about his mother, it was the sporadic concern of a pleasure-bent college student. With Ala in Europe most of the time and Mrs. Aitken in bad health herself, the only one constantly concerned about Sunny was Maria Schrallhammer. Maria wrote a letter to a friend that summarized the ominous situation in the Von Bülow household and Maria's most gothic fears:

Dear Erika,

Unfortunately not everything is rosy here. . . . Monday night at about 11 P.M. Mr. Bülow came to my room and told me something had happened, but it was nothing bad. As I entered the bedroom, Mrs. was laying on the bed covered with blood, with an injury on the back of her head. On the carpet also bloodstain and a towel soaked with blood. He already had called the ambulance which arrived very shortly. Mrs. Bülow was in a complete daze and mumbled some words you could not understand. They took her to Lenox Hill Hospital two blocks away and next day transferred her to the Medical Center. There she regained consciousness and could recall nothing. She was till Thursday under intensive care with poisoning symptoms and very, very weak. She is feeling better. Her husband said she fell and injured herself.

Last December 27 I found her unconscious in a bedroom at Newport. I went to my room after my boss told me that Mrs. had a throat ache and would not get up. He told me specifically that I don't have to come. As I stood in front of the locked door I heard her moaning. Determined, I knocked on the door and went in. He lay next to her and tried to convince me that she was asleep. It went on all day. He refused to call a doctor and she sank deeper in her coma. At 6 P.M. I held her groaning in my arms as the doctor finally came through the door.

My God, was that a relief. She literally was rescued from death. With an ambulance from the Fire Department she was taken to a hospital. Thank God she recovered slowly. They found out that her blood sugar level was very low. At least a plus for him.

I found that her condition in February was very peculiar. I went secretly to Mrs. Aitken and told her the truth. Bülow and I are at daggers' points. In April Mrs. Bülow spent almost two weeks at the Medical Center for tests. They diagnosed that her blood sugar was unstable. But at the hospital she was feeling rather well. Sometimes I get sick thinking what is going to happen next. Mrs. trusts her husband blindly and is totally dependent. He of course has a girl friend. The whole life has changed. No more parties, and they don't go out either. She gained a lot of weight and is very unhappy about it.

A few days before Von Bülow was to drive to Newport for a pre-Christmas weekend with Sunny, Alexandra Isles invited him to a carol service in which her son Adam was playing in the orchestra. Afterwards, Von Bülow returned to Alexandra's apartment for dinner. The evening was a typical Alexandra mockup of family life. A day or two later he was with Alexandra at a dinner party given by friends, which suggests how far they had progressed as an open couple.

Still, relations between Claus and Alexandra were not fully repaired. The Watergate coffee shop declarations had not succeeded in mollifying her. For the opening of the play she was working on in Washington, she received a telegram from Von Bülow: "Break a leg, break a heart." This was followed by a note from him saying that Sunny had been hospitalized with an aspirin overdose; it's effect was to drive Alexandra back into her old fears that her affair was causing Sunny's health crises.

Since this had once before caused a rift in their affair, it seems odd Von Bülow felt obliged to keep Alexandra, with whom he was now having such spotty communications, so well informed about Sunny's difficulties.

Christmas softened Alexandra's heart, however, resulting in two conciliatory gestures: the invitation to the carol service and two Christmas presents for Von Bülow, which she dropped off at 960 Fifth Avenue. Inside the package was one gift-wrapped present to which she had affixed a cut-out heart torn in half but crudely rejoined with a Band-Aid; the other present had the recklessly indiscreet inscription "To *my* favorite manic depressive." Alexandra would later characterize these gifts as "a peace offering."

Nevertheless, the affair, which for a good part of its two-year duration had been tormented, now seemed to be at its most agonized. Each of Alexandra's actions suggest her pain and confusion. How much longer could Von Bülow hold in abeyance this woman who had already been heroically patient and forgiving?

It was in an anguished state of mind that he prepared to climb into the Mercedes with Sunny and Cosima to drive to Newport for a family holiday weekend. (Alexander would come down from Providence.) Because Mrs. Aitken was ill and had to remain in her apartment, the plan was to spend the weekend of December 20 and 21 at Clarendon Court and then return to New York for Christmas dinner with the Aitkens.

Just before leaving, Sunny phoned Isabel Glover at her antique store on Manhattan's 57th Street. Sunny seemed in a mood to talk about herself; this happened so rarely that Isabel took the time from a working morning to chat with her old friend.

Sunny was preoccupied with her erratic health; she wished she could find out what was wrong with her, she told Isabel. On one point Sunny was emphatic: she would not return to a hospital. During her treatment for aspirin toxicity earlier in the month, nurses had had trouble finding Sunny's veins and "those needles hurt." In talking about this conversation later, Isabel said, "Sunny was very stoic. If she said the needles hurt, they must have been excruciating."

Isabel went on to say that Sunny never leaned on her friends; if something was bothering her, she invariably kept it to herself. She never mentioned to Isabel, for instance, that she was contemplating divorce. "But in that case," Isabel added, "she didn't have to. It was obvious something was wrong."

Maria was to have accompanied the family for the Newport weekend, but at the last minute Von Bülow urged that she stay behind. Maria was overworked, he said; if she went up to Newport, she "would just catch flu again." Sunny, who had asked Maria to come, agreed it was a good idea to give Maria a few days off.

As Maria was helping her employers get off, she took some of their bags down in the elevator. Among them was Von Bülow's customary open satchel, this one a white canvas bag that had METROPOLITAN OPERA printed on it. Among the items inside, Maria spotted the black bag. She opened it and saw that it contained the syringes and vials, among them the one marked INSULIN. Alarming as this was, Maria tried to allay her fears by telling herself he wouldn't dare try to do it again.

The day after the Von Bülows arrived in Newport—Saturday, December 20, 1980—would be Sunny's last day of consciousness. Although the family was planning to remain at Clarendon Court only three days, Sunny had phoned ahead for a Christmas tree. In the morning she sent Cosima and the houseman, John Berdy, up to the third floor to bring down the tree ornaments; a good part of the day was spent decorating the tree and festooning the house with flowers and greenery.

Dinner that evening was earlier than usual so the family could get to the first show at the Jane Pickens Theatre of the Dolly Parton, Lily Tomlin, Jane Fonda film, 9 to 5. At the dinner table Sunny complained of a headache but was otherwise in good spirits. She didn't eat her main course; when it was time for dessert, she asked the butler to bring her a large plate of vanilla ice cream with the caramel sauce Sunny asked her cook, Irene, to make up and keep in jars in the refrigerator.

(Later, when Alexander was relating these events to Richard Kuh, the lawyer he hired to investigate his mother's comas, Kuh asked, "Why didn't *you* try to stop her from eating the sundae?" Alexander replied that he had no idea she was forbidden sweets.)

As Alexander and Von Bülow stood waiting for Sunny to get her coat, they had an odd conversation in which Von Bülow told his stepson he was not comfortable with his life: he felt he was living off Sunny and knew most people in Newport felt the same way about him. Alexander was at a loss what to say and was relieved when his mother arrived and the family set out for the film.

Just after nine o'clock the chauffeur brought them back to Clarendon Court. On entering the house, Von Bülow excused himself to do some work in his study; Sunny, Alexander, and Cosima decided to have a chat in the library, Sunny saying she first wanted to stop off at her bathroom.

She returned in a few minutes having changed into a dressing gown and carrying a glass of something Alexander later said he thought was ginger ale that she had fixed from a table of such beverages set up in her bedroom.

Fifteen months later, at the end of Von Bülow's trial, one of the few unexplained mysteries of the case was, if Sunny was injected with insulin, when did the injection occur? In the next half hour, while Sunny was conversing with her two children, Alexander again noticed the speech distortions she had shown the year before.

Since the family had been together for the past three and a half hours, an opportunity for a "surreptitious" injection would seem to have been nonexistent. Von Bülow's prosecutors held the theory that the slurred speech and other symptoms Alexander was about to see resulted from barbiturates or tranquilizers that Sunny either took or was given by her husband—that the injections of insulin came later, when she had retired for the night.

Another possibility is that Sunny, in her brief excursion to the bathroom, either gave herself an injection or was given one by her husband, whose study, where he had gone, was right off the bedroom and only accessible from it. Von Bülow could have offered Sunny something for her headache, to give her a sound sleep, or whatever. If that was the case, Sunny would not necessarily know what drugs her body was receiving.

She settled in the library, where she talked with Alexander and Cosima for about half an hour, at which point Von Bülow entered and asked Sunny if she wanted anything. She told him if there was any chicken soup left she would love a cup. He left to get it. It was then that Alexander noticed that her voice was growing so weak he had trouble hearing her. This was a bit of timing that tended to exonerate the cup of soup as the prime cause of her decline, although after she drank it, Sunny's condition deteriorated rapidly until she was too weak to lift her glass of ginger ale.

Von Bülow returned to his study. Sunny's voice grew fainter. Alexander asked if she felt all right. She said she did. Had she taken a barbiturate? No, she said. Alexander suggested she go to bed.

Sunny got up, staggered, and almost fell. Her son picked her up and carried her to the bedroom. This irritated Sunny, and she protested vigorously, insisting she be allowed to walk.

When he got her into her bedroom, Alexander put her down. She went into the bathroom. Alexander went to get Von Bülow and found him in his study on the phone. (Von Bülow was talking to an American Express co-worker about a business deal.) Alexander interrupted to say that his mother was very weak and possibly ill.

Von Bülow continued his conversation and Alexander returned to the bedroom, where he found his mother out of the bathroom and struggling to get into her bed. She managed to sit on the unusually high bed but was unable to lift her legs. Alexander got her under the covers and talked with her for a few minutes when Von Bülow entered.

She asked Claus whom he had been talking to. An office colleague, he told her. While they spoke, Alexander glanced in the bathroom and around the bedside tables to see if he could spot any sign of a drug she might have taken to explain her condition; he saw nothing.

Alexander, assured that his stepfather would now be staying with her, said good night. Even though it was below freezing outside, Sunny asked him to open the windows. She liked sleeping in a cold bedroom with an electric blanket turned high. Alexander left his mother and stepfather in their bedroom, closing the door behind him. He would not see her conscious again.

Alexander went upstairs to his bedroom; after about an hour and a half—close to midnight—he went out for a drink at a favorite waterfront haunt of young Newporters, the Clarke Cooke House. Here again is an aspect of the story that was never satisfactorily explained. If Alexander was so worried about his mother, why would he leave her with Von Bülow, whom he suspected of trying to harm her?

When he testified, he answered this by saying that he informed his stepfather that his mother was ill and "to be careful." The most salient factor would seem to have been his exclusion from the master bedroom, which eliminated any influence he might have had on what occurred inside it. For the hour before his decision to go out he was isolated in his own part of the house—a large house that remained still, that appeared to be asleep.

Two years later, looking back on that evening, Alexander remembers feeling worried and powerless. As for a specific reason for going out, he does not recall having one.

Von Bülow claims he awoke at 5:30 the next morning, December 21, and saw Sunny still asleep. He first let the dogs out of the bedroom, then showered and shaved. He went out for a walk, came back, read the paper. Shortly after eight he encountered houseman Berdy. Von Bülow passed through the bedroom to phone his Shearson–American Express co-worker, Margaret Neilly, to resume the conversation that had been interrupted the night before.

They spoke for just over an hour about a financial report concerning an R. J. Reynolds deal they were working on together. Von Bülow could make no sense of the report; the first two pages were clear, but the third page was gibberish to him. Neilly had as much trouble with the third page as he did. They finally discovered the problem: someone had collated into the report a page three from an altogether different report. Von Bülow was furious.

Around nine o'clock the butler, Robert Biastre, ran into Von Bülow in the pantry on his way out for another walk. At 10:30 John Berdy came into the library to vacuum it and found Von Bülow.

"Unfortunately, John, Mrs. Von Bülow is still asleep," he told the houseman.

Berdy knew the family was planning to leave for New York around noon. He also knew that on days when they were traveling Mrs. Von Bülow usually arose earlier than usual, not later.

Around eleven o'clock Alexander woke up. On his way downstairs he happened to look out the window at the frigid, bleak day; he saw his stepfather walking back toward the house from the ocean, the four labradors scampering around him. Alexander went into the dining room and found his sister Cosima alone eating her breakfast. He ordered his and asked Cosima if their mother was awake. Not yet, she said.

Von Bülow arrived from his walk outside and wished them both good morning. Alexander asked if his mother was up yet. Von Bülow, expressing surprise that Alexander had not seen her, said he would go to the bedroom to check on her. Von Bülow was gone, by Alexander's estimate, ten to fifteen minutes, a length of time long enough to increase his apprehensions that something was wrong. Finally Von Bülow appeared in the dining room doorway, invisible to Cosima, whose back was to the door, and motioned silently to Alexander.

When Alexander joined him in the hall, Von Bülow whispered, "Something's happened, but I don't want to upset Cosima."

He led his stepson through the master bedroom and into the bath, the door of which was open. Sprawled diagonally across the pink-marble floor was Sunny, her calf-length nightgown pushed to the top of her underpants, her head under the toilet. She was unconscious and had urinated on the floor. Water was running in the basin.

Von Bülow knelt and put his finger under her nose. "She's still breathing," he said.

Alexander could see that her lip was swollen and there was some blood around her gums. He placed his hand under her head and was struck by how cold she was; he decided against trying to move her. Von Bülow said he was going to phone a doctor and told Alexander to place a throw over her.

At 11:21 Lieutenant Paul Ripa of the Newport Fire Department received an emergency call from Newport Hospital to go immediately to Clarendon Court. He arrived six minutes later and was shown to the bathroom. He noted that the woman had a split upper lip and was wearing men's athletic socks. He marked very slow pulse and respiration rates and an extremely cold body temperature. With the help of his driver, he got her onto a stretcher and made the drive to Newport Hospital in about three minutes, Von Bülow riding in the ambulance with her.

Dr. Gerhard Meier, the chief physician on duty that day, had received a message on his answering machine that Martha Von Bülow was being rushed to the emergency room. When she arrived he gave her body a quick examination and commented, "This is an obvious drug overdose case." He ordered the routine blood tests for unexplained unconsciousness. He told the technician to draw more than the customary number of tubes.

Dr. Meier took Von Bülow into a nearby room to ask him about his wife's history, particularly about alcohol and drugs. Von Bülow told the doctor that as far as he knew his wife had not drunk anything; he knew of no drugs either. She may have had one Seconal a few days earlier.

While they were talking, a nurse rushed in to say that Mrs. Von Bülow had gone into cardiac arrest. Meier sprinted to the emergency room and, with the help of another doctor he grabbed on the way, made a frantic resuscitation effort; they administered pure oxygen.

By about 12:30 Sunny's breathing had been stabilized, and Meier moved her to the intensive care unit. It was at this point he ordered the first "push" of glucose. This is a standard procedure given unconscious patients on the possibility that their condition involves low blood sugar—which turned out to be precisely Sunny's situation. The theory is that if sugar deficiency is *not* the problem, adding sugar to the blood will do no harm, but if it *is* the problem, irreparable harm can be done while waiting for sugar level test results. Several more massive doses of sugar were given during the next twelve hours in addition to a slow glucose drip administered intravenously.

Meier's examination on arrival showed that Sunny had a body temperature of 81.6°, a pulse rate of 36–40, highly constricted pupils, only a slight response to light. He judged her to be deeply comatose. He did not go over her body with a magnifying glass looking for needle marks. He later explained that in an emergency situation such as this doctors must make certain snap assumptions based on the patient's social and economic background, meaning that Sunny did not appear to be a junkie.

When Dr. Gailitis, who had treated Sunny a year earlier, arrived at Newport Hospital at 8:30 the following morning, he went immediately to examine her and found her still deeply comatose but with her vital signs stabilized. He ordered a second insulin level test and the c-peptide test to determine the presence of synthetic insulin.

As he grew convinced throughout the day that Sunny was not going to emerge from her coma naturally, the decision was made to transfer her to the Peter Bent Brigham Hospital in Boston (now named the Brigham and Women's Hospital) where she could receive the care of specialists in coma and blood sugar problems.

At 8:15 that evening an ambulance carrying Sunny left for Boston with Dr. Gailitis, a nurse, a technician, a driver, and Von Bülow.

Preparing for a vigil, Von Bülow got a room in a motel across the street from the hospital, then discovered he had come away with no money. He borrowed fifty cents from Dr. Gailitis to make some phone calls.

When Sunny had been examined by the Boston specialists, Dr. Gailitis told Von Bülow they had given Sunny a fifty-fifty chance of living. Von Bülow burst into tears. It occurred to no one witnessing this that there may have been doubt about which fifty caused his outburst.

XI

DEBRA Azevedo and Cheryl Edwards worked as technicians at the Newport Hospital. Debra, thirty, was heavy-set and brunette. She was single. Cheryl, twenty-five, was also brunette, with striking brown eyes. She was married. Both women had been born and raised in Newport, had graduated from local high schools, and led the job, supermarket, weekend-social-event lives of working women—far removed from Sunny Von Bülow's Bellevue Avenue existence.

Both Cheryl and Debra received their technical training while working at the hospital. They valued their jobs. The pay was good for the area, which had been economically depressed since the Navy curtailed its local operation. The hospital working conditions were pleasant, sometimes exciting, and there were always plenty of people around. A disadvantage to hospital work was having to work an occasional weekend.

The Sunday before Christmas 1980, it was dark and bitter cold when both women arose to go to work at 5:30—the same hour when, on the other side of town, Claus Von Bülow was awaking and letting out the dogs. Sundays were usually slow. Unless there was an emergency, doctors waited till weekdays to run tests on their patients. The doctors preferred admitting patients to the hospital on weekdays, and tests were usually run on arrival. Little happened on Sundays.

As they hung up their coats and got themselves coffee, Cheryl and Debra were beginning a work day that would change both their lives drastically. Their recollections of this day's commonplace activities—when called forth by law thirteen months later —would have a crucial importance to the large number of family and law-enforcement officials hoping to bring an attempted murderer to justice—and even greater importance to the man accused.

Among the aspects of their lives that would be permanently altered was the way in which Cheryl and Debra viewed the tiresome procedures in the performance of their routine tasks—drawing blood in the case of Cheryl, who was a phlobotomist, and analyzing it in the case of Debra. The tedious record-keeping would take on a significance that the two women would never forget—and that would be used by the hospital for years to come as illustration to newcomers of the importance of such paperwork.

Even for a Sunday the morning had been quiet. Sometime between 11:45 and noon Cheryl was thinking about what she would have for lunch when she heard her name being called over the hospital intercom. She was to go immediately to the emergency room.

There she found Dr. Meier and about six others working frantically over a newly arrived patient, an unconscious woman. Someone whispered to Cheryl that it was Martha Von Bülow. At first the name was only vaguely familiar; then Cheryl remembered: the woman was a prominent socialite who had been brought to the hospital in a coma a year earlier. The unexplained coma had been the subject of much talk around the hospital.

Meier ordered Cheryl to draw blood immediately; she was to draw the amount needed for the usual tests as well as a few extra tubes. Each tube had sufficient blood for a number of tests. Five tubes was the customary amount, so Cheryl pulled seven, first labeling each tube "Von Bülow, Martha."

She affixed the needle into the unconscious woman's arm, which was extremely cold. As each tube was filled, Cheryl placed it in a rack and started filling another. She managed to fill all seven tubes without changing the needle's position in the woman's arm. She carried the rack the short distance to the lab, where she placed it on a work counter.

Debra Azevedo and Mary Beth Brucker were the only two technicians on duty in the lab, which usually has a staff of nine.

They went to work immediately to centrifuge the blood, spinning it down to separate the red and white corpuscles.

Around 1:30 P.M. Cheryl Edwards again was paged on the intercom, this time to go immediately to the receptionist, where she picked up a request slip from Dr. Meier asking her to draw more blood from Mrs. Von Bülow, who had now been moved to the intensive care unit.

On her way to intensive care to comply with this order, she was almost knocked down by Dr. Meier, who burst out of the ICU highly agitated.

"Stop whatever you're doing," he barked. "I want an insulin level test on Mrs. Von Bülow right away, and I want it on one of the original blood samples."

Cheryl rushed back to the laboratory and relayed Dr. Meier's message to Debra: she should stop what she was doing and prepare one of Mrs. Von Bülow's blood samples for an insulin level test. Debra had just finished the qualitative part of the chemical analysis and was about to begin on the quantitative part: having determined which of the extraneous substances tested for were present, she was now going to determine how much.

Debra was not sure if Dr. Meier remembered that her lab was not equipped to test for insulin levels; she phoned to ask him if the test was urgent. Sending blood out to private labs for tests meant that results might not come back for a week. He told her yes, the tests were urgent, but if they took a week, then they took a week. She should, however, waste no time freezing the samples to be sent out.

As Cheryl went off to the intensive care unit to draw the second round of blood samples from Mrs. Von Bülow, Debra prepared the tubes to be sent the next day to the Boston Medical Labratory. She poured a small amount of blood from her rack of tubes into a fresh tube, labeled it, then placed it in her freezer. She resumed her toxology tests. By three o'clock she had the results.

Aside from the extremely low blood sugar, the only significant finding was a modest barbiturate level of 1.06 in the blood and 2.15 in the urine. The potassium level was very low. Azevedo found no traces of aspirin, alcohol, Valium, or any of the other substances for which comatose patients are routinely tested.

Followers of the Von Bülow trial would later learn aspects of health care procedures hospitals would prefer keeping from the public, such as the automatic doubling of outside laboratory bills before passing them along to the patient.

Then there was the unexplained time lag between Debra Azevedo's completing her tests at 3 P.M. and their not reaching Dr. Meier until 4:30. This meant that important information about a patient—perhaps lifesaving information—remained with a hospital technician rather than being rushed to the doctor charged with saving that patient's life. The laboratory was perhaps a two-minute walk from Meier's office, but the test results sat for an hour and a half before being relayed to him.

When Debra and Cheryl left that afternoon, well after their usual 3:30 quitting time, they gave little thought to the woman under the respirator in the intensive care unit except that she had given them a far busier Sunday than usual. They had no idea that the sequence of their chores—did they prepare the blood sample for the insulin test before or after drawing the second batch of blood samples?—would be of enormous interest to a great many people.

The two technicians had even less reason to think that the small tube of yellow blood serum they were leaving behind in the laboratory freezer and that was about to begin a journey from Newport to Boston to Los Angeles—that fragment of Sunny Crawford Von Bülow—would affect the life of everyone it encountered.

Inside the glass cylinder the organic matter drawn from Sunny's body by Cheryl Edwards and started on its clinical odyssey by Debra Azevedo contained the evidence that would prove this woman was in her vegetative condition, not from natural causes, but because someone had injected her with a drug in an attempt to kill her.

XII

WITH Sunny at the Peter Bent Brigham Hospital in Boston, in the hands of specialists who saw less and less chance of her emerging from the coma, individual eddies of suspicion began to converge. Phone calls flew between Newport, Boston, New York, and Austria; the callers minced no words about what crime they believed had been committed. While they still had little idea *how* it had happened, they had little doubt about the agent.

At his first opportunity after his mother was rushed to the hospital, Alexander had searched her bedroom looking for some sign that she had taken a drug or done something else to harm herself. In particular, Alexander was looking for sleeping pills; he found only a bottle of Inderal on her bedside table. He left it there.

He also looked in his stepfather's closet for the black bag. He glanced around quickly, but saw nothing. He resolved to make a more thorough search when he had the chance. It came when Von Bülow left for Boston. Going to the closet, Alexander now found it locked.

A few hours after Sunny had been rushed to Newport Hospital, Maria answered the phone at 960 Fifth Avenue to hear Von Bülow's voice. Knowing the family should have been en route to New York, she knew something terrible had happened.

Maria flew to Newport to take care of Cosima and to be on hand when Sunny came out of the coma. Von Bülow, who had scarcely been on speaking terms with Maria, now changed abruptly, losing no opportunity to flatter and cheer her. "If you hadn't come up," he told her over the phone from Boston, "I don't know what we would have done." He paid her similar compliments when he returned to Clarendon Court.

Christmas came and went with Von Bülow in a Boston motel, Alexander, Cosima, and Maria in Newport, and the Aitkens, numb with worry, in Manhattan. When Ala was first informed about the coma, she was told it was less serious than the previous year's; when she phoned from Austria to wish her mother Merry Christmas and learned she was still unconscious, she took the next plane to America.

The first week Sunny was in the Boston hospital, Alexander made several trips to see her, one of them to relieve Von Bülow so he could return to Clarendon Court for clean clothes.

When it began to appear Sunny's condition was not temporary, those in Newport returned to New York. In the last days of December a meeting was held at Mrs. Aitken's apartment to discuss what should be done. Present were Alexander, Ala, Russell and Annie Laurie Aitken, and Morris Gurley, the Chemical Bank trust officer for both Sunny and Mrs. Aitken and a good family friend.

The people who met in the Louis Quinze splendor of the Aitkens' drawing room were shocked, confused, and frightened. Overriding their tangled thoughts was the nightmare of Sunny deliberately having been put into this condition by one who not only might get away with the crime but might profit enormously from it. Close behind this agonizing specter was the fear that their efforts for justice might bring down on them enormous scandal yet achieve nothing; they might be unable to prove their suspicions.

An overriding concern of the family was what the scandal and the incrimination of Von Bülow would do to Cosima. They were naturally afraid it would alienate the girl from the rest of them, but they were more concerned about the psychological havoc the exposure of her father might cause.

Alexander had a different way of looking at this problem. "Should we let her spend her life," he asked, "with a man who tried to kill her mother?"

Still, the family determined to keep their suspicions as secret as possible for as long as possible. Morris Gurley suggested that one step they could take without sacrificing secrecy was to seek legal advice. All agreed it was a good idea. The family lawyer, Sims Farr, was preoccupied with a personal matter. They decided they would do better consulting someone with broader experience than divorce, wills, and real estate practice of polite law. After a few days Morris Gurley came up with the name of Richard Kuh, a former District Attorney of the County of New York, who was now with the general-practice firm of Warshaw Burstein, but whose background gave him a solid grounding in criminal law. An appointment was set up for Alexander and Ala to meet with Kuh in his office on January 5, a mere two weeks after the onset of Sunny's final coma.

Although the family now had no doubt they were finally seeing clearly the strange events of the past thirteen months, a succession of occurrences reinforced their suspicions. The doctor in charge of Sunny at the Peter Bent Brigham Hospital was Harris Funkenstein, a prominent neurologist. After studying Sunny's condition at the outset of this and her previous coma and after running extensive tests on her, Funkenstein became convinced that she had received insulin by injection. He arrived at this conclusion with no knowledge of black bags, Alexandra Isles, or fifteen-million-dollar bequests.

When Ala visited the Boston hospital, Funkenstein asked if her mother might have had access to insulin.

"Not as far as I know," Ala replied.

Even more conclusive for the family was a campaign launched by Von Bülow, within a few days of Sunny's arrival at the Boston hospital, to have her life-support systems removed. He argued that since it was clear she would remain a vegetable and wasn't even able to breathe without artificial help, she should be allowed to die. The doctors in Boston had suggested this to Von Bülow as an option; he picked it up and pushed the idea with considerable vigor.

When the family in New York heard of this effort, they sent word that under no circumstances was such action to be contemplated. Von Bülow did not let up. "In England, they know how to handle these matters," was one of his themes.

His campaign went on through the first week in January. He would frequently drop down at Ala's apartment or she and Alexander would receive calls from him as often as two or three times a day urging the wisdom of letting Sunny die. He said for them to keep their mother alive was an act of selfishness. He frightened and confused them with stories of how Sunny's organs would deteriorate and have to be removed one by one. When they learned that this was not true, they stiffened their resolve not to let their mother die.

Von Bülow tried another tack. He wrote his stepchildren a letter outlining how much it would cost to keep Sunny alive. Sunny had debts, he told them; they would have to reduce their life-style drastically. Many changes would have to be made. Alexander, for instance, whose college tuition was now paid from Sunny's trusts, would have to start paying his own tuition (Alexander and Ala both had modest incomes).

When they consulted their mother's lawyer and banker about this, Alexander and Ala learned that Von Bülow's representations were totally untrue: their mother had ample money for any eventuality. When Ala saw the basic figures, she was particularly incensed that her stepfather would rely on their being unable to read a financial statement or add a column of figures.

In kicking up dust about money, Von Bülow appears to have been appealing to his stepchildren's greed. His zeal approached frenzy proportions when the decision was made to move Sunny from Boston to the Columbia Presbyterian Hospital in upper Manhattan, where Sunny could be under the care of her own doctor and where it would be far easier for the family to visit her. (Alexander and Ala were spending a lot of their time on the Boston–New York shuttle.)

Stating that the hospital had a strongly Christian orientation, Von Bülow argued that once Sunny was admitted there, religious prohibitions would keep her alive indefinitely. Kuh thinks Claus did not really believe this but was merely using it as a further ploy to pressure the children into the difficult decision.

With Claus's campaign to pull the plug on Sunny reverberating in their ears, Alexander and Ala made their first visit to Richard H. Kuh. Kuh had been born on Manhattan's West 110th Street. He graduated Phi Beta Kappa from Columbia University, and after serving as a combat infantryman in Europe during World

War II, he returned to graduate magna cum laude from the Harvard Law School in 1948.

Despite eleven years of distinguished service as an Assistant New York District Attorney, Kuh achieved most public attention, to his regret, when he successfully prosecuted comedian Lenny Bruce on an obscenity charge. When Frank Hogan resigned as District Attorney in 1974 due to bad health, the governor appointed Kuh to finish his term. At the next election, Kuh ran against Robert Morgenthau, who beat Kuh resoundingly. Since leaving office, Kuh had been in private practice.

At fifty-nine, Dick Kuh was a handsome man, with a decidedly gentle personal style that belied his many years as a big-city prosecutor. His manner was calm and steady. While the two young von Auerspergs were remarkably self-possessed themselves, this quality in their chosen adviser would be put to good use before their business together was completed.

Alexander and Ala told Kuh all their suspicions, starting with events prior to the 1979 coma, Maria's discovery of the black bag, her finding insulin in it later, Sunny's aspirin overdose of December 1980, and her entering a coma at Christmas, from which she showed no signs of emerging. Could they discover, they asked Kuh, whether the comas were natural or "unnatural" without making a public scandal? Could they investigate without bringing in the police? Kuh assured them they could.

He asked to speak with Maria, who came to his office three days later and related everything she had observed during the past year that fueled her suspicions.

Kuh spoke with Alexander and Ala several times on the phone, then met with them again a week after the first visit. Kuh then had lunch with Gurley in an executive dining room of the Chemical Bank, where they discussed at length the drama they were confronting.

With a formal investigation now in motion, Alexander and Ala still had to contend with a Von Bülow intent on persuading them to do "the sensible thing" about Sunny. He would ask them to meet with him to discuss "family matters," which invariably turned out to be the terrible burden to the family finances of a prolonged hospitalization. (As it happened, the matter of life-support efforts shortly became moot. Once Sunny was taken off a drug that facilitated tests by making her brain swell, she stabilized and was able to stay alive without a respirator.)

At one meeting, Von Bülow spelled out the terms of Sunny's will saying that on her death they would each—Cosima included —receive fifteen million dollars. He would receive the same amount, plus the apartment, Clarendon Court, and all furnishings.

The von Auerspergs, now aware that he had misrepresented both the financial problems and Sunny's inevitable deterioration, no longer argued his positions; instead they allowed him to play the paterfamilias role for fear of alerting him to their investigation.

Hostility found other outlets. At one of these talks Ala told her stepfather she had heard he was having an affair with another woman. With no loss of equilibrium Von Bülow replied that he *had* had an affair but that the woman and he were now just good friends.

Smoothly Von Bülow went on to explain that, after the birth of Cosima, Sunny felt herself unable to have sex and had given Von Bülow his freedom in this department. This announcement came as a surprise to Ala, who had trouble believing her still attractive mother had not made love in fourteen years.

Within two weeks of first talking with Alexander and Ala, Kuh felt there was ample evidence of what came to be called Von Bülow's "unhusbandly behavior"—watching Sunny dying in 1979 and forbidding Maria to call the doctor—but there was still no hard evidence.

Thoughts focused on the black bag. Maria had reported sighting it regularly in Von Bülow's possession up until she saw it leave for Newport in his open canvas satchel on December 19, 1980, three days before Sunny's final hospitalization. The black bag had not been seen since then either in Newport or New York. There was a chance, of course, Von Bülow had the bag in his private apartment, but it probably would have been sighted by Maria as it passed from Newport through the Fifth Avenue apartment—he never made any attempt to hide it.

Kuh engaged detectives to investigate Von Bülow. Foremost among them was a retired New York policeman with whom Kuh had worked in the past, Edwin Lambert. To Kuh's frustration, Lambert and his colleagues were unable to gain access to Von Bülow's East 69th Street apartment.

Another fact, however, pointed to the black bag's having been left behind in Newport. When Alexander searched his parents' quarters while Von Bülow accompanied Sunny to Boston, he found Von Bülow's closet locked. Not only had it been unlocked when he left the house at the onset of his mother's coma, he never recalled its ever being locked when the family was in residence.

At a family council on January 22, Alexander suggested that on his return to college he go down to Clarendon Court and get a locksmith to open the closet. All agreed that this was a good plan, but Mrs. Aitken insisted that her grandson not go alone. Kuh said he would send Eddie Lambert with Alexander and they should leave without delay. If they found the black bag, they should bring it to New York where the contents could be analyzed.

The next afternoon around four, Alexander and Lambert met in Kuh's Fifth Avenue office, mapped out their plan, and left for Newport in Alexander's car. They went first to Alexander's apartment in Providence, arriving about 8:30 P.M. Providence was out of the way, but the plan had been to pick up a locksmith there rather than in Newport, where it could cause gossip.

They opened the Yellow Pages and called the first locksmith they saw, one Marshall Salzman of Central Falls, a somewhat rough section of Providence. They offered Salzman three hundred dollars if he would drive with them to Newport and open a locked closet in the house of one of the two people requesting his services.

Salzman thought the deal sounded suspicious, but three hundred dollars was three hundred dollars. As a precaution, he asked one of them to drive in his van with him. Alexander drove with Salzman, Lambert following in Alexander's Fiat. They arrived at Clarendon Court between 10:00 and 10:30 in the evening.

Alexander, Salzman, and Lambert were admitted at the kitchen entrance by houseman John Berdy, and made their way to the opposite side of the sprawling house, where the master bedroom apartments were located.

Arriving at the closet, which was off the corridor connecting Sunny's bedroom with Von Bülow's study, the locksmith suggested that, before trying his skills on the locked door, they look around for a key.

Alexander went off to the kitchen to get cigarettes; Salzman and Lambert went into Von Bülow's study and almost immediately found some keys in his desk. Salzman started trying them in the closet door. With the second key the lock turned effortlessly. Lambert said they should wait till Alexander returned before opening the door.

What happened next was later disputed by the locksmith. Alexander and Lambert maintain that at this point they paid the locksmith and told him to leave, which he did.

As soon as they were alone, they decided that, before searching the closet, they would search other likely areas. They went through Von Bülow's desk and found a vial with yellow powder marked, in French, Valium. In Von Bülow's bathroom they found a black-leather bag which Alexander could see was larger than the one Maria had shown him. It was empty.

Finally they entered the closet, Lambert searching one side, Alexander the other. In the pocket of one of Von Bülow's jackets they found another French pharmaceutical container marked Valium, this one empty.

Alexander was finding nothing on his side. Turning, he saw that Lambert had pulled a large box of black metal from under a low shoe shelf. He had opened it and was removing a small leather bag.

"That may be it," Alex said.

The bag was about four by seven inches with a zipper around three sides and embossed with the word *Bowmar* (a manufacturer of calculators, it turned out).

Inside were bottles of pills, a vial with blue liquid, two packets of ampules, a cardboard box marked Lidocaine, a syringe, and three hypodermic needles. Two of the needles were sealed in their plastic containers; one was loose and looked dirty, as though it had been used.

They put the items back in the bag and zipped it shut. They next went into the bedroom and searched it thoroughly. From the few pill containers they found, they took sample pills and put them in a matchbox. They left Clarendon Court around midnight.

Fearing gun laws, Lambert had left his revolver in Alexander's apartment, necessitating a fifty-minute drive north to Providence before they headed back to New York. Dawn was breaking over the Manhattan skyline as they drove over the Triboro Bridge. Alexander dropped off Lambert, then, with the bag and other items, he went to the apartment of his sister, who was in Europe, and went to sleep.

The next day, together with Richard Kuh, Alexander took the black bag to the offices of Kuh's brother, a doctor with offices on East 91st Street. They examined the bag's contents more thoroughly. Dr. Kuh was most struck by the form of the drugs —a blue liquid and a bluish-white powder, which later turned out to be Valium.

Dr. Kuh assured his visitors the drugs they suspected the substances to be were not available commercially in these forms. The suggestion was made that perhaps they were adulterated in this way to put them into food; they conjectured further that the yellow paste found earlier by Maria and which tests showed to be Valium, might have been spread on toast. Farfetched as this is, no other explanation has ever been made of this bizarre alteration of a substance always taken in pill form. Dr. Kuh suggested they have the drugs and the one used needle analyzed by professional laboratories set up for this purpose. This would best be done through the family's own doctor.

The following week, Alexander, learning that Dr. Stock was on duty at Columbia Presbyterian Hospital, went there with the black-bag items now removed from the bag and in a manila envelope marked "Dr. Stock." When the doctor saw what Alexander had brought, he told him to take the envelope home and bring it to his East Side office the following day. When Alexander arrived the next morning with the manila envelope, Stock was with a patient. Alexander left the envelope with the receptionist.

When Dr. Richard Stock received the black-bag items in Alexander's manila envelope, he packed them carefully and called the Bio-Science Laboratories on Long Island to send a messenger for them. Stock had frequently done business with Dr. Ronald Gamberdella of Bio-Science, which was a subdivision of Dow Chemical and in Stock's opinion the premier lab in the country.

Six days after he sent off the items, February 9, Stock received the test results. The bluish-white powder was amobarbitol, the blue liquid a mixture of Valium and amobarbitol. The used needle contained a high concentration of insulin.

In studying the circumstances of Sunny's recent coma, Stock had been struck by one aspect more than others: her extremely low body temperature of 81° when found on the bathroom floor at

II A.M. For a body to reach such a degree of cold it would require many hours of unconsciousness, but Von Bülow said he had seen her asleep in bed when he arose at six. Four hours did not seem enough for such a temperature drop. Stock suspected Von Bülow was lying.

Now with the insulin reading on the needle, he wasted no time in phoning Richard Kuh and delivering a short message:

"Either you go to the police or I will."

Two days after Stock's ultimatum, Claus and Alexandra Isles checked into a room at the exclusive Lyford Cay Club for a midwinter tropical idyll. Unaware he was being stalked, Von Bülow had only one worry: that people might think it odd his going off on vacation while his wife was seriously ill in the hospital. He solved this by saying he was going to New Orleans on business.

One person who might think his going on a vacation at that time particularly odd was his daughter Cosima. Sunny's doctors had just come to the conclusion that the coma was permanent and Cosima had been told she had lost her mother. In addition, two days before Von Bülow was scheduled to fly south, the girl came down with chicken pox. The double calamities for a daughter he would later claim was "the center of his universe" did nothing to alter Von Bülow's travel plans.

Everyone else knew exactly where Von Bülow was going. While Alexander was away at college, Von Bülow used his room in the apartment as a study. Cleaning it, Maria had spotted three plane tickets for Nassau, one for Claus, the others for an Alexandra Isles and her son.

While the couple was relaxing in the sun, the forces aligned against Von Bülow were trying to exercise their final degree of control over the scandal that was about to break. Richard Kuh's clients urged him to launch the criminal action in New York rather than Rhode Island; their belief was that the case would attract less notice in sensation-numbed, scandal-plagued New York.

Kuh felt certain such a course was futile, but obliged his clients by first contacting his old office, that of the New York District Attorney. As he expected, he received a letter saying that the New

York authorities had no jurisdiction in such a matter; he must pursue his case in Rhode Island.

On February 23, Kuh telephoned the Rhode Island Attorney General's Office and was told that that office did no investigating; he should take his case to the Rhode Island State Police. But the Rhode Island Attorney General's Office assumed they would eventually become involved, and the case was assigned to a young lawyer in the office, Stephen Famiglietti.

Although he was enmeshed in other cases, Famiglietti was asked to keep abreast of the police's Von Bülow investigation in case anything came of it. Famiglietti sat in on a meeting at State Police Headquarters between the State Police Chief, Captain Edward Pare, Richard Kuh, and others of the police department. Captain Pare had decided to assign the case to one of his top detectives, Sergeant Jack Reise, who at that time was with his partner, Detective Joe Miranda, in Plattsburgh, New York, picking up a rapist to bring him back to Rhode Island.

On February 17, a week before this meeting at the Rhode Island police headquarters, a birthday party was held for Maria Schrallhammer at 960 Fifth Avenue. Present were Alexander, Ala, Cosima, and Franz Kneissl. Just after "Happy Birthday" had been sung and the cake candles blown out, the front door of the apartment opened and Von Bülow entered, returning a day early from his "business" trip. While the awkwardness of his arrival into the group would have been apparent to anyone, Von Bülow himself could not know how unwelcome he was. To avoid arousing his suspicions, Alexander and Ala made an effort to appear cordial. (His decision to return a day early had also upset plans of Richard Kuh, who now had Von Bülow under sporadic surveillance and had arranged for a photographer to be at the Newark airport to get a picture of Claus and Alexandra returning from their trip.)

Cosima was the only one present who still believed anything Von Bülow said and she was also the only one not upset by his surprise entrance. She asked the pointed question, "How come you have a tan?"

With his usual evenness, Von Bülow replied that he *had* gone to New Orleans on business as intended; once there, however, the man with whom he was conferring suggested they should continue their talks in the Bahamas, where he had a house. Von Bülow wished Maria a happy birthday and excused himself.

A short time later Maria again wrote her friend a letter:

> The news I am writing is unbelievable. Mrs. Von Bülow is since December 21 in a coma. Her condition is hopeless. It happened in Newport and I was in New York. The whole thing is very mysterious and criminal. There are police investigations but they take a long time. This is still a secret. I am almost sure that her unfaithful husband is guilty of the whole thing. I made many observations during the past year. I know too that the marriage was unhappy. On this December 21 (at 11 AM) she was found unconscious with a body temperature of 81° in her bathroom. They took her to Newport Hospital same as in December 79. They could not get her out of her coma.
>
> Mr. Bülow wanted to turn off the respirator to let her die. The children, Mrs. Aitken and I spoke against it. On January 13 she was transferred to New York.
>
> Mr. Bülow in the meantime passes the time with his girl-friend.
>
> It is correct Mrs. Bülow had very low blood sugar as she went to the hospital, but she must have been laying there for a long time. How did she get to the bathroom? There are a few things which don't seem to fit.

unny's father, utilities magnate George Crawford, the late 1920s.

unny and her mother, Annie Laurie Crawford, ding at Tamerlane, their Connecticut estate.

Sunny with a skating instructor at a New York rink.

Sunny in Greenwich, Connecticut.

Sunny and Prince Alfie von Auersperg at the time they met in 1956.

The late 1950s: the Princess von Auersperg in her new country.

Sunny with Alexander and Ala in New York after the failure of her European marriage.

Aerial view of Clarendon Court, the Von Bülows' Newport house on the Atlantic (© Providence Journal/Picture Group) →

The christening of Cosima Von Bülow. In front: Ala holding the baby, with Alexander at her side. Second row, from left, Viscount Lambton, Isabel Glover, Sunny, Annabel Berley (now Lady Goldsmith), J. Paul Getty, and Claus Von Bülow.

Another view of Clarendon Court, showing the pool that Sunny added.
(© Providence Journal/Picture Group)

Princess Annie Laurie von Auersperg (Ala) at her New York debut.

Sunny and Claus arriving at the Newport Music Festival, 1979. (© Providence Journal/Picture Group)

The drawing room at Clarendon Court. (© Picture Group)

XIII

SERGEANT John Reise had been with the Rhode Island police since he got out of the U.S. Marines in 1959: nine years as a patrolman, later as a detective. For a man who had devoted his adult life to two organizations with such authoritarian themes, Reise was an easy-going sort who seemed at peace with his fellow man.

He had grown up in Newport, the oldest of five brothers, and married a local girl, Susan Sullivan, by whom he had three children. The Reises lived not far from Bellevue Avenue on Annandale Road, in an attractive, immaculate house that could fit into the dining room of one of the summer mansions farther up the street.

Like many boys who grew up in Newport, Reise had frequent contacts with the multimillionaires living around him. He caddied for them, crewed for their yachts, and labored for landscape and construction firms doing work on their estates. He boasted that he had seen the inside of almost every Newport mansion. His mother had worked, from time to time, in the households of summer colonists and was now a tour guide at Hammersmith Farm, the former home of Jackie Onassis's mother.

Rather than having any animosity toward the rich, Reise quotes with approval his father's philosophy: "If it weren't for the rich, who would we work for?" Reise adds, "They have their part of town and we have ours. They have a lot, but their money cuts them off from a lot too."

When Reise was put on the Von Bülow case, his superior, Captain Edward Pare, told him he should be able to wrap it up "in a couple of weeks." His initial reaction on getting the assignment was that the Newport-based case would give him a break from the daily forty-two mile drive to police headquarters.

His first step in the investigation was to meet with Richard Kuh, then with Alexander von Auersperg. He studied their stories carefully, and because Alexander was so crucial to the case, Reise studied him as well. In judging the reliability of witnesses, Reise knew certain things to look for. Among the two hundred questions he had written down for Alexander was "Maria says that when she showed you the black bag, there was insulin in it. Is that true?"

Alexander was apologetic; he said that, although it might have been, he had no recollection of seeing it.

Alexander, Reise knew, was aware of how helpful to the case his "recalling" seeing the insulin would be. It would have been a simple matter for him to have manufactured a recollection to reinforce that of his ally, Maria. His not doing so convinced Reise of his honesty.

Several other times Alexander had a clear shot at bolstering his story with a specific memory but instead answered, "I'm sorry, it may have been that way, but it didn't seem important at the time and I'm not sure enough to testify to that under oath."

His impression of Ala, when he met her later, was equally positive. And when he listened at length to Maria Schrallhammer's hard-to-believe story, Reise never doubted for a moment she was telling the truth. His sidekick, Joe Miranda, agreed: "Over the years you get a gut feeling of whether someone's telling the truth or not."

When armchair spectators of the Von Bülow trial later aired their theories of a conspiracy against Von Bülow, they could not be expected to have a reading—as Reise and Miranda did—on the characters of those they were accusing of such villainy. They might, however, have had more of an idea of *how many* people they were impugning.

In order for Von Bülow to be convicted of attempting to murder his wife, his accusers had first to convince each other they had a case and were telling the truth. Then they had to convince Richard Kuh, then Sergeant Reise, then the Rhode Island Attorney General's Office, then a grand jury, then a jury, and in Rhode Island they had to convince the trial judge as well, for he can overrule the jury's verdict.

While it is possible for all these people to be wrong, the odds against collusion or falling-in-line gullibility increase with the addition of each new faction.

As Reise studied the medical records of the victim—whom he always referred to by her formal name, Martha—he was immediately struck by a discrepancy. The health records spoke of problems with alcohol and drugs, yet the toxology reports for both comas called the amounts of these substances "insignificant" in the 1980 coma, nonexistent in the 1979 coma. He was quick to pick up on the origin of all information about Mrs. Von Bülow's "problems": Mr. Von Bülow.

From the beginning of his investigation, Reise pursued this oddity, always making it a point to ask doctors if they had any firsthand knowledge of alcohol or drug problems in Mrs. Von Bülow or if they had learned of them elsewhere. The answer was invariably that they had heard of them directly from Mr. Von Bülow or had seen references to them in her medical records—which came down to the same thing, since Von Bülow had been the source of them as well.

When Reise later interviewed servants and found that they all testified that Mrs. Von Bülow drank almost nothing, he still did not rule out the possibility that they were lying to protect either their jobs or their mistress, although claiming she drank "next to nothing" would, he knew, have been much more easily disproved than saying she drank "normally."

Doggedly skeptical, Reise made a point of interviewing servants who no longer worked for the Von Bülows in an attempt to eliminate the job-fear motive for withholding information. Every one of them agreed that Mrs. Von Bülow hardly drank at all.

In his effort to learn about Sunny, Reise spoke with numerous people who were never called as witnesses. Among them was Sunny's hairdresser, Eve of New York, who said that Sunny had confided fears of falling into another coma; because of this she was afraid of going out during her final year.

Reise found this revealing for several reasons. Doctors had told him that among the first casualties of low blood sugar are the brain's memory centers. This would explain Sunny's not remembering events leading up to her first coma. Such retrograde amnesia, doctors said, is common among coma victims. This forgetfulness did not mean that Sunny had shrugged off her coma; although she was frightened and preoccupied with it, she was of no help in tracing its cause. (While Von Bülow, in talking about Sunny, made her record of last-minute party cancellations sound like a long-standing failing, it had actually been typical of her only during her final year; her dread of another coma makes a plausible explanation.)

Reise's ruminations kept returning to the odd position in which Mrs. Von Bülow had been found by her husband and son on the occasion of her final collapse. Her head was well under a toilet bowl that jutted out farther than most. Although her lip was cut, no trace of blood was found on the floor or on any fixture. Her head was close to the door, her feet farthest from it. Her nightgown was up around her waist. All these factors made Reise suspect she had been carried through the door and placed on the floor.

As Jack and Susan Reise prepared for bed one night, he picked up his wife and carried her into their bathroom. His experiment established two things: when carrying someone in your arms, it is most natural to bring them through a doorway feet first; as he lowered Susan onto the floor, her nightgown caught on his arm and rose up her body waist high.

Steve Famiglietti later decided that Reise's deductions were not sufficiently substantial to be used in the state's case against Von Bülow. They served, however, to remove any uncertainty Reise still felt about the cause of Mrs. Von Bülow's condition.

Before Reise could get very far into the medical aspects of the case, he had to master the medical terms "exogenous" and "endogenous" when referring to insulin. The first means administered from outside the body, the second means produced naturally inside the body. The two words would be crucial to the case.

The insulin information on Sunny's two admissions for coma were quite different. In 1979 Dr. Gailitis did not order an insulin test until midnight, almost six hours after her admission and more than twelve hours after Maria first reported believing her mistress to be in serious trouble. The results, 72 micro-units per milliliter on the first test, 54 micro-units on the second, were not that extraordinary and, because the tests were given so late, prove nothing either way. The result of Dr. Meier's more immediate test a year later was far more conclusive: an astoundingly high 216.

Reise was struck that Sunny's Boston doctor, Harris Funkenstein, had asked Ala if her mother had access to insulin. Reise knew that Funkenstein, when he voiced this suspicion of exogenous insulin, had no knowledge of the black bag, of a history of syringes and needles in the Von Bülow family, or of Von Bülow's suspicious behavior at the time of the first coma. Funkenstein's arrival at the injected-insulin notion was based entirely on his examination of the patient and her immediate record.

Even though Reise had been presented with substantial evidence on receiving this case—primarily the lab reports on the black-bag substances—his procedure was to start again from the beginning. Despite the impressive credentials of Richard Kuh and Reise's belief in Kuh's three clients, he treated the information and evidence as he would "that of any other informants."

When Reise received the black bag and its contents on March 13, he had everything tested again by the state's toxicologist, with the exception of the used needle. Once the needle washings had been tested for Dr. Stock at Bio-Science labs in Maryland and Boston, they had been discarded as a matter of routine. Reise considered their findings reliable enough to stand up in court; so did Famiglietti.

All the prescription vials in the black bag (and those seen there earlier) had Claus Von Bülow's name on them with one exception: the prescription vial of Valium made out to a Leslie Baxter. The name meant nothing to Reise, who now knew the names of most of the people in the Von Bülows' life. The address which Maria had copied from the vial proved to be false.

The more Reise inquired, and the more people who said the name meant nothing, the more mysterious Leslie Baxter appeared. Reise visited the pharmacy in the hope that someone there might remember the customer. Not knowing if Leslie Baxter was a man or a woman, a ten-year-old or an eighty-year-old, Reise could not help the druggist's recollection.

The only other bit of information Maria had jotted down from the vial was the prescribing doctor: Dr. Rosenberg. With a doggedness that the others came to see as typical, Reise began phoning every Dr. Rosenberg in New York. Remarkably, he found one who had prescribed Valium to Leslie Baxter. Reise got a phone number but no address. Dialing it, he heard an adult woman's voice become pleasantly evasive when Reise identified himself as a policeman involved in a criminal investigation. Reise quickly assured the woman that he was not interested in drug dealing, did not have any authority in the state of New York, but was simply involved in an investigation and was seeking informa- tion. She refused to let him come to her apartment, but agreed to meet him on a street corner on the Upper East Side.

Waiting on the corner, Jack Reise and Joe Miranda watched several women approach only to pass on by. Suddenly Joe said, "There she is."

"You've got to be kidding," Reise replied.

Reise saw a woman about forty, not bad looking, but quite heavy. The odd thing about her was not her corpulence but her get-up. She had on a short skirt, white leather boots, and a coarsely knitted white shawl under which something heavy dan- gled on her bosom. Reise saw that it was a large crystal pendant, which she fingered throughout their talk.

At first Leslie Baxter was wary and stiff. Yes, she knew a Claus that fit their description, a tall businessman from some Scan- danavian country—or was it England? Von Bülow? She didn't know his last name. She saw him maybe six times a year "when he came to town." Leslie was surprised but not flabbergasted to learn he lived in the neighborhood.

After a bit more cat and mouse, Reise said, "Come on, Leslie, what are we talking here, prostitution?"

Her response was a smile, but no comment.

Although Reise was not uninterested in Leslie's role, his main objective was to learn how Valium with her name on it ended up in Claus's pharmaceutical kit. Leslie admitted she had obtained the Valium for Claus. Reise's main purpose of this wild-*poule* chase was to prove that every item in the black bag belonged to Claus, not to Sunny or any other member of the household. He was now satisfied that the black bag belonged to Von Bülow and no one else.

* * *

In March, while Jack Reise was deep in his investigation, Claus and Alexandra returned to Nassau, this time taking along their two children. Alexandra's idea was to see how they all functioned as a family. "Building bridges" was the phrase she used for the holiday experiment. Claus flew directly to Nassau from Europe, where he had gone on business; Alexandra flew down from New York with her son and Cosima, whom she picked up at 960 Fifth Avenue. Maria brought Cosima down in the elevator and turned her over to the woman she had never seen before.

By the middle of April, Reise and Miranda had been working on the Von Bülow case night and day for seven weeks. They considered the medical evidence strong that Sunny's comas were caused by the injection of insulin. They were convinced the lab report on an insulin-stained needle was accurate and that the black bag in which it was found belonged to Von Bülow.

From talks with Sunny's trust officer they knew that Von Bülow stood to inherit "many millions" at Sunny's death, that the two children pursuing the investigation would each inherit the same amount, and stood to gain, if Von Bülow were eliminated from the will, a relatively small amount of additional money. More important, they would not receive it for twenty-one years. He knew that Von Bülow was in love with another woman and that both he and Sunny wanted a divorce. Reise felt it was time to talk with his suspect.

For their first confrontation, police invariably try to take a suspect by surprise. Making an appointment in advance allows those suspected of crimes time to arrange their defenses and alibis, or perhaps consult a lawyer, who will tell them under no circumstances to say anything to the police. Since Fifth Avenue apartment houses are set up to avoid drop-in visits, from police or anyone else, a strategy had to be devised for Reise to have an impromptu face-to-face encounter with Von Bülow. He met the day before in Kuh's office with Alexander and Ala, and they worked out a scheme.

Reise was to arrive at 960 Fifth Avenue early the next morning, just before Von Bülow usually left for his office, and wait on the street. Alexander would hang a red towel from his bedroom window. He would remove it when Von Bülow got into the elevator. This would enable Reise (and a New York detective) to intercept Von Bülow as he came out the door.

The plan had one problem. The building had two entrances—one on Fifth Avenue, another around the corner on 77th Street. To cover both exits, Richard Kuh was to sit across Fifth Avenue on a park bench, from which he could see the 77th Street entrance and also could spot Alexander's bedroom window.

When Kuh saw the signal, he was to remove a white handkerchief from his pocket and, with as much flourish as possible, blow his nose. This would enable Sergeant Reise and the New York state policeman accompanying him to wait in their car, from which they could see Kuh. Joe Miranda would be stationed farther up Fifth Avenue with another New York trooper.

The following morning—April 17—it was raining. Fortunately for Kuh, none of his Harvard classmates happened to pass as he sat on the park bench in the rain at 8 A.M. reading a newspaper. Reise and the New York policeman sat in a car parked across the street. The two officers must have interrupted their vigil on Kuh's nose. When Reise looked, Kuh was waving his handkerchief in total surrender.

They jumped out of the car and went to the doorman and told him they wanted to speak with Mr. Von Bülow. He just left, the doorman replied; if they headed up 77th Street, they could possibly catch him. As they rounded the corner into an almost empty street, Reise saw far up the block the striding figure of Von Bülow, his height identifying him.

As Reise caught a glimpse of the face, he realized he had seen the man around Newport, but had not known who he was. Before the police caught up with him, Von Bülow reached Madison Avenue and crossed it just as the light changed. Rush hour traffic prevented the two officers from crossing, so they kept abreast of Von Bülow on their side of the street as he walked rapidly south.

Finally the light changed and they crossed over and stopped him. Reise introduced himself as a Rhode Island detective looking into the circumstances surrounding Mrs. Von Bülow's coma. Could he ask him a few questions? Von Bülow replied he was on his way to his acupuncturist. When Reise said he had come all the way from Rhode Island to talk with him, Von Bülow said he could phone and cancel the appointment. The three men returned to the apartment and settled into the library.

After admiring the apartment, Reise went to pains to conceal that he suspected Von Bülow, although he conceded that everyone in the household was technically suspect. Reise presented himself not as a policeman stalking a criminal but as someone who was baffled by what had happened to Mrs. Von Bülow and who would be grateful for any light Mr. Von Bülow might throw on the puzzling matter.

Although Von Bülow was visibly nervous—stammering occasionally and digressing constantly—he nevertheless seemed confident that he could manipulate Reise, could lead this Rhode Island detective in any direction he chose.

Several times Von Bülow referred to his wife's problem with drugs and alcohol; when pressed on dates, however, he said that she had had no problem with these things since her first coma in 1979. Later on, after discussion about a number of other matters, Von Bülow referred to having been forced to remove drugs and alcohol from his wife's possession during 1980, a direct contradiction of what he had just said.

Von Bülow put most stress on his wife's hypoglycemia. She had been under a doctor's orders not to eat sweets, he told Reise, yet the night before her final coma she had eaten a caramel sundae in addition to a number of glasses of eggnog.

Reise moved in. Would his wife have any reason to inject herself with insulin?

"My God!" Von Bülow exclaimed. "That's the last thing she should have!"

Reise knew he had scored an important victory. Von Bülow's awareness of how harmful insulin would be to a hypoglycemic eliminated any possible defense that he gave it to her in the mistaken belief that it would benefit her in some way.

The exchange was an even greater victory. Reise could not know that at one point Von Bülow's lawyers would try to prove that Sunny injected herself regularly with insulin to lose weight. It would be difficult for her to engage in such a practice without the knowledge of a husband with whom she shared a bedroom. Or, to look at it another way, if she were injecting herself with insulin for such an innocent purpose, what reason would she have had to go to the pains necessary to hide such a routine from her husband?

If instead of expressing alarm at the notion that Sunny took insulin he had said "Yes, my wife takes it to lose weight," the investigation—and therefore the case—might well have ended right there.

With each exchange Von Bülow talked himself into a tighter corner. At the start of their conversation, Reise had read Von Bülow the Miranda warnings. ("You and I are going to talk. I have no idea what you'll be saying, so just as a precaution . . ." "Of course, Sergeant.")

Von Bülow was determined not to appear evasive or uncooperative. A hardened criminal, Reise knew, would have refused to say a word. Von Bülow's tenacious hold on the gentlemanly façade probably did more than any one thing to destroy him.

Von Bülow never got irritated or defensive at any of the questions (as had many Reise had interrogated), but rather talked to the policeman as if conversing with an old friend. Reise was impressed with Von Bülow's knowledge of hypoglycemia.

Afraid of silencing Von Bülow, Reise went to great pains never to say anything like "But Mr. Von Bülow, if what you say is true, how come . . . ?" Instead, he feigned total credulity, maintaining the pose of one seeking the guidance Von Bülow was only too happy to give.

"Now, Sergeant, you're making a mountain out of a molehill there."

Or more positively, Von Bülow would say, "If you'll just pursue this avenue, I'm sure you'll discover exactly what happened."

Looking back on this crucial meeting after the trial, Reise said, "Everyone talks about how intelligent Von Bülow is. Maybe he is, but more important than his brain is the *way* he talks. He's a master of speech. He has the words, the phrases. Talking is his forte. That's the way he operates. And I guess it works in his world. He thought it was working with us."

Then, in reference to Von Bülow's various contradictions, Reise added, "The beauty of telling the truth is that you don't have to remember what you said."

When Reise finally got up to leave in less than an hour, Von Bülow offered a concluding observation. "This whole thing," he said sadly, "is a vendetta on the part of Sunny's family. In a crisis such as this, a family should unite and pull together. This one isn't doing that."

Although Von Bülow did not name the object of the vendetta and Reise was careful not to ask, Reise felt that this was as close as Von Bülow came to acknowledging he was a suspect. This was the first evidence that Von Bülow was aware of the family's efforts against him. It is more than likely he knew nothing about it when he and the Rhode Island policeman sat down to talk an hour earlier. As the awareness came over him that forces were bent on connecting him with Sunny's illness, he had no difficulty concluding who those forces might be.

Relating the conversation to Joe Miranda immediately afterwards, Reise clung to his belief that he had not completely revealed his hand, that Von Bülow did not consider himself the primary focus of their investigation—not yet at any rate.

"But I'll make you a promise, Joe," Reise said. "Von Bülow is going to go to Newport in the next few days to get the black bag."

XIV

J ACK Reise had been back from New York four days when his son called him to the phone at quarter to nine in the evening of April 21, 1981.

"It's for you, Dad. It's important."

The caller told Reise that a taxi had just driven up to Clarendon Court and a tall man had gotten out. For the detective who for two months had thought about little except this case, the moment was intense. Ninety-nine percent suspicion is one thing, but accurately predicting the guilty moves of your prey is another. He had to get to Clarendon Court as soon as possible.

Reise won't say who gave him the tip, but acknowledges that a formal, round-the-clock stakeout would have been too costly and too impractical for such a free-based hunch. As with police work anywhere, friendships are crucial, and Newport was a small town in which Jack Reise had many friends. Also, his wife's parents lived across the street from Clarendon Court.

Reise was on the phone immediately to Miranda, who lived in the nearby town of Bristol. "Joe," he said, "get down to my house as fast as you can."

Reise already had in his possession a search warrant for Clarendon Court, but wanted to obtain from Von Bülow a consent-to-search signature. He also intended to tell Von Bülow he was a suspect, read him his warnings, and try to elicit a statement. He had no intention of arresting him.

For this program he needed at least two other officers. Without delay, he dialed the numbers and gave the same message he had given Miranda to two nearby police colleagues he had alerted to this possibility. More than anything else, Reise wanted to get to Clarendon Court before Von Bülow discovered that the black bag was no longer there.

Reise had learned that even when the mansion was unused—none of the family had been in the house since Alexander's January 23 visit—at least one servant was in it twenty-four hours a day.

The entrance gates were closed; Reise and the three men with him went around to the side street, Yzanga Avenue, to a small entrance in the wall, where an illuminated doorbell signaled that the door was in use. Within thirty minutes of receiving the call, Reise and his men were admitted into the kitchen by houseman John Berdy.

Reise identified himself and said he wanted to speak with Mr. Von Bülow. Berdy asked them to wait a moment. In a few moments Von Bülow came into the kitchen. He had removed his suit coat and put on a wine-red silk dressing gown over his shirt and pants.

"Ah, Sergeant Reise!" Von Bülow beamed. "How nice to see you again."

Reise later said he would never forget those words or Von Bülow's effusiveness in delivering them. "No one had ever spoken to me like that before," he said.

Both men knew that one was attempting to bring down the other. The suspect's unruffled and hearty cordiality toward the policeman was heavy with condescension and disdain. Not a jot of this escaped Reise.

Von Bülow said he had come to Rhode Island for the express purpose of seeing Reise, that he had attempted to phone his Providence attorney, John Sheehan, to learn how to reach Reise, whose name, Von Bülow apologized, he had neglected to write down.

When Reise said he wanted to ask a few more questions, Von Bülow led the four officers into the library. Reise and Von Bülow sat facing each other in chairs about five feet apart. The purpose of his visit was twofold, Reise said. He wanted to inform Von

Bülow he was a suspect. The charge, Reise said slowly, was in the area of assault with intent to kill.

Von Bülow showed no reaction.

"It was as though he hadn't heard me," Reise said later.

Reise then declared the other reason for his visit: to obtain permission to search the house. Von Bülow said he had no objection and signed the form. Joe Miranda and one of the officers left to start the search.

Reise produced a pocket tape recorder. When the machine was on, Reise asked if he recalled having been read his rights in New York. Von Bülow said he did. As a formality, Reise said, and to get it on the record, he wanted to read them again.

Reise produced a card from his pocket and started reading the Miranda warnings. Von Bülow, recovered from his initial freeze, now spurted reactions, which interrupted Reise's ceremony.

"I had no idea when we spoke in New York, the nature of the charges or of possibilities. . . . This is taking me back . . ."

When these interjections promised to be more than a word or two, Reise would snap off his recorder.

When the machine was turned on after one of these pauses, it had missed a section of the warnings. When Reise finally finished the warnings, he indicated he would like to get a statement although Mr. Von Bülow was under no obligation to say anything.

Von Bülow's replies to this option, repeated several times, were equivocal. "It never occurred to me in New York the nature of your investigation. . . ."

"Do you want your lawyer present?"

"It's hopeless. I can't get hold of Mr. Sheehan tonight."

"If you want him," Reise said, "we can stop right here."

Von Bülow interrupted. "Oh, you don't have to stop."

"You can make the call."

"It's hopeless to reach Sheehan now," Von Bülow said again.

The curious game continued—all of it on the tape—with Reise indicating that their talking was not obligatory but that he wanted to continue taking a statement. Von Bülow, on the other hand, confused and off-guard, was determined not to appear evasive and uncooperative.

At one point Von Bülow said, "I am prepared to stay over to have my lawyer present."

"Are you requesting a lawyer now?" Reise asked.

"Well, I've been a lawyer myself, you know. Isn't it customary? Haven't I got to have time to get my attorney?"

"Yes," Reise said. "You can make the phone call." Then he added, with more than a trace of guile, "But we are still in the investigatory stage, not the accusatory stage."

Von Bülow relaxed somewhat. "Well, let's see how we get along," he said. "You might reach a point in your questions when I say 'Make a note of that and ask me later.' Is that fair?"

"Yes," Reise said. "But let me clarify one thing. Do you want a lawyer present now?"

"No," Von Bülow replied. "Not if I can reserve the answers to some questions."

"You understand," Reise said, "you can stop at any point."

"Yes," Von Bülow said.

Finally putting to rest the matter of whether they should or should not be talking, Reise proceeded to ask specific questions about Mrs. Von Bülow, her habits, their life together, and the circumstances of her two comas. All in all, Reise and his police were in the house about three hours; the taped interview, however, lasts only about an hour and forty minutes.

Occasionally Von Bülow and Reise would digress. For example, Von Bülow told how he and Sunny frequently played backgammon, then pointed out the table across the library where they played. In describing the angle at which his wife was found lying on the bathroom floor, Von Bülow used a large weather vane set into the library ceiling as a point of reference. Reise was fascinated by the ornamental object. A gold pointer, about four or five feet across, was set into a large painted rose, around which clouds had been painted. Reise's digression was no Colombo Gee-nice-place-you-got-here routine, but genuine admiration for a bit of ornamentation whose like he had never before seen. Von Bülow was happy to discuss it.

When they returned to the subject of Sunny's final coma, Reise asked how she was found. Von Bülow started to describe his wife lying on the bathroom floor, then said, "Why don't you let me show you the exact place? It will make it easier."

They got up and headed for the bedroom area off the living room.

As they arrived in the bedroom, Von Bülow excused himself, saying he was going into his study to get cigarettes, then disappeared down the connecting corridor. While Von Bülow was out of the bedroom, Detective Miranda stuck his head into the room.

"What did you find, Joe?" Reise asked.

"The metal box is still in the closet," Miranda replied, then added he didn't want to move anything in the closet until the police photographer arrived. He also reported that in Von Bülow's study some clothes and a murder mystery had been tossed on the bed. Inside a black briefcase Miranda had found five pill vials. One, labeled with a prescription for 2 mg Valium, contained 10-mg pills (Dr. Stock never prescribed more than 5 mg) mingled with some 2-mg pills.

When Von Bülow came back into the bedroom after a few moments, he showed Reise how he had found Sunny lying in the bathroom on the morning of December 21. They returned to the library and sat down again and resumed their conversation, first turning on the tape recorder.

A half hour later, the police photographer arrived and went off with Joe Miranda. Within a few moments Miranda returned to the library and said, "Sergeant Reise, can I interrupt you for a moment?"

Reise followed his partner into the living room. When they were out of earshot of Von Bülow, Miranda said, "That son of a bitch locked the closet on me!"

"Are you sure, Joe?" Reise said.

"It was unlocked. I was inside it. I saw the metal box where Alexander said they'd left it. Now it's locked!"

"I'll be damned," Reise said.

Reise and Miranda had been not more than twenty feet from the closet, but out of sight of it, when Von Bülow had gone for cigarettes. Neither had heard the click of a key turning.

When he was later confronted with this incriminating action, Von Bülow said he kept a shotgun in that closet and, as it was not licensed, did not want the police to see it.

Aside from the fact that shotguns do not require licenses in Rhode Island, it is remarkable that Von Bülow should think to deceive the police over such a minor matter when he was at the moment being accused of a major one.

Locking the closet would under any circumstances seem a highly suspect action. When it is coupled with Reise's prediction that Von Bülow would make this off-season visit to Clarendon Court to retrieve the bag, the two actions seem redolent of guilt, but were not emphasized at the trial.

Von Bülow's version is that he came to Rhode Island to find Sergeant Reise and locked his closet to conceal an unregistered shotgun. Reise's version is that Von Bülow, learning he was a suspect, came to Rhode Island for the sole purpose of retrieving and perhaps destroying incriminating evidence, the black bag, was interrupted in this errand by the police, then slipped off to lock the closet in which he thought the bag to be, unaware that the bag had been removed a month earlier by Alexander and Detective Lambert.

Perhaps the most likely version would be that in the approximate half hour between his taxi pulling up to Clarendon Court and the arrival of Reise and his men, Von Bülow removed his outer coat, conferring with the butler, Robert Biastre (whom he sent out to buy him a razor), then went to his study, removed his jacket, donned the dressing gown, and unpacked a few clothes, which he tossed on the bed. (The houseman, John Berdy, unaware that Von Bülow had arrived and hearing noises from the bedroom wing of the first floor, went to investigate and was surprised to find Von Bülow there.)

When left alone by Berdy, it is possible that Von Bülow had gone to the closet, which Alexander and Lambert had left locked, and had not found the black bag where he remembered leaving it. He may have thought either that his memory was mistaken as to precisely where in the closet he'd left it (the handwritten reminder, "Metal Box," found on his desk suggests Von Bülow did not trust his memory, even about important matters) or thought that a servant had perhaps rearranged things (Biastre had been told about the key in the desk so that he would always have access to the closet).

With this hypothetical construction, Von Bülow may well have been in the closet starting to look for the bag when the buzzer sounded and Berdy returned to tell him he had visitors.

* * *

Jack Reise was startled in his sleep that night by a noise. Looking up he saw Claus Von Bülow standing over him with a slight smile. In his hand he held a syringe and needle.

"Sergeant Reise, how nice to see you again."

Reise threw a punch and caught his wife in the abdomen, close to the scar of a recent gallbladder operation.

XV

AFTER Reise's April 17 visit to 960 Fifth Avenue, Richard Kuh insisted that his clients who were still living there—Alexander and Maria—move out. Kuh later stated his reason bluntly: "We were convinced Claus was a bad guy. Now that he knew he was under investigation, I didn't want Maria and Alexander in his clutches."

Within hours of Reise's visit, Alexander had moved his things down to his sister's. Maria left but returned when she realized that Von Bülow would be away most of the weekend and Cosima would be alone for Easter. By Monday, only Von Bülow and his daughter remained in the fourteen-room apartment.

Now aware Sunny's family were trying to establish that he had tried to murder her, Claus's reaction was odd. Instead of confronting the two children he had reared for fourteen years with outrage that they should suspect him of such villainy, he went to Morris Gurley, the family trust officer, and asked what the children were seeking. What did they want to drop their investigation of him? Was it Clarendon Court? The Fifth Avenue apartment? Whatever it was, he told Gurley, he would be glad to give it to them. Getting nowhere with Gurley, Von Bülow tried other tactics.

He took Sunny's oldest friend, Ruth Flood, to lunch at the Knickerbocker Club. He told her what was happening and added, "When calamities strike families, it either draws them together or splits them apart. Unfortunately, with this family it is the latter." He urged Ruth to persuade the Aitkens to drop the campaign against him. Von Bülow made the same appeal to Isabel Glover.

For a time here Von Bülow told *his* friends that the entire effort to destroy him was a plot on the part of Russell Aitken, who he implied had a complicated financial motive. Von Bülow also started a program of vilification about Alexander, Ala, and Maria.

In May of 1981, another of Sunny's old friends, Alan Murphy, went to a large cocktail party at the palatial Fifth Avenue apartment of Mark Millard and spotted Von Bülow among the guests. Murphy was accustomed to the curt nod he got from Claus whenever they encountered each other at a social gathering where some sort of greeting was unavoidable (as opposed to on the street, where Von Bülow never even acknowledged Murphy). He was therefore surprised to have Von Bülow come directly to him and say "Hello, Alan. As an old friend, I must talk to you."

The "old friend" label was as astonishing as the use of the first name, since it was the first time Claus had addressed him by name in the thirteen years they had known each other. Von Bülow pulled Murphy into a corner and began telling him how rich Sunny was, how spoiled, and how much she had been drinking before going into her second coma.

Murphy had heard about the investigation of Von Bülow from Sunny's friend Ruth Flood, but he was still unprepared for the conversation's destination.

"The Aitkens are launching an investigation aimed at implicating me in Sunny's condition," Claus said. "Since you are an old friend of the family, I want you to persuade them that this will only bring them scandal and embarrassment. You've got to make them call it off."

Murphy was incensed. He told Von Bülow that if Sunny *had* been drinking, he should be dedicated to keeping her weakness silent, especially now that Sunny was in a coma and couldn't defend herself. But more important than that, if Von Bülow was innocent of doing anything to Sunny, he should be eager for the most thorough investigation.

Von Bülow glared at him, then turned without a word and walked away.

* * *

At this point the investigation of Von Bülow was being conducted with total secrecy. Not only was the press unaware of the suspicions aimed at the prominent socialite, but the rumor mongers of the party circuit were equally oblivious. Ruth Flood and Alan Murphy had learned about it only because they had been approached by *him.*

Not all of Von Bülow's responses to being the target of a criminal investigation were so arcane. Immediately after Reise's first visit, he had phoned his friend and fellow Newporter, Rhode Island Senator Claiborne Pell, and related his predicament. Could Pell recommend a good Rhode Island criminal lawyer? Pell told him to contact John Sheehan in Providence.

Sheehan was a sad-eyed Irishman in his mid-fifties who had come from a poor family in Springfield, Massachusetts, had been a paratrooper and later put himself through law school working as a bartender in a Providence dive that turned out to have among its clientele a number of criminals who started Sheehan on his way to a highly successful private practice.

By the time Sheehan had his first meeting with Von Bülow on April 24, the Cambridge law graduate and London barrister had already given a total of three and a half hours of statement to the police, a fact that did not delight the Providence lawyer. They set to work.

As Sergeant Jack Reise delved deeper into the medical complexities of the Von Bülow case—talking with doctors about insulin levels, hemoturia, and pancreatic disorders—he realized he was technically out of his depth and would need expert help in assembling the scientific evidence and testimony.

Richard Kuh suggested a Harvard professor, William Curran, a lawyer who specialized in medical cases; on behalf of his clients, Kuh hired Curran to assist Reise. When Reise first met with Curran and outlined the Von Bülow events, Curran was fascinated by the story and threw himself into the project with vigor.

Foremost among the many contributions Curran made to the prosecution was leading Reise to Dr. George Cahill, who was affiliated with the Harvard Medical School and who was now director of research at the Howard Hughes Medical Institute; he was among the world's top blood sugar experts.

When Cahill was asked to review the medical history of Mrs. Von Bülow, the position of Reise and of Steve Famiglietti was that, while they were convinced Von Bülow made the attempt on his wife's life at Christmas 1979 and 1980 and possibly other times, they only had sufficient evidence to bring one of these charges: the 1980 assault. They reached this conclusion because an insulin level test had not been taken on Sunny's admission to Newport Hospital on the occasion of her first coma.

Cahill felt the facts at their disposal about 1979 more conclusive. He was struck by her alarming low blood sugar, 41 mg per centum on admission; then after being pumped full of glucose, her blood sugar had *dropped* on the next reading to an even more shocking 20 mg per centum. To lose sugar at that rate, Cahill contended, the blood had to be loaded with a "sugar-eating" agent, that is to say, insulin.

Dr. Cahill told Reise and Famiglietti that in his opinion they had ample evidence to prosecute the first attempt as well. Reise was vastly heartened that Cahill made this judgment solely on the basis of medical evidence and with no knowledge of Maria Schrallhammer's account of Von Bülow's obstructive behavior prior to the 1979 coma.

As Reise and Miranda were getting close to having sufficient evidence to present to a grand jury, they increasingly had to consult Famiglietti, who was deeply involved in other cases and was increasingly troubled with a recurring back problem. Finally he was able to give the Von Bülow case his full attention. A round of meetings with his case's principals convinced him they would soon be ready to go to the grand jury.

Stephen Famiglietti had been born in a poor Italian section of Providence thirty-four years earlier, the son of Rocco and Angela Famiglietti. Rocco was a bricklayer, and Angela worked as a seamstress in a dress factory.

From earliest childhood Famiglietti was bright and cocky—yet well liked. He flirted with a career as a troublemaker, but changed his mind when he was about six. In a vacant lot close by his house, Steve started a brush fire which was serious enough to bring the police to the Famiglietti house looking for the "little boy who started it." Without a moment's hesitation, Angela Famiglietti pointed across her living room and said, "He's there, behind the sofa."

Famiglietti put himself through Providence College and later Suffolk University Law School in Boston by working at construction, catering and other odd jobs. After receiving his law degree, he joined the Attorney General's Office and in his seven years as a prosecutor had earned a reputation as one of the department's best.

Famiglietti became aware of the Newport of legend "as soon as I could read," but was somewhat older before he realized that the resort was one of his state's main claims to nationwide fame. Famiglietti had an instinctive man-of-the-people disdain for the summer colonists, attributing to them feelings of superiority over their fellow men, but whatever antagonisms he may have harbored toward the rich, he quickly developed a liking and a respect for the two von Auerspergs, finding them "remarkably mature, unassuming, and courageous."

They were quick to return the respect. They were particularly struck by his all-business single-mindedness about the issue at hand, which he softened with a quick humor that, for one so sure of himself, could be winningly self-deprecating.

Early in the summer a lunch was given at Clarendon Court for the principal players on the legal side to meet the family, particularly Mrs. Aitken, whom none of the representatives of authority had met before. Famiglietti was quick to see the older woman's great charm and graciousness, but figured that was what these people were good at.

He was overwhelmed by Clarendon Court, never having been in a home so magnificent. At one point during a casual meal served by the pool Famiglietti got up and walked alone across the immaculate, tree-framed lawn to the ocean, perhaps on the subconscious calculation that he could learn less by conversing with the people he was championing than by contemplating their setting.

The grand jury convened in June of 1981 on the second floor of the Colony House, the historic Newport statehouse adjacent to the courthouse in which, seven months later, the Von Bülow trial would take place. The proceedings of course were secret, but one witness who testified at them was impressed not only by the number of questions jurors asked but by their astuteness as well.

After listening to the evidence for several days, the grand jury came to the same conclusion as Dr. Cahill: the Attorney General's Office had enough evidence to indict Von Bülow on two counts of injecting his wife with insulin—in December of 1979 and again in December of 1980—his intention both times to kill her.

John Sheehan was notified by phone on July 6 and told to present his client in the Providence courthouse—Newport's was closed for the summer—on July 14 for his arraignment.

While the grand jury was deliberating, Alexander's and Ala's worries mounted about Cosima. If an indictment was handed down, newspapers would have the story, making it impossible to put off any longer telling their half-sister their role in the business. They were so anxious about the effect of the revelation on the young girl that they made an appointment with a New York child psychologist for advice on how to explain the matter to help her cope with this to-the-death battle between the three people closest to her in the world over the fate of the fourth.

Alexander and Ala were exceptionally fond of Cosima, and they were fearful of losing her love. In this regard, however, their concern was more for her. They at least had each other, Ala had her husband, Alexander had a girlfriend, they had their grandparents, they had Maria. In addition, both Alexander and Ala were as good as out of the home and embarked on their own lives.

Cosima was still at home. And now, cut off from Alexander, Ala, Maria, and her grandparents, she was at home alone with a man who may have tried to kill her mother.

When on the evening of the indictment Ala and Alexander finally told Cosima, the scene, which took place by Clarendon Court's swimming pool, was highly emotional despite Cosima's saying she had known from the beginning. The trepidation felt by Alexander and Ala about the effect of the grizzly business on Cosima was not felt by her father, who had immediately unburdened himself to his thirteen-year-old daughter and asked her to share his distress.

Cosima told Alexander and Ala that she knew what they believed her father had done. While she was convinced they were mistaken, she knew they would not be taking the action they had unless they believed they were right. She cried and told them she understood how much the whole thing must hurt them and how much pain they must feel in having to tell her. All three of Sunny's children found themselves hugging and crying.

In the days, then the weeks, that passed, Alexander and Ala kept bracing themselves for the anger they expected to burst forth from Cosima; indeed, the psychologist had told them to expect it. To their amazement, it did not come. Throughout the trial Cosima remained as she always had been with her half-brother and half-sister—warm, in frequent touch. She avoided any discussion, however, of the bitter business that was permanently upsetting all three of their lives.

Such equanimity may have required some dissembling on Cosima's part. She had lunch one day with her godmother, Isabel Glover, who asked that Cosima forgive her but she would not be able to see her father until the business was cleared up; she found it too difficult to be around him.

"I understand," Cosima replied. "I feel the same way about being around Alexander and Ala."

The day after the indictment, July 8, newspapers across the country ran the story, but often in baffled little articles in back pages. *The New York Times* was typical: under the headline FINANCIER INDICTED ON CHARGE OF TRYING TWICE TO KILL WIFE the article didn't mention the accused's name until the second paragraph, which quoted a spokesman of the State Attorney General's Office as saying "We allege that Claus Von Bülow, knowing that his wife was hypoglycemic, injected her with insulin, knowing it could be fatal."

Two days after the indictment, Jack Reise got a phone call from a reporter asking if Reise knew whom he was going to be up against in the courtroom. Reise said that he knew: John Sheehan.

"That's what you think," gloated the reporter. "You face Sheehan, but you also face Herald Fahringer."

"Who the hell is that?" asked Reise.

"He's only one of the top criminal lawyers in the country,"

gloated the reporter. Reise hung up the phone, sighed, and went back to work.

Until about this time, few people had heard about Fahringer; his recent selection to handle the appeal of Jean Harris and to defend Claus Von Bülow had put him in a position to become one of the best-known lawyers in the country.

Fahringer was born to a poor family in Williamsport, Pennsylvania, of the German ancestry known as the Pennsylvania Dutch. He graduated from Penn State and spent the three years before deciding to enter law school attempting an acting career, getting occasional work in radio, television, and summer stock. After earning his law degree, he settled in Buffalo, where he joined a firm and specialized in criminal law.

The success he brought them was such that he opened a New York City branch in 1975—because "the criminals pay better there." He became an expert in pornography cases, some with a Mafia stripe, pleading several before the U.S. Supreme Court. He also defended such independent flesh documentarians as Larry Flynt and Al Goldstein. While handling a less high-toned pornography case in New England, Fahringer found himself working with Providence lawyer John Sheehan. They decided they worked well together.

Now in his late fifties, Fahringer was a striking figure with a neat head of hair that might, except for its whiteness, have graced a preppie, a handsome face of like boyishness, a trim figure, and fastidious formality of dress (although he claimed he varied his wardrobe according to the case and its jury).

Fahringer admits to being obsessive about his career. He states his ambition simply: "I want to be the best lawyer in America." Now in charge of two criminal defendants of nationwide interest, Fahringer was within striking distance of this goal.

In the midst of his Von Bülow involvement, Fahringer lost his appeal for Mrs. Harris, which put him under even greater pressure to score a victory in Newport.

Immediately upon taking the case, Fahringer wanted to visit Clarendon Court, the scene of the alleged crimes. Without warning, Von Bülow, Sheehan, and Fahringer arrived at the Bellevue Avenue mansion and encountered Alexander and Ala by the swimming pool with a friend. Startled as they were, the two accusers, according to John Sheehan, showed great politeness, almost graciousness, to the enemy party.

If civility marked Von Bülow's first public appearance as an accused criminal, indignities marked his second, the arraignment in Providence on July 14 at which he was released on one hundred thousand dollars bail and had his passport lifted.

The press was excited by word of a Newport socialite who had been indicted a week earlier for trying to murder his enormously rich wife and so the arraignment would have been a carnival in any event, but what turned it into a dangerous melee was a small logistical fact: the newspapers had no file photos of Von Bülow and had sent out their photographers with orders to come back with a good clear shot of him. The usual jostling and elbowing became a life-threatening stampede.

Few people witnessing the scene could not feel pity for the accused, regardless of what they felt about his guilt or innocence, as he found himself pushed, pawed at, and pursued both on entering and leaving the courthouse.

As he was trying to get back to his car, a man emerged from the crowd and screamed in German, "You pig! You killed Sunny!" The man was hustled off and, after refusing to tell reporters his name for fear of reprisals from "Von Bülow's powerful friends," disappeared into the story's misty edges as a bizarre curtain-raiser to the drama's public phase.

Even when Von Bülow made it into John Sheehan's car, he was still not safe. A carload of European journalists set out in pursuit and gave a high-speed chase on Providence's crisscrossing freeways. Throughout this and all that preceded, Von Bülow appeared to be in shock. He could not know that in the months that followed nothing would approach this affront to his finely tuned sensibilities. The civilized mood of his Clarendon Court visit would be more typical of the trial to come.

The day after the arraignment, the story was trumpeted in the area's newspapers and given good play in big-city papers across the country. Extensive as the coverage was—particularly for a small-town unsuccessful murder attempt—it was little more than a discreet drum roll for the subsequent press tattoo, a media thunder that would be heard from Berlin to Hong Kong.

* * *

Whatever shock Von Bülow felt at all that was happening to him, he recovered from it enough to seek from the enemy camp the use of Clarendon Court for the week of his birthday in August. There is something grotesque about this concern with a week's free use of a vacation house when his world was collapsing.

Von Bülow's requesting Clarendon Court for a week was a foretaste of the proprietary complications that would ensue from this litigation. Even his conviction would not automatically evict him from the two houses, nor, for that matter, from the will. Legal machinery existed to formalize such exclusions, but they needed activation by court action.

It was all too far off to worry much about, and he was given Clarendon Court for the week. For the same reason, no one suggested he should move out of Sunny's palatial Manhattan apartment.

While the Aitkens and von Auerspergs were trying to behave in as gentlemanly a manner as possible, they no longer credited him with doing the same. After Von Bülow's week at Clarendon Court, Alexander had Detective Eddie Lambert go over the house to check for listening devices.

Some Newporters found his presence embarrassing. Others of his circle were doggedly loyal. Mrs. John Nicholas Brown invited him to lunch, and afterwards commented on his admirable spirit and undaunted sense of humor.

Another woman, who had known him years before he married Sunny, invited both Claus and Cosima for dinner. Admirable as her show of solidarity was, she reported later she was so nervous, she didn't stop talking all evening. The woman learned quickly how courageous her gesture was. The next day she dropped by Bailey's Beach and greeted Russell Aitken, a friend of many years, and watched in disbelief as he turned his back on her.

Unlike the rest of Sunny's family, Aitken had never liked Von Bülow. Now, convinced along with the rest of them that his step-son-in-law had tried to kill Sunny, he was anything but reticent in voicing his loathing around Newport. As for friends showing Von Bülow kindness, Aitken clearly felt there was such a thing as being too "civilized."

Those who angrily rejected the possibility of Claus's guilt did not stop to consider that such a judgment ipso facto incriminated others, also popular in Newport, of another dastardly crime: framing an innocent person. It was not just a matter, therefore, of pronouncing one of their number guilty or innocent; the guilt they lifted from him had to land, like the dreaded tarot card, on someone else in the group.

Newporters in general deplored the scandal brought down on them, but they were more concerned with the culpability issue and, by extension, the moral issue. Curiously enough, the moral issue swung around and returned, with crazed frivolity, to the social issue. What would his guilt say about their cherished exclusivity? Even the self-congratulatory Newporters might ask what kind of club it is that would accept a man who killed his wife for profit but would exclude a Jew or a Catholic. The cherished "standards," flimsy enough under normal circumstances, might collapse under the corrosive contamination of an attempted murderer.

Not all the summer people were so concerned with the moral ramifications. Some Newporters accused others of choosing sides on the basis of who they thought would win—with an eye to future dinner invitations. Never mind who did what to whom, the question was said to be, Which side will emerge with Clarendon Court and the money?

Perhaps the most bizarre reaction among the coinhabitants of the Von Bülows' strata was the feeling, expressed by more than a few, that police investigations and trials were for the rabble; *their* sort did not air its dirty linen in such a vulgar way. Those advocating sweeping the whole mess under the Aubusson invoked the example of Elsie Woodward, the society leader who was said to have believed her daughter-in-law had murdered her son, but who, for the sake of her grandchildren, had embraced Ann Woodward and avowed belief in her innocence.

Now *that,* her admirers claimed, was the aristocratic way of dealing with family murders.

Alexander, responding to swipes from wealthy cronies about causing a public scandal, said simply, "What would you do if someone tried to kill your mother?"

He would also claim that a strong motivation on the part of him and his sister was a desire "to vindicate our mother" (against Von

Bülow's charge that she was alcoholic, depressive, and suicidal). But more than anything, they wanted Von Bülow punished. After it was all over, Alexander said, "For us, it was a moral issue right down the line."

Ever since Von Bülow had become aware of the family's investigation against him, he had made no effort to communicate with Ala and Alexander. Ala was startled to receive a call from him late one evening to express his outrage over a newspaper quote attributed to her. She broke into his diatribe and said, "If you want to discuss Cosima, I will talk to you. If not, I'm going to hang up." He kept on with the diatribe, so she hung up. That was the last contact between the adversaries.

XVI

FOR several reasons the defense lawyers of Claus Von Bülow wanted to avoid a postponement of the trial, which was scheduled to start in mid-November of 1981. Since it was estimated that the trial would run from four to six weeks, the November starting date could mean sending the jury into deliberation just at the approach of Christmas—a difficult period, the reasoning went, to condemn a fellow creature to jail, particularly the father of a fourteen-year-old girl.

While lawyers rarely make light of such sentimental influences, a tangible legal consideration was of greater concern. The defense wanted proceedings to begin as soon as possible for fear Mrs. Von Bülow might die before the start of the trial; if she did, it would be a relatively simple matter for the state to revise the charge to murder. If she died while the trial was under way, altering the charge would become a far more complicated matter. In fact, the snarl of motions and countermotions might eject the defendant altogether from the state's grasp.

The prosecution was eager for a delay in order to fortify its case, which was complex and circumstantial; both qualities tended to keep the goal of sufficient evidence out of reach. The prosecution prevailed, and the trial was postponed until January.

Another problem that needed resolving, then re-resolving throughout the pretrial months, was the trial's location. Neither side pushed for a change of venue. The defense argued that Newport probably had a sophisticated populace, tolerant of the upper crust's eccentric ways. The prosecution felt that, in principle, trials were best conducted where the alleged crime had taken place: locals might feel that wife-murdering was all right for Providence but should be stopped in Newport.

Both legal teams were a bit stunned when the Superior Court judge selected to hear the case, Justice Thomas H. Needham, announced he was moving the trial from Newport to Providence. Since the arraignment in July, Needham's office had been receiving requests from journalists for seats in his court. By late fall the number of such requests had reached fifty; the courtroom, the only full-sized courtroom in Newport, held a total of fifty-four spectators. Assuming that as the trial progressed even more press people would be seeking admittance, the judge decided that Newport's modest facilities would prove inadequate.

Unfortunately, Needham's decision got to the press before his colleagues in Rhode Island's judiciary had granted him an alternative courtroom. They were less than thrilled to learn that the Von Bülow circus was going to land in their midst. Not too cordially, they declined the honor, saying there was no available court. So it was back to Newport.

The trial date was set for Monday, January 11, 1982, with pretrial motions set for the Thursday preceding. The only matter of any substance to be decided that day was a defense motion to ban television and still cameras from the courtroom. Rhode Island had adopted a one-year experiment in which television cameras would be permitted in courtrooms during trials. Even though twenty-six other states already allowed in-court cameras, the Von Bülow case loomed as the first trial of national interest in which cameras would be permitted. The trial augured to be of the magnitude of the trials of Patty Hearst, Mrs. Harris, and, concurrently, Wayne Williams—none of which had allowed cameras in their courtrooms.

Legal experts were of mixed opinions about the pros and cons of the TV phenomenon and of what effect it might have on the judicial process. All agreed it was a potent and unknown force. Rhode Island and the entire legal community, therefore, were watching the television camera with a good deal of apprehension.

Herald Fahringer had written a paper for the ABA in which

he presented the arguments against cameras in courtrooms. At the beginning of the essay, he stated that he was as yet undecided whether he was for or against in-court cameras, but felt final decisions should take into consideration the following dangers: the creation of a showboat atmosphere; the temptation for witnesses and lawyers to "act up"; the pressure on these groups, and on judges themselves, to abandon their true opinions if they felt the opinions were unpopular. He also maintained that the relative anonymity of the courtroom made it less frightening for a witness to come forward and, once on the stand, to speak with candor. Would the television cameras inhibit witnesses from speaking frankly or speaking at all? All those involved in the Von Bülow trial were considering these issues; under the state's one-year experiment these were the possible ramifications that would be watched for particularly by those deciding television's courtroom future.

Practical, logistical problems of television coverage were soon overshadowing the abstract ones. Foremost was the problem of accommodating all the television stations and networks that wanted to cover the Von Bülow trial. A system was worked out whereby the three local TV stations would provide a pool cameraman to man the courtroom camera, each station taking a week. The electronic results would be flashed on a monitor in the Colony House, the large building adjacent to the courthouse that had been designated the press headquarters for the trial. Up to twelve stations (or networks) desiring trial footage could plug into this master monitor. Eventually, when nationwide interest in the case grew intense, an elaborate system was set up for relaying the courtroom proceedings to a Providence transmitter, from which it could be broadcast anywhere in the country.

Fahringer had filed a motion to forbid television at the Von Bülow trial but had predicted to colleagues that his request would be denied. When his prediction proved correct, it was good news to the stations that had already spent six thousand dollars to rewire the eighteenth-century Colony House for their twentieth-century power needs.

The defense made a motion for an individual voir dire, the right to interrogate each prospective juror individually rather than in front of all the others. Since the questions are basically the same, it can be highly tedious to sit through this process. More importantly, hearing the questions many times before having to answer them, jurors can rehearse their responses and figure out the "correct" response for getting on or being excused. The defense also felt that a large audience might inhibit candor with the more personal questions. Judge Needham granted the request.

The judge postponed ruling on a defense motion as to the number of peremptory challenges allowed each side, from eight to sixteen; he would decide on that after sixteen panelists had been interrogated.

The other pretrial motions, all of much greater importance for the trial itself, were postponed until after the jury was selected. This was decided in conference in the judge's chamber. The defense agreed to let the press be present for the motion arguments if the jury selections came first. The reasoning was that, once chosen, the jury would be forbidden by the judge to view the media and would therefore remain ignorant of the pretrial hearings.

The defense had three important motions: to bar as evidence the notorious black bag with its incriminating drugs and hypodermics on the grounds that it had been illegally obtained; to bar the statement made by Von Bülow to the police on the grounds that he had not been given his warnings properly; and to bar medical evidence as it violated a Rhode Island law against revealing privileged patient-doctor information without the patient's consent.

With the postponing of the key motions, the pretrial day had importance simply as a shakedown runthrough for the long spectacle about to begin. For the relative handful of press and spectators who gathered for the pretrial motions, the big event was the first glimpse of Von Bülow. The other leading participants who also made their first appearances that day—the defense counsel, the prosecution team, Judge Needham, all of whom would become almost as celebrated as Von Bülow himself—were at that time not recognizable to most spectators.

As Von Bülow strode into court the most remarked-on impression by the neck-craners was his height, a feature photographs rarely indicated. A shade over six foot three, he loomed majestically over both of his lawyers. Secondly, he marched into court with a ramrod carriage that bordered on a parody of military bearing. This oddity was intensified by a defense strategy, quickly abandoned, of entering the courtroom in a miniparade—Fahringer leading, followed by Von Bülow, then his second counsel, John Sheehan, the rear brought up by Mary McGann, Sheehan's secretary.

Whether this was to convoy Von Bülow through crowds containing who-knew-what menace, or merely to impart some dignity to the visiting team, it was clearly out of key with the relaxed mood that would dominate the proceedings. Fahringer would frequently prove adept at sensing similar missteps and quickly altering his strategy.

A defense policy apparent that first day that never altered throughout the trial pertained to the defendant's, and to a lesser degree his lawyer's, dress. Von Bülow, who was famous among his circles as an innovative, almost eccentric, dresser—much given to polka-dot shirts, brocade jackets, and frilled cuffs—was now trotted out in a black suit of worsted wool, beautifully tailored to be sure, but, with a stark white shirt and a gray tie, funereal in effect. It was an odd way to present a man about whom Lally Weymouth in an informed article in *New York* magazine, the first full-scale press review of the case, had raised the specter of the necrophilia rumors that had clung to him for years. Even though Weymouth had been firm in disclaiming the rumors as having originated in a joke, it was strange of Fahringer and Sheehan to allow their client to dress himself in a style suggestive of potted palms, fragrant lilies, and open caskets.

Another curious aspect of Von Bülow was a single row of hair transplants which ran in a straight line across the top of his head, directly above his ears. Because of his height, this oddity would be noticed by few. In the courtroom, however, the slight elevation of the press box gave fourteen journalists a clear view of a bald front half of his head, then the file of brave transplants, with partial baldness behind them. It appeared he had started the transplant process, then abandoned it, leaving this one outpost to fight baldness alone.

Other than his suit's tailoring, the only suggestion of wealth was a Cartier wristwatch. A final touch to his courtroom rig was, although small, perhaps the most telling. On the third finger of his left hand he wore a somewhat chunky gold wedding band. Being the only hint of color in his entire get-up, the yellow metal hit the eye forcefully. Considering the circumstances of Von Bülow's presence in court, the ring had an even greater impact.

Among the events of that first coming together of trial elements was a cat-and-mouse game Von Bülow and his legal entourage played with the photographers waiting outside the courthouse. Having been caught and photographed as he entered the side door (the usual entrance for judges, witnesses, and other proceeding principals), he foiled the camera people by exiting through the front door. The courthouse had only two doors; with many more days of entrances and exits and a growing army of photographers who would remain on length-of-trial duty, such feints proved futile. When it became evident that the photographers sought only their daily photo, Von Bülow stopped ducking them and became an ever more agreeable subject.

If Von Bülow was overly evasive with the newspaper photographers on the pretrial day, he was overly cooperative with the television cameramen. His cheerful availability caused the day's only serious upset.

In the general milling about after the day's proceedings, the pool TV cameraman, Jim Taracani of WJAR-TV in Providence, asked Von Bülow, who was standing idly at the prosecution table, if he might put a few questions to him. Von Bülow agreed. With the camera on him, Von Bülow gave his opinions about television in the courtroom. He was disappointed at the judge's decision to allow the cameras, he said, as it would be too easy for an unfriendly station to show him in a bad light, "picking his nose" for example.

The pool cameraman was delighted with his unexpected interview and refused to share his coup with the other stations. The pool arrangement, he argued, dealt only with the gavel-to-gavel court proceedings. Once the judge had left the bench, the cameraman on duty was free to forage for whatever nuggets he could for his station.

A cry of "dirty pool" went up from all stations and crescendoed mightily when the interview was run that evening on WJAR-TV and no other station. As it became clear the ruckus was threatening the entire TV deal, WJAR backed down rapidly, indicated a willingness to compromise, and agreed when Judge Needham announced a new rule: no corridor interviews by the pool cameraman.

The judge's decision pointed up the underlying reason for allowing cameras in the courtroom: the constitutionally protected right of an accused to an open trial and the public's right to know how their judiciary was carrying out its trust. The Constitution guaranteed no one exclusive interviews with the principals in a given action. It was not hard to see what havoc such open-season license might create.

As the dust settled, the television people realized they had had a close call and that their no-holds competitiveness could end this fragile experiment abruptly. Needham made it clear if another flare-up like this one occurred, the cameras would be tossed out of his court without ceremony. The mood quickly became, and remained, one of mutual cooperation and mindful observance of the rules.

Monday morning, January 11, 1982, the first day of the Von Bülow trial, was a face-stinging two degrees above zero in Newport. At 7 A.M. the photographers outside the courthouse shifted from leg to leg and hunched their shoulders to combat the icy winds. One said to a colleague, "I can see why the rich prefer this place in the summer."

Across Washington Square to the right of the courthouse, the marquee of the Jane Pickens Theatre announced *Raiders of the Lost Ark;* the theater would figure in the trial as the last public place Sunny Von Bülow visited. At 7:15 a growing number of solitary figures pressed into the wind and made their way across the square to the courthouse. By 7:30, the time jurors had been told to arrive, almost a hundred of them crowded outside the courthouse. They shivered in the cold until the doors opened at 8:00.

The small street that entered the square between the courthouse and the adjacent Colony House was blocked off to traffic. Several of Judge Needham's sheriffs paced behind the barricades waiting for a crush of traffic that was not to come. Inside the main entrance to the courthouse another sheriff asked those entering if they had camera or tape recorders; the sheriffs confiscated a few and looked over the press credentials of the reporters. Judge Needham's crowd-handling systems were in place.

By 9:30, the time for the start of the trial, a fair-sized group, mostly press people, waited in the corridor outside the second-floor courtroom. Those called for jury panels were seated inside; no one else was admitted. The prospective jurors had been seated in the courtroom, it turned out, for lack of any other place to put them. The lawyers were thrashing out procedural matters in Judge Needham's chambers and continued to do so until lunch time.

This gave the fifteen or twenty reporters accumulated outside the doors a chance to get acquainted. Some had recently covered the Jean Harris trial together; their greetings gave the corridor the convivial air of a sophomore fall registration. Even these reunions ran out of steam as the morning progressed with no activity from the courtroom. Finally, at 12:30, the jurors were dismissed for lunch having heard or done nothing.

When the court reassembled at two o'clock, the press and the jurors were admitted to the courtroom. It was a well proportioned room about sixty feet square. Oak paneling rose along the walls to a height of about six feet, then white stucco continued another twenty feet to the ceilings. Six large colonial-style brass chandeliers illuminated the room with rings of naked bulbs. Four tall windows that ran down one side of the room had venetian blinds that were kept closed, an accommodation to the television cameraman stationed on the opposite wall, next to the room's entrance. His permanent spot gave a clear shot of the judge and the witness box and a profile shot of the legal counsel teams starting with Jack Reise (now a lieutenant), followed by Susan McGuirl, Famiglietti, Fahringer, Sheehan, and at the far end, almost at the press box, Von Bülow.

This phalanx of adversaries sat at two side-by-side tables facing the bench but twenty feet back from it. This placed them close to the middle of the courtroom. Behind them was a railing, then five benches for spectators. About a dozen of these seats were reserved for press not designated a permanent seat.

The judge's bench was raised two steps. In front of it sat the court clerk and, a little to one side, the stenographer. All three had green-visored lamps on their desks. Along the inside wall to one side of the bench was the jury box in which the jury would sit. On the facing side was an identical jury box where the fourteen press people selected by Judge Needham were given the much-coveted guaranteed seats. Positioned midway between the judge and Von Bülow and facing the jury and witness box, these were ideal seats for viewing the proceedings. Not so good, it turned out, for hearing them, being in somewhat of an acoustical dead spot. Intensifying this problem, the street outside was a staging area for Newport buses. Just as the most intimate whispers were wafting from the witness stand, buses would rev and gun their motors, thereby driving some with daily deadlines into the electronic security of the Colony House, where every witness came across on the monitor with *Tonight Show* clarity.

With everyone in place and quieted, a sheriff popped out of a door to the right of the bench and bellowed, "Rise, please." Judge Needham darted through the door and, gathering his black robe around him, negotiated the steps to his seat. He closed his eyes as the sheriff intoned, as he would at the start of every day, an invocation that concluded with "God save the State of Rhode Island and Providence Plantations," with which Judge Needham crossed himself and sat down.

It was his practice, he explained in a slightly gruff voice, a grammatical Archie Bunker, to have the defendant rearraigned at the start of the trial. Would the defendant come forward? Von Bülow sprang to his feet and strode to a spot before the bench, his two lawyers arriving quickly at his side.

The clerk asked his name, age, and address. When he said "Claus Von Bülow, fifty-five, 960 Fifth Avenue, New York," his voice was clear, slightly British, and a bit hesitant.

The clerk read the indictment—remarkably brief for a legal composition. It spelled out the offense with which he was charged: that on two separate dates—December 26, 1979, and December 21, 1980—Claus Von Bülow did assault his wife Martha with an intent to kill her. Judge Needham asked, "How do you plead?"

"I am not guilty." His voice was now even firmer, slightly louder, the third word emphasized just perceptibly; most remarkably his tone carried a hint of weariness, suggesting sad resignation to the clumsy, hurtful errors of ordinary men.

Whatever Claus Von Bülow thought of those who were "trying" him or indeed of the laws of this foreign country, as a lawyer he was surely aware that his pronouncement of innocence brought into effect an array of rights, a kind of legalistic circle of fire designed to protect him from injustice.

Judge Needham asked counsel if they were ready to proceed. They said they were and took their seats. Needham now addressed the jurors about those rights of the defendant that they must keep in mind. They must, for example, presume him to be innocent; if they thought him "a little bit guilty" in order for matters to have progressed this far, they must banish such thoughts from their minds. They must also realize that the defense must prove nothing; they can sit throughout the trial without offering a word in their client's defense; if the jurors feel the prosecution has not proved its case, they must acquit him. Neither is the defendant obliged to say one word.

Needham asked the defendant to rise and face the jurors. "Do any of you know the defendant, *Carlos* Von Bülow?" Two jurors raised their hands. They knew him, it turned out, only from having seen his picture in the papers. The judge then asked the prosecutor to name the witnesses he planned to call. Steve Famiglietti rose and read a list of over forty names.

When Judge Needham asked if any of the potential jurors knew any of the witnesses, there was almost a unanimous show of hands. Newport is a small town. A poll was taken and it turned out that each hand indicated an acquaintance with one of the many witnesses to be called from the Newport Hospital. The juror's number was recorded along with the name of the witness familiar to each. One girl, when asked which people on the list she knew, replied, "All of the doctors."

This brought a laugh from the courtroom and the first smile to Von Bülow's face. Up till then he had sat impassively, occasionally making a ticklike grimace, a thrusting out of his jaw and lower lip followed by a clenching. It became as regular in the courtroom as the click of the still camera or the gunning of a bus motor outside.

A pitfall in the courtroom setup was discovered when a bench conference was called over the motion for individual voir dire. After the confidential huddle between counsel and Judge Needham, someone came rushing across the street from the Colony House to warn that every one of their whispered words was broadcast loud and clear to the reporters watching the TV monitor.

From then on, bench conferences were at the side of the bench away from the microphone.

When the judge recessed the court until 9:30 the following morning, there was a jovial air in the courtroom, like the end of school's first day. Nothing had been done but the mere act of "getting into" such a long-anticipated happening gave everyone a feeling of progress.

XVII

STUDENTS of jury trial often say that the process of jury selection, the voir dire, is the most important part of the case. Defense lawyer Herald Fahringer stated this opinion several times while interrogating prospective jurors; from the length of time both he and Famiglietti spent with each panelist, it appeared Famiglietti felt the same way.

In many trials, much that happens is inevitable. There is an inexorable unfolding of witnesses and evidence over which lawyers have some control, but not always a lot. The voir dire gives the lawyers a say in who sits on the jury; nothing, of course, is more important to them. The voir dire is their one chance to fine-tune the legal machine in their favor.

In trials where large amounts of money are involved—and this was certainly one—it is not unknown for counsel to hire research firms to profile the ideal juror from their point of view. Fahringer would not say if he had done this for Von Bülow, but he clearly went into his questioning with a clear idea of what he did and did not want in a juror, as did Famiglietti.

Fahringer's concept of what to look for in jurors was, it turned out, based on more than guesswork. In the days prior to the trial's start, about a hundred Newporters received phone calls from a New Jersey market research firm who politely asked if they might pose a few questions about the Von Bülow affair. This firm had been hired by the defense team to get a reading on community attitudes toward the case and their client. Apparently the results were not discouraging to Fahringer and Sheehan, who did not move for a change of venue nor to sequester the jury—both moves they probably would have made had they felt Newporters were strongly against Von Bülow.

Judge Needham had scheduled the second morning's starting time for 9:30 but did not take the bench until 10:40. When he did, the courtroom had five spectators. Since the motion for individual voir dire had been granted, all of the one hundred prospective jurors were kept in another room. The press box, full with its complement of fourteen, gave the room a lopsided appearance.

Von Bülow again wore the black suit, the only difference the replacement of his gray tie with a black one. It did not seem possible to improve on the solemnity of the previous day's costume, but he had found a way. He opted for another change from the day before: he turned his chair slightly, so that his back was more toward the press, his front more toward the TV camera, making it impossible to conclude whether this revealed shyness or vainglory. It didn't matter, as he soon abandoned the awkward angle.

From a revolving drum the court clerk drew the name of Donald W. Zuercher, a bachelor of early middle age who had been a photographer for many years in another state; since moving to Newport, he had worked as head of the housekeeping department at the Sheraton-Islander Hotel, where Von Bülow and his lawyers were staying. Such coincidences would become common.

Judge Needham asked him a few questions. Would he have trouble with the presumption of innocence? No. Ever served on a jury? No. Then Needham explained the TV and still camera in the courtroom as departures for Rhode Island's criminal justice system. Under the state's guidelines, jurors could elect not to be photographed. Would he permit himself to be photographed? He would.

Needham would ask this question of every juror. The final twelve jurors and four alternates were split evenly on this, eight forbidding pictures and eight allowing. This explained the positioning of the cameras, which looked over the jurors' shoulders.

As Steve Famiglietti and Herald Fahringer launched into their questionings, their difference in courtroom style became quickly apparent. Both appeared intent on ingratiating themselves with the jurors, but Famiglietti confined himself to straightforward, respectful questioning; his rather considerable personality didn't appear until later in the trial.

Fahringer on the other hand bristled with energy and bumptuousness. As he walked toward each juror introducing himself, he did it with a twinkle that seemed to suggest Fahringer and the juror shared some delicious secret, that they were in reality brother and sister and would explode this hilarious fact on the courtroom after pulling its leg for a bit. Because of his reputation as a high-powered New York lawyer, the love-me tail-wagging was no doubt sound strategy, but some of the crustier Yankees looked at Fahringer's hearty approach with suspicion.

Famiglietti started out with Zuercher by saying the prosecution was looking for a good cross section of the community. He then dove into a series of questions that would remain more or less constant with each of the thirty-five jurors interrogated in the eight days it would take to arrive at sixteen jurors the two legal teams could agree upon.

Both Famiglietti and his adversary asked panelists about their familiarity with witnesses or with other aspects of the case. Had they read much in the press? If the jury was sequestered, would that pose a problem for them?

Steve Famiglietti's questioning had variations from panelist to panelist, but always touched upon certain points, foremost the matter of circumstantial evidence. Did they have a problem with Rhode Island's law making circumstantial the equal of direct evidence? That doesn't mean, Famiglietti was quick to add, the prosecution doesn't have to prove its case beyond reasonable doubt, it only means that the one kind of evidence has the legal weight of the other.

Many panelists looked puzzled at this, but usually said they had no difficulty with the principle. Occasionally panelists would admit they considered circumstantial evidence inferior to direct evidence, with which Famiglietti would try to steer them through the abstract concept. Direct evidence can be mistaken or it can be untrue; it must be weighed just as circumstantial evidence must be weighed.

If the panelist remained unconvinced, Judge Needham would come to Famiglietti's assistance with further elucidation of this elusive legal point. If the prospective juror remained unconvinced, he or she was dismissed.

On about the third morning of questioning, Famiglietti arrived at the courthouse with an analogy obviously inspired by the local weather. When he launched into his circumstantial evidence line, he asked a panelist, "Suppose you went to bed at night and the ground was clear. You get up the next morning and it is covered with snow. Don't you conclude that during the night it snowed? You didn't actually see it snow, but you are certain? Right?"

Sometimes he would ask if it were not logical for one planning to commit murder to do it when there were no witnesses around, making sure the prospective juror got his point that, without a jury's willingness to consider circumstantial evidence, most murderers would go free.

Famiglietti asked all the panelists if they were familiar with insulin and if they understood the term "motive." Here he would usually throw in that under state law the prosecution was not obliged to prove motive but could introduce it if it chose, to reinforce its case.

There would be days of medical testimony that might become tedious and difficult to follow. Could Famiglietti have the prospective juror's assurance he or she would give this important material full attention?

Generally Famiglietti would finish by asking whether the panelist would have difficulty, if finding Von Bülow guilty, in standing up in court and saying so. All announced they would have no trouble. Famiglietti's questions seemed aimed more at educating prospective jurors to their responsibilities and proper mental set than in learning specifics of a particular panelist's life and attitude.

Herald Fahringer was less abstract in his approach. He was more concerned than his opponent about jurors' exposure to press accounts of the case. He was curious about whether panelists owned or rented their houses (for attitudes toward the rich?); about whether others worked under them (leadership?); about how much schooling they had had (intelligence?); about their hobbies and pastimes. Were they knowledgeable about chemistry? Did they take tranquilizers or sleeping pills? Had they been treated at Newport Hospital? Was it a satisfactory experience? Were their dealings with doctors in general satisfactory?

Then Fahringer would zero in on the questions aimed at uncovering attitudes that could be crucial in this case. Were the panelists familiar with what was called Newport's summer colony? (Some had to have this term explained.) How did they feel about them? How did they feel about the rich in general? Did they feel that rich people were entitled to the same justice as poor people?

Of all the panelists questioned, only one came anywhere near warming distance of the social fires on Bellevue Avenue. That was Barbara Connett, later to be jury foreman, whose husband taught at the fashionable St. George's School.

Other than Connett, about as close to the Bellevue Avenue crowd any panelist came was one woman who had once helped clean Mrs. John Slocum's Bellevue Avenue mansion and another who had once worked as a ticket taker at the Breakers, the Vanderbilt palace now open to the public.

For the most part the panelists were middle- or lower-middle-class jobholders, housewives, and a farmer. Only four of some twenty men wore neckties, and most of the women wore polyester pants suits. The majority of the panelists professed to having only the dimmest notion that people of wealth came to Newport each summer; if aware of them at all, the townspeople didn't give them a thought.

As for feelings about the rich in general, it was unanimously a matter of live and let live. This line of questions produced a number of statements that might have been dictated by Andrew Carnegie into a primer for his workers' children: "If you are rich, that's fine; if you are not, you're not." "I have nothing against the rich, I wish I were one of them." And so on.

It was a chorus of satisfaction with one's lot and knowing one's place that seemed straight out of Dickens. Nowhere was there a hint of the bitterness said to poison the affability of many year-round Newporters. Such bitterness was rarely found among the third- and fourth-generation islanders, whose parents and grandparents probably worked for one of the great Newport households and who knew something of the splendor, not just the residual arrogance.

Waxing confidential, Fahringer would tell the perspective juror that Mr. Von Bülow, although a United States resident for fourteen years, had never taken out citizenship. Would the juror think less of him because of this? Several had a problem with this until it was pointed out either by Fahringer or Judge Needham that Mr. Von Bülow was not on trial for his lack of citizenship and that his reasons for not becoming naturalized would not be permitted as evidence. Even after such explanations, one woman stuck doggedly to her disapproval. She was dismissed.

Lowering his voice to the intimacy of a Côte Basque banquet, Fahringer said, "It might come out during the trial that Mr. Von Bülow had an affair with another woman while married to Mrs. Von Bülow. Would that affect your opinion of Mr. Von Bülow, or your ability to judge him fairly in this case?"

Now the reporters had their day's headline. The existence of an affair had rarely risen above the level of rumor, but here was Von Bülow's own lawyer talking in court about one. The tabloids were delighted.

It was fascinating to see the effect of this "other woman" on female jurors. They all echoed the male panelists in assuring Fahringer that Von Bülow's infidelities would not affect their judgment, but with almost every woman the mention of his having an affair while married produced a visible tightening of the facial muscles or a set to the jaw.

It was a wonderful demonstration of instinctive response, of the entire organism contradicting its own utterances with a visceral reaction, invisible to some but to others as apparent as the shudder of a sea anemone when touched by an alien body. While vocally claiming indifference, female panelists gave off waves of outrage that permeated the courtroom.

There was a curious fascination to the voir dire interrogations despite the tedious repetition. Ordinary citizens were standing up before a room full of strangers and sketching quick and surprisingly intimate portraits of themselves. Panelists revealed their social and economic levels, their intelligence and educational levels, whether they owned or rented, were married, single, divorced, or widowed; their health problems and how they felt about doctors; what they liked to do in the evenings.

It was like riding a subway car and suddenly having the anonymous faces start talking, one by one, offering little monologues on who they were, what their lives were, and how they thought. *A Chorus Line* without the dancing.

Even when the panelists were coloring an opinion, the manner in which they did it was almost as revealing as the unvarnished truth would have been. One man, when asked if he was bothered by Von Bülow having money, snapped, "Not at all. I wish I had it!" On other occasions the panelists almost overdid the candor. A bouncy middle-aged woman, when asked if she objected to Von Bülow's having an affair, replied, "Doesn't bother me at all." Then she added a postscript her husband probably could have done without: "People who live in glass houses . . ."

For those listening to these endless self-revelations, it proved educational. We learned that a foreigner could live in the United States for forty-four years without learning English. We learned that some people believed whatever a doctor told them, that some people read motor manuals and electronic textbooks for fun, and that some people don't think *anyone* could attempt to murder his wife.

Another interesting thing to come out of the voir dire is that not one of the thirty-five panelists interrogated ever watched television. None mentioned it as a pastime; when asked if they had seen anything about the case in the media, all answered they had seen nothing or almost nothing, which ruled out their ever having seen television news. This freedom from television was particularly remarkable in light of a study recently released stating that the average American watches over five hours of television each day.

Something else besides jury selection was happening in the Von Bülow trial that first week in the courtroom. The participants were becoming acquainted. Herald Fahringer established that he could be a scrappy adversary from the beginning. A fair number of sarcastic remarks aimed at his opponents bordered on the contemptuous.

Judge Needham can be given some of the credit for setting the tone in his courtroom. He was known in Rhode Island as being tough on lawyers and not hesitating to dress them down in public. But in the matter of moving Fahringer into a more gentlemanly stance, most of the credit must go to Steve Famiglietti.

The Providence prosecutor showed he wasn't to be cowed with Madison Avenue venom but neither was he going to offer the Rhode Island variety in return. By the last days of January, Fahringer was even complimenting Famiglietti on his scrupulousness and his courtroom sense of decorum.

Famiglietti and Sheehan knew each other from the relatively small Rhode Island criminal justice world. Needham claimed not to know any of the participants; Famiglietti forgave the judge for not remembering his pleading the first case Needham heard eight years earlier. After the first few days the frequent bench conferences between the lawyers and Judge Needham were often marked by laughter and back slaps. At these moments of adversary bonhomie, Von Bülow, left alone at the long defense table, appeared the world's loneliest man.

The defendant, as it turned out, was making a few friends on his own. In the first day or two, Fahringer had tried to keep the press from Von Bülow, but the informality of those first days made this difficult. A recess would be announced and there were ten minutes of milling around when anyone was free to approach the lawyers' table and address whomever they chose. Most chose Von Bülow, who turned out to be all too willing to flex his verbal muscles.

At the first of these breaks, Von Bülow, who had reverted to chain smoking after three years of abstinence, would move directly from the courtroom to the private room reserved for the defense team. But after one or two recesses isolated in this way, he took to lighting his cigarette in the corridor, where he would amble among the spectators and the press. Because of his height and his formal outfitting he stood out as much as a costumed performer would strolling among an intermission crowd.

Once he made himself available in this way, it wasn't long before a reporter was upon him. If a question was trial related, like that of a young woman who asked him if he would take the stand in his own defense, Von Bülow would smile icily and say, "I think you'd better ask my attorneys that." If the question was more neutral, he was affability itself.

"How do you find Newport this time of year?"

"I couldn't say. My lawyers have kept me busy at the hotel every moment I'm not in court."

Of course, when Von Bülow spoke to anyone, everyone else watched from the corner of their eye. As soon as it was established that he was civil, anyone who had the slightest remark to make to him soon showed no hesitancy about doing so. Groups of housewives, opting for the Von Bülow trial instead of an afternoon movie, would push one of their group forward to ask him how his daughter was.

Although he was genial with all, he showed a nimble-footedness in making escapes that reflected years of navigation through the treacherous cocktail bores of two continents.

The recesses, for all their fluidity, were brief minutes in six-hour courtroom days, during which Von Bülow sat stonily at the defense table staring without expression at the motley parade of prospective jurors.

What must Von Bülow have thought as he watched these drab lives unfold? The short, fat wife of a bus driver, her main recreation Tuesday night bowling; the sixtyish factory worker who was just laid off after seventeen years—these were people who join Christmas clubs, who cut money-saving coupons from newspapers, who dream of converting their basements to playrooms, who socialize through their churches, and who retire on social security. These were the people Von Bülow had dedicated his life to escaping, putting as much distance as possible between their shabby existences and his own resplendent one.

He sat and stared sullenly at each panelist, knowing that twelve of them would be deciding whether he would lead out his life in gilt-heavy, servant-soothed palaces or in a cell at Rhode Island's Adult Correctional Institution.

Needham had earlier granted a defense request to designate the first twelve jurors selected as the deciding jurors, making the remaining four selected alternates. This broke with the Rhode Island tradition of not naming alternates until the jury went out for deliberation.

Like most trial lawyers, Fahringer put great store in his ability to establish rapport with jurors; he was reluctant to expend this effort on four jurors who ended up with no vote. On such small matters as this, Needham seemed to be straining to accommodate the distinguished out-of-state lawyer.

Small matter or not, Needham brought himself under criticism from judicial colleagues in the state for his reversal of the customary procedure. One judge was quoted in the *Providence Journal* as saying Needham lacked the authority to make such a change.

Needham was furious at this attack on his judgment from a colleague while a trial was in progress, stating publicly his belief that such conduct undermined the judicial process. Nerves were raw in these first days of the trial. Despite ever-mounting press attention, however, dispositions calmed as the participants—judge, prosecution, defense, jurors, press, spectators—each with a potential for making trouble—came to know the outer limits of each others' bad behavior and the prevalence of their good.

On January 20, after eight days of interrogation, both the defense and the prosecution had exhausted their peremptory challenges and arrived at twelve jurors and four alternates. Of the nine men and seven women, all were white and all were year-round Newport residents, although a majority were not natives.

The unexpected selection of Barbara Connett as jury foreman was thought to have been Judge Needham's way of compensating her for serving against her will. Throughout the voir dire, Connett had made daily pleas to the judge to excuse her on the grounds that she might lose a new job if forced to sit through a long trial. After one of these unsuccessful sessions, she was seen crying on a corridor bench.

Judge Needham was determined not to countenance career inconvenience, a problem most people could claim, as reason for dismissal; he also hinted publicly that he would intercede with her employers if they should try to fire her on such grounds. An irony of Connett's conscription was that both defense lawyers had wanted to eliminate her but had been overruled by Von Bülow who, it seems, admired the tweed-jacketed, lovely mother of two young children and wanted to have something pleasing to look at throughout the trial.

Everyone had expected juror Robert Kirkwood to be made foreman. Kirkwood was an older man of impressive dignity, a retired Navy officer (Needham was a retired army colonel) and the father of six children, who had indicated during the questioning that he had little interest in news stories like the Von Bülow case.

In the same age bracket was Walter Jablonski, a Newporter of Polish extraction with two middle-aged children, who was retired after thirty-two years with the Naval Underwater Systems Company, one of several Navy-oriented firms in the area. During questioning he had shown a lively sense of humor ("Affair? I wish *I* were in his shoes") and a live-and-let-live outlook.

Juror Arthur Hull was in his thirty-first year as a mechanical engineer with the same company. He lived with his wife and daughter (a son was away in the Army) across the bay in Jamestown, where he was the leader of a scout troop and an active churchgoer.

Among the jurors who impressed their colleagues with their intelligence was Fred Nussbaum, who had been brought from Germany by his parents when a small child but who seemed as much a Rhode Islander as the others. He held a master's degree in business administration and worked as an engineer in the same department as Hull at Naval Underwater Systems. Nussbaum, who was around forty, proved a likable, easy-going sort despite a trial-long expression of pained concern on his good-looking face, even when he was ogling, along with the other male jurors, Shalla Pacia; Famiglietti's eye-catching paralegal.

Another juror won a reputation for intelligence: David Taffs, perhaps the least prepossessing in appearance. In his late twenties, Taffs's ungainly girth, offhand dress, and straggly ponytail gave him the look of a tattooless Hell's Angel. Looks notwithstanding, he was a Brown graduate and worked as a computer analyst, as did his wife.

Pierce Gafgen was a gentle, quiet type in his mid-thirties, who worked as a photographer for the Raytheon Corporation and repaired cameras on the side. Thick glasses gave him a quizzical, professorial look that was counterbalanced by an athletic build, the result of an enthusiasm for long-distance bicycling. His wife was a lecturer for Weight Watchers.

The remaining male juror selected was Donald Zuercher, a bachelor who had moved to Newport six years earlier from upstate New York where for twenty-five years he had worked as a baby and wedding photographer. A World War II veteran, he was a former Lions Club president who had an enthusiasm for music and theater. He would live up to his self-designation as "a happy person."

Besides Barbara Connett, the jury would have four other women. Winifred Shaw was a thin, intense woman with close-cropped hair and a slightly askew approach to the world around her that, along with a quiet nature, tended to conceal a keen mind. Married and in her thirties, she had no children and worked as a secretary for Naval Underwater Systems.

Aldina Paiva, a grandmother who worked as a kitchen aide in a nursing home, was a representative of the region's large Portuguese population. She loved her native Rhode Island and was delighted to be back after "thirty miserable years in New York."

Of all the female jurors, Barbara Silvia was the closest to a "typical" housewife in that her life focused on her two children and her husband, who drove a truck for a soda company. She had mentioned Friday night bowling as her main recreation.

Constance Jennrette was a large, handsome woman whose warmth and affability contradicted a high-strung nature. She had worked at various jobs while raising six children and looking after a husband, now retired from the Navy, where he had been a boatswain's mate. Within a year of the trial's end, the Jennrettes would be moving to Florida.

Though few of the selected jurors qualified as Yankees, most showed the firm-footed individuality that characterizes the breed. Two of the women and one of the men would show a nervous, emotional side that appeared to result less from personality defect than from the strain of the jury ordeal late in strain-free lives. While holding the task before them in the utmost seriousness, the jurors maintained a sense of humor and a relaxed camaraderie among themselves.

The twelve men and women with lives far removed from Von Bülow's were deemed his peers in the eyes of the law, the same law that was demanding that for a period of weeks, maybe months, they suspend these lives and determine the future life—free or jailed—of a fellow human.

XVIII

WITH all the eagerness to delve into the crime at hand it is often frustrating that pretrial motions concern themselves not with the one question in which everyone is interested—the guilt or innocence of the accused—but with whether the incriminating evidence was illegally obtained or is otherwise inadmissible. And while this may be a noble struggle from the constitutional point of view, it tends to sully the defendant's façade of outraged innocence.

If there are legal loopholes afoot, lawyers must dive for them. While we are not supposed to think any worse of a defendant for availing himself of one of these constitutional protections—for instance, to plead the Fifth Amendment against self-incrimination and refuse to answer a question—we tend to assume such a defendant has things to hide.

It was not surprising, therefore, that Herald Fahringer moved to bar the press from the pretrial hearings. If the press remained to witness the struggle to keep certain facts and objects from the jury, this defense-repugnant evidence would be spotlighted and revealed to everyone in the world except the jurors. And *they* would remain ignorant only if they followed the judge's admonition to avoid press exposure.

Even this early in the trial, the press box had an unofficial alarm-sounder. Theo Wilson, the respected New York *Daily News* veteran of twenty-five years, had established herself as the most sensitive to infringements of press rights. For the other journalists, she was the caged canary who would first react to constitutionally noxious fumes.

With this antipress move of Fahringer's, not only Theo but many journalists covering the trial flapped into impressive action. The reporters of both the *Boston Globe* and the *Providence Journal* rushed to phones at the morning recess (Judge Needham forbade any entering or exiting while he was on the bench) and reported to their newspapers on the possibility that the press would be excluded.

Gayle Gertler of the *Providence Journal* called her boss at 10:50 A.M. at his office an hour's drive from Newport and was told the paper would have a lawyer in the Newport courthouse by 12:15. Judge Needham recessed for lunch at noon, enabling lawyers representing three newspapers and a wire service to be on hand, ready to argue for admitting the press, when Judge Needham took the bench again at 2 P.M.

As court resumed, the interloping lawyers launched into their defense of the press with a vigor and thoroughness that suggested they did nothing but wait for calls for help from judge-threatened reporters. They invoked the traditional right of public access to courtroom proceedings, the First Amendment's superiority to the Sixth Amendment's guaranteeing a defendant a fair trial, an argument that irked Theo Wilson, who insisted there was no conflict between the First and Sixth Amendments.

Because Fahringer was risking antagonizing the press early in the game, he clearly felt strongly about this motion. As he argued his position, he reached levels of exasperated passion better suited to summations. He was asking only that the press be excluded for *two days.* (The pretrial motions required, as it turned out, seven days.) Wasn't it enough that the press had full access to the rest of the proceedings? "Just two days," he pleaded, "to give a fellow citizen a fair trial."

"A fellow citizen?" Judge Needham corrected.

"I was speaking generally to mean a fellow member of the human race." As he returned to his seat he added in a stage whisper, "Which we all belong to, I hope."

The arguments went on all afternoon. Finally, Judge Needham decided. After reviewing the arguments as well as the various precedents invoked by counsel, Judge Needham ruled that the press would *not* be barred from the pretrial hearings: his main reason was that the jurors were already selected and under court orders to avoid media accounts of the trial.

Friday afternoon was taken up with squabbles about the prosecution not turning over to the defense everything it had turned up in the investigation that might be exculpatory. This was required in criminal cases under the Brady rule, which later in the trial would again play an interesting role. Famiglietti argued that the state had turned over everything as required under Brady. Fahringer reminded him of two statements from the doorman at the Von Bülow Fifth Avenue apartment that Lieutenant Reise had taped. Famiglietti said these were of no consequence, but agreed to turn over the tapes. Spectators were getting a glimpse of each side's awareness of the other's activities.

Fahringer then moved to have certain evidence barred from the trial on the grounds that the materials on which it was based had been destroyed. He was talking about items tested in laboratories —the blood samples and the used needles—items that, once tested, are discarded as a matter of course. Judge Needham denied this motion saying that if the laboratories were bona fide, "a degree of reliability is established whether the substances are destroyed or not."

On Monday morning, January 25, the court got down to the defense's three principal pretrial motions: to suppress evidence obtained by the private investigation, to suppress Von Bülow's statement to the police, and to suppress patient/doctor information. Richard Kuh was called to the stand.

When the first stories of the Von Bülow affair broke in the newspapers at the time of the indictment the previous July, Kuh was the legal name most mentioned in connection with the case. He had launched the investigation that resulted in the indictment, he was available to reporters, and he was not an anonymous lawyer but a former District Attorney of Manhattan.

Indeed, some observers speculated that the Kuh name had something to do with the press's immediate interest in the bizarre case. Rich stepchildren accusing their rich stepfather of trying to murder their rich mother might have been dismissed as pampered hysteria or, at best, greed-propelled plotting. The name Richard Kuh jumped out of the confusing and unlikely tales earning them a serious consideration that otherwise might have been far slower coming. It was therefore fitting that Kuh was the first witness called, as though both the defendant and the state of Rhode Island were giving a courteous nod to his paramount role in their legal spectacular.

Fahringer kept Kuh on the stand the entire morning quizzing him about his participation in the Von Bülow case, the questions aimed at substantiating Fahringer's charge that Kuh had acted as a "private prosecutor." In the entire trial this epithet would be one of Fahringer's most effective phrases, falling on the ears with the clank of unfair privilege, conjuring up the nation's feudal period when the great poltroon families had private militias to patrol their vast New York estates.

Fahringer walked Kuh through his step-by-step involvement in the case: his being hired by Alexander and Ala von Auersperg and their grandmother Mrs. Aitken to investigate the circumstances of Sunny Von Bülow's coma, Kuh's subsequent hiring of others to assist in the investigation, his seizure and examination of evidence (the black bag) and his turning over his findings first to the New York authorities and finally to the Rhode Island authorities.

At times the exchange grew sharp, revealing more hostility between Fahringer and Kuh than between any other two participants throughout the trial. At one point Kuh was asked about discarding trial-related medical documents.

"Nothing was thrown away, Herald," Kuh replied, his voice rising, "and in light of what I read in the papers, I emphasize *nothing* was thrown away."

"Don't get excited, Mr. Kuh," Fahringer replied.

On another occasion, Kuh was attempting to explain his continuing involvement with the case after the Rhode Island police had taken over the investigation. He said, "There was some concern whether Rhode Island would have the budget for a prolonged New York investigation."

"So, Mr. Kuh, you were helping the Rhode Island police?" Fahringer asked.

"Helping the cause of justice," Kuh replied.

"I understand," Fahringer said angrily. "That is very pleasant."

"It is not pleasant at all, Mr. Fahringer," Kuh said grimly, abandoning for the first time his interrogator's first name.

Fahringer got Kuh to describe hiring a private detective to accompany Alexander von Auersperg to Clarendon Court to find the black bag, its discovery in Von Bülow's closet, their bringing the bag to Kuh in New York, his turning it over to doctors for analysis, and his eventual turning over of all his evidence to the Rhode Island police.

Most of the information was in the court record, available for months to anyone who cared to see it. As a result, most of these facts or allegations had already appeared in the newspapers. Some interesting information was new, however. Kuh told of hiring detectives to follow Von Bülow in New York and, when Von Bülow returned from Nassau with Alexandra Isles, to photograph the couple.

Kuh's detective spent an entire day outside Von Bülow's office only to report that he emerged at the end of the office day and went home. As for the return from Nassau, Von Bülow and Isles, for reasons of their own, decided to take an earlier plane than originally planned, and so eluded the photographer. The detective did learn one thing: Von Bülow had rented an East Side studio apartment.

Kuh also acknowledged that he had hired a detective in England to look into rumors about Von Bülow, "ugly and otherwise." Fahringer hurried away from this dangerous area.

Fahringer finished with Kuh by appealing to the court for permission to look at Kuh's notes and records, arguing that ordinary attorney-client privilege did not apply because Kuh was acting in concert with the Rhode Island authorities. This motion was denied.

When Kuh stepped down, Fahringer called to the stand Edwin Lambert, the private investigator who had accompanied Alexander to Clarendon Court. This was the first of many coups de theatre throughout the trial. Having just heard about "a detective" who played a small but swashbuckling role in one of the saga's most dramatic episodes, courtroom spectators were thrilled to see this man materialize so promptly.

But instead of a Sam Spade they got a funeral director—which turned out to be a second occupation of Lambert's since retiring from the New York City police. A conservative gray suit and rimless spectacles made him look as though he had spent his life behind a desk rather than a gun.

With the aplomb of one used to testifying, Lambert gave his account of the Newport expedition. Fahringer asked him if he had gotten a search warrant.

"I didn't need one," Lambert replied.

"I didn't ask you that," Fahringer snapped.

When Alexander von Auersperg took the witness stand on January 25 as a pretrial witness, Judge Needham's court had, with jury selection and pretrial hearings to date, devoted two weeks to the Von Bülow case. In that time, the participants, now acquainted, had become relaxed with each other; the courtroom had taken on an air of happy excitement that smacked of carnival.

Alexander steadfastly refused to adapt himself to this easy mood. Throughout his long testimony he was unshakably grim. Part of this, he later admitted, was nervousness, although the twenty-one-year old did not appear the least nervous. His dark good looks had their strongest feature in his eyes, blue and penetrating, perfect for glowering, which is what he appeared to be doing throughout his testimony.

To all subsequent witnesses, even those most pained at testifying, some quirk of interrogation would eventually bring a smile, but not to young von Auersperg. Several of his terse answers amused the courtroom, but he would not acknowledge the friendly chuckles.

His solemnity was impressive and perhaps a salubrious reminder to the courtroom that this was, despite the media hoopla over the trial's yeasty and glamorous aspects, a bitter litigation of the utmost seriousness, an adversary proceeding in which either Von Bülow or his accusers would be destroyed. In order for others to think Von Bülow innocent, they had to think Alexander guilty of villainy of comparable ruthlessness: framing another for a crime he did not commit. Alexander could no longer be unaware that he had to clear his own name of the ugliest suspicions. Indeed, Kuh had already told him that counteraccusations against him were likely.

From time to time Alexander glanced at his stepfather, who in turn seemed to look less at the witness than he usually did but would instead find reasons to glance around the room or stare at the empty legal pad on the table before him.

Since the questioning of Kuh had taken up the entire morning and part of the afternoon, Fahringer, in the remainder of the day, was only able to cover with Alexander the early suspicions against his stepfather and his hiring of Kuh.

As court resumed the following morning, Fahringer pounced into a quite different theme. Did you see Richard Kuh last night? Yes, they were both staying at Mrs. Aitken's house on Bellevue Avenue. Did they dine together? Yes, at a restaurant. Did they discuss the case? In general, yes. They also discussed Mrs. Von Bülow's condition.

"You were together six or seven hours," Fahringer snapped, "and that's all you talked about?"

"Regarding the case, yes."

"Mr. Kuh did not give you advice on your testimony?"

"No."

"Did he discuss differences between Detective Lambert's testimony and yours?"

"No."

Having gotten nowhere with dinner, Fahringer tried breakfast —with no more success. Alexander and Kuh had discussed nothing about Alexander's testimony at breakfast. Had Alexander talked with Steve Famiglietti? Not about my testimony. Did you ask Mr. Kuh to be here today? No.

Throughout the trial, Richard Kuh would be present whenever any of his clients testified. This fact seemed to irritate Herald Fahringer. He would invariably ask the witness about Mr. Kuh's presence as though it were somehow improper.

Throughout such verbal advances against his clients, Kuh sat with folded arms, his head tilted upward, and with a slight smile on his face. Often this expression would suggest no more than compassionate humor for the extremes some lawyers are driven to, but when Fahringer's aggression was at its most threatening, the smile would broaden, the head tilt more heavenward until Kuh appeared to be listening to a particularly rhapsodic passage of music. Whether or not Kuh's smile had any effect on spectators, it infuriated the defense table.

After hammering away at the relationship between Kuh and his clients, Fahringer took Alexander back to his evolving suspicions of his stepfather. Immediately they struck a crucial point of the prosecution's case. When Maria had shown Alexander the black bag, had Alexander seen insulin in it? Could he say positively he saw a bottle of insulin?

"No," Alexander answered.

It is likely the jury was impressed, as Jack Reise had been, to see Alexander pass up an opportunity for a risk-free lie, an unchallengeable reworking of the facts that would strengthen his side's case. Maria would testify, as Alexander well knew, that she had seen insulin in the black bag on more than one occasion. Alexander trusted Maria and believed what she said. Still, he told the court he could not recall seeing insulin, which at that time had no special significance either to him or Maria.

For the rest of the morning Alexander recounted, with as few words as Fahringer would allow him, his version of journeying to Clarendon Court with Lambert to get the black bag.

Up till this point the Von Bülow trial had been marked by the easy availability of all the major participants, including Von Bülow. Much as reporters would have liked to get their hands on Alexander von Auersperg as he came off the stand, they were frustrated. He disappeared into the prosecution room as soon as he left the stand and, almost immediately thereafter, exited the courthouse by the side door.

Alexander was the last witness on the motion to suppress evidence obtained by the private investigation. Because Judge Needham had said he would rule on all motions simultaneously, no ruling was made and the court proceeded directly to arguments for the next motion: to suppress Von Bülow's statement to the police. Lieutenant John Reise was called to the stand.

None of the courtroom spectators and few of the press had a clear idea of who this handsome man was who had sat with Famiglietti at the prosecution table since the trial's beginning. And even with his testimony that he had been the one to arrest Von Bülow, that information did little to throw light on his important role in the whole affair, a role that never was fully clarified by the long weeks of testimony ahead.

What credit the press gave for uncovering the facts of the case was accorded Richard Kuh, who was presented as having deposited a relatively airtight case on the desk of this lucky Rhode Island State Police sergeant, recently promoted to lieutenant. This was a distortion. Not only was there still much information to be uncovered before the Attorney General's Office could proceed with a case, but Reise had to start his investigation again at the beginning.

Lieutenant Reise's investigation, as Kuh was the first to admit, made up the backbone of the Von Bülow case. Throughout the trial a number of spectators, learning Reise was with the Rhode Island police, wondered why he was sitting at the prosecution table day after day instead of issuing speeding tickets. The answer was that he probably knew more about the case than anyone in the room, with the exception of Von Bülow, but not excepting Famiglietti, Kuh, Fahringer, and Sheehan. Famiglietti relied on this backup support of information.

For the interrogation of Lieutenant Reise, Fahringer yielded the floor to his co-counsel, John Sheehan. If there was a pattern to the relief hitting, it was that Sheehan was apt to handle witnesses with a strongly local orientation such as a state police officer. For the most part, Fahringer was the courtroom defense spokesman.

Sheehan had an entirely different style than Fahringer. He was as low-keyed as Fahringer was keyed up. Leaning on the jury box rail, he would lower his head, then look up at the witnesses as though over the top of reading glasses.

Despite Sheehan's renown as one of the state's top criminal lawyers, he would not justify that reputation in the Von Bülow case. Perhaps he found the second-banana role debilitating, or perhaps there was truth to rumors of a lack of rapport between Sheehan and his client. In any case, Sheehan entered most of his in-court chores with a faltering listlessness. If he got through two questions without an objection, he would usually ask the court for a minute or two to collect himself, even when he had not asked anything beyond the obligatory setting-up questions.

With Reise, Sheehan built a certain momentum and extracted a detailed retelling of Reise's involvement with the case, his investigation, and his two meetings with Von Bülow, the first at the Fifth Avenue apartment when Reise did not inform Von Bülow he was a suspect, and the April 21 encounter at Clarendon Court when Reise did tell him.

Sheehan zeroed in on Reise's observance of proper constitutional form in confronting a suspect. The first interview, being merely an investigational interrogation, did not require Reise's reading Von Bülow the Miranda warnings, but Reise gave them anyway, saying it was merely a precaution.

On the second interview, Reise said, he read Von Bülow his warnings into the tape recorder when Von Bülow had consented to its use—even though there was a question of whether the warnings were necessary since Von Bülow was not arrested or placed in custody, the conditions that mandate the formal warning.

Sheehan argued to play the entire tape, which ran an hour and forty minutes, but finally agreed to play only the first portion, dealing with the reading of rights and whether or not Von Bülow should proceed without a lawyer.

As the tiny machine clicked on, it was electrifying to hear Von Bülow's voice. Despite his daily presence, he had not spoken in the courtroom since his "I am not guilty" two weeks earlier. Except for those who chatted with him during recesses, no one had heard him speak conversationally, nor would they again.

Even more startling than the voice itself was the recreation of a climactic moment in the drama, the moment when authority was dropping its mask of seeking Von Bülow's cooperation and seeking instead his hide. The courtroom sat rapt as Reise's voice came over the tiny loudspeaker telling Von Bülow he was here to talk about Mrs. Von Bülow's illness, that Von Bülow was a suspect, that the charge was "in the area of attempted murder." He would again inform Von Bülow of his constitutional rights, but first asked, "You recall me advising you of your rights when we spoke in New York?"

"Yes," Von Bülow replied, then went on, "I had no idea when we spoke in New York, the nature of the charges or of possibilities. . . . This is taking me back a bit. . . . It never occurred to me in New York the nature of your investigation. . . ."

"Do you want your lawyer present?"

"It's hopeless. I can't get hold of Mr. Sheehan tonight."

"If you want him, we can stop right here."

"Oh, you don't have to stop."

"You can make the call."

"It's hopeless to reach Sheehan now. . . . I am prepared to stay over to have my lawyer present."

"Are you requesting a lawyer now?"

"Well, I've been a lawyer myself, you know. Isn't it customary? Haven't I got to have time to get my attorney?"

In reviewing this exchange, it seems odd how Von Bülow seems to have assumed an immediacy problem. Reise made clear that if Von Bülow chose to wait until his lawyer was present, the entire discussion could be postponed until that time. Although Reise, as he later admitted, was hoping Von Bülow would proceed with a statement, a number of times he offered him the opportunity of discontinuing their talk.

The state of being under custody is, under certain circumstances, vague and arguable. If there are a number of police present, as was the case that night at Clarendon Court, does the suspect feel free to leave?

John Sheehan was hoping to prove first that Von Bülow considered himself under custody and, second, that he had been given his rights improperly. The first allegation was destroyed by Reise's many offers to await a lawyer, plus Von Bülow's movements around the house (he excused himself for cigarettes at one point and to get a soft drink at another). The two readings of the rights before witnesses, once in New York, and once that evening at Clarendon Court, were put forward by the prosecution as sufficient warning.

Sheehan made much of one of the Miranda warnings not being on the tape. Reise's explanation was that, after an interruption, he had briefly forgotten to turn the machine back on, but the missing right had, indeed, been read—and read in front of another police officer who could testify to that effect. Still on the witness stand, Reise pulled a card from his wallet that had the Miranda warnings typed onto it. He always carried the card with him. It was submitted as evidence.

Sheehan then called Detective Joseph Miranda, Reise's sidekick on the Rhode Island police, whose surname was an odd coincidence. Sheehan had no more luck with Miranda than with Reise in establishing that Von Bülow's rights had somehow been violated the night the policemen appeared at Clarendon Court to accuse him.

When Reise was called back to the stand, Judge Needham, noting that Reise was coming to the witness stand from the prosecution table, said, "I thought there was an arrangement between counsel that two testifying officers would not be in court at the same time."

This gave spectators a rare glimpse of the kind of procedural deals that make up most of the bench or in-chambers conferences between the judge and the opposing legal teams. Famiglietti apologized, murmuring something about not anticipating Officer Miranda being called.

The last questioning of Reise addressed the lesser motion about his having failed to get a search warrant in order to test the medicines and other substances from the black bag that had been turned over to him by von Auersperg and Kuh. Reise's position was that he had never been required to get a search warrant for this sort of routine follow-through in an investigation.

Finally came Fahringer's and Famiglietti's summary arguments on each motion presented so far. Fahringer started off arguing his motion to suppress seized evidence. This was the first demonstration of Fahringer's prowess at sustained argument and he was impressive. The gist of his reasoning was that the Fourth Amendment, while specifically forbidding unreasonable search by *governmental* authorities, could not be construed to allow private citizens to do what the government was forbidden to do. Such an interpretation, he said, would bring us to "George Orwell's world."

Famiglietti insisted that the Fourth Amendment applied *only* to government agencies although that principle had been "much criticized by defense attorneys over the years." In a reference to a Montana decision supporting Fahringer's position, Famiglietti said, "There is no reason for Rhode Island to join Montana in going against the Supreme Court, whose decision may make no sense to Mr. Fahringer—many don't make sense to me—but we must live with them."

Judge Needham then launched into a full review of the testimony and the arguments of both counsel, paying particular attention to the precedents invoked. The defense, he said, had not shown complicity between Kuh's forces and the state of Rhode

Island *prior* to the date the black bag was seized; the purpose of seizing the bag was to collect evidence which was not turned over to the police until some time much later.

Needham concluded, "I reject the argument that because the material was headed for the police department that should make the prior actions subject to the Fourth Amendment. The court denies the motion."

Summary arguments for the next motion, that analysis of the black-bag contents constituted illegal search, were briefer. Needham boiled the arguments down to two main points: Was it a search, and was it unreasonable? After a further review of both positions, he ruled no to both questions and denied the motion.

As for the motions to suppress Von Bülow's two statements to Lieutenant Reise, Needham first posited that the Miranda warnings were limited to a "coercive environment." As the earlier interrogation was in New York State, where Reise had no authority to arrest, there could be no question of coercion. As for the second meeting, Needham concluded that the evidence on tape and Von Bülow's free actions within his house indicated he did not consider himself under custody; in addition, the Miranda warnings were given. He denied the motion to suppress these statements.

It is ironic that having fought so hard to keep the statements from being introduced, Fahringer would later move to place them in evidence, and be blocked by Famiglietti. Somewhere during the trial, Fahringer decided that much of Von Bülow's statement to Reise was exculpatory; Famiglietti argued that for defense to introduce these statements was a way to allow the defendant to "testify" without subjecting him to cross-examination.

Needham agreed, saying it was all right for the prosecution to introduce Von Bülow's statements (which they elected not to do), but not for the defense. This reversal on both sides revealed how neither side felt confined by predetermined strategies, how both stood ready to alter directions or reverse themselves. This was particularly true of the defense, as would be shown by several switches in game plans, sometimes mid-witness.

Judge Needham invited the defense to present arguments for their motion to bar evidence gathered by the grand jury that violated confidentiality of patient-doctor relationship. Sheehan leaped into this one with the news that divulging such information in court was, under Rhode Island law, a *criminal* act. The grand jury's use of such illicit information was grounds for dismissing their indictment, he argued.

There was a brief exchange on this, but the arguments on the motion were postponed till the following day to give the prosecution team the chance to research their rebuttal.

The next day, the prosecution's arguments were presented by Susan McGuirl. Although McGuirl had been in the courtroom at Famiglietti's side nearly every day since the trial's start, she had kept an almost Von Bülow-like silence. Her wholesome good looks gave the twenty-nine-year-old lawyer the look of an athletic college student rather than the number-two figure in the State Attorney General's Office.

In a machine-gun monotone, McGuirl delivered a denunciation of the defense's medical-evidence motion that bordered on scathing. The defendant, she said, is *not* the patient, so does not have standing to make this motion. That he was married to the patient does not apply when his spouse is the victim.

"If the defendant objected to the state's using this information," she said, "he should have objected seven months ago, in the spring of 1981, when he signed a waiver allowing us to examine these medical records."

She finished up by saying the defendant's attempt to hide behind a law that was clearly intended to protect the person he is accused of trying to kill was "an outrage."

For all of McGuirl's informed indignation, Sheehan, when he rose to rebut her, was anything but daunted. The idea of invoking this law was not the defendant's idea, but his lawyers'. They did not raise this point last spring as they were waiting till jeopardy was attached at the trial. The defendant does not need standing for this motion; the court has standing to eliminate evidence that was "criminally obtained."

Judge Needham gave the debate his fullest attention. Without showing a hint of incredulity, he engaged Sheehan in a dialogue on his motion. "You are saying," he said, "that regardless of what the medical testimony says about the guilt or innocence of the defendant, the victim, if alive, could refuse to allow its being used? You are saying that if the victim cannot assent or refuse, then the court must assert that right and tell doctors they cannot testify?"

"Yes," Sheehan said doggedly, "the court on its own initiative must stop its use until consent can be obtained. That is a right the waiver of which cannot be assumed."

This led into a discussion of the feasibility of appointing a conservator or guardian of the victim, a suggestion Susan McGuirl had made in her argument.

Needham got back to what he considered the underlying point of this discussion. "Am I not facing a situation," he said to Sheehan, "were I to adopt your motion, where I would be permitting a statute designed to protect a victim to protect the accused?"

"We must assume," Sheehan responded, "that Martha Von Bülow would not want the record read. Also, were you to allow it, you would be permitting a crime to be perpetrated from the witness stand."

Needham was not going to allow Sheehan too much pristine indignation. "Didn't I hear about an overdose of aspirin? Didn't that come from your side of the aisle? Isn't that the sort of information you are now claiming would be against Mrs. Von Bülow's wishes?"

"We both committed a crime, your honor, and we should stop," Sheehan said with unabashed righteousness.

Susan McGuirl was back on her feet. "It is ludicrous, your honor, to say the victim would prefer no discussion of medical matters already made public, rather than to have the man accused of trying to kill her brought to trial. If we cannot use the medical records, we cannot prosecute the case."

Judge Needham then brought the jury into the courtroom. They had been told to stay home for the past few days, but had been called in today, Thursday, in anticipation of the conclusion of the pretrial motions. The next agenda item was for them to tour Clarendon Court. Judge Needham had to disappoint them. Arguments were going on longer than anticipated and it would be another two days before they would be finished. Jurors should go home again and return Monday at 2 P.M. to be sworn in and then tour the Von Bülow mansion.

Judge Needham took the opportunity to get in a swipe at the press. "There was an item in the newspapers yesterday saying you had already toured Clarendon Court. Nothing I could say to you could better illustrate that what you read in the papers ain't necessarily so. This is one of the reasons we cannot allow jurors to follow the press coverage during the trial."

Although Needham said this with a twinkle, the reaction in the press box was sour. This group, some among them stars in their profession, were bright and sophisticated journalists who maintained a lively sense of humor about the trial while working hard to report it correctly. About themselves and their profession, however, they were exceedingly thin-skinned. A local paper was being kidded about an inconsequential error—kidded from the bench, to be sure—but a few of the nation's major dailies and wire services were reacting like offended dowagers.

More arguments were presented the next day on the inadmissibility of medical evidence. John Sheehan had driven to the law library at the Providence courthouse and come back armed with precedents; basically, he rested his argument on the *illegality* of divulging confidential medical information.

The Rhode Island law, it had already been pointed out, had fourteen exceptions, instances in which the confidentiality could be waived. Surprisingly, the patient's being the victim was not one of them. A zealous reporter had tracked down the judge who framed this law with its exceptions. When asked why this exception was not included, the judge replied, "We couldn't think of everything."

Susan McGuirl ended her two-day battle by zeroing in on the evidence in question having already been made public. "All the material we seek to introduce," she said, "was in the court record, a record open to the press. It is not confidential anymore. To make confidential what has already been in the press is an absurdity and would make a mockery of the court's purpose, the execution of criminal justice."

Both Sheehan and Fahringer had many more points to make on this motion, but were finally ruled down by Judge Needham saying that were courts to adopt the defense position, they could not introduce evidence of medical examiners in a homicide case without the victim's permission. Needham did not think "any such thing was intended."

The trial's third week was ending. All of the defense motions had been denied. Medical evidence was admissible as was the evidence gathered by Richard Kuh's preliminary investigation and the statements made by Von Bülow to Lieutenant Reise. When the trial itself got under way the following week, these legal points would be forgotten.

At the trial's end, however, if Von Bülow should be found guilty, these legal issues would rise from the dead to positions of even greater importance. If a higher court decided Judge Needham had been in error and that certain evidence had been incorrectly allowed, it could cause a new trial or, more likely, the end of Rhode Island's efforts to put Claus Von Bülow in jail.

XIX

MANY of the reporters covering the Von Bülow trial had, before arriving, only the vaguest knowledge about Newport. Like most Americans, they thought of it as a place where the rich used to summer and some still do. In those first weeks of the trial, gray, icy January weather gave the shuttered mansions of Bellevue Avenue a foreboding grimness. The winter weather made them evoke, not gilded dinners and sparkling balls, but leaky roofs and ruinous fuel bills. In the dark of winter they appeared good places for murders and little else.

This uninviting aspect of the mansions enabled the reporters, not a group known for partiality to the wealthy, to look on those houses as eccentric throwbacks rather than objects for envy. The same was probably true of the jurors, most of whom claimed to have barely noticed their town's unique concentration of marble palaces.

It was ironic therefore that the day designated for the jury to tour Clarendon Court was the only fine day in several weeks. It was the first time since the beginning of the trial that the temperature rose above freezing and the sky cleared to a full-force blue. With the bright sunlight giving a logic to the formal gardens that stretched from the manors to the sea cliff, and the white caps dancing on the ocean beyond, these Bellevue Avenue showplaces looked like very pleasant places to live indeed.

To the reporters, finally released after two foul-weather weeks in the public-building shabbiness of the Newport courthouse, it seemed that the weather was far better in the smart end of town.

It is interesting to speculate on what this minor meteorological fluke had on the jurors, most of whom had never been inside a house of the scale of Clarendon Court. Perhaps the beauty and comfort of Sunny Von Bülow's interior trappings would have been enough to impress them, but it is possible that the cosmetic effect of the clear sun on the formidable estate enhanced the attractiveness of great wealth.

Shortly before the jurors arrived, the area around Clarendon Court buzzed with the activity of a sports stadium before a game. Reporters and spectators had exhausted nearby parking spaces and, leaving their cars some distance, were walking up side streets toward the mansion. Three trucks outfitted as cherry pickers, their cranes manned by photographers, were positioned across Bellevue Avenue from the mansion, each trying for peeks over its wall. The small, dead-end street alongside Clarendon Court, Yzanga Avenue, usually closed to the public by a wooden horse, now had in addition a court sheriff on hand to bar reporters and photographers.

Judge Needham had denied a press request to join the house tour, and denied as well a press compromise suggestion that one of their number be permitted to represent them. Needham argued that a tour is not evidence; it is aimed only at helping the jury to understand testimony by showing the relationship of one room to another. The public needs to know nothing about the interior of Clarendon Court, so there is no reason to violate the wishes of Mrs. Von Bülow, whose determination for privacy caused her to refuse repeated requests from magazines to photograph her house.

No lawyers rushed to fight this ruling.

The press may have ceded any rights in the matter, but not its interest. In addition to the scores of reporters and photographers who waited outside the barricade, two network helicopters circled overhead, providing otherwise unobtainable views of the grounds and the building itself. When the jury disappeared into the house, the press wandered off feeling a bit foolish for having flocked to this non-event.

Entering the house through the kitchen as the family always did, the jurors were led through the ground-floor rooms—sometimes by Famiglietti, sometimes by Fahringer—to the breakfast room, the dining room, the living room and the library. A ground-floor lavatory had a framed sign, "Fuck Communism," which turned out to be a bit of Von Bülow's whimsy, and somewhat gratuitous in that setting. The focus of the tour was the ground-floor bedroom beyond the living room, where Mrs. Von Bülow had entered into both comas.

Jurors were shown the bathroom where she was found on the floor, December 21, 1980; they went down the hall from her bedroom to Von Bülow's study, where they saw the large, ornate desk in which the closet key was found. Finally, two at a time, they were allowed to enter the closet where Alexander and Lambert had found the black bag. Except for the lawyers' comments, the tour was silent; the jurors had been forbidden to ask questions.

The Clarendon Court tour, whatever help it gave the jury, provided the Von Bülow trial with one of its funniest moments. A few days later, with the trial in progress, Judge Needham returned from lunch, had the jury brought in, and addressed the court in his gruff deadpan about a newspaper story concerning the house tour that appeared in the *Boston Herald American*.

On a page of satiric jibes at the week's news, an article was headlined VON BÜLOW JURORS TO GO ON TRIAL. The article described how Clarendon Court servants were distressed to find that on the tour of the mansion the jurors had "collected more than evidence." Missing, the article said, were two crystal pitchers, an onyx paperweight, a gold candlestick, a silver cigarette lighter, a gold letter opener, a small jade statue, a chandelier, two Matisse prints . . .

As the list grew in preposterousness, everyone in the courtroom appreciated the humor, but none more than the jurors, who tried to conceal smiles with their hands but were soon laughing out loud. As the list of missing items concluded with "two polo ponies and a small Rolls-Royce," the courtroom was raucous with laughter. It was abruptly silenced by Judge Needham, saying, "I don't think that's at all funny."

Every laughing face in the room sobered. No school of tropical fish ever responded so instantly to an unexpected maneuver of the alpha fish.

Somewhat defensively, Judge Needham explained that although the article's humorous intention would be clear to most, some might take it seriously. Indeed, at lunch he had been approached by two jurors who angrily said they had heard about such a *news* story. Their anger was most justified, he said. It was wrong, he lectured, to subject citizens doing their civic duty to this kind of ridicule or perhaps suspicion.

When Steve Famiglietti approached the jury on February 2 to make his opening statement, his manner was straightforward. Famiglietti's only tilt toward flamboyance was in his personal appearance: his jackets were impeccably and stylishly tailored. He also spent time in the courthouse men's room before each day's session working with a can of hairspray to camouflage an incipient bald spot in his mane of dark hair.

Famiglietti told the jury that with the testimony of its witnesses the prosecution would prove the following: Martha Von Bülow was in a hopeless coma that was the result of an ingenious attempt to end her life by insulin injection; insulin can be fatal to ordinary people; up until recently, it was almost undetectable in the human body; one year earlier she suffered a similar coma of twenty-four-hours' duration after which she suffered retrograde amnesia in that she could recall no events prior to entering the coma. The state would prove that the defendant placed her in that condition as well.

It is not necessary, Famiglietti went on, for the state to prove a motive. Nevertheless, it will present evidence of a motive. The victim was an extremely wealthy woman while Von Bülow had no significant wealth of his own. Martha Von Bülow's will leaves him approximately fifteen million dollars, which he was aware of because he took part in making this will. The marriage was not happy, a condition aggravated by his love for another woman. Divorce "would not benefit the defendant."

Physicians will testify that Sunny's coma was caused by exogenous insulin (from *outside* the body) and that those studying her case have exhausted all other possible causes. The doctors and their tests will be proved to be competent and accurate. She will be presented as a shy, withdrawn woman; but she was in fact psychologically sound and had every reason to live. Her condition is the result of a deliberate and malicious act of another individual.

The prosecution will also establish that the defendant was familiar with needles and syringes, that the maid, Maria Schrallhammer, became suspicious and started to monitor his belongings;
that she found the black bag with needles, several drugs, and a vial
of insulin which can be purchased *without* a prescription [this was
the first time many in the courtroom knew this]; that she told the
family about the black bag.

The maid and Mrs. Von Bülow's family did not realize the
significance of what they saw, Famiglietti continued; they hesitated because they did not want to come between husband and
wife. After the second coma, they hired Richard Kuh to look into
the circumstances surrounding the comas. Alexander von Auersperg went to Clarendon Court and in Von Bülow's closet found
the black bag, which was brought to New York, analyzed, and
found to have traces of insulin on one used needle.

The prosecution will also show that at the time of both comas
the defendant conducted himself in a suspicious, unhusbandly
way. At the time of the 1979 coma he made efforts to keep Maria
from the bedroom. Only when she insisted did he admit her and
only after five hours' delay, in response to her pleading, did he call
a doctor. The prosecution will show that in statements to doctors
on both of his wife's two admissions to the hospital he gave false
accounts of her history and of his activities prior to the comas.

"He generally conducted himself," Famiglietti said, "in a manner not consistent with that of an innocent man."

With this slur, Von Bülow showed a reaction he would show
frequently throughout the trial: he reddened.

Famiglietti concluded by warning the jurors that some of the
medical testimony would be difficult to follow; he asked their full
attention for this important part of the case. They would then
arrive at the inescapable conclusion that, beyond a reasonable
doubt, the defendant on two occasions assaulted his wife in an
attempt to commit murder.

Fahringer's style was quite different than Famiglietti's in that
he often reached outside the facts of the case to matters of personal
involvement. His first paragraph, for example, referred to the
effect of the case on him personally, and on his client. He spoke
of the "awesome responsibility" that he, Fahringer, had under-

taken and pointed out that the trial would be "the most important moment in Von Bülow's life."

Another difference in courtroom style was Fahringer's skill at modulating his voice. Having trumpeted the importance of the case to him and Von Bülow, he decrescendoed abruptly to an intimate level as he said to the jury, "Three weeks ago we were strangers. I'd like to start our relationship on a note of frankness and candor. . . ."

The frankness turned out to be the somewhat defiant claim that the defense lawyers were not required to make an opening statement or, in fact, do anything on behalf of their client. They would, as it turned out, do a lot; they wanted the jury to know right now what they would prove.

First, he had a few kind words for the jurors themselves. Much time and effort went into their selection and they "are the chosen few." He reminded them they had sworn they could be fair and impartial in a case trailing "clouds of suspicion and rumor," that they would not be distracted by these irrelevancies. Observing such pure-minded principles "raises the stature of each of us and our confidence in government."

As for the prosecution's claims, Famiglietti was not present for these events; he has learned of the case from others. Fahringer shot his hand flat into the air. "What do you see? Your hand, you say. Not true. You see only *one side* of my hand."

Fahringer then traced a biographical sketch of Von Bülow, his escape from Nazi-occupied Denmark, his English education, his success in London as Getty's assistant, his wealth and high life-style. "He was not a fortune hunter."

Fahringer switched to Sunny's background, emphasizing her great wealth. He spoke of her first marriage and lobbed a few gratuitous shots at Alfie von Auersperg: at the time of the divorce, he confided, she gave this husband one million dollars plus two European homes worth another million. (The family denies that Alfie received any cash settlement, just the real estate.)

Von Bülow, on the other hand, insisted before marrying Sunny that they execute a premarital agreement in which he relinquished any claim to her wealth. With audible pride, Fahringer added that Von Bülow allowed this agreement to stand for the first three years of the marriage.

When Von Bülow married Sunny, he willingly gave up his good job and his good life in England in his devotion to her. The marriage was happy and he acted as father to her children. Fahringer quoted a remark Sunny once made that Claus was a better father to these children than was their own father.

After a time Von Bülow got restless staying at home looking after her; he wanted to work, but she wouldn't let him. Fahringer quoted Thomas Carlyle: "He who has found his work is blessed." As for Sunny, she had no hobbies or other interests. Her daily routine was to rise at eleven and have her chauffeur drive her to exercise class—then shopping, hairdresser, and home by 3:30. She would nap till 5:30 then spend the evening with the family, often without getting dressed again. "Her greatest enemy was time."

After Cosima's birth she lost interest in sex and told Von Bülow he could do what he wanted as long as he was discreet. She gave Von Bülow the interest on a million dollars to discourage him from working. Still, he went to work for financier Mark Millard. She was unhappy about this.

She was not healthy as Famiglietti stated. She was a terribly disturbed, unhappy person. Even her children said she couldn't hold liquor. She was hypoglycemic, which means she couldn't eat or drink sweets; she did both. She took twenty aspirin a day. She once overdosed on aspirin, at which time Von Bülow saved her life. She relied heavily on laxatives. She used barbiturates and tranquilizers. When hospitalized for the first coma, she had a 1.06 barbiturate level, a level high enough to kill in some cases.

Fahringer gave names to the three critical episodes in Sunny Von Bülow's decline into permanent coma: the eggnog episode, the aspirin overdose, and the amobarbitol overdose. The defense will prove that the harm to her was *unconsciously self-induced*. Before the first episode she had consumed, Von Bülow told us, ten glasses of eggnog and was helped to bed. The next morning, Von Bülow was awakened when the four labrador retrievers who slept with them made noise to indicate they wanted to go out.

Astoundingly, Fahringer here seemed to feel it would help win his client acquittal if he imitated the sound of pleading dogs. The courtroom was enthralled by Fahringer's dog whimpers, and yet looked perplexed by the relevance of this imitation. He continued his logging of the first coma, arriving finally at another large accusation: "We know Martha Von Bülow was drinking the entire day before. The one and only witness to say Martha was ill was . . . *Maria Schrallhammer!*"

Fahringer spat out the name with venomous force. Maria tells us, he continued, that Von Bülow was lying on the bed beside his wife with his clothes on. Fahringer explained Von Bülow often lay beside his wife reading in order to be there when she awoke. There is "nothing sinister about this, nothing ominous."

When Maria, who entered the room at eleven, not nine as she had stated, said, "Madam does not look right," Mr. Von Bülow replied, "Maria, you've gone through this twelve times before." When Von Bülow did call the doctor, he was advised to let Mrs. Von Bülow sleep. When she was eventually rushed to the hospital she was given blood tests and Dr. Gailitis looked for signs of drug overdose, but found no needle marks. When she awoke, he recommended she talk with a psychiatrist. She spoke with Dr. John Carr, who recommended psychotherapy. Von Bülow encouraged her, saying he would do likewise.

Fahringer interrupted his narrative to say, "Something important happened at that point." Von Bülow went to Mrs. Aitken to say we must get Sunny to stop drinking. Mrs. Aitken was unwilling to do anything about the problem. Von Bülow wrote Dr. Gailitis and laid out the facts of his actions prior to his wife's coma. Von Bülow asked the doctor, tell me frankly, did I do wrong? Was I too late? Dr. Gailitis responded that *he had saved his wife's life!*

Fahringer then introduced his version of Sunny's aspirin overdose three weeks before she went into her final coma at Christmas 1980. Von Bülow was in his bedroom at the Fifth Avenue apartment. It was 11 P.M. He heard a cry from his wife's room. He rushed in to find her on the floor, her head bleeding. He lifted her and put a pillow under her head.

Had he wanted her to die ("I hate to even say this"), he could have left her there hopeless, but instead he phoned the ambulance. He summoned Maria. Sunny was rushed to Lenox Hill Hospital. Immediate blood tests revealed her aspirin overdose.

As she was recuperating in the hospital, Von Bülow asked for a private chat with his wife's doctor, Richard Stock. He and Sunny were talking of divorce. Was she well enough to undergo the rigors? Stock thought she was. This shows Von Bülow's concern for her.

Fahringer traced the events of the evening before her final coma. The caramel sundae at dinner, the film *9 to 5,* returning home at nine o'clock. Sunny went to the bathroom. What did she do there? We don't know. Von Bülow was in his study. Mrs. Von Bülow went to the library to chat with her son. He noticed her speech growing slurred. Von Bülow came in to see if she needed anything. She asked for chicken soup. He brought her a cup.

"There was nothing in that soup!" Fahringer said impassionedly. "She had the symptoms *before* she drank the soup. But that is the kind of suspicion we are dealing with!"

Sunny reeled; her son helped her to bed. He reported to Von Bülow that his mother was ill. Von Bülow asked his wife how she felt. She felt much better, she said. He did not behave in an unhusbandly fashion on either occasion. They both went to bed.

When he awoke at 5:30 in the morning, it was pitch dark. Von Bülow thinks his wife was in bed with him. He went to his study, where he cannot know if she is in bed or not. He did the calisthenics that he did every day. He spoke on the phone for an hour and six minutes with Margaret Neilly from his office, then at 9:30 went to breakfast. When he returned to his bedroom it was daylight. The bed was empty. He heard water running in the bathroom. The door was closed. He took the dogs for a walk.

At eleven he returned to the house and asked Cosima and Alexander, who were eating breakfast, where their mother was. Not up, they said. He went to the bedroom. The bed was still empty. He pushed open the bathroom door and found her lying face down on the cold floor. He saw her head was cut; he knows not to move a person with a head injury. He got Alexander and they called an ambulance.

At the hospital her blood was tested and found to have 156 milligrams per centum aspirin and 1.06 milligrams per centum amobarbitol. They found only a small amount of alcohol. Alcohol metabolizes very quickly, Fahringer explained; it is not odd to find only a little.

What caused her coma, Fahringer asked? One of four things: low body temperature, the aspirin, the barbiturates, or the low blood sugar. The hospital tests were important. They showed a high insulin level and a low blood sugar. Fearlessly, Fahringer proceeded to write the exact chemical percentages on a large blackboard that had been set up in front of the press box.

Fahringer had barely entered the dreaded technical area when Famiglietti, who had just pleaded with the jury for careful attention to *his* technical evidence, yawned conspicuously.

Fahringer painted a picture of blood testing at Newport Hospital that could have been a scenario for *The Three Stooges Play Lab Technicians*. Workers pulling tubes from random racks, not labeling them, not caring when they were drawn (before or after the glucose injections), the tubes later destroyed. He built to the contention that the high insulin level was read on blood drawn *after* the massive glucose infusions; this would naturally drive up the insulin level.

At this, Famiglietti turned his head up from his legal pad and gave Fahringer a look of happy astonishment.

Fahringer was winding up. This case had been a private prosecution. This was the first case in Rhode Island history in which all the evidence had been collected by a private investigator.

Famiglietti abandoned his amused posture abruptly and was on his feet with a vociferous objection. Judge Needham allowed Fahringer's remark but warned Fahringer about taking too many liberties.

Fahringer saved some of his most audacious claims for the end. He promised the jurors he would produce some surprises. Whatever was in that black bag belonged *to Martha Von Bülow* and not to the defendant. And when Alexander and the detective seized the black bag, they took no fingerprints so we could know (his voice rising to a near shout) *who put that bag there!*

For two months, he went on, the evidence was molested by all kinds of people before it was turned over to the police. ("Outrageous.") When Von Bülow was interrogated by the police, he answered every question.

To come to a verdict, you must ask these questions: Why did he save her life on December 1? Why would he ask her doctor if she was strong enough for a divorce? Why was there a high level of amobarbitol in her blood? A high level of aspirin? Why would an intelligent woman not complain of feeling funny?

Where Mr. Von Bülow sits, Fahringer said with climactic lyricism, is the loneliest place in the world. You jurors must make sure that no person in this country can be convicted unjustly on circumstantial evidence. Claus Von Bülow did not cause his wife's coma. If you follow the law and obey your consciences, you will have to find him innocent.

When he had sat down, Judge Needham turned toward the jurors and reminded them that whatever the two counsel said was not necessarily true—which seemed a rather mean comment after two such impressive performances. When he declared a recess, the reporters rushed to file their stories on the opening statements. They did not return to hear Needham's charge to the jury, which consisted mainly of defining the charge, telling the jurors they were the sole judge of witnesses' credibility, and that they were not obliged to solve the mystery, only to decide if Von Bülow had tried to kill his wife.

XX

AT two o'clock on February 2, nine days short of a month after the trial began, the prosecution called the first of its thirty-nine witnesses. Rules of courtroom procedure forbid any explanation of a witness's presence, or what counsel hopes to prove by this testimony. With so many witnesses, some of whom were obscure indeed, it was often hard to determine either the reason for their presence or the line of questioning. Famiglietti had warned jurors that they sometimes would not understand particular questions but that eventually all the pieces would fall into place.

The order of the witnesses loosely followed the logic of the prosecution's argument. Famiglietti called first the persons closest to the situation, Alexander and Maria, who were most familiar with the events leading up to the two comas; then a number of witnesses to corroborate their testimony; next, the Newport Hospital people, to establish the treatment and tests administered to Sunny; then a number of hospital personnel for further corroboration.

These were followed by Lieutenant Reise and Sergeant Miranda to establish details of the investigation and their talks with Von Bülow, then a series of medical expert witnesses to prove the comas were caused by insulin injection, and finally, Sunny's trust officer to give details of the financial situation of Claus and Sunny Von Bülow as well as their children.

A casual observer might have felt that a sense of theater influenced this agenda. Two of the most sensational witnesses, Alexander and Maria, appeared at the outset; the single most dramatic, Alexandra Isles, just after the halfway point; and two other equally sensational appeared at the end: Ala and Chemical Bank vice-president Gurley, who spelled out exactly what kind of money was being discussed.

Whether by design or not it broke down into a strong opening to win the nation's attention, the plodding, fact-building witnesses while the public was held enthralled, then, before resting the case in the face of spent interest, a few concluding bombshells.

When Alexander von Auersperg took the stand as the state's first witness, he was familiar to everyone in the courtroom except the jury. While Alexander may not have been the prosecution's most important witness from the standpoint of incriminating the defendant, he was in terms of involvement with the overall drama. Unlike his sister or Maria, he had been present on both occasions when his mother went into a coma.

Famiglietti laboriously took Alexander over his family relationships. He asked about his mother's present condition. He established that Alexander had never seen his mother inebriated and that prior to the first coma Alexander had felt no hostility toward his stepfather. They went through the events of the evening of December 26, 1979: Alexander chatting with his mother at Clarendon Court, her slurred speech, his putting her to bed, his returning from tennis the next afternoon to find Maria in tears.

Famiglietti then asked, "Why was Maria in tears?"

Fahringer objected, but Judge Needham told Alexander he could answer.

"Because my mother was sick and the doctor was not being called."

Fahringer objected again; Needham instructed the jury to disregard the second portion of Alexander's remark.

Alexander described the doctor's arrival, the rushing of his mother to Newport Hospital, and the later conversation in which Von Bülow told him of being "uncomfortable" in his marriage to Sunny.

Did he talk later to his mother about her coma?

"I don't recall any conversation about it or the events leading up to it."

"Did she say anything about not having slept for two nights?"

"No."

When Alexander told how Maria later pointed out the black bag to him and aroused his suspicions, Famiglietti said, "Did you ever go to your mother and tell her about seeing the black bag?"

"No."

"Why not?"

"I told my sister and my grandmother about it, but I did not feel I had sufficient evidence to risk alienating myself from my family."

Famiglietti was establishing early in his parade of witnesses an adeptness at asking hard questions about the weakest or most puzzling aspects of their stories; this served to diffuse Fahringer's inevitable attack on the same points. It would also make him appear repetitious, an irritating offense in a trial that threatened to be prolonged.

The courtroom was mesmerized when Alexander told of the conversation he had with his mother at Thanksgiving of 1980, when she said she planned to divorce Von Bülow for a reason "too horrible" to tell. The press and spectators were frustrated that Alexander never did learn what this unspeakable revelation had been. The conversational fragment hung over the trial and over the head of the defendant from this point on.

Alexander described in detail the events of his mother's final coma—her weakening condition after they had all attended 9 to 5, his carrying her to bed, his leaving the house for a drink after an hour or two in his room.

"If you were so worried about her," Famiglietti asked, "why did you leave her?"

"I had warned my stepfather that my mother was not feeling well," Alexander replied. "I thought he would be careful."

Alexander's choice of the words "warned" and "careful" had, for the situation, an off-kilter ring. A more natural remark would have been, "Mother is unwell; look after her." It is odd, however, he felt it necessary to admonish in any way a husband to look after his wife.

Still without any emotion, Alexander related his being brought by Von Bülow the following morning to his mother's bathroom, where he found her lying unconscious on the floor; the dash to Newport Hospital; the transfer the next day to Boston with Von Bülow accompanying her.

Famiglietti asked Alexander about his looking in his stepfather's closet immediately following the coma, not finding the black bag, but returning for a more thorough search after Von Bülow had gone to Boston, to find the closet locked.

"When you were in the closet, did you look under the lower shelf?" Famiglietti asked, referring to the spot where it was later found.

"No," Alexander replied.

When Alexander returned to the courtroom the next morning, every seat was full of press and spectators (as it would be till the trial's conclusion) except for the six chairs at the two counsel tables. The lawyers were conferring in Judge Needham's chambers. Alexander sat on the last chair at the prosecution table. Next to him was a row of four empty chairs stretching across the two tables to the last chair of the defense table, which was occupied by Von Bülow. The two adversaries—stepfather and stepson—sat staring straight ahead for a good fifteen minutes until the lawyers emerged, Judge Needham took the bench, and Alexander was called to the stand.

Famiglietti started the day's testimony by leading Alexander through the circumstances of how he, along with his sister and grandmother, hired Richard Kuh, their reasons for seeking this aid, and the advice Kuh gave them. They went over Alexander's trip to Clarendon Court with Detective Lambert ("It had been my idea to go but my grandmother wanted someone to go with me"), hiring the locksmith in Providence, driving to Newport, getting into and searching the closet with Detective Lambert, finding the black bag, bringing it back to New York, and giving it to Dr. Stock for an analysis of the contents.

At this point Famiglietti produced the black bag and asked Alex to identify first it, then its contents. About four by seven inches, perhaps three inches thick, it was a bag of soft black leather with a zipper running around its side like a case for an electric razor. It had actually been a case for a pocket calculator and had the word *Bowmar* imprinted on its back. Jurors and spectators stretched to get a look at this much-written-about object, which could be, in effect, the murder weapon.

As vials of pills, packets of needles, and unused syringes were logged and entered as exhibits, the clerk's desk before Judge Needham's bench began to look like a pharmaceutical smorgasbord.

For days of testimony, until the clerk's desk got overloaded with exhibits, the black bag sat in plain view of all, mute yet engrossing, rather like the defendant himself.

All of this was covered in meticulous detail. Famiglietti concluded with some questions about Alexander when he was about six or seven having seen his mother and stepfather with needles and syringes while on vacation in Majorca. At that time he saw his stepfather inject himself with vitamins.

When Fahringer rose to cross-examine Alexander, his voice was menacingly loud. "You are not a party to these proceedings," he boomed, "just a witness, is that right? Why do you feel it necessary to have Mr. Kuh here? How much are you paying him?"

Alexander, undaunted by the lawyer's volume, said he, his sister, and his grandmother had paid Kuh around $100,000. This produced a gasp from the spectators and Alexander said it was probably closer to $70,000, including the cost of investigators.

"After your testimony yesterday, didn't you go to the prosecution office across the hall with the entire prosecution team to go over questions you might be asked?"

"Yes, I did."

"And didn't they tell you to be prepared on this subject and to be ready to give this answer?" Fahringer quivered with indignation.

"That's garbage," Alexander said quietly. "No."

After equally fruitless questioning about Alexander's coaching by Kuh, Fahringer plunged into Sunny's drinking and fondness for sweets. When he got to the caramel sundae prior to the final coma, Fahringer said, "You had special ice cream at Clarendon Court, didn't you?"

"I thought we had Newport Creamery ice cream," Alexander replied, naming the most common local brand.

"Isn't that special ice cream?" snapped Fahringer, sure of his ground.

"It's ice cream," Alexander replied with a let's-cut-the-crap shrug in his tone that clearly delighted the jurors. For all the grandeur of Clarendon Court and the noble title, this handsome young prince ate the same ice cream they did.

Fahringer asked Alexander about his mother's use of pills but could turn up little more than the Bufferin she liked to have nearby. He reminded Alexander that he had spoken to his mother by phone early in December of 1980, that her voice had grown slurred and he had asked her, several times during the conversation, if she had taken a sleeping pill. She had denied it. In answering, Alexander managed to get across two points detrimental to the defense: that he suspected sleeping pills only because his stepfather had told him she used them; and that he had never heard her voice slurred in this manner before the 1979 coma.

They spoke of a meeting with Von Bülow after the final coma in which the family's finances were discussed and Von Bülow had told Alexander and his sister how costly Sunny's care would be, that readjustments would be necessary. In an attempt to show Alexander's acquisitive side, he quoted Alexander as asking if they would be able to keep Clarendon Court. His acknowledgment suggested little more than Alexander's fondness for the house.

Fahringer seemed slow to realize when a line was taking him nowhere. But didn't you and your sister use the house the summer of 1981, have parties there? Alexander said they had indeed used it and may have had informal gatherings there.

Fahringer established that Von Bülow had told Alexander and his sister the degree of participation in their mother's will. Then Fahringer threw a curve. Did you know, he asked Alexander, that Von Bülow had made a will leaving you, Ala, and Cosima everything he owned? Alexander had not known.

"No one told you? You are not interested?" Fahringer was incredulous.

"My stepfather's will?" Alexander said with his usual lack of expression. "Why should I be interested in it?"

"Do you have any reason to doubt that it is true?"

"Yes," said Alexander.

"Would you like to see the will?" Fahringer asked, moving toward a briefcase.

"No," Alexander said forcefully.

A wan smile came over Von Bülow's face, the irate smile of someone just slapped.

Hostility came out at other moments. Several times, Fahringer, whether from strategy or carelessness, referred to Von Bülow as Alexander's "father." With a steady voice Alexander would quickly interrupt and say, "My stepfather."

When Fahringer was working in other ways to establish Von Bülow's role as Alexander's father, the witness admitted that he called Von Bülow Uncle Claus, that Von Bülow helped him get a Senate page job with Claiborne Pell and perhaps helped him win admission to Brown University; with all this, he steadfastly refused to admit Von Bülow had been a father to him.

"Wasn't he the only man in the house?" Fahringer cried, hoping to win by default.

"Perhaps in the literal sense," Alexander sneered.

Ordinarily, lawyers are not happy to see their witnesses show too much hostility; it undermines credibility. If this person is that bitter, jurors might think, perhaps he is coloring his testimony. In Alexander's case, however, his bitterness added credence to his performance. If indeed Von Bülow was guilty of what Alexander claimed to believe—trying to kill his mother for her money—an absence of hostility would have been carrying courtroom decorum to an absurd degree.

If Fahringer was having little success in burnishing Von Bülow's image, he managed to sully Alexander's a bit—although to nowhere near the degree the prosecution feared. Fahringer brought out that Sunny had her chauffeur deliver a new car to Alexander at Deerfield as a graduation present (spoiled), he later wrecked the car (wild), and when his mother gave him a twenty-first birthday party in Paris, he failed to show up (inconsiderate). Such victories for Fahringer, however, fell far short of his goal: to make Alexander appear the kind of scoundrel who could frame another human being for a major crime.

Fahringer continued to retrace the most familiar parts of Alexander's testimony, particularly about the discovery and later handling of the famous black bag. Several times Fahringer misunderstood something Alexander said and was corrected by his witness. He returned to one of Alexander's winning subjects —ice cream—and the milkshakes his mother used to make with it. He intended to ask if Alexander's mother hadn't been in the habit of making her milkshakes richer but instead said "make her ice cream richer."

"How do you make ice cream richer?" Alexander said in his flat, disinterested voice.

"By adding more ice cream," Fahringer snapped impatiently.

"Oh," said Alexander with the aplomb of a cat playing with a particularly foolish mouse.

Fahringer's biggest bungle came at the end, when he asked perhaps his most incisive question, "If you thought someone were trying to kill your mother, wouldn't you go to her?"

"Only if you were sure," Alexander replied, then added, "It is not a very nice thing to accuse anyone of."

To everyone in the courtroom it was clear Alexander was saying that accusing his stepfather or anyone else of attempted murder is not something done lightly, but Fahringer misunderstood and all but roared at Alexander, *"I'm not accusing you of anything!"*

So direct were the young man's answers that for most who heard his testimony, Alexander the archschemer no longer existed. The only possibility that seemed to remain was that Alexander was the unwitting dupe of a plotting Maria Schrallhammer or of a Maria who had seriously misinterpreted a series of circumstances.

Detective Lambert was brought on the stand briefly to corroborate Alexander's version of the expedition to Clarendon Court for the black bag. He was systematically taken through an inventory of what they found in the black bag and elsewhere in Von Bülow's study and bath.

Given his turn with Lambert, Fahringer hammered away at his not taking fingerprints from the bag. Lambert defused this thrust to an extent by saying that even when he had been a policeman he had taken prints one out of ten times; he took them only if there was a good chance of getting prints. This developed into an argument over whether or not a soft leather surface preserved prints. It seems it may or may not. All in all, Lambert's answers were not convincing about why no fingerprints had been taken.

Excitement mounted as the appearance of Maria Schrallhammer approached, especially among the growing number of photographers stationed outside the courthouse, who were under orders to get a shot of the German maid who had yet to be shown in the newspapers. To fulfill this simple assignment they confronted a major problem: not one of them had the vaguest idea of what she looked like.

Photos of almost everyone connected with the case had appeared in the newspapers; all of the principals had been photographed—except Maria. Because of this, the photographers were frantic that the maid of the century might slip past them. Every woman over thirty-five was suspect; many were nonplussed to have their pictures taken.

When Maria approached the courthouse in a car with Kuh, he suggested she get out a block from the courthouse and, instead of going in the side entrance used by witnesses, where the press waited, enter by the courthouse's main entrance. His ploy almost succeeded. In the company of Alexander's girlfriend, also unknown to the press, she made it up the long walk and almost to the doors before a sharp-eyed journalist spotted her and snapped a few pictures. The others made up for it when she emerged later.

Anyone following this case since it broke into the papers the previous summer was familiar with the name Maria Schrallhammer. Her role in the entire affair was the stuff of vintage Agatha Christie or Daphne du Maurier. Indeed, Von Bülow now referred to Maria among friends as "Mrs. Danvers." In reading about her, her name, nothing more than a configuration of letters, stood for an entity capable of the most Machiavellian plottings, twisted allegiances, and vicious acts. Seeing this small, frail, pretty, not-young woman with a shaky, slightly accented voice—highly ladylike in a printed black dress with long sleeves and a small ruffle around its high neck—the possibilities narrowed resoundingly.

Much of Maria's long testimony would be extremely damaging to Von Bülow, but it is fair to venture that nothing she said hurt him as much as the woman herself. Had she been overbearing, assertive, truculent or abrasive, it would have been far easier to dismiss her testimony. But this fragile, soft-spoken, feminine figure before the hushed court was sympathetic and believable. The defendant's backers had had considerable success in projecting their man onto the public's consciousness as the solitary, friendless foreigner, beleagured by imposing forces of wealth and influence. He had now been upstaged by the dainty Maria; if anyone was to be bullied by cruel oppressors, it was going to be she, not he.

Maria's manifest pain at having to air private matters served to underline her sense of outrage at the crime she believed had been committed. The hostility she revealed toward Von Bülow appeared to be secondary to her adoration of her mistress.

Maria testified from midmorning Thursday till the end of the day; she was on the stand the entire next day and for a portion of the morning of Monday, February 8. During those twelve hours on the witness stand she painted a vivid picture of her mistress's personality and life and, with scant emotion, of a sinister Von Bülow who at best was indifferent to his wife's well-being and at worst was trying to kill her.

Famiglietti first traced Maria's history with Martha Von Bülow, her going to work for Sunny in Germany twenty-three years earlier, her service throughout the marriage to von Auersperg, her help in raising the two children, her devotion to her mistress, which never compromised a servant-master relationship ("She rarely confided in me").

She described her duties: looking after Mrs. Von Bülow and her personal possessions, particularly tending to the many cleaning, pressing, and maintenance chores that go with servicing a large wardrobe, cleaning her bedroom and bath, helping her to arrange flowers (at which the two women would often spend several hours a day). She told of having complete access to every cranny of Mrs. Von Bülow's life, including the contents of her handbag. Like other witnesses, Maria was unwittingly painting a picture of the life of the very rich.

She described Mrs. Von Bülow as an athletic woman who in the summer swam daily and, until she broke her hip, played golf, a woman who kept weights and an exercise slant board in her bedroom. She was prone to headaches and adored sweets although Maria added, "I ate ten times more sweets than she did." Her mistress had no alcohol problem, drinking only rarely. If she had two drinks, however, she showed the effects—not by a weakening voice or slurred speech but by becoming uncharacteristically talkative.

Maria was led into what was perhaps the most crucial testimony of the trial, her description of the events leading up to her mistress's first coma just after Christmas 1979. Much had been said about the evidence against Von Bülow being entirely circumstantial, a designation that sounds more pejorative to the general public than it does to the legally sophisticated, who know the flimsiness of much direct testimony. Still, there is something in all our natures that rebels against a certainty about events to which no eyewitness exists.

Maria's description of Von Bülow's refusal to assist or call a doctor for his obviously failing wife was as close to direct evidence as could exist without someone actually witnessing a murderous act. She was, in effect, describing Von Bülow actively abetting his wife's death.

As the courtroom held its breath, Maria described her mistress's wooziness on the night of December 26, her unprecedented failure to rise the next morning, Maria's hearing moans inside the bedroom and forcing her way in to find an unconscious mistress guarded by a Von Bülow who denied anything was wrong or that she required help, the day-long battle between Maria and Von Bülow about calling a doctor, Maria finally prevailing when her mistress's breathing became erratic around six in the evening, Von Bülow urging the doctor to come immediately, saying he would "pay him anything," the coarse breathing turning into a "rattle," Von Bülow refusing to help Maria lift her mistress, the arrival of Dr. Gailitis, Sunny's going into cardiac arrest.

Throughout this tale, Maria spoke in a soft, flat voice with just a hint of a whine—as though she were complaining respectfully about a master who dirtied too many towels. Occasionally a bus would rev its motor outside the courtroom causing gasps from reporters, terrified of missing a word.

After the lunch recess Maria described an episode in February 1980, when her mistress had shown many of the same symptoms, Von Bülow's explanation that Sunny had eaten a greasy hamburger the night before and was on antibiotics, Mrs. Aitken's being phoned about this.

The courtroom had barely calmed down from the drama of the first coma when Maria was led by Famiglietti into the circumstances of her discovering the black bag. While cleaning Von Bülow's closet in which her mistress's evening dresses were kept, she noticed a canvas traveling bag; inside was a small black leather bag. Saying she didn't know why she did it, she opened the bag to find several prescription vials made out to Von Bülow and one to Leslie Baxter.

In the midst of this gripping narration, Famiglietti, as if by afterthought, threw in a significant but out-of-place question.

"When *you* would get sick, Miss Schrallhammer, would Mr. Von Bülow call a doctor?"

"Right away," she responded without hesitation.

She went on to describe the various sightings of the black bag (including the one on Thanksgiving of 1980 when she saw the insulin for the first time), her writing down the prescription drugs and eventually getting Ala to take samples of them to the family doctor for analysis. (Famiglietti would leave to medical witnesses the description of the drugs.)

In her statement to the Rhode Island police that was typed into the court record, Maria had quoted herself as saying, "What for insulin?" This version had an indelible ring, clearly being a mistranslation of a German asking "Why insulin?" and a sublimely succinct summation of the mystery. Perhaps because of Maria's two versions, the line appeared in many forms, even to a totally altered version in one newspaper that had it "What is insulin for?" None of the variations had the lapidary perfection of "What for insulin?" Her changing the phrase on repetition in court was unfortunate, almost a breach of orthodoxy.

Maria told of seeing the black bag again just before the Von Bülows' left for Newport the final Christmas, when Mrs. Von Bülow had wanted Maria to go with them but Von Bülow had squelched the idea.

Famiglietti then switched Maria back to the episode in April of 1980 when Mrs. Von Bülow had felt extremely shaky and weak and had been subsequently put into the hospital for tests by Dr. Stock.

Maria also told of frequently seeing needles or syringes among Mr. Von Bülow's toilet articles but never with her mistress's; but she recalled one time years earlier in London Mrs. Von Bülow complaining to Von Bülow of fatigue and asking him for a vitamin shot. This was extremely important testimony as it corroborated the childhood recollections of Alexander and later Ala that needles and syringes were part of the life of their mother and stepfather, a fact that Truman Capote "revealed" weeks after the verdict by way of crashing a celebrated affair from which he felt wrongfully excluded.

Maria's memory on this point went far toward explaining how Von Bülow would be able to inject his wife with insulin without her knowing it (as did the presence in the black bag of the local anesthetic Lidocaine). For the recipient, one injection is pretty much like another.

Maria talked of her mistress's love for Christmas, how happy she had been as she departed for Newport her last week of consciousness. Famiglietti brought up the aspirin overdose of December 1, 1980, when Maria was puzzled how her mistress had cut her head, or why her speech was so slurred Maria was unable to understand her, and her lack of any recollection afterwards as to what had occurred.

Much general talk followed about Martha Von Bülow—her dieting, her love of privacy, her talk of divorce, her insistence on a cold bedroom for sleeping, and such bizarre details as her sleeping with her four yellow labradors, whose snoring drove the Von Bülows to earplugs.

Maria's first day on the stand wound up with a discussion of Von Bülow's trips to Nassau and Florida in February and March 1981, when his wife was in a coma. Maria had seen Alexandra Isles when she came to pick up Cosima for the March trip.

All the television networks showed samples of Maria's testimony that evening and there were few newspapers that didn't summarize her damning testimony. The *Boston Herald American,* which later in the trial came close to running the full-page headline CLAUS SPOUSE NO SOUSE, on this day ran MAID: CLAUS WAS A LOUSE.

The next day when Maria left Mrs. Aitken's Bellevue Avenue mansion to come to the courthouse she asked the driver to wait a moment: she had forgotten to light a candle to her patron saint, a ritual that had helped her, she was convinced, on the stand the day before. She disappeared into the house and emerged a few minutes later ready to face cross-examination.

Famiglietti had a few more questions to ask Maria before turning her over to Fahringer. Hadn't the 1979 coma changed Mrs. Von Bülow's social habits? Yes, she became more reclusive, but she only canceled at the last minute twice in that entire year. Von Bülow's hotel bill at Lyford Cay had been $970.40; Mrs. Von Bülow did not know that Von Bülow was having an affair.

How did it happen, Famiglietti wanted to know, that Von Bülow allowed Maria to pack his suitcase for European trips? "He liked the way I packed his suits." Von Bülow, who had sat impassively throughout Maria's incriminating narrative, now smiled broadly.

Fahringer started off his cross-examination by establishing some current information. Maria was staying at Mrs. Aitken's; she now worked for Ala Kneissl for $887 per month plus board; she didn't recall if she had told police investigators she regretted having gotten involved in this case.

Had she ever seen her mistress intoxicated during her marriage to von Auersperg? Yes. Very intoxicated? No. Had Mrs. Von Bülow frequently used pills? No. Hadn't von Auersperg shown up in the United States to get money from his former wife? Maria knew nothing about that but managed to get in that in the seven years of the Austrian marriage she had never once seen her mistress cry.

Fahringer switched to the early days in London of Sunny's marriage to Von Bülow, trying to establish how graciously Von Bülow lived before marrying Sunny. He introduced photos and a floor plan of the Belgravia apartment. The apartment was indeed large, but the photos of the lavish furnishings were discredited as proof of his point—they turned out to have been taken *after* the marriage and the arrival of the Crawford millions.

In Fahringer's every attempt to extract a concession from Maria he was not only unsuccessful but was usually knocked back a few paces. Didn't Von Bülow pick out a car for Alexander? No, Sunny and the chauffeur picked it out. Hadn't the Von Bülows given a party in his London flat for 280 people? No, maybe 200. With each of Maria's counterpunches, Famiglietti smiled up from the prosecution table.

Perhaps to establish animosity between Maria and Von Bülow, Fahringer brought up the episode in which Maria had noticed some watches missing from her mistress's jewelry box and indirectly accused Von Bülow of taking them. Sunny had confronted Von Bülow about them; he had said he had taken them to get measurements for an anniversary gift for Sunny.

This was an astounding thing for Fahringer to have introduced about his client. In addition to the ugly suspicion the story stimulated, it revealed a startling facet to the Von Bülow marriage: that this shy, passive woman did not flinch at accusing her aristocratic husband of petty theft.

Whatever gains Fahringer hoped to win by this subject, the risks were enormous—and, it appeared, fully realized.

Maria's most overwhelming rout of the New York lawyer was when he brought up a fire that had occurred in the dressing room of the Von Bülows' Fifth Avenue apartment fourteen years earlier, when Sunny was pregnant with Cosima. "The fire was in a large container," Fahringer said, "which Von Bülow took and emptied, putting the fire out, causing his hands to be burned."

"This is not correct," Maria said firmly.

"Did he put the fire out?"

"No, he didn't. He took the laundry basket and tried to put out the fire," she explained patiently, "but then dropped it in the bedroom, then partly got it into the bathroom, but it was still burning. Mrs. Von Bülow came yelling to the kitchen, 'Maria the house is on fire.' I took the fire extinguisher and I killed the fire."

"Didn't Mr. Von Bülow have to go to the hospital to have his hand treated?" asked Fahringer, now desperate.

"He had a little burn on his finger, yes." With which Maria held a finger up to the jury which was now, along with the entire courtroom, laughing heartily.

"Mrs. Schrallhammer"—Fahringer calling "Mrs." the woman who had never married—"when he came back were his hands bandaged?"

"No."

"Oh," said Fahringer in total defeat.

Fahringer had more success in trying to establish that Sunny was slow to seek medical help (after breaking her hip, she had waited two days before calling a doctor) and was not a complainer, which raised the possibility that she was in poorer health and mental condition than Maria realized.

"Were you like sisters?"

"No. We liked each other."

"If you thought for a moment Mrs. Von Bülow was going to die, wouldn't you phone a doctor?"

"No, for fear of Mr. Von Bülow. I always obeyed him."

Fahringer switched to the episode in April of 1980 when Maria had phoned Mrs. Aitken to report her daughter's alarming condition. "Did Mrs. Von Bülow tell you never again to call her mother?"

Maria blurted out, "He made her say that!"

"Your honor . . ." Fahringer pleaded to Judge Needham for help with this uncontainable woman.

Throughout the long day on the stand, Maria had shown none of the shaky emotion she had shown with Famiglietti's gentle questioning. She answered each of Fahringer's questions in a steady and imperturbable manner. If Fahringer had won a few points, Maria had won many.

Other lawyers witnessing Fahringer's prolonged and counter-productive stint with Maria were of the opinion that once he saw how unflappable she was, he should have asked her a few questions to establish her dogged devotion to Mrs. Von Bülow and gotten her off the stand and out of town as fast as possible. His prolonged and deteriorating effort to score from her appeared more a result of wounded vanity than a desire to help his client.

Fahringer apparently spent a long weekend poring over court records in an effort to turn up something he might use to lay a glove on Maria. Retaking the stand Monday in an equally prim outfit, Maria was asked by Fahringer if in her previous week's testimony she hadn't said that Mrs. Von Bülow had told her she wanted to divorce Mr. Von Bülow as she felt she was standing in his way and that the next time she would like to marry a successful businessman.

And didn't Maria say in her grand jury testimony that when Mrs. Von Bülow discussed divorce, no reason was given? Which version is the truth? Maria used as her defense that she had sworn to Mrs. Von Bülow never to divulge what had been told in confidence. "I didn't want to betray her. I thought she would recover."

"But now you say that Mrs. Von Bülow didn't want to stand in his way and she wanted to marry a rich businessman!" Fahringer had built so much steam and was quivering with such indignation that when Maria said quietly "But those are not reasons" he did not appear to hear her, nor did anyone else. This was unfortunate, as those words would seem a more telling rebuttal of the inconsistency charge than the pledge of secrecy (Fahringer indeed asked why Maria had not simply said to the grand jury that she had sworn not to discuss such private matters).

Maria's unheard interjection raised the interpretation that Sunny had wanted a divorce for reasons, even now, still unmentioned. To justify ending her marriage she had added a "besides," to wit, her feeling of obstructing her husband's career hopes. Furthermore, if she did divorce and marry again, next time she would like to marry a successful businessman. Neither of these contingencies, seeing it Maria's way, were the *reason* Sunny wanted a divorce.

Nevertheless, Fahringer, for the first time, had succeeded in confounding Maria and making her appear to some as though she had been less than honest in her grand jury testimony.

Energized by this success, Fahringer bounded on to other matters and almost immediately found himself in the same kind of Maria trouble he had been unable to escape for the five preceding hours. He asked Maria about Sunny's having had a facelift. On this turf Maria dug in and doggedly refused to discuss the matter: her mistress, who hadn't even wanted her children to know, had sworn Maria to secrecy. Maria remained adamant against Fahringer's persistence, a persistence that allowed Maria to prove her recent claim: she was ready to go to jail rather than betray a confidence from her "lady."

Fahringer catalogued other health mishaps in an effort to show Sunny's erratic physical condition and how much was going wrong with her in which Von Bülow had no part. Alluding to Sunny's February 1980 illness, which Von Bülow attributed to a greasy hamburger, Fahringer listed the symptoms—weakness, failing vision, slurred speech—and got Maria to renounce suspicion that Von Bülow was responsible.

Still, she managed to blurt out, "I don't think you get all that from a greasy hamburger"—which drew a dangerous laugh from the courtroom.

How about the aspirin overdose? Was that Von Bülow's fault? Maria did not think so.

Fahringer's sarcastic tone and his willingness to raise these dark suggestions indicated that he, at least, believed any involvement of Von Bülow's in these illnesses to be totally out of the question.

Before relinquishing Maria for good, Fahringer returned again to his one victory, Maria's "altered" testimony about Sunny's reasons for wanting a divorce. "Was that as honest as the rest of your testimony here today?"

"Yes," she replied.

"Thank you," Fahringer snapped, as though this one discrepancy in a matter far removed from the alleged crimes had unraveled Maria's voluminous testimony that related directly to them.

On his redirect, Famiglietti leaped through the door Fahringer had inexplicably opened with the missing wristwatches. He naturally found it irresistible to luxuriate in such a defense-damaging subject, a subject the prosecution would have been forbidden to introduce because of its irrelevance to the crimes under discussion.

He brought up Maria's letter to a friend written several weeks before the final coma in which she summarized her suspicions about Von Bülow. Then Famiglietti concluded with a sprinkling of random items that, if not incriminating, were certainly intriguing: the only locked closet at Clarendon Court was Von Bülow's; nothing in the black bag belonged to Sunny; Maria never saw tranquilizers in her mistress's possession after the first coma; Maria had seen needles in Von Bülow's bathroom in England and Spain.

As Judge Needham recessed the court at the conclusion of Maria's testimony, a reporter stood at the clerk's desk examining the photos of Von Bülow's London apartment.

"Nice place," he commented to himself.

Von Bülow, who was standing next to him, added sotto voce, "For a man who had nothing."

XXI

AFTER the bravura performances of Alexander and Maria, anything short of a surprise appearance by the victim would have been anticlimactic. But so overwhelming were Maria and Alexander's stories that the succession of household servants brought on by the prosecution had a steadying as well as the intended corroborating effect. It again gave glimpses of the Von Bülows' nineteenth-century living style as well as the human faces of those who maintained it. If the story lacked the scene in the drawing room where the detective assembles all members of the household staff, the prosecution would now present them one at a time.

Few people who listened to the testimony of houseman John Berdy, cook Irene Silvia, or the maid Mrs. Sullivan didn't reflect on how nice it would be to be looked after by such decent, kindly people.

Houseman Berdy confirmed that on the fateful morning at the end of 1979 when Maria felt her mistress was in trouble Von Bülow had told him about 10:30 or 11:00 that Mrs. Von Bülow was still asleep; Berdy had seen Maria four or five times that day; she was upset but did not specifically complain to him that it was because Von Bülow was not phoning the doctor; in all the time Berdy worked for her, he never saw Mrs. Von Bülow take a drink.

Mrs. Sullivan affirmed that Maria had indeed been tearfully upset that day, at first because she was barred from the bedroom, later because no doctor was called; she testified that she had seen nothing unusual about Mrs. Von Bülow the day before; she had been kept from cleaning the bedroom the entire day of December 27, 1979; when she did (after her mistress was rushed to the hospital), the bed was wet, as was the bathroom floor; she had seen no empty vials, no needles, nothing unusual.

Perhaps the most significant part of Mrs. Sullivan's testimony from the prosecution's point of view was her claim that, as she waited in the library from nine to eleven o'clock that final morning for Mrs. Von Bülow to emerge so that she could clean the bedroom, she saw Mr. Von Bülow go in and out of the bedroom three separate times, not the one time he stated.

On cross-examination she revealed a hint of disapproval of Sunny's treatment of her husband. "She wanted him with her at all times," the tiny, white-haired woman sniffed. "That's why he went for walks early in the morning. It was the only time he could get away from her." Mrs. Sullivan reinstated herself as a prosecution witness by admitting she had never seen Mrs. Von Bülow take a drink.

When Famiglietti rose to ask Mrs. Sullivan a final question he slapped his vest pockets looking for something, then stunned the courtroom as well as the seventy-eight-year-old woman by saying "Mrs. Sullivan, did you take my pen?" This was the first of several attacks of Famiglietti's playfulness.

Lieutenant Ripa of the Newport Fire Department took the stand to describe receiving the emergency call from Clarendon Court on December 21, 1980, finding Mrs. Von Bülow unconscious in a puddle of urine on the bathroom floor, and rushing her to the Newport Hospital, where the doctor on duty, Gerhard Meier, had taken one look at her and said, "This is an obvious drug overdose."

With that lead-in, the next day's testimony started off with Dr. Gerhard Meier. It seemed the merest reference to a player in the drama evoked that player's instant appearance in the courtroom.

Dr. Meier's forty-three years and dark beard did not conceal a babyish face and a somewhat petulant manner. The condescension Europeans sometimes feel toward Americans—especially cosmopolitan Europeans transplanted to small American towns—spilled over in the doctor's apparent attitude toward the Von Bülow trial.

He maintained an air of bemused toleration toward the proceedings as well as a puzzling flippancy toward both counsel.

The most important part of his lengthy testimony was that because of a conversation he had had with one of the doctors treating Mrs. Von Bülow's coma the previous year, Meier, as soon as he received Mrs. Von Bülow in the emergency room, made plans to test her insulin level. The earlier conversation had been with a Dr. Marc Feller, who had expressed bafflement as to the cause of his coma patient's low blood sugar. At the time Meier had said to him, "Do not rule out the surreptitious administration of medication."

Famiglietti did not ask him the reason for this suspicion, but asked instead if insulin was a blood sugar–lowering agent.

"It is," said Meier as if to a child who had caught on.

Meier made a firm point that on December 21, 1980, his immediate concern was saving the life of this woman whose heartbeat of a faint 35 to 40 per minute and whose body temperature of 81.6°—seventeen degrees below normal—put her near death. Still, when a technician was drawing the usual blood samples for testing patients inexplicably unconscious, he told her to draw a few extra tubes of blood. When asked if he had specifically at this time mentioned an insulin test, he replied, "That was what I had in mind and I may have mumbled something."

Shortly after Mrs. Von Bülow's arrival Meier had asked her husband for background information. Von Bülow said that his wife had not, to his knowledge, taken any pills that might have caused her coma, nor had she drunk any alcohol. (This would have been a good time for Von Bülow to have told the doctor about the black bag with its drugs and needles that his lawyers were now claiming belonged to his wife. For some reason, Famiglietti did not point out this omission.)

After five minutes of conversation with Von Bülow, Meier was interrupted by a nurse who told him to return to the emergency room immediately: Mrs. Von Bülow had gone into cardiac arrest. He rushed to her and successfully resuscitated her.

When the results of the insulin tests came in days later from the laboratory in California they showed that Sunny's blood on admission to the hospital contained 216 milligrams per centum of insulin, a level Dr. Meier termed "incredibly high." This crucial fact had been brought out in Famiglietti's opening statement and was referred to frequently by Fahringer, who in his cross-examination of Meier didn't contest the figure but only the blood sample it described.

At 1:15 ("give or take fifteen minutes") Meier ordered an insulin level test taken on original blood. He did this verbally to a technician whose name he couldn't recall and he didn't write down the order on a request slip until 2 P.M. He had not ordered the patient's stomach pumped and he admitted forgetting to order the c-peptide test which would have shown whether her system contained exogenous as opposed to natural insulin (and which would have saved the prosecution the considerable time and effort they spent proving the insulin had been injected rather than naturally produced).

At 3:30 Meier called Dr. Stock in New York for further background information on the patient and heard again about the hypoglycemia diagnosis. He had definitely ordered the insulin test before talking with Stock, although tests showed she had an amobarbitol level in her blood of 1.06 mg per centum, which Meier now testified was not a toxic level (although he had told the grand jury that in one case a similar level had been "related" to a patient's death).

Famiglietti used Meier to begin his course in insulin endocrinology for the jurors' benefit; there would be much more of this with later witnesses.

When his turn with Meier came, Fahringer pounced on the surreptitious-administration suspicion, asking Meier if he had any judgments about who had administered the medication. Meier said he did not.

"And," Fahringer went on, "a surreptitious administration could be self-induced, couldn't it?"

"Of course." Meier smiled.

Fahringer roamed over considerable territory with Meier, but his main points were the high level of amobarbitol in Sunny's blood and the possibility that the insulin tests had been performed on blood taken *after* the glucose pushes, which would make her high insulin level far less extraordinary. Indeed, the prosecution's case for the second count relied heavily on the high insulin and low blood sugar levels in Sunny *on admission* to the hospital. He also got Meier to admit that Sunny's coma may have been caused by a combination of factors: her low body temperature, barbiturates, excessive aspirin (156 mg per centum was found in her urine, a high but not toxic level).

When Famiglietti reexamined the witness he asked if Meier believed barbiturates were the sole cause of Sunny's coma. Meier did not. The doctor told of a case in which the patient had survived unharmed a hundred times Sunny's barbiturate level, adding that the damage done by barbiturates depends on many other factors, such as the patient's age, general health, underlying disease, presence of other agents. In Sunny's case these things pointed to her barbiturate level as unimportant.

Did Meier think the low body temperature was the coma's *cause*? "In all likelihood," he replied, "it was the *effect.*"

Next on the stand were the technicians from Newport Hospital who had handled the blood tests on Sunny: Cheryl Edwards and Debra Azevedo. They confirmed the prosecution's version of the events: that Cheryl had been ordered by Meier to draw extra blood from Mrs. Von Bülow on admission well before the first glucose push and Debra had indeed drawn tubes from this initial rack of virgin blood, and not from samples that would reflect the pumped glucose. They easily assented to Famiglietti's hints that Dr. Meier was a man who expected his orders carried out instantly.

Fahringer went at Cheryl Edwards. Hadn't she told him and his colleague John Sheehan when they had interviewed her last August that she had received the order to run the insulin test *while* she was drawing her second round of blood samples? Yes, but ... And hadn't she said that she had been carrying those samples back to the lab when she went to tell the others about the insulin test order? Yes, but ...

While this version didn't by any means prove the insulin test had been taken on the second rather than the first blood samples, it went far toward raising the possibility of such a mixup. In defending Von Bülow, all the defense had to do was establish reasonable doubt that things happened as the prosecution maintained. Fahringer was cutting the technician's answers short. It became clear she wanted to explain something.

When Famiglietti got her back, she blurted her story. When

Fahringer and Sheehan had interviewed her last summer, she was intimidated and confused. At home later the same evening, she thought through her movements on December 21, 1980, and realized that she had misspoken to Fahringer about the day's sequence of events. She had encountered Meier as she was on her way to pick up request slips. The time was about 1:20. On hearing the urgency of his order, Edwards changed course and returned to the laboratory to pass along his instructions before returning to draw more blood.

When she realized her mistake in her account to the lawyers, Edwards made several attempts to reach John Sheehan to tell him but was unsuccessful. In somewhat of a panic, Edwards phoned Lieutenant Reise to tell him of the altered version she had given the defense lawyers. Reise said, "Don't worry about it."

Famiglietti also extracted the curious information that after giving their stories to Fahringer and Sheehan the lab technicians received a dozen red roses from the lawyers. Cheryl Edwards now took this opportunity to thank Herald Fahringer across the courtroom. The Rhode Islanders were showing the New York lawyer no mercy.

Debra Azevedo, too, testified that she had been confused by Fahringer the previous August into allowing for the possibility of a blood sample mixup, having told him that perhaps Cheryl Edwards had arrived in the lab with the second batch of samples while she was still spinning the first batch down into serum, that the two batches may have been intermingled.

Azevedo, however, was more specific in describing Fahringer's role in the confusion by his insistence "Couldn't it have happened this way?" Finally she agreed that maybe it could have, but in a calmer moment she remembered it was as she told Lieutenant Reise and as she was now testifying here in court: she got the order for the insulin test *before* there was any blood other than the first, virginal batch. She had immediately taken blood sufficient for an insulin test, which had to be performed in Boston, and frozen it to be shipped the next day, the Newport Hospital not being equipped for the insulin test.

Fahringer said he had no idea he had intimidated or confused either woman.

"Well, you did," Azevedo said.

A third woman who was on duty with the other two that Sunday, Mary Beth Brucker, was put on the stand to corroborate the final, unconfused versions of her two colleagues. She did so with no doubt or hesitation.

During her brief testimony, Brucker made reference to the hospital's Stanton Room. Famiglietti, to avoid confusion, asked her about the room's name.

"That was named after someone, wasn't it?" he said, then added, "Some *rich* person?"

Von Bülow, who up till now had sat through the trial rarely reacting to anything that was said by more than a reddening, now reacted vociferously with a kind of silent but visible outrage at Famiglietti's slur on those Von Bülow considered to be his people.

A final hospital employee was brought on with her record books to corroborate the timing of medical testimony so far. It was discovered that three out of four entries she was required to log were mistaken. It was a chilling glimpse at the listless execution of clerical tasks which one day, today for instance, might be very important. Two other Newport Hospital employees reinforced the testimony of Edwards and Azevedo.

Famiglietti brought on a series of witnesses to establish the "chain of custody" of Sunny Von Bülow's blood sample that had to leave Newport Hospital in order to be tested for insulin level. With two of the witnesses flown in from California for no more than ten minutes' testimony apiece, it was an impressive display of the care and expense the state of Rhode Island was prepared to go to to leave no weakness in its case against Claus Von Bülow.

They traced the shipping procedures—packing the tubes in dry ice and Styrofoam; driving the package to the Boston Medical Laboratory, where it was decided to reship the sample to the Bio-Science Laboratory in Anaheim, California; the repacking and forwarding by commercial airliner which was met by a delivery truck at the Los Angeles airport and driven to the Anaheim laboratory. Any impression Fahringer may have hoped to create of a test tube of frozen blood being thrown to who-knew-what winds was dispelled by the precise, fastidious procedures recapitulated by the Boston and California technicians.

Before Dr. Janis Gailitis, Sunny Von Bülow's Newport doctor, took the stand Tuesday morning, February 16, there was a two-hour conference in Judge Needham's chambers that culminated in the jurors' being summoned one at a time. No one knew what was going on, but rumors of mistrial filled the air.

When the lawyers emerged they were tightlipped in their refusal to discuss what went on. The press were beside themselves. At the lunch recess, a large group of them, looking a little like a South American coup d'état, barged into Judge Needham's chambers and were pushed back by a one man counterrevolution. Standing in shirt-sleeves in the door to his chambers he blasted the reporters' affrontery in storming his private rooms demanding information.

"This was an in-chambers conference," he snarled. "That's all you're entitled to report. You can speculate any God-damned way you want!"

Later, when he took the bench, he again expressed his outrage at the press's "invasion," saying that if it happened again the press would find its numbers seriously curtailed.

Word came out that the conference concerned defense anger over an interview Famiglietti had given over the weekend naming future defense witnesses and mentioning that one of the witnesses they might call was a prostitute. This apparently violated a pledge to keep these names secret in case the defense lawyers wanted to alter their strategy or if a witness, for one reason or another, became unavailable. As for the prostitute, Fahringer feared linking her to Von Bülow might tarnish his client's image—although it developed that this image, with certain segments of the public at least, was untarnishable.

Each juror was brought in and asked if he or she had heard anything about the Famiglietti interview. It was a lesson in courtroom skirmishes. The disagreement between counsel passed without a trace; the hostility it set in motion between Needham and the press lingered.

Dr. Janis Gailitis is chief of medicine at Newport Hospital, where he has a reputation as an exacting professional. The tall, balding doctor spent the first thirty-five of his sixty-seven years in Europe, having been born in Latvia. When the Russians absorbed the small country in 1944, he emigrated to Germany. He came to America in 1950 and served an internship at Newport Hospital, where he remained. His Newport personal life overlapped that of the Von Bülows in only one area: the Newport Music Festival, of which they support and of which he is vice-president.

On the stand he was led by Famiglietti through his key involvement with Sunny Von Bülow's two comas. He described in detail the phone call from Von Bülow on December 27, 1979, in which Von Bülow described his wife as being unconscious from liquor, adding that she was an alcoholic. He told of the later, more frantic phone call in which Von Bülow urged him to come immediately; of finding Sunny gasping, near death; of resuscitating her and rushing her to Newport Hospital.

In detail he described the extraordinary test findings: a low blood sugar level (41 mg per centum), which prompted a massive glucose (25 grams) injection; when her sugar level was tested *after* this, it was found to be *far lower* (20 mg per centum). (This was one of the main indicators that her blood sugar was being rapidly "eaten" by something in her system, most likely a large amount of insulin.)

Gailitis said he only ordered an insulin test after the glucose push failed to raise the patient's blood sugar, which meant it was too late to reveal the insulin level on her admission to the hospital. Famiglietti asked if he got the results of the insulin tests.

Gailitis said, "I certainly did."

There was a long pause in which Gailitis and Famiglietti stared at each other. Finally Famiglietti said, "I thought you were going to give me the results."

"You didn't ask me," Gailitis smiled. "I was told not to volunteer anything." Charming as this was, it was dangerous ground as it betrayed a degree of coaching on the part of the prosecutor which the defense could have taken as a glimpse of a much larger conspiracy. But the doctor's ingenuousness, coupled with his obvious intelligence, served to defuse the moment and it passed with merely a chuckle from Fahringer and the courtroom.

Gailitis continued. The first insulin test taken at midnight showed a level of 72 micro-units per milliliter, a high but not alarming amount; the one done at 7 A.M. showed a level of 54 micro-units per milliliter, indicating her system was returning to normal. The other tests showed Sunny had had no alcohol (Gailitis adding that alcohol clears the system quickly), no oral antidiabetic agents, and only a small level of aspirin.

He talked of the meeting with Von Bülow in which he was told of Sunny's alcoholism, her shyness, her depression, her use of tranquilizers. Gailitis was so alarmed by this briefing that he went directly to talk with the patient. It wasn't till Fahringer's cross-examination, however, that Gailitis was allowed to say how he recounted her husband's accusations to Sunny, who denied only the alcoholism.

Ironically, Gailitis was somewhat of a specialist in alcoholism; in this case, however, his wide experience may have led him from the truth rather than toward it. It is most common, he testified, for alcoholics to deny their condition.

If, in hindsight, we see Sunny's denial as a feeble protest against her husband's lie, we have to bemoan its failure as a distress signal that the husband was conspiring against her; the other charges—shyness, depression—were vague, alcoholism specific. It is logical that she settled on this for denial. It is also possible that the other charges—unlike the alcoholism—had some truth. As this campaign of Von Bülow's to label his wife an alcoholic was perhaps the most flagrant symptom of his alleged plot, it is tragic that Gailitis disbelieved Sunny's denial.

Fahringer got Gailitis to recall telling the state police that at no time did he suspect foul play; but Famiglietti countered this with another recollection: his saying at the time that Sunny's illness was "most puzzling."

Perhaps the most intriguing part of Gailitis's four hours of testimony was his reading of Von Bülow's letter to him, written four weeks after his wife's first coma. Von Bülow wrote his version of what happened on the fateful day: he assumed his wife was sleeping off a drunk, as he had seen her do many times before; only when her breathing became erratic did he have any reason for alarm, at which point he urged Dr. Gailitis to come immediately.

As Gailitis read the plaintive phrases "Have I stated everything fairly? Was I to blame?" the totally contradictory testimony of Maria Schrallhammer was still reverberating in courtroom ears. It was indeed the most head-on confrontation between two "testimonies"— and a rare instance of the court hearing Von Bülow's version of anything. Where Maria had described Mrs. Von Bülow throughout that long day as moaning, unmoving in an uncomfortable position, cold and completely unconscious, Von Bülow wrote to Gailitis that she had been merely sleeping, that she had gotten up from time to time to go to the bathroom.

The defense clearly felt the letter was exculpatory; Famiglietti referred to it off the record as a "cover-your-ass letter."

The two versions might still be viewed as two different interpretations of the same thing (except for Von Bülow's asserting that Sunny had gotten out of bed several times) until the third-party, eyewitness testimony that definitely reinforced Maria's version of what happened throughout the day and threw heavy doubt on Von Bülow's: Gailitis's harrowing story of finding Sunny gasping, turning blue, and almost immediately upon his arrival going into cardiac arrest.

Before finishing with Newport Hospital, Famiglietti brought on another of its doctors, Marvin Chernow, who related the results of the blood tests that were taken on Mrs. Von Bülow, tests he oversaw on Monday following her Sunday collapse, when the hospital returned to more normal, weekday operations. Chernow turned out to be a stand-in for one of his employees who had actually run the tests, a Nigerian exchange student who had since returned to Nigeria, with the unexportable name Chukwemaka Onyenokoproh. (When Famiglietti tripped this name effortlessly from his tongue, Judge Needham said to the courtroom, "He's spent a month practicing that pronunciation.")

And so the polyglot procession of witnesses, which had already brought in an Austrian prince, a German maid, Latvian and German doctors, and Chicano and South Korean lab technicians, was now broadened still further by an African lost in a steaming Nigerian jungle, who possibly had information relevant to the comas of Sunny Von Bülow.

Outside the courtroom the seemingly endless winter had vanished and been replaced by a sunny day with temperatures climbing into the fifties. Reporters and jurors trotted off for lunch at nearby restaurants leaving overcoats in the courthouse, sheriffs opened the courthouse windows to flush out January air with the more benevolent February stuff.

The pretty day was merely a respite, of course. Rhode Island had plenty of winter in store; but the spring preview was a strong reminder that time passes, the slowest trials move toward a conclusion, and the most snarled mysteries eventually unravel.

XXII

THE Von Bülow trial had been going six weeks; the days when spectators could wander in at any time and find a seat were long over. Crowds now lined up outside the courthouse as early as 6 A.M. to assure seats when the doors opened at 8:30. Some were regulars; others were people who wanted to experience just one day of the famous case.

The journalists with fixed seats in the alternate jury box, having started the trial carrying the entire journalistic burden, were now the merest nucleus of a press army bivouacked in the Colony House from which they phoned or word-processed their dispatches to newspapers and news shows around the globe. Some of the original fourteen journalists were outranked by newcomers, in this case the mighty network stars who were now ambling into town.

Regardless of power pecking order, the journalists present from the start developed a camaraderie with each other and with the trial's principals that the late arrivals never achieved. To the important parvenues the principals would make formal pronouncements; to the pioneers they would make offhand remarks.

In these informal asides, Von Bülow lost no opportunity to kick the prosecution. When someone remarked to him about the icy weather, he replied, "If they'd had the trial in November as we wanted you wouldn't have to suffer through this, but that was their ploy" (meaning that the delay gave them more time to gather evidence against him).

For the most part he was genial and in good spirits, even when coming fresh from devastating courtroom assaults. After a long morning's testimony about opening his closet and finding the black bag, Von Bülow said to a reporter, "Do you know what they found when they finally got into my closet? A closet queen!" His attempting humor at all was remarkable, if the wit was not.

Another Von Bülow conversational ploy was to twist the attention to his predicament. A female reporter, known to the defense as a walking ambush of trial-related questions, approached him with "Mr. Von Bülow, I hate to ask you this"—Von Bülow stiffened— "but do you have a light?" He chuckled in relief. "Of course," he said smoothly. "Unless of course I am to be accused of arson."

Von Bülow, often artfully down-to-earth in his exchanges with the press, could sometimes be remarkably tactless. Once, talking with a writer about journalistic errors, he mentioned a magazine article on Palm Beach. "It was extraordinary," he said. "When the article came out full of quotes from Palm Beachers, no one knew *any* of them." He'd forgotten he was talking to a working journalist and not Gloria Vanderbilt.

The most revealing snatches of conversation were perhaps those furthest removed from the business at hand. He once got into a monologue on America's coal resources, how "we" hadn't scratched the surface of this asset or exploited it to motivate Poles and Russians and other governments "as we do with grain." It was a virtuoso turn of big-think, statesmanlike vocalizing, the kind that over brandy and cigars would have comforted a power dinner in Washington or London.

Another time he ruminated with equal eloquence over the United States government's folly in breaking up IBM. Von Bülow would address these remarks to writers with the courteous condescension of the head of a vast corporation dealing with a not-too-bright board of directors.

Affable and relaxed as Von Bülow was during these recesses, conversing with him was unnerving and perilous. Just below the surface lurked attitudes that could abruptly end the civility that enabled communication.

Of all the leading players Herald Fahringer was perhaps the least communicative to the press. Unlike his client and his legal sidekick, he never loitered in the corridor during recess (for that matter neither did Famiglietti).

He was aware, however, of the ready access he had to national media by the simple act of raising his head from his briefcase as he packed it to leave his table. If he wanted input in the next day's accounts of the Von Bülow trial, he merely lingered at the defense table until a reporter approached him. As soon as he was seen talking to one, the others would quickly cluster around him.

Journalists tugging at the principals' sleeves for exclusive tidbits diminished after the first weeks. And the sleeve-tugging was not all on one side. Lieutenant Reise revealed a proprietary interest in the case he had such a major role in assembling by chiding a writer for missing the first part of Dr. Gailitis's testimony.

"You weren't in the press box this morning," he said despairingly. "This is very important testimony." The writer assured Reise he had watched Gailitis on the Colony House monitor.

For the most part the adversaries kept a gentlemanly distance. One place this was not possible was the men's room which was the setting for some close encounters. At one point the hunter and his prey, Famiglietti and Von Bülow, found themselves standing side by side. Famiglietti greeted the defendant cheerfully and Von Bülow replied, "I'm saying nothing or you'll consider it a statement."

This jibe prompted Famiglietti to tell Von Bülow a joke. A peasant from the Russian outlands visits Moscow and at a lunch counter finds himself sitting next to a famous commissar. The rustic rejoices that in this wonderful country he, a peasant, can find himself next to such an important man. The peasant's experience is repeated with a ballet star and an astronaut. Finally he finds himself standing at a urinal next to a general, a hero of the revolution. Again he praises the egalitarian society but adds, "Tell me, General, why it is that with me there is a splashing sound and with you there is none?"

"Because I am pissing on your coat, you lowly cur of a peasant."

Von Bülow laughed and reciprocated with a story about Henry Ford II offering an official who impressed him a gift of a new Lincoln. The official said it would be improper to accept such a thing without paying for it. "All right," Ford replied, "pay me five dollars."

"In that case," said the official, "I'll take two."

* * *

A large number of press people stayed at the well-known Newport hotel, the Viking, which was a short walk from the courthouse and which offered reporters a good rate. Those with fatter expense accounts, the television people mostly, stayed with Von Bülow and his lawyers at the Sheraton Islander; the bar then became an evening hangout, even after it was apparent neither Von Bülow or Fahringer would amble in for a nightcap.

Jack Reise was the only one of the prosecution principals who lived in Newport, but he was a family man not given to bar-sitting. Famiglietti and Susan McGuirl both drove considerable distances each night to homes in the Providence area, as did Judge Needham. John Sheehan had the press to himself at night in the Sheraton bar; it soon evolved, however, that if they weren't mad at him for a bum lead, he was mad at them for a slur on his client.

Very shortly after the trial's beginning, a number of townspeople would wait to see Von Bülow enter the courthouse or, if they encountered him on the street, would greet him encouragingly. He was, after all, the star of the biggest spectacle Newport had ever hosted. As the trial progressed and each day's paper had accounts of two or three new witnesses incriminating him, Von Bülow became more and more of a martyred hero to a growing body of Newporters.

While the defense had been unable to impeach either the judgments or the actions of the two Newport doctors, Meier and Gailitis, they did not enjoy the professional standing of the prosecution's next witness, Dr. Harris Funkenstein, a prominent neurologist who had treated Sunny Von Bülow on her arrival at Boston's Peter Bent Brigham Hospital. Short, bald, and with rimless glasses, Funkenstein looked every bit the punctilious scientist.

Funkenstein's main testimony was that Sunny's coma was caused beyond doubt by her drastically low blood sugar, which in turn had caused permanent brain damage. He told of three causes for such hypoglycemic comas: an insulin-secreting tumor; an unusual form of alcoholism coupled with a liver disorder; and insulin injected from outside the body (exogenous).

A number of tests had ruled out both a tumor or liver dysfunction, leaving, in Funkenstein's opinion, only one possibility: exogenous insulin. Barbiturates had been eliminated, as the test results had shown the level to be of dubious significance; more to the point, had barbiturates been involved, Funkenstein said, the victim would have been at her worst state when the rescue squad arrived at Clarendon Court (at which time she showed a normal blood pressure), not later in the hospital, where her coma *deepened*.

Had Dr. Funkenstein been alerted to the possibility of aspirin overdose? Of subdural hemotoma? Of the low body temperature? All these possibilities had been explored in an effort to discover how a "woman previously healthy had, within a matter of hours, developed a coma which appeared to be irreversible."

Famiglietti was savoring the moment. "You came to the medical conclusion," he said, his pace slower than usual, "that the only viable diagnosis for her coma was exogenous insulin?"

"That is correct," Funkenstein said matter-of-factly.

After a pause, Famiglietti asked the doctor if he had relayed this opinion to any family member. Yes, Funkenstein had asked the patient's daughter, Mrs. Kneissl, if her mother had access to insulin. The daughter knew of no way her mother could have gotten it or, indeed, wanted it.

Before turning the witness over to the defense, Famiglietti extracted some interesting information on another issue, the retrograde amnesia that had been offered as one explanation for Sunny's not having any recollection of events preceding her first coma. Funkenstein stated that such forgetfulness is common with coma victims. He also testified that he experienced about two cases a year of coma caused by diabetics injecting too much insulin into themselves.

Fahringer went at the Boston doctor with an energy that seemed an acknowledgment of the harm being done his client. The New York lawyer also revealed having done a formidable amount of medical homework.

Had Dr. Funkenstein seen the results of the tests done on Sunny in April of 1980? The tests had shown an equally low blood sugar level of 23 and 28 mg per centum, yet she had shown no symptoms whatsoever. The doctor was aware of those tests but said the present coma was caused by low blood sugar working *in conjunction* with other factors—the cold floor, the barbiturates—but that the blood sugar was the primary cause.

At one point Fahringer asked Dr. Funkenstein if Mr. Von

Bülow had accompanied his comatose wife to the Boston hospital. Funkenstein said he did not recall seeing him. At this Von Bülow showed one of his rare reactions: from his seat at the defense table he shook his head vigorously "no."

It was later established he had indeed ridden in the ambulance to Boston, making it even odder he would choose this unimportant fact to protest after the hours of incriminating testimony he had suffered impassively from Alexander, Maria, and the two Newport doctors. Later, during recess, a writer remarked to Von Bülow that Funkenstein was a good witness in that he could render complicated medical material understandable to laymen.

"Yes," said Von Bülow loftily, "he's a good presenter." He maintained his connoisseur's appreciation of style—even for his own executioner.

Fahringer launched his main attack. If Dr. Funkenstein had suspected exogenous insulin, *why had he not mentioned it in his report*? Funkenstein was ready. First, he had not come to this conclusion until after several days' reflection. There were other reasons. "We did not know the woman well," he said. "We had heard conflicting stories . . ."

Fahringer pounced. What stories? From whom?

They had heard about "prior illnesses," the doctor said delicately and about "depression." Fahringer clearly felt Funkenstein had heard harsh accusations about his client, but the doctor emphasized the possibility of depression. "We believe her coma was from exogenous insulin. Our leading hypothesis was that this had been self-induced."

Fahringer was dumbfounded. "But you would not put *that* in your hospital records, these complete records that go on for two weeks?"

Calmly, Funkenstein lifted the issue from the emotional to the coldly practical level. "Questions about suicide are only relevant if the patient is alive to . . . require further treatment. It did not seem important in terms of managing her at that point."

This unprepossessing witness, so damaging to many of the defense theories on how Sunny went into coma (barbiturates, eating sweets, alcoholism), reached a climax of drama that bordered on catharsis. Fahringer took him again through the other extraordinary circumstances leading to the coma. If high enough, couldn't amobarbitol cause coma? Well, yes, but . . . if high enough, could aspirin in the blood cause coma? Yes, but . . . if high enough, couldn't low body temperature cause coma? Yes. It was apparent Funkenstein was eager to say more.

Famiglietti leaped to his feet. "*Were* they high enough?"

"No!" Funkenstein nearly yelled.

Famiglietti next called Lieutenant Reise and Detective Joseph Miranda, who spoke of Alexander von Auersperg's bringing the black bag and its contents to police headquarters on March 13, 1981, Reise turning it over to the state toxicologist on March 20.

Miranda told of accompanying Reise to Clarendon Court on the night of April 21, 1981, and setting out to search the house while Reise interviewed Von Bülow in the library. Miranda went directly to Von Bülow's closet, which was unlocked. Miranda spoke of leaving the closet briefly while he awaited the arrival of the police photographer, during which time Von Bülow ducked past the closet on his way to his study to get cigarettes. Miranda returned after only two or three minutes to find the closet locked.

With this, as with the other most damaging revelations about his behavior, courtroom spectators glanced at Von Bülow. As usual, he sat impassively and, on this instance, maintained his normal color.

Dr. Ronald Gamberdella of the Bio-Science Laboratory in Long Island related having received a used needle plus several substances for analysis from Dr. Stock. He did a washing of the needle, sending one sample to their lab in Maryland, another to their lab in Boston for further analysis.

So far the Von Bülow trial had given the press and public so much drama that the courtroom had grown accustomed to its daily ration of sensation. Still, as the rumors of the imminent appearance of Von Bülow's love, Alexandra Isles, crescendoed, excitement mounted apace.

Up to now the trial had focused on *whether* Von Bülow did what the state accused him of and *how* he might have done it. Now it would perhaps be seen *why* he did it—at least for those to whom fifteen million dollars was insufficient motive. Besides, Alexandra Isles was a good-looking television actress and to date the unfolding story, which lacked little else, lacked a romantic angle.

The press particularly was thrilled. Lovers are to tabloid readers what miracles are to the devout: they can exist without them, but when they turn up, they validate the preoccupation.

One person—Alexandra herself—was not so enthusiastic about this appearance, and her reluctance caused considerable behind-the-scenes drama that never got into the newspapers. When she refused to come voluntarily, Famiglietti served her with a subpoena. Accompanied by a lawyer, she headed for Rhode Island but was still determined to offer the minimum the law allowed.

When hotel accommodations were discussed with the Attorney General's Office, she opted to stay at the Sheraton Islander, but they vetoed that foolhardy notion. (Her lawyer later denied that Alexandra was aware Von Bülow was staying there.) She was put instead in the Biltmore in Providence—for one reason, to keep her from the press until Famiglietti had a chance to talk with her.

The prosecutor was determined to get some idea of her testimony before actually calling her to the stand; a woman who had been in love with the defendant (and might still be) could be dangerous before a jury. Once on the stand she could make statements that would disrupt a case that was going quite well without her.

Famiglietti delegated Deputy Attorney General Susan McGuirl to feel out Alexandra's state of mind and her trustworthiness as a witness. Here again Alexandra was less than cooperative. When she and her lawyer arrived in the rooms reserved for them, they were immediately "out." Susan was told they were in the coffee shop; arriving there, she was told they had just left.

Susan finally caught Alexandra in her room around 10 P.M. Through a slightly cracked door she told Susan she would not talk with her, but her attorney would. The attorney came to the door and told McGuirl his client would not speak with anyone until she was on the witness stand.

Susan consulted with Famiglietti, who held to his determination to talk with Alexandra before calling her to the witness stand. They decided to move Alexandra and her attorney down to Newport's Treadway Inn where, according to Famiglietti, "they'd be stuck." When they were ensconced there, Susan McGuirl tried again to confer with them, but met equal determination to do only what the law demanded.

Susan applied pressure. "Look," she told them
"I can continue your subpoena and keep you h
cooperate with us, we won't cooperate with yo
out of Newport."

It began to look like an impasse, but finally the out-of-tow..
players weakened; Susan was granted a meeting, not with Alexandra, but with her lawyer. When Susan arrived at the Treadway
room for the interview she was pleased to see that Alexandra was
present. In a dark skirt and dark printed blouse, she was prettier
than Susan had thought from her photos. Alexandra was pleasant
to Susan, almost gracious. Susan sat in one of the room's two easy
chairs facing the lawyer, who sat in the other. Alexandra sat
quietly on the edge of the bed.

Ignoring the fact that the meeting was supposed to be between
the two lawyers, Susan addressed her questions to Alexandra; the
lawyer answered.

Alexandra merely watched and would occasionally nod as
Susan outlined the areas the prosecution hoped to cover in her
testimony. At one point the lawyer hesitated in a reply and Alexandra broke in, answering for him. Little by little, Alexandra took
over the conversation, especially as it approached the aspects of
testifying that most worried her.

She had a twelve-year-old son, she told Susan; she was anxious
to keep him out of the testimony. Would they agree not to ask any
questions about him? Susan was delighted to be able to accommodate the woman's concern for her family. Isles was particularly
anxious not to be made to appear a kept woman. But would
Alexandra be willing to be open about the nature of the relationship? Susan asked, recalling that Alexandra had told state police
she and Von Bülow were "just good friends."

Yes, Alexandra replied, she was not ashamed of that, but she
hated the press's use of the word "mistress," which to her meant
somebody who is supported financially by a married man.

And that was not the case?

No, it wasn't, Alexandra said firmly.

Susan saw no problem. She would see to it that the prosecutor
asked Alexandra questions establishing her financial independence. With each assurance Susan could see she was making more
of an ally of Alexandra. At the same time, Susan was growing

...easingly secure that Alexandra would make a good witness for
..e prosecution. She seemed honest and decent. On the other
hand, Susan worried that these good qualities might rub off on
Von Bülow; jurors might feel such a sweet, lovely woman couldn't
have a prolonged love affair with a murderer. Nevertheless,
Susan's inclination was to take the chance.

Receiving news of the breakthrough from Susan, Famiglietti
was hopeful but wanted to see for himself. He had spent a long
morning in court getting important testimony from Joe Miranda.
As soon as Judge Needham recessed for lunch, Famiglietti jumped
in his Volvo and drove the short distance to the Treadway Inn.

After listening to Alexandra's candid account of her affair,
Famiglietti agreed with McGuirl that this testimony would help
the prosecution. Without intending it to come across this way,
Alexandra was painting a picture of a trusting woman being
strung along by a scoundrel. That she related the facts with no
rancor—quite the opposite—made the testimony even more potent.

Still, Famiglietti wanted more. He asked her a risky question.
"But at some point, Mrs. Isles, you must have put it to Claus."

"What do you mean?"

"Delivered him an ultimatum."

To the surprise and delight of the two prosecutors, Alexandra
said that she had. She proceeded to tell Steve of not one but two
occasions when she had told Von Bülow either to terminate his
marriage to Sunny or stop seeing her. This was new information
and very damaging to Von Bülow. Famiglietti was ecstatic.

"Will you come back to the courthouse with me and testify this
afternoon?"

She nodded yes. Famiglietti offered to have her spirited away
from the Treadway so that she could avoid reporters. He arranged
for state police to take her down a back way, where an unmarked
brown police car waited to take her the short distance to the
courthouse.

When Famiglietti reached the hotel lobby, the large group of
waiting reporters were frantic to know what had happened. The
prosecutor was beaming but would say nothing more than that
Mrs. Isles would be testifying that afternoon.

For her courtoom appearance Alexandra had added only a

black cardigan sweater to her ensemble of black skirt and dark, printed blouse with a bow of the same fabric at the neck. She wore her shoulder-length dark hair pulled back from her broad forehead revealing the only flaw in an otherwise exquisite face: slightly protruding ears. Under the high sweater collar a double strand of large pearls was just visible; she wore single-pearl earrings.

All of this served to point up the lovely eyes which, throughout her testimony, conveyed sadness and innocence. Her appearance had a definite effect on Von Bülow. As she took the stand he reddened; during her testimony he stared sullenly at the blank legal pad on the table before him; sometimes he closed his eyes; only occasionally would he sneak glances at her. (A few newspapers reported that he never once looked at her.)

She spoke in a soft voice; even Famiglietti, standing a few feet in front of her, had to ask her to repeat statements. She led the hushed courtroom through their two-year affair, the meeting, the lunches, the eventual declaration from Von Bülow.

Famiglietti asked if, when Von Bülow told her he loved her, she replied in kind.

"No," she said, "but I didn't do anything to dissuade him."

Von Bülow smiled.

Famiglietti asked at what point they had become *intimate* (early March 1979) then went on to put considerable strain on that euphemism by asking at important subsequent meetings in the on-and-off affair if they had "been intimate." She always answered forthrightly.

At the end of March 1979, Von Bülow had brought up marriage. Alexandra told the court the idea surprised and delighted her because, she said, "I loved him."

"Did you tell him you loved him?" asked Famiglietti.

"I hope so," she said softly.

Throughout her testimony Alexandra maintained a look of wide-eyed distress, the look of a child called on the carpet for a misdemeanor she never dreamed would have such repercussions. That appeared to be her precise situation. It is unlikely she had any inkling of what Von Bülow might have been plotting because of her. Their dilemma was too easily solved by the simple act of divorce. She was also a woman for whom money was always "around." Her parents were wealthy and so was her former husband. Unlike Von Bülow, she had never endured a moment's deprivation.

Famiglietti asked what Von Bülow had said to her about divorce. He was thoughtful of his wife, she said; it would save face for her if *she* were allowed to initiate the divorce. Alexandra admitted that they discussed his getting a divorce each time they met.

"Did you give him an ultimatum?"

"Yes," she replied. "I told him I thought six months would be suitable." That would put his deadline shortly before Christmas, the time of Sunny's first coma. In case that interesting juxtaposition escaped any in the courtroom, Famiglietti made a strong point of it in his summation.

Then she related her disillusion with Von Bülow's intentions, saying that she didn't doubt his sincerity so much as his ability to make a break with Sunny. At every opportunity to affix blame on Von Bülow, she dodged the implication and presented the action from his point of view.

She told of his announcing he had finally moved out of the Fifth Avenue apartment, her doubting him and phoning the apartment after a few days to be told by a servant that Mr. Von Bülow was expected home by dinnertime. When she confronted him, he had said that he *had* moved out, but returned to his family when Alexandra didn't call.

While she made it sound in the courtroom as though she had believed his excuses, the chronological events indicated otherwise. After his explanation for still living with Sunny when he had told Alexandra he had moved out, she took a job in Washington and took pains to place herself beyond Von Bülow's reach.

She told the court about his finding her in Washington, the Watergate love scene, and his offer to go to a pay phone and ask Sunny for a divorce with Alexandra standing by.

She told of her fears that Sunny's first coma was related to unhappiness over her marriage, perhaps awareness of the affair with Alexandra. It is interesting that though Von Bülow in recent months had frequently stated that Sunny had "released" him sexually, he didn't mention this to Alexandra. Those listening to her story had to wonder why she worried so about Sunny's collapses—which elsewhere she speculated might be "passive" if not active suicide attempts—if she had been assured by Von Bülow that, if something was upsetting Sunny, it was definitely *not* his love interests. Similarly, he could have reassured her that the problem could not be the threat of divorce, which Sunny now wanted more than he did.

Either Alexandra didn't believe him when he told her these things, or he didn't tell her. He was quick to reassure her, on the other hand, when the doctors concluded that Sunny's first coma had physical origins, not emotional ones. He seems to have been treading a narrow course. Having told Alexandra that Sunny's devotion to him was a problem needing time for undoing, he couldn't then turn and say their marriage plans wouldn't bother his wife in the slightest.

Of all the revelations Alexandra was making, none were more startling than the juxtaposition of dates: The climactic scene in the Watergate coffee shop, in which Alexandra portrayed Von Bülow as a man desperately in love, occurred in November, less than a month before the Von Bülows departed for Newport for Sunny's last Christmas; the deadline for her first ultimatum occurred a month before Sunny's first coma.

In recounting their winter vacations together, Alexandra's determination not to appear a loose woman worked directly against Von Bülow. By establishing that she was striving to build a family —by bringing along her child and his, for example—she was substantiating the seriousness and long-range nature of her hopes.

One of the most dramatic moments of the trial occurred when Famiglietti asked his witness if she was still seeing the defendant. She said that on the advice of lawyers she had stopped seeing him "when all this began."

"What had she thought of 'all this'?"

Without hesitation, Alexandra answered, "I thought it was a pack of nonsense."

"Do you still think it is a pack of nonsense?"

There was a long pause. Her eyes shifted and remained on Von Bülow, who doodled on his legal pad. "I don't know," she said quietly.

Famiglietti later said he fully expected her to say "Yes, I still think it is a pack of nonsense." In his summation, he would have overcome this by saying "Of course she would think it was a pack of nonsense. She was in love with the man." Her unexpected admission that the man she knew so intimately might be capable of murder was devastating for Von Bülow and a triumph for Famiglietti.

Almost immediately, the strength of Von Bülow's hold over her was underlined by her telling the court of meetings with Von Bülow after the indictment and the lawyer's admonition to stop seeing him. The effect of this shocking admission was heightened by Famiglietti's extracting from her a mention of a meeting at Christmas 1981—less than three weeks before the start of the trial —at which time they had been intimate. Even though many would admire her loyalty, there was a curious indecency to this admission of sex after their romance was exposed in the newspapers.

Famiglietti had earlier asked the promised questions that enabled her to establish her financial independence, but he clearly knew something related to money matters that he was determined to bring out. He asked if Mr. Von Bülow had given her money to buy a car. Yes, a BMW, but it was to have been used by both of them; when his leaving home looked unlikely, she offered to repay the money, but he said it was a gift. How much had it cost?

Alexandra turned plaintively to Judge Needham. "Do I have to say?"

Judge Needham asked her to answer.

"Twelve thousand dollars," she said sadly.

Perhaps realizing that this impinged on his agreement not to suggest a financial basis for the affair, Famiglietti asked her if she considered herself Von Bulow's mistress.

"Not by my standards," she replied.

"What are your standards?"

"Someone who is kept."

The spectacle of this lovely actress telling a roomful of people —and in effect the world—the most intimate details of her affair with a married man, from school Christmas programs with the kids to each time they made love—and airing before an audience feelings that are often hard for lovers to verbalize to each other —made it hard to remember that this was real and not television drama. Aside from being a major part of the saga, her courtroom appearance set up the next development, the end of her friendship with Von Bülow. Although they had made love only days before he left for Newport to stand trial, the friendship would not continue past this day.

Altogether, the testimony of Alexandra Isles was a major advance for Famiglietti. Her beauty alone made her a walking motive, but added to that was her sweetness, sincerity, refinement, motherly instincts, concern for the defendant—and the lethal testimony that at the time of the two alleged attempts Alexandra was holding a gun to Von Bülow's head. No prosecutor could have hoped for more. Before letting Alexandra off the stand, Famiglietti nonetheless tried for more—a final endorsement of her testimony's validity.

"Mrs. Isles," he said, "I have one final question. Are you still in love with the defendant?"

As she again turned her eyes to the now deeply red Von Bülow, even the buses outside seemed afraid to move. She said something inaudible which sounded like "No."

Famiglietti snapped, almost barked, "I'm sorry. Would you repeat that?"

With her eyes fixed on Von Bülow she again said, still quietly but now audibly, "I don't know."

Because Alexandra's appearance had taken the defense lawyers by surprise, Judge Needham allowed them overnight to prepare a cross-examination. To fill out the time left, George Nitis, a Ph.D. in chemistry and director of the Bio-Science Laboratory in Columbia, Maryland, testified that insulin had indeed been found on the needle forwarded to him by Dr. Ronald Gamberdella in February 1981.

When court resumed the next day, Fahringer stood and told Judge Needham that his client asked if they could waive the right to cross-examine Mrs. Isles, because his client felt "she had been put through too much already."

The state called Dr. V. J. Aggarwal of the Boston Medical Lab, who had received washings from the used needle from Dr. Gamberdella of Long Island's Bio-Science Laboratories. Aggarwal had tested the substances for toxicity—finding them to be amobarbitol and Valium—both chemicals which were also found in the needle washing.

While the courtroom drama was at its most intense, another drama had occurred behind the scenes that, had it gotten into the newspapers, would have been explosive. Defense attorney John Sheehan received a phone call in his Providence office from a man in Pennsylvania who claimed to have one of the Von Bülow jurors "in his hip pocket." For $50,000 he could fix the jury, that is, guarantee Von Bülow a hung jury.

Sheehan immediately went to Judge Needham and the prosecution. All were quick to realize that if word of the extortion plot became known, it would permanently render suspect a verdict in Von Bülow's favor and undermine the trial. The police were brought in and an effort was made to play along with the man in the hopes of arresting him. Probably smelling a setup, he abruptly stopped after three calls and was never heard from again.

XXIII

IF Alexander von Auersperg had introduced hostility into the Von Bülow courtroom, it had been controlled and civil. His mother's doctor of twenty-six years, Richard Stock, on the other hand, allowed his animosity to erupt in bitter exchanges with counsel for both sides.

Famiglietti started off by asking about Mrs. Von Bülow's present condition. As the doctor told of visiting her now every day, adding details about her appalling state, tears came to his eyes, forcing him to remove and wipe his glasses.

Stock's testimony was strong. In twenty-six years he had never seen in Mrs. Von Bülow any signs of the depression, alcoholism, or drug abuse the defense was alleging. He enumerated the signs of these problems that make them difficult to conceal, especially from a doctor. He had prescribed Valium for her, but not since 1977, two years before her first coma. In all the years he treated her he was never asked by her for drug prescriptions; it was always Von Bülow who called, sometimes for himself, sometimes for his wife.

He saw Sunny in his office two months before her 1979 coma; she was in excellent health and spirits as she always was. He received a call from Von Bülow saying that Sunny had been admitted to the Newport Hospital "in a drunken stupor." Von Bülow later elaborated on this to the doctor, affirming that Sunny's alcoholism was the reason she was rushed to the hospital.

When asked if he had relayed these allegations to Sunny, Stock said he had not wanted to jeopardize the Von Bülows' marriage;

he didn't think it was his place. Stock said that during his talks with Sunny, Von Bülow was always present, to the doctor's annoyance, implying that Von Bülow was working to avoid a confidential chat between his wife and the doctor.

Stock later admitted seeing Sunny alone on one occasion, December 18, 1980, a mere three days before she went into her final coma. At that time he found her in good health and in fine spirits. Referring to Sunny's aspirin overdose of December 1, 1980, Stock emphasized his annoyance at Von Bülow phoning the emergency number instead of phoning Stock himself, who lived only a few blocks from the Von Bülows.

When Famiglietti brought up the large number of laxatives Sunny would sometimes take, Stock grew angry and with a raised voice said, "I was not concerned with this kind of minutiae. If my patients want a doctor concerned with how many laxatives they take, they'd better go to another doctor!"

There was a long discussion of his receiving the black-bag contents from Alexander, his decision to send it to the Bio-Science Laboratory for testing ("I think they are the premier lab in the country"), the results which showed the one used needle to contain "a high concentration of insulin." When Stock learned of this, he said, he phoned Richard Kuh and told him, "Either you go to the police or I will."

At one point, Famiglietti got Stock to state that Sunny had never shown any symptoms of alcoholism, not even on her return from Austria. Von Bülow had expressed particular concern to Stock that his wife would get drunk and disgrace herself at Ala's debut, but Stock, who was present for that party, said he watched Sunny and saw her drink almost nothing.

Famiglietti moved to kill off for good Sunny's drinking problem. "Did anyone else ever indicate to you that she drank?"

Judge Needham sustained Fahringer's objection.

Famiglietti tried again. "Who was the source of information about her alcoholism?"

"Only Mr. Von Bülow," Stock said, as pleased as Famiglietti to finally get this out.

After about over an hour with Dr. Stock, Famiglietti discussed the April 1980 test results that led to the diagnosis of reactive hypoglycemia. He chose an uncharacteristically oblique form for a crucial question:

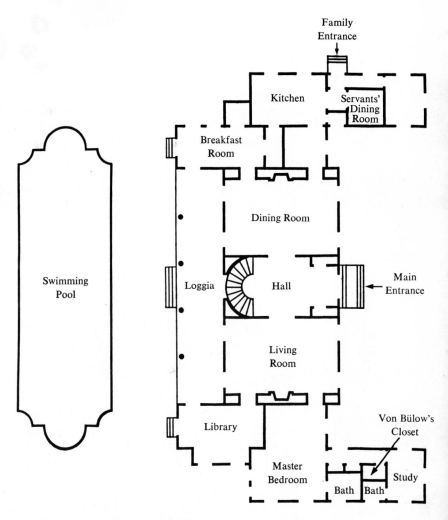

Family
Entrance

Kitchen

Servants'
Dining
Room

Breakfast
Room

Dining Room

Swimming
Pool

Loggia

Hall

Main
Entrance

Living
Room

Library

Von Bülow's
Closet

Master
Bedroom

Bath Bath

Study

Ground-floor plan of Clarendon Court.

The black bag in which the drugs and the incriminating needle were found.
(© Bryce Flynn/Picture Group)

Lieutenant Jack Reise, sitting next to the subject of his investigation at a pretrial hearing. Herald Price Fahringer, Von Bülow's lawyer, on the right.
(© Paniccia-Providence Journal/Picture Group)

A typical bench conference during the trial. From left: Judge Thomas Needham, prosecutor Stephen Famiglietti, defense lawyers Herald Price Fahringer
and John Sheehan. (© 1982 Michael Grecco/Picture Group)

Maria Schrallhammer identifies items from the black bag for Herald Fahringer. (© Sylvia-Providence Journal/Picture Group)

Prince Alexander von Auersperg testifies against his stepfather. (© 1982 Bryce Flynn/Picture Group)

Claus Von Bülow's lover, Alexandra Isles, a reluctant witness for the prosecution. (© 1982 Bryce Flynn/Picture Group)→

Alexander's sister, Ala Kneissl, during her cross-examination. (© Sylvia-Providence Journal/Picture Group)

Joy O'Neill, Sunny's exercise instructor, testifies for the defense. (© Providence Journal/Picture Group)

Von Bülow's accusers in the courtroom for the jury charge. Left to right, second row: Ala and Franz Kneissl, Maria Schrallhammer, Alexander von Auersperg, and their attorney, Richard Kuh. (© Providence Journal/Picture Group)

s hold a press conference after de-
ng their verdict. From left: Walter
nski, Barbara Connett, Pierce Gaf-
Arthur Hull, and David Taffs.
Providence Journal/Picture Group)

na Von Bülow, Claus's only child,
ng the courthouse with defense law-
ohn Sheehan after the sentencing of
ather. This was her single appearance
s trial. (© Picture Group)

Claus Von Bülow arrives at the Newport courthouse. (© Ron Manville/ Picture Group)

FAMIGLIETTI: At the time she was discharged from the hospital after the tests were performed, did you intend that that diagnosis [of hypoglycemia] apply to the cause of her coma on December 27, 1979?

STOCK: There were too many things to be established that were not established to link her reactive hypoglycemia to her coma.

FAMIGLIETTI: In your opinion, did the results of the tests performed in April and May of 1980 satisfactorily explain the 1979 coma?

FAHRINGER: Objection.

NEEDHAM: I'll allow it.

STOCK: [after asking Famiglietti to repeat the question] In my opinion they did not satisfactorily explain the cause of Martha Von Bülow's coma.

FAMIGLIETTI: At the time she was released from the hospital were you satisfied there was *any* explanation for her 1979 coma?

STOCK: [after a pause] The explanation was unpalatable to me, sir.

FAMIGLIETTI: What do you mean by "unpalatable," Doctor?

FAHRINGER: Objection.

NEEDHAM: Is that a medical opinion you're about to give, Doctor?

STOCK: Yes.

NEEDHAM: Overruled.

STOCK: I did not like to consider it. It was not something I had previously experienced in the practice of medicine. It was morally and ethically outside my experience and it was something I just found distasteful.

FAMIGLIETTI: And what was this you found distasteful?

NEEDHAM: [when Fahringer started to rise] I'm going to allow it.

STOCK: It was the surreptitious administration of insulin.

If the significance of what the doctor had just said—that he suspected that his patient while still a reasonably healthy woman was being secretly injected with insulin—had not sunk in on the courtroom, the vehemence with which Fahringer went at the witness served to underscore it.

After first attacking Stock's expertise in endocrinology, he established that in the twenty-six years he had been Sunny's doctor he saw her on an average of two hours a year. When Stock mentioned that he had seen Sunny every day during the ten days of tests in April with Von Bülow always present, Stock threw in a comment contrasting this solicitude with the scarcity of Von Bülow's hospital visits since she went into coma.

Fahringer couldn't let this pass and got off into a squabble with the doctor about the slur just as he was moving toward his main attack. When Needham broke up the off-the-point sparring, Fahringer threw himself at Stock's most alarming statement.

FAHRINGER: Do you mean to tell me that in all of 1980—and incidentally, you saw Mrs. Von Bülow alone on December eighteenth, didn't you?

STOCK: No, sir. Well, he was . . . December eighteenth, yes.

FAHRINGER: She was all by herself, wasn't she?

STOCK: Yes.

FAHRINGER: He wasn't there, was he?

STOCK: Yes. [As Fahringer started to interrupt, Stock smiled.] Yes, he wasn't there.

FAHRINGER: On that occasion, did you indicate to her in any way at all that you were concerned for her because of this yellow paste and white powder?

STOCK: I do not think it is my position as a physician to bring up things that might trouble or fracture their marriage.

FAHRINGER: Well, if you thought it was going to cause her death?

STOCK: I did not think that at that time.

FAHRINGER: During the period of these comas, did anyone ever tell you they had found insulin in a black pouch at 960 Fifth Avenue?

STOCK: No, never.

FAHRINGER: If you thought that anyone, during 1979 or 1980, was trying to poison Mrs. Von Bülow, wouldn't you have done something?

STOCK: You're on a very sensitive subject, counselor. If you're going to blow the whistle, you better make darn sure you're correct. I cannot go to one of my patients and say "I suspect your mate may be doing something harmful to you" unless I have absolute proof. I could have a suspicion and not act. We have libel laws in this country, counselor. I can't afford to make an accusation that I can't back up in court.

FAHRINGER: But you don't operate in court, do you?

STOCK: I sure am.

FAHRINGER: But you're practicing in a Park Avenue office. You're not going down to a courtroom?

STOCK: After today, every single note I write on the chart, I'm going to make sure I can read it out loud and clear in a courtroom.

FAHRINGER: Doctor, let me put this question to you. If you had suspicions that someone was trying to kill Mrs. Von Bülow in 1979 and 1980, wouldn't you have gone to her and told her?

STOCK: I'm a physician. I don't act on suspicion, sir. If I *knew,* I would have. If I suspected and couldn't prove it, no.

As Fahringer neared the end of his questions for Stock, he returned to his strongest point. "Somewhere between April and June of 1980 you became suspicious of surreptitious administration of insulin into Mrs. Von Bülow. Did you mention it to her, yes or no?"

"Counselor," said Stock in a quavering voice, "don't you think that I wish to heck I *had* mentioned it? Every time I go into her hospital room now I say to myself, 'Why didn't I mention this?' "

In the onrush of information of the Von Bülow trial, and the confusion of who-knew-what-when, Dr. Stock's astounding admission was all but overlooked. Stock was quite different from the others who had suspicions in 1980. He was a physician who had treated Sunny for twenty-six years, and his suspicion was not unformed like the others' but highly specific. His testimony also left little doubt who he thought was doing the injecting.

Stock's reasons for his inaction—his lack of proof, his reluctance to "fracture" the marriage, the fear of libel—hindered him from efforts to save his patient's life. He would not have needed proof simply to tell Sunny he believed she was being injected with insulin. Either she was doing it, he could have told her, or someone else was, but it had to stop as it was destroying her health.

Such a statement might well have brought from Sunny information about vitamin shots Claus was giving her, perhaps pointing to a connection between such shots and her woozy spells, or it might have merely served notice to whoever was doing the injecting that he was under scrutiny.

Stock seemed to be seriously overemphasizing the dangers of

speaking out and seriously underemphasizing the life-saving potential of such a course.

Long after the trial this inaction of Stock's remained one of the most puzzling facets of the case. In looking back at Stock's admission in court, the suspicion arose that he had mistestified, that in 1980 he had *not* suspected insulin injections. At the time of the April 1980 tests, Dr. Kermit Pines, one of the specialists Stock had brought in to examine Sunny, had asked Stock in a casual conversation if there was any possibility Sunny was getting insulin injections. Stock had been aghast at the suggestion, adding that the Von Bülows were very fine people and such a thing was unthinkable. Lawyers know that it often happens during the pressures of a trial that witnesses say things they do not mean to say.

In an interview six months after the trial Dr. Stock declined to avail himself of this explanation. He insisted he *did* suspect insulin injections, but the suspicions were too unformed and hazy to act upon. He reiterated his courtroom view that to make such an accusation you have to be prepared to defend it in court.

When it was suggested he did not have to accuse a specific person, he replied, "What good would that do?"

Presented with the possibilities that might open up, he thought for a minute and said, "Suppose Sunny had told me about the injections. What do I do then? Ask her to bring in samples?"

Stock clearly felt that such actions on his part would be detective work outside the doctor's role. After more discussion of the possibilities he said, "Look, let me state one thing categorically. I never in my wildest dreams thought Von Bülow was a murderer, that he was trying to kill Sunny."

Yet Stock suspected he was injecting her with insulin. What other reason could he have?

"How would I know?" Stock demanded.

So the position emerged that he did not equate insulin injections with murder attempts. He did not deny that such injections, if they were occurring, were endangering her health. Her worrying health was what prompted the speculations in the first place.

Perhaps the most haunting picture to emerge from the entire story is that of Maria perplexed and stymied by a bottle of insulin she discovers in Von Bülow's bag and, a few blocks away, Dr. Stock perplexed and stymied by the thought his patient might be receiving insulin injections. And it seems odd Maria mentioned the insulin to no one but Von Bülow's stepchildren when, with their help, she had had the substances discovered earlier analyzed professionally. The difference seems to be they had no idea what the earlier substances were; the insulin was labeled and, in their mind, not harmful.

At the end of the post-trial interview about his silence to Mrs. Von Bülow, Stock mentioned, as he had in court, the difficulty of seeing Mrs. Von Bülow alone. This led him to a concluding thought: "You've got to remember that the investigation into Mrs. Von Bülow's health was not an ongoing business. After the April tests I had little opportunity to see her. And you know, out of sight, out of mind."

The next witness was Dr. Kermit Pines, the specialist in metabolic diseases who concluded from his examination of Sunny in April of 1980 that she suffered from reactive hypoglycemia. The diagnosis, he now told the court, had not pleased him; several pieces did not fit. Also, he had not known at the time that previously, during her 1979 coma, her blood sugar had *dropped* after several glucose pushes. The only explanation for this, he said, "would have to be insulin."

Although he had worked in the field since 1946, he had never heard of anyone injecting themselves with insulin either for weight loss or to make themselves sick. Neither had he ever known a patient suffering from hypoglycemia to go into a coma because of something he or she ate or drank.

Next in Famiglietti's battery of expert medical witnesses was Dr. Donald Holub, a professor of medicine at Columbia University who has been treating Sunny Von Bülow since her arrival in New York in the final comatose state. Throughout the past year, he testified, he had repeatedly tested her blood sugar and insulin levels, which had never been anything but normal. He explored the possibility that her problem was related to hormone deficiency, but tests showed no hormonal dysfunction. Like other doctors, he checked for insulin-producing tumors but was satisfied she had none.

When Fahringer tried several hypotheses on him, including that the tests showing the high insulin level had been incorrect, Holub doggedly maintained that the sugar levels *alone* pointed to exogenous insulin, that no other explanation made sense.

The prosecution's medical evidence seemed conclusive when the last and strongest of the battery of specialists took the stand. He was Dr. George Cahill, who was affiliated with the Harvard Medical School, a former president of the American Diabetes Association, and one of the world's top experts in blood sugar disorders. Cahill was dispassionate, even genial, as he insisted that injected insulin was the only possible explanation of Sunny Von Bülow's coma.

Dr. Cahill was any prosecutor's dream witness. In addition to his unequivocal credentials and a pleasant appearance, he presented his expertise in terms laymen could understand without the condescension that usually accompanies such gulf-bridging. He addressed most of his responses directly to the jury and at one point apologized to them for trying to cram a year of medical school into ten minutes. Early on it was apparent they were with him.

Famiglietti took Cahill through a "hypothetical" situation, describing all the circumstances leading to Sunny's 1979 coma; he then asked Cahill's conclusions. Exogenous insulin, came the unhesitating reply. For the low blood sugar to persist *after* glucose injections, he added, can only be explained by injected insulin. As for alcoholic intake, Cahill was satisfied the amounts in the preceding twenty-four hours were trivial, not only because almost none was found in the blood (he acknowledged that it can be absorbed quickly) but because she had none of the residual "garbage" that alcohol leaves in the system.

As for the eggnog, Cahill could not think of a better way for a hypoglycemic to ingest liquor, as it contains large quantities of fat and protein to buffer the alcohol. The consumption of sweets such as the caramel sundae "means nothing," he said, because reactive hypoglycemia does not in itself cause coma. Barbiturates may have contributed to the second coma, but could not have caused it, because barbiturates do nothing to blood sugar concentration.

"Doctor," Famiglietti suddenly asked, "can insulin injections cause death?"

Cahill said that they could and that he knew of instances.

When Fahringer rose to cross-examine Cahill, he looked like he was about to demolish a giant. "Isn't it true, Doctor," he began slowly, "that if the insulin test was invalid, your theory that insulin was injected falls apart?"

"No, that is not correct," Cahill said, unperturbed.

Fahringer paused. "You could still give that opinion?"

"Yes, sir," Cahill said brightly. "The sugar levels alone would lead me to suspect insulin."

Later, in discussing the insulin test level of 216, Cahill said that such a high level is almost impossible to obtain in a normal patient —the level was "way out of bounds."

With far less bravado than when he began with Cahill twenty minutes earlier, Fahringer asked if the insulin could have been injected by Mrs. Von Bülow. "Of course," was the reply.

The prosecution finally arrived at the end of its medical testimony with the state toxicologist who returned from his vacation to confirm the private-laboratory findings after his testing of the black-bag contents. In order to remove the private-investigation stigma, Famiglietti needed the report of the police's chemists as well as Dr. Stock's laboratories.

One point the witness emphasized was the commercial unavailability of the black-bag drug mixtures. Although relatively common substances, they could not be purchased in those forms. This information conjured up bizarre pictures of Von Bülow the home pharmacist.

At this point in the trial, rumors began circulating about a 1950s trial in England involving murder by insulin injection. Von Bülow was working as a barrister in London at the time; some versions of the rumor had his firm connected with the case. (It was true. The judge, Mr. Kenneth Diplock, was also in Lord Hailsham's chambers.)

The crime in question concerned one Kenneth Barlow, a hospital attendant, whose wife was found dead in her bathtub on May 3, 1957. She appeared to have drowned, but when police found needle marks on her buttocks, they ran tests that showed she had died of insulin injections. Among several factors making the case celebrated, it was a landmark of forensic crime-detection techniques.

In addition to substantial forensic evidence that led to his conviction, Barlow was greatly damaged by a co-worker's testimony that Barlow had spoken to him about insulin's ability to kill and its impossibility to trace. Also incriminating Barlow were his wife's sweat-soaked pajamas found by the tub and her widely dilated pupils—both symptoms of insulin overdose.

Adding to Barlow's legend, if not the case against him, was the mysterious death of his former wife, aged thirty-three, the previous year; police, lacking any other explanation, had termed her death "natural." The death of the second wife was said to have been the first known instance of murder by insulin injection.

Although proof of Barlow's knowledge of insulin's ability to kill went far toward convicting him, such evidence would not be permitted against Von Bülow. Even though it was highly unlikely that Von Bülow was ignorant of the Barlow case, Judge Needham forbade any reference to Barlow in the trial of Claus Von Bülow for attempting to murder his wife by insulin injection.

It is doubtful if every judge would have been so quick to designate this evidence inadmissible. It could be argued that Von Bülow's prior awareness of insulin's murderous potential was as relevant as a poisoning case defendant's knowledge of poisons. Indeed, proof of such prior knowledge had been instrumental in convicting Kenneth Barlow.*

---

*I learned about the Barlow case in a curious fashion. During a recess Von Bülow had advised me, to broaden my background on criminal trials, to find a book series called *Famous British Trials* and read the case of one Elizabeth Seddens, an Edinborough woman accused of murdering her lover by arsenic poisoning. "It is," Von Bülow told me, "the finest piece of advocacy I know." At the first opportunity I took myself to the New York Public Library; finding no series of that name, I requested a five-volume set called *Famous Criminal Cases* on the chance that Von Bülow had mistaken the title. When the books arrived from the stacks, I opened the top volume at random and was stunned to see a chapter heading "Murder by Insulin Injection." It was an account of the 1957 Barlow case. With mounting excitement I read the details of the crime that so closely paralleled the one for which Von Bülow was standing trial. Because of the juxtaposition of time and place, I decided I had to mention it to the prosecution. Trepidations at introducing myself into the judicial fray were allayed when I learned Famiglietti was fully aware of the case. I shouldn't have been surprised at the prosecutor's broad knowledge of matters that could throw light on the Von Bülow mystery. Some months before the trial I had asked if he was aware of a section in Thomas Thompson's 1976 best seller, *Blood and Money,* in which a doctor, speculating on methods of murder, says, "Maybe an overdose of insulin. It's a natural substance and impossible to trace." Famiglietti said, "I know about it. Page 135."

XXIV

CLOSE followers of the Von Bülow case got a sharp lesson in public misconceptions about major news stories, not because the press was doing a bad job, but because the public fell victim to aspects of the case being more arresting and more memorable than others.

One arresting fact, perhaps the most arresting, was the huge amount of money involved. Early on, there had been speculations (fueled by Von Bülow's lawyers) that the whole affair resulted from the children trying to wrest from their stepfather his share of their mother's fortune. This was not a bad plot: what it lacked in originality was made up for by its feasibility. It was natural that it stuck.

Natural, that is, until Morris Gurley, Sunny Von Bülow's trust officer at Chemical Bank, took the stand and made nonsense of the theory by spelling out exactly how rich Alexander and Ala were and would inevitably be, then showing how little they would benefit from Von Bülow's removal from the will.

The interesting part of the misapprehension lesson was still to come. Even after this unequivocal testimony, people could still voice the opinion that greed motivated the children's struggle with him. The injustice of it suggested legislation forbidding people to voice opinions on trials unless they were conversant with the testimony of all the witnesses. Perhaps the most curious part of this phenomenon was the absence of anyone—ignorant or well-versed—who did not have a strong opinion.

Gurley's testimony also provided an excellent example of the perpetuation of errors in the press. If a fact is mistaken in an early account, it is often repeated again and again by newspaper and television news writers who recycle it for lack of any other source.

It would be amusing to tabulate how many times Sunny Von Bülow's fortune was estimated at $30 million. *The New York Times,* true to form, allowed for human gush and reduced the figure to $25 million. Morris Gurley took the stand and said in plain terms she was worth $75 million. Fortunately for press vanity, there were extenuating facts: $30 million was Sunny's outright and $45 million was in trust, with Sunny receiving the interest. This meant she received each year the income from $75 million—even allowing for non-income-yielding assets, that would engender many millions each year—and no one would consider her hands unreasonably tied if she had only $30 million with which to indulge her investment whims. (It is revealing of the enormous amount of money behind Sunny that the $30 million was money Annie Laurie put aside from the income from Sunny's trusts during her daughter's minority.)

The $30 million broke down into $2 million worth of art and $1 million for each of the two residences (very conservative); the remainder was in investments. Her will, which Von Bülow helped write, avoids taxes by a number of stratagems. She leaves half her personal estate—which, with executors' fees, etc., shrinks to $28 million—to Von Bülow. This sum includes the $4 million worth of houses and art which are left to him specifically, thereby rendering his cash inheritance $10 million.

But the will has more for Von Bülow, Gurley tells a reverential courtroom. The other half of Sunny's personal money, the other $14 million, goes into a charitable trust whose income is designated by Von Bülow alone. In Von Bülow's circles, to be able to give each year upwards of $2 million to your favorite opera company or art museum represents formidable social power, the kind of outlay new millionaires wrench from their own hard-won fortunes to gain admittance to the circles they crave. Von Bülow would have this social clout without spending a penny of his own $10 million. The fact was lost on no one in the courtroom that Sunny's death would make Claus Von Bülow an enormously rich and powerful man.

If for some reason he was excluded from the will (by his death, would be one way), his share went into the charitable trust, where it remained for twenty-one years, and then was distributed to the three children—but only if *they* had no children; otherwise, Claus's share would pass immediately to Sunny's grandchildren. The money's twenty-one years of charitable service is the device by which the will pays not one penny to the United States government, a ploy for which Von Bülow takes credit. This is a great irony, since it was the twenty-one-year delay that virtually removed suspicion from Alexander and Ala that they were after his share. Most people in their early twenties view twenty-one more years as putting them well beyond their capacity to enjoy life.

As for provision for the three children after Sunny's death, they would divide equally the $45 million trust. Skipping generations is another way the very rich reduce the government's share. Of course, to do this, you must have enough money for two fortunes to be leapfrogging each other but never touching.

To sum up the part of Gurley's testimony that related to the crime: Von Bülow gets upwards of $14 million the day Sunny dies and the children each get the same. If Von Bülow is eliminated from the will, each child will get an additional $4.6 million but not until the money does its twenty-one years of charitable service.

Conclusive as all this was, it omitted one very salient fact. The three children's grandmother, Mrs. Aitken, was in all likelihood richer than her daughter. She was in her eighties and in poor health; when she died, the chances were strong that Alexander, Ala, and Cosima would inherit amounts as large as they would receive from their mother's will. Gurley demolished the notion that Alexander and Ala, who could not escape becoming enormously wealthy, were plotting in a criminal way to get a little more money twenty-one years after their mother died.

Another fact that touched on this lack of motive, yet was not mentioned, was the two older children's disinterested attitude toward money and the enormous importance given it by Von Bülow. The closest testimony came to this was when Gurley made the point that the children were ignorant about their mother's will and expressed no interest and that Von Bülow was far more interested in money matters than Sunny had been.

As if all this wasn't devastating enough, Gurley then led the courtroom through a series of excruciating statistics on Von Bülow's pathetic earning record. Taking his tax returns for every year since 1968, when he still worked for Getty, Gurley showed that Von Bülow never earned more than $33,000 in any one year (1980, after working for Shearson–American Express) and most years earned nothing.

Before being turned over to the defense's cross-examination, Gurley established that he had a warm, friendly relationship with Sunny, being frequently invited to family functions with the Von Bülows and the Aitkens. He had never known Sunny to drink more than moderately and he had never known her to be depressed.

Fahringer was unable to damage even slightly Gurley's statement of facts and figures. He tried to show that Von Bülow would only get 6.8 percent of all the money that would pass when Sunny dies, but Gurley pointed out that that only spoke of the outright cash, adding that what he would get in trust brought the figure up to 13 percent.

Fahringer was finally reduced to showing that Von Bülow's elimination would mean his eviction from Clarendon Court and the Fifth Avenue apartment and that the kids would have their "exclusive use." Given the wealth of Alexander and Ala, it was hard to credit their going to such lengths over the use of their mother's real estate.

Greatly adding to Gurley's effectiveness for the prosecution was his manner, which was unemotional and businesslike. He simply stated the figures with no show of hostility toward Von Bülow. Talking informally after his testimony he revealed his close personal relationship with Sunny and considerable emotion about her fate.

The majority of Famiglietti's witnesses had been behind-the-scenes people—doctors, technicians, servants. The only actual players in the drama were Alexander, Maria, and Alexandra. It showed a nice sense of balance to conclude with a major player: Annie Laurie von Auersperg, now Mrs. Franz Kneissl, nicknamed Ala.

Just as the presence of Von Bülow himself triggered conflicting thoughts of martyred innocence or coldblooded murderer, so did Ala present the dilemma of warring alternatives: ruthless plotter or one who had lost her mother to another's greed.

As she took the stand, the beauty of her face overcame the somberness of a brown tailored suit and a black blouse. Her broad face was saved from an appearance of heaviness by delicate features, particularly remarkable blue eyes, which seemed to draw on the beauty of both her parents.

She appeared a bit more relaxed than her brother and established a note of forthrightness by saying she had been an obnoxious child and had quarrelled often with her mother, but never seriously enough to stop speaking. She affirmed she had seen her mother use Valium but that her mother's health and mental state were good, that she rarely consumed alcohol, and that when she did her tolerance was low.

Ala was in Austria at the time of the first coma and learned about it by phone after it was over. She said her mother had no recollection of what had preceded her collapse. Her spending Christmas in Austria the following year, 1980, did not upset her mother, as the defense maintained; Ala would only be away a few weeks and her "mother knew there would be other Christmases."

When she spoke of phoning her mother to wish her a Merry Christmas and learning from Alexander that she had again gone into a coma, Ala started to cry. She quickly recovered and went on to describe flying immediately home.

She related Maria's showing her the black-bag contents, their taking samples to Dr. Stock for analysis, and Maria's overall suspicions about the situation. Ala discussed with her mother the reasons for her wanting to divorce Von Bülow, Ala adding to other testimony on this that because of Von Bülow's feelings of uselessness and his inability to find a job, her mother feared he was on the verge of a nervous breakdown. She didn't feel, Ala said, any of this was her fault, but would oblige him if he felt their separating was necessary. Ala denied her mother objected to his working.

Ala told of a meeting with Von Bülow in which he asked her and her brother not to believe rumors that he was telling others Sunny was an alcoholic. He was appalled they could think such a thing of him because, she quoted him as saying, he "had raised us both for fourteen years and we all knew [the alcoholism charge] was not true."

Famiglietti asked her if she was familiar with her mother's will. She was not, but had heard from Morris Gurley that she would come into considerable money. She also knew that her share was virtually unaffected by Von Bülow's fate.

Ala confirmed her brother's recollection of seeing needles and syringes on vacation in Majorca when they were children, adding that she knew her stepfather gave her mother vitamin injections. She admitted that she never actually witnessed him giving a shot. When Judge Needham called a recess, Ala headed for the sanctuary of the prosecution room; as she worked her way through the crowd she again broke into tears.

When she returned to the stand fifteen minutes later, however, she was composed to face her stepfather's lawyer. Fahringer first attacked the proposition that Sunny liked Kneissl, Ala's husband, and approved of the marriage, a thrust made more poignant by the presence of the handsome young man close by the prosecution table. Hadn't Sunny been upset by the financial difficulties of the Kneissl family's ski manufacturing business, and hadn't she insisted on his signing a prenuptial agreement? Her mother had suggested such an agreement, but when Ala indicated she didn't want it, her mother acquiesced.

As for her mother's drinking, hadn't Mrs. Kneissl said to the grand jury that she had on several occasions seen her mother drunk? Ala said she had seen her *inebriated*.

"Doesn't that mean drunk?" Fahringer asked.

"If it does then she was never inebriated," Ala said, "only tipsy. I now say I never saw her drunk."

But couldn't a low tolerance for alchohol be described as a drinking problem, Fahringer persisted, now driven into semantic desperation by the stream of witnesses who denied Sunny drank even a moderate amount. Fahringer's question was tacit admission he had given up on the charge she drank excessively.

Fahringer talked about the broken hip, when Sunny put off calling a doctor for two days. Ala acknowledged this but denied her mother had an aversion to doctors. He returned to the subject of needles, giving her an opportunity to emphasize she had never seen needles around her mother other than the one time years earlier in Majorca and that she had never seen her mother inject herself.

When Ala left the stand, she took the seat beside her husband who took her hand and squeezed it. She gave him a look of relief; for the next few moments both Ala and Kneissl stared at Von Bülow.

Before resting his case Famiglietti got the defense to stipulate that Leslie Baxter had given him the vial of Valium that had her name on it. This meant that Miss Baxter would not have to take the stand, which was a blow to the press box, one of whom during the dog days of lab technicians had wanted to hold up a sign saying "Bring on Leslie!"

Another journalist, on hearing that she would not be called as a witness, suggested to Famiglietti that she at least be entered as an exhibit. Since the jury is allowed to keep exhibits in the jury room, handling them at will, this could present certain problems of civil liberties.

The prosecution witnesses concluded on Thursday, February 25. Judge Needham recessed his court until Tuesday, March 2, to give the defense a long weekend to marshal its counterattack. When Tuesday arrived, Needham granted Famiglietti's request to reopen his case briefly. Dr. Aggarwal of the Boston Medical Lab was called again to the stand.

Famiglietti was concerned because his understanding was that Sunny's blood sample taken after the 1980 coma had been forwarded by the Boston Medical Laboratory immediately to California for the insulin test; he had now learned it had first been tested in Boston. Could the doctor explain?

Aggarwal expanded his earlier testimony: his lab had decided to stop insulin testing just at that time and only had left a small amount of the necessary reagent. They had used this to test the two samples, one of which had been low in insulin, the other too high for them to read. Since they had now exhausted the reagent, they were unable to repeat the test and had to send the blood on to Anaheim.

Uninteresting as this prosecution finale was, it reflected the only major disagreement within the prosecution forces. Although Famiglietti was technically the subordinate of Deputy Attorney General Susan McGuirl, he had been given a free hand with this case and she had assumed the role of backup counsel. On this one point, however, they were in sharp disagreement. Famiglietti felt the discrepancy to be unimportant; Susan felt it could be grounds for a mistrial. Neither would yield, so Susan suggested they submit the issue to their boss, the Attorney General, who agreed that Famiglietti should reopen the case and amend Dr. Aggarwal's story.

If the doctor's new testimony was not earth-shaking, it still contained a nugget of the kind of intriguing mystery Von Bülow followers had come to expect. After explaining what had happened at the lab, Aggarwal told the court that he was unable to show the medical records that confirmed his testimony. After leaving the lab the previous day, he had put the records in his car to bring them today to Newport; while he was eating dinner in a restaurant, his car had been stolen. The trial regulars, with imaginations already inflamed by the labyrinthine plot of the case, quickly scanned the possibilities for further intrigue or villainy, but could come up with nothing but a random car theft. So, along with the Nigerian lab technician, a Boston car thief also was missing in action with information relevant to the Von Bülow case.

XXV

FAHRINGER'S first defense witness was the Providence locksmith Marshall Salzman, whose account of being called by Alexander and Detective Lambert paralleled their version until one crucial moment, when it diverged diametrically. Salzman recalled thinking that the request was odd. After all, Newport had locksmiths; Salzman had insisted that Alex drive with him in his van. ("People zoom off.")

At Clarendon Court, Salzman found the closet key on the desk. Lambert asked him to open the closet, but Salzman insisted on waiting until Alexander returned from the kitchen. Once the closet was open, he said, Alexander and Lambert did not enter and begin searching as they had testified; only the detective went in. Alexander remained outside in the corridor, where Salzman "made conversation" with him, asking him about Clarendon Court, its size, its history. While they were talking, Lambert emerged from the closet and said to Alexander, "It's not here."

Was Salzman sure of those words? Fahringer asked. He was.

He concluded his testimony by saying they all went down to the kitchen for soft drinks, after which he left.

Famiglietti asked the locksmith how his recollection was so sharp about something that had happened two years earlier. He had made notes. Did he have them now? No, he threw them away. Why had he not come forward before? He had consulted a lawyer friend who told him, "They'll contact you if they need you."

Famiglietti brought out that Alexander had not called a Newport locksmith in order to avoid gossip in the small town. Salzman then added a remarkable coda to his story. He was so suspicious of the call from Alexander that he had phoned the Newport police to report what he had been asked to do; they had given him the names of Clarendon Court's yellow labradors for the locksmith to use as test questions on Alexander. Alexander had passed, which relieved Salzman only partially. He was bothered anew by the closet's key being discovered nearby. ("If it was his house he should have known about the key.")

Famiglietti asked if after Salzman left Clarendon Court that night he had any idea of what Lambert and von Auersperg did. No, he didn't. The inference was clear. After he left, the other two might have returned to the closet, searched it as they claimed, and found the black bag. With this interpretation, the two versions differed only in Alexander and Lambert not mentioning the abortive first look.

Salzman's story of Alexander's actions was hard to believe. For the twenty-one year old college sophomore, his arrival at Clarendon Court the night of January 23, 1981, must have been a moment of high drama. He was on an errand to collect evidence he had been told would incriminate his stepfather in attempting to murder his mother.

The elaborate preparations of hiring a detective, going first to Providence, then backtracking down to Newport, all indicate the mission was not a casual one. They indeed found the closet locked but found the means to open it. At the moment of actually opening the door, the drama for Alexander must have been at its most intense. He should have been frantic to learn if this journey was in vain or if Maria's suspicions proved correct.

Yet Salzman asked the jury to believe that Alexander at that instant was not curious enough to enter the closet, instead preferring to loiter outside chatting with an unknown locksmith about the number of rooms in Clarendon Court. It also does not make sense that Alexander was trying to distract the locksmith. If they had reason to fear a third presence, why bring one to the scene? Lambert surely knew "safe" locksmiths in New York, or they could have resorted to the simpler precaution of asking Salzman to leave once the closet was unlocked.

Other aspects of his version didn't jibe. Salzman claimed the closet was in total disarray, implying someone had already ransacked it. Putting aside the fact that nothing of Von Bülow's or Sunny's was ever known to be in disarray, the houseman and others testified that neither Von Bülow or anyone else had been to the house since the family's Christmas visit. If Alexander and the detective had already been inside the closet, what need did they have for a locksmith?

Salzman said something else that could have easily been impeached, according to Lieutenant Reise. His story about phoning the Newport police and getting the dogs' names was to Reise, a nineteen-year veteran of the Rhode Island police, an absurdity. If the police received such a call from a stranger telling them he was being asked to enter a Newport mansion to open a locked closet, the first thing the police would do (after logging the call) would be to call the house and ask what was happening. The Newport police had a greater obligation to local residents than they did to anonymous callers.

Secondly, Reise said it was even more absurd to think that the night dispatcher would have the vaguest notion about the names of the Von Bülows' four dogs. When Reise was asked why he didn't seize on this weakness in Salzman's testimony, at least producing the police record of calls, he said simply, "I didn't hear him say it, and Steve let it pass. We missed it."

The defense's next witness was the Clarendon Court butler, Robert Biastre. He testified that he served Mrs. Von Bülow drinks but rarely, that he never saw her inebriated, that the only sign she had consumed a few drinks was her "feeling good." She may have had three or four glasses of eggnog on December 26, 1979. Yes, the next day Maria had tried to enter Mrs. Von Bülow's bedroom. Biastre was present when the rescue squad arrived. At dinner the night before she had eaten vanilla ice cream and marshmallow fluff, *not* caramel sauce.

Fahringer asked about Mr. Von Bülow's closet; Biastre said that the shotgun was kept in there (as well as the items everyone in America now knew about). He described the Von Bülows' life together.

Since Biastre was confirming most of the prosecution's contentions, it was difficult to discern his usefulness to the defense until

Fahringer asked the butler if Mr. Von Bülow seemed concerned for Mrs. Von Bülow's welfare. Yes. Do you think he would have harmed her?

Biastre, looking frightened by the very suggestion, said, "I never saw any indication."

Famiglietti asked how many drinks he would serve Mrs. Von Bülow in the course of a year. Ten to twelve, adding that she often took the second before finishing the first. Did he ever know Mrs. Von Bülow to get drinks on her own? No. Did she drink regularly? No. Did she have a drinking problem? "I'd say no," he replied.

The Von Bülows' chauffeur, Charlie Roberts, was next called to the stand. Fahringer established the man's practice of driving Mrs. Von Bülow for her morning routine when in Manhattan. This was leading up to Roberts's saying he had often taken her to several addresses on Central Park South, the implication being that this street had a number of doctors, some of whom might be "Feelgoods" and sources of drugs.

The only evidence that she was stopping at these apartment buildings to see drug-dispensing doctors rather than an astrologer, a school friend, or a lover was that she sometimes asked the chauffeur to stop at a pharmacy afterwards, which he assumed was to fill a prescription.

Roberts's principal claim to witness distinction was that he was the only person the defense was able to produce to say he had seen Mrs. Von Bülow under the influence of alcohol. The eight years he drove for them, he recalled *one* evening driving the Von Bülows home from a dinner at Mrs. Aitken's when Mrs. Von Bülow had slumped to one side of the back seat. When Von Bülow had helped her from the car, Roberts heard him say, "Come, darling, not now."

Famiglietti got Roberts to say he liked both Von Bülows and he hated to see Mr. Von Bülow accused of something if he didn't do it. When he said that he took Mrs. Von Bülow to visit Dr. Stock "about every two weeks," Famiglietti did a good job of discrediting him by pointing out that Stock (and his records) said that Mrs. Von Bülow visited his office twenty-six times in twenty-five years.

Inconsequential as this witness had been, the prosecution went to considerable pains to produce witnesses to rebut his testimony.

By now the followers of the Von Bülow trial were accustomed to surprises and dramatic appearances, but none of them were prepared for the next witness, an exercise instructor from the Manya Kahn Body Rhythm Exercise Studio, a health establishment well known to Manhattan's wealthy women.

Shortly before her appearance, two journalists were speculating on what would be the strongest possible evidence for the defense. They both agreed that, after the conclusive medical testimony, the only thing that could save Von Bülow was a witness who would have firsthand knowledge that Sunny injected herself with insulin. Enter Joy O'Neill to say precisely that.

Joy O'Neill was a striking woman, about forty, whose dark hair was pulled back severely into a bun, giving her the sleek, arch look of a ballerina, which she had indeed been for the American Ballet Theatre. Sunny Von Bülow, O'Neill said, quickly singled out Joy as her favorite instructress at Manya Kahn's and took a private class with Joy five days a week for five years. Of course, sometimes Sunny would be in Newport; other times Joy was busy and Sunny would be forced to take another instructor. For the most part, she exercised with Joy O'Neill.

The two women became close friends, "like sisters," Sunny confiding in Joy about her marriage, her children. Sunny offered to set Joy up in business. When Joy lost her mother, Sunny sent flowers and a note inviting her to come spend the summer at Clarendon Court, adding "It would be good for you to get away."

As she talked, a curious theme kept cropping up. Asked the day of the week of an occurrence, she responded, "I've sworn to tell the truth, it was Friday." Other superfluous prefaces suggested a preoccupation with truth. "I just want to tell the truth and get out of here." "The truth is . . ."

One time she and Sunny had been sitting on the gym floor and Joy, looking at her own stomach, bemoaned how fat she was becoming. Joy knew the problem: the wine she needed to calm her nerves. She couldn't think of giving it up.

What you need, Sunny told her, is a shot of insulin. Sunny

went on to explain how insulin consumed sugar in one's system. By injecting it you could eat what you want, "sweets and everything."

Fahringer asked her why she had been so slow coming forward with this highly relevant testimony. She now worked for the Harkness organization, she said; their lawyer had told her not to get involved. Fahringer asked if she knew the defendant, gesturing toward him. Saying they had never met, Joy looked at him brightly and said, "Good morning, Mr. Von Bülow." He looked homicidal as he nodded curtly at this woman who had done more to save him than anyone so far.

Famiglietti immediately questioned Joy O'Neill about her coming forward to testify so late in the day. Apparently she had heard nothing about the Von Bülow case until she read the article in *New York* magazine at the start of the trial. When she got to the part about Sunny's coma resulting from insulin injection, she felt she should come forward. Had she seen none of the many news stories about the case that had appeared in the five months prior to the trial? No.

Even after seeing the article she had vacillated, consulting first friends, next a lawyer, then calling the Rhode Island Attorney General's Office to offer her new evidence. Having made this major step, she still wavered. After telling Susan McGuirl over the phone that she would see her, she refused to when Susan arrived in New York.

Joy O'Neill entered the case through the *prosecution,* despite her evidence that was so helpful to the defense. The damage to their case notwithstanding, the prosecution turned O'Neill over to the defense team under the Brady rule, which requires prosecutors to inform their opponents of anything exculpatory they might uncover in their investigation. Fahringer and Sheehan snatched at O'Neill but ended up less than grateful for the prosecution's scrupulousness. O'Neill backfired so badly for them, they suspected a trap.

Famiglietti began his attack on the witness by alluding to Joy's claim to have been the top instructress at Manya Kahn's. "What would you say," he said slyly, "if I told you Miss Kahn said you were one of the worst instructors in her establishment?"

"It would be a lie," O'Neill said with curious equanimity. Miss

Kahn and she had money differences. The eighty-year-old woman was envious of Joy; indeed, Joy had caught her listening at the door of her class; they had parted badly. Going back to her reluctance to testify, she said, "I felt like a criminal. I'm not used to that. You people frighten me."

"Weren't you aware that insulin was critical in this case?"

"I didn't read the whole article," she said. "I was in shock. I couldn't believe it. I'll probably be in court for the rest of my life."

Famiglietti got her to admit that she took tranquilizers herself, indeed had taken a small amount before coming to court today. As usual after responding in a harmless way, O'Neill added a postscript that accelerated her destruction: "Dancers are very hyper people. Someone is always trying to shoot you down before you even get onto the stage."

The secret to discrediting Joy O'Neill seemed to be to wait a few seconds after she appeared to have finished a response; she would quickly fill the hiatus with hard-to-believe postscripts or alarming mental spasms. After Famiglietti concluded with O'Neill, Fahringer passed by the defense table on his way out of the courthouse for the next recess. Leaning over his adversary, he said, "I was trying to get her to shut up; you did a good job of opening her up."

After this high-strung testimony, the solid dignity of financier Mark Millard calmed the courtroom. Millard, one of the country's top investment bankers, specialized in energy finance, working through Shearson–American Express. In a deep, slightly Russian accent, Millard recounted Von Bülow's persistence in seeking a job, his capability, and his salary expectations, which Millard calculated between $100,000 and $200,000. Millard testified to learning that Von Bülow was well regarded by the Getty people, later confirming this when he and Von Bülow visited the Los Angeles Getty office, where Von Bülow was "treated like a member of the family."

Just as the bank officer's testimony did little to still the trial kibitzers who suspected the stepchildren of plotting for Von Bülow's share of the fortune, so did this unequivocal testimony do little to the Von Bülow haters who scoffed at his Getty role or claimed his services to Paul Getty had nothing to do with oil, crude or otherwise. But Millard's testimony also showed how trial intricacies can obliterate the central issue: Von Bülow's success with Getty no more exonerated him from the attempted-murder charge than Sunny's supposed melancholia (or drinking, or whatever) proved she wasn't a victim.

Millard's main assistance to Von Bülow was as a character witness and to attest to Von Bülow's earning capability. High as his estimates may have seemed to the wage earners in the courtroom, the upwards of $100,000 Von Bülow could hope for by working full time did little to eliminate as a motive the upwards of one million dollars in annual interest he would get from his share of Sunny's will. More helpful perhaps was Millard's obvious regard for Von Bülow. As a witness he was an impressive presence; it was unfortunate for Von Bülow that his employer didn't have more to say.

Next to testify for the defense was a Millard associate, Margaret Neilly, who had worked closely with Von Bülow on several deals. It was Neilly with whom Von Bülow had the long phone conversation the night before and the morning of the final coma. As Neilly traced the substance of their conversation, Von Bülow's difficulty with figures on a report, it was staggering to think he could preoccupy himself, indeed get upset over, columns of dollar figures when, according to the prosecution, he was busy doing in his wife.

In recalling the Boston phone conversation, she said she could tell Von Bülow had been weeping and that he was deeply despondent about his wife's calamity. Famiglietti did little damage to her testimony except to bring out that, according to his phone bill, Von Bülow had called Neilly a third time, the evening of December 21, and spoke for eight minutes. The call had slipped her mind; she had gone to Christmas lunch with a friend that day and drunk considerable champagne.

Eugene Thaw was, like Millard, a social contact that Von Bülow had converted into a business colleague. Also like Millard, Thaw was brought in to substantiate the defense claims of Von Bülow's financial potential, but throwing no direct light on whether or not Von Bülow tried to murder his wife. Thaw was a prominent Manhattan art dealer who was vice-chairman of the board of an art-buying syndicate called Artemis. Von Bülow had sat on the board of Artemis since 1978, which earned him nothing; Thaw, however, was setting up a new art firm for which Von Bülow would be financial administrator, eventually receiving a fee of $150,000 per year.

Thaw's most direct involvement with the case was his selling, at Von Bülow's request, a million dollars' worth of art Von Bülow had acquired while living in London. He did this in July, 1981, just after Von Bülow's indictment, when Von Bülow needed funds for his defense. Famiglietti's cross-examination concerned itself with the ownership of this art. Was it Von Bülow's, or in reality *Mrs.* Von Bülow's?

Thaw's evidence that it belonged to the defendant was his knowledge of the art market and his recollection of these items becoming available in the early 1950s. Some of the works were prominent enough, if placed on sale, to attract his attention and perhaps remain in his memory for thirty years. Others would have been in the one- to two-thousand-dollar range at that time and if put on the market would hardly make international art news.

Famiglietti also brought out that Thaw did not know if Von Bülow had bought the items at the time, only that they were available. Nothing was said about the possibility of subsequent private sales about which Thaw would know nothing.

With the subject of ownership in the air, Thaw, in response to one of Fahringer's questions, referred to Clarendon Court as "Mr. Von Bülow's residence." Famiglietti was on his feet. "*Mrs.* Von Bülow's residence!" he all but shouted.

Thaw's testimony threw light, if not on Von Bülow's guilt or innocence, on the source of the funds which seemed to be so ample for his legal defense. In addition to the high-priced lawyers, the research firms, and the expensive hotel accommodations, a small story best illustrates the unrestrained spending.

A courthouse employee was moonlighting for Von Bülow, typing up transcripts of the trial. As she would deliver a portion, she would present him with an invoice for the work, usually in the area of two or three hundred dollars. Once when she did this, he scrawled her a check for five thousand dollars and said, "Here. I might not always have a check with me. Let me know when you need more."

* * *

To prove that Sunny Von Bülow's coma was caused by insulin injection, the prosecution had produced seven medical doctors, two more doctors in chemistry, and an array of laboratory technicians. To counter this scientific regiment the defense produced one man, Dr. Milton Hamolsky, who practiced at Rhode Island Hospital and taught medicine at Brown University.

Two of Famiglietti's medical witnesses, Cahill and Funkenstein, were among the world's top experts in blood sugar and hypoglycemia. Hamolsky was an endocrinologist with no special knowledge of blood sugar. The doctor had undertaken a lot.

The basis of Hamolsky's testimony, which went on all Thursday afternoon and part of Friday morning, was that one could not say conclusively that Sunny's two comas were caused by exogenous insulin. He did not, however, rule out the possibility. His main argument was that unless the insulin and sugar levels were tested on the same blood sample, results were inconclusive.

As Famiglietti rose for his cross-examination, his father, Rocco Famiglietti, who was in court that day, was heard to say "Go get him, boy!"

The prosecutor attacked first the same-sample contention. The tests at the time of the second coma had been taken from the same *batch* of samples; on the first coma, even though the insulin was not tested until hours after her admission, Sunny's drop in blood sugar after being given massive glucose injections allowed no other conclusion, according to three experts, except a high insulin level. No, insisted Hamolsky, other factors might have contributed to the drop in blood sugar.

Before calling Hamolsky to the stand, Fahringer had asked the doctor to study Sunny's medical records and point out things to the court that bothered him. The court was taken again on a tour through Sunny Von Bülow's health eccentricities—the aspirin reliance, the "twenty-four laxatives a day," the psychiatrist's diagnosis of neurosis.

The short, owl-like doctor spoke of an episode in 1966 just after the birth of Cosima in which Sunny had suffered a "total paralysis." When Famiglietti questioned him on this, he asked the doctor if a person *totally* paralyzed wouldn't have to be put on a respirator in order to breathe? Yes, he answered. And didn't you know that Mrs. Von Bülow was *not* on a respirator? The doctor admitted he had known it. But you told the court that she was *totally* paralyzed?

"I was just reading from the record," the doctor said.

"Why hadn't Dr. Hamolsky read a little further on, that her paralysis was in her legs only?" Famiglietti revealed the same sort of bias in this witness a number of times.

When, with exasperation, the doctor referred to Sunny taking "twenty-four laxatives a day for twenty years," Famiglietti said the testimony had been "*up to* twenty-four a day," and Famiglietti added a postscript that if anyone took twenty-four laxatives a day for twenty years they would have spent eighteen years on the toilet.

The doctor had cited Sunny's 1977 fractured hip as an element of her history that "bothered" him. When Famiglietti got to this he said sarcastically, "That's a real significant fact, isn't it, Doctor?"

Famiglietti moved to another item in the record that alarmed Hamolsky: Sunny's "frequent episodes of ataxia and confusion." "Where in the record," Famiglietti said, placing a report in front of the witness, "does it say 'frequent'?"

"I may have been in error," Hamolsky replied.

It was an extraordinary performance on both sides. With none of the prosecution's thirty-nine witnesses had Fahringer succeeded in revealing their bias and distortions as Famiglietti had with Hamolsky—not even with witnesses who had better reasons for bias: the victim's two children for example. The closest Fahringer had come was the discrepency he found in Maria's testimony about Sunny's reasons for wanting a divorce, but that area had been far removed from issues central to the case. Hamolsky, on the other hand, seemed to be bending every fact to depict Sunny Von Bülow as a mentally and physically messed-up woman; with the "total paralysis" charge, he seemed to be flirting with perjury.

Throughout his testimony, Hamolsky looked straight ahead and, because of his shortness, slightly upward, giving him the look of a bird defending a nest. Not once did he glance at the jury, a few feet off his right shoulder. (Jurors later remarked that his ignoring them had affected their overall evaluation of him, just as Cahill's focusing on them had helped to win them over.)

At the end of Famiglietti's cross-examination he asked Dr. Hamolsky if he was familiar with England's famous Barlow case (the insulin-injection murder that occurred in London when Von Bülow was working there). Fahringer objected vociferously and was sustained. Famiglietti rephrased the question and was again stilled by Judge Needham, who said, "I think you'd better abandon that line of questioning."

Another witness drama had been occurring behind the scenes over the past two days. A young man named Robert Huggins, who worked as a technician for the Newport Hospital, was discussing the Von Bülow case with a close friend when he boasted that he knew something that could affect the trial. The friend coaxed Huggins to tell him. It seems that after Mrs. Von Bülow's first coma in 1979 Huggins had been sent to her room to draw blood for tests. To make conversation, he asked her why she was there. She replied that she had tried to kill herself.

The friend passed the story along to his wife, who turned out to have once worked as a baby-sitter for defense lawyer John Sheehan. The wife immediately called Sheehan, who wasted no time subpoenaing Huggins.

Huggins's testimony was perhaps the most damaging to the prosecution's case. If Sunny could be proved to be depressed or alcoholic, it said nothing definite, finally, about how the comas were caused. But if her first coma could be proven a suicide attempt, it would strongly suggest that the second one was as well.

When Fahringer got Huggins to repeat the story on the stand, he said that when he entered the hospital room to draw blood, December 30, 1979, Sunny had looked distant. He had asked why she was in the hospital. She had replied that she had tried to kill herself.

"You shouldn't have done that," Huggins said he replied, adding, "I'd like to have you around."

"Yeah, sure," was Sunny's response.

Fahringer almost immediately turned Huggins over to Famiglietti. Why had he waited two years before telling anyone? Huggins said he had told a fellow employee at the time. Who? He couldn't remember. Didn't Huggins know that Mr. Von Bülow was on trial for two very serious crimes? Why had he said nothing to Lieutenant Reise, who spent weeks at Newport Hospital the previous summer interviewing anyone who could throw light on the case? (A suicide attempt was a possibility that particularly interested Reise.) Everyone in the hospital knew the reason the police were there. Why had Huggins not come forward? He had not wanted to get involved.

Under Famiglietti's pressure he added, "I figured if she told me, she would have told the nurses. And without the nurses to back me up, my story would sound a little incredible."

"You can say that again," Famiglietti said in a stage whisper.

Reise, somewhat floored by the surprise testimony, took solace in the timing: it was Friday, the weekend was coming up and would give the prosecution two days to find a witness to rebut Huggins.

Sheila Anne Passante, another defense witness from the Manya Kahn Body Rhythm Studio, recalled that Joy O'Neill and Martha Von Bülow were "synonymous" and that Joy had received a Christmas gift from her client. On cross-examination Famiglietti gave a taste of the ammunition he had in store when he referred to the Manya Kahn appointment books for the years 1976 through 1980, which indicated that Joy had given instruction to Sunny only a handful of times in those years. Passante did not dispute this, in fact testified to the accuracy of the record books.

This last day of the defense case was shaping up to be one of the most varied of the trial, having started off with the conclusion of Dr. Hamolsky's single-handed assault on the prosecution's medical testimony, followed by the bombshell of Robert Huggins's suicide story, and ending with now partial corroboration of Joy O'Neill's strange tale.

Perhaps due to the variety of the witnesses on a personal level, few in the court seemed to notice the disparity of their testimonies' aim; each of the defense witnesses was launching a *different* theory on how Sunny fell into permanent coma. The locksmith was implying that Von Bülow had been framed, Huggins was saying she had tried to kill herself, and O'Neill was implying she had accidentally overdosed on insulin. While the theories weren't in complete contradiction to each other, neither did they do anything to reinforce each other.

From the start of the trial, rumors had circulated that Newport's venerable dowager, Mrs. John Nicholas Brown, would be taking the stand on Von Bülow's behalf. After the exhaustive prosecution, the even split of social Newport over Claus's guilt was a total fiction, if indeed it had ever been true. The majority of the summer people either suspected his guilt or were certain of it. A small group of loyalists, however, still insisted on his innocence. Of these, seventy-six-year-old Ann Brown was the most prominent.

A Kinsolving from Baltimore ("Pauline de Rothschild and I worked on the same newspaper there"), she had married the enormously rich and well liked John Nicholas Brown, giving her a social power base which she used with gusto.

In a long interview months before the trial she had indicated her belief that the whole case was a nasty vendetta on the part of the Aitkens and von Auerspergs. This, of course, is a far uglier countercharge than charging them with merely being mistaken. Ann Brown felt Von Bülow's accusers knew, as she did perfectly well, that he was not guilty of these crimes, but for reasons of their own wanted him destroyed. It is understandable the two factions weren't speaking.

In her conversations about the case, her major theme was that Von Bülow couldn't possibly have done such a thing because he was a friend of *hers*. What's more, he came to her house for *dinner*. So the state of Rhode Island, which happened to be the crucible of the Brown fortune, could just close up its courthouse and send everybody home.

In relating her friendship with Von Bülow, it appeared Von Bülow had set out to make a friend of the social queen when he first came to Newport. Given the smallness of the summer colony, it was inevitable the two would meet; being of different generations and both married, it was less inevitable they would become friends.

Mrs. Brown is known to have an impressive collection of books on military history; at a dinner party one night, Von Bülow indicated that military history was a great interest; might he drop by some afternoon and look at her books? Naturally, she gave him tea and the friendship blossomed.

After so much talk about Newport's fabled summer colony, the courtroom was excited to be visited by a prime specimen. Suspense was high as both swinging doors were flung open and, after a pause, Ann Brown made her entrance.

A tall, good-looking woman, she was an impressive figure as she walked toward the witness stand with John Sheehan just behind her. As she was halfway across the open space between the bench and the lawyers' tables, she stopped abruptly, turned, and holding out her leather handbag to John Sheehan, snapped in a tone surely known to every butler in Newport, "Here. Take this."

John Sheehan had to turn and traverse the empty distance carrying a brown alligator purse. He deftly turned disaster into glory by waiting until the courtroom stopped laughing to say, "This is the one moment of me television will show."

The thrust of Ann Brown's testimony was that Von Bülow was a very good and dutiful husband, that he was as concerned about Sunny's well-being as he was about his daughter's. As for his having a mistress, she allowed that if she had denied John Nicholas Brown her bed for fourteen years, as Sunny had Claus, he would have been justified in straying. Fahringer wound up his investigation by asking Mrs. Brown if she had any indication Von Bülow would do anything to harm his wife.

"Absolutely not!" came her reply.

Famiglietti stood up and without hesitation said, "Mrs. Brown, do you think if Mr. Von Bülow was attempting to murder his wife, he would tell you?"

There were laughs from the courtroom. When they subsided, she said sternly, "That's a silly question." This provoked an even bigger laugh.

Without laughing at all, Famiglietti said, "Give me a silly answer."

"I refuse to answer a silly question like that," she snapped.

Throughout her testimony Ann Brown was rude to the point of abusiveness to Famiglietti, saying things like "I can't tell you how many times I saw him, I'm not a mathematician," and "If you'll *listen* the next time I talk . . ."

Famiglietti, as everyone in the courtroom now knew, had a cutting tongue and wasn't above scrapping with defense witnesses. Not once, however, did he return a sally of Mrs. Brown's. His handling of her was perhaps his most admirable courtroom moment; with his one "silly" question he had made nonsense of her entire testimony, and his refusal to match her truculence made her appear gratuitously imperious and overbearing. It is not easy for a thirty-four-year-old man to win a struggle for juror sympathy with a seventy-six-year-old woman, but Famiglietti had done it.

However misguided her testimony was, it took Mrs. Brown courage to appear ("John Brown would kill me if he knew I was doing this"). Her family, it was said, did everything they could to dissuade her. It would have been far easier for her to abandon Von Bülow. Putting herself out in such a peril-filled fashion for a friend had the ring of nobility about it. Furthermore, the underlying message was not lost on the jury. A person of her caliber was willing to expose herself to ridicule and embarrassment for Claus Von Bülow.

The final witness in the defense's case was Dr. John Thomas Carr, the chief psychiatrist at Newport Hospital at the time of Sunny's first coma. On Dr. Gailitis's recommendation, Carr had visited Sunny when she was convalescing after this coma. He determined that she "was neurotic and desperately in need of psychotherapy." She had denied trying to kill herself, but said to the doctor "she often wished herself dead." Sunny also had told Carr she hoped her future would be more fulfilling than her past; she had almost never been happy and she had not slept with her husband in five years.

Famiglietti, as he often did, started out with his most damaging question. How long had Dr. Carr been with Mrs. Von Bülow? Twenty minutes. He'd asked how many questions? Twelve to fifteen. Famiglietti proceeded to other matters, frequently returning to the duration of his visit. "And you were able to tell all that in twenty minutes?"

"Yes."

"That's amazing," Famiglietti said.

"Yes it is," the doctor replied.

Famiglietti reminded Carr that he had told Lieutenant Reise

last summer that most of the information he had obtained from Sunny had "been of little value in making a diagnosis"; he had based his conclusion more on "intuition." Why had the doctor not mentioned to Lieutenant Reise that he considered Mrs. Von Bülow "suicidal"?

"I only answered his questions," Carr replied.

Was Dr. Carr's evaluation of Mrs. Von Bülow's psychological state colored by his briefing from Dr. Gailitis about her alcoholism and other failings—all of which her husband had placed in her medical record? Only to a certain extent.

It was a point for Famiglietti, a point for Carr—until a bizarre thing occurred. Famiglietti asked why a woman of Mrs. Von Bülow's resources, if she was so disturbed, wouldn't at one point have sought professional counseling? All the people who are neurotic can't be under a doctor's care, Carr replied, then added, "You're neurotic, I'm neurotic, the judge is neurotic . . ."

"Thank you, Doctor," Famiglietti said, abruptly returning to his table to allow the strange outburst to permeate the courtroom. Thoughtfully, Famiglietti repeated the doctor's words, "You're neurotic, I'm neurotic, the judge . . ."

"Let's just talk about you two," Needham snapped, to the delight of the courtroom. Funny as his remark was, it detracted from the prosecutor's windfall. Carr made his sweeping diagnosis just at the point when many in the courtroom were reminding themselves that psychiatrists generally consider *everyone* neurotic; indeed, Famiglietti's questions seemed headed in that direction. Carr saved him the trouble.

At 3:55 on Friday, March 5, Fahringer told the court that the defense rested its case. It had been extremely short, twelve witnesses to the prosecution's thirty-nine, and had lasted only four days. The strangest aspect was that its two strongest witnesses— Joy O'Neill and Robert Huggins—had only recently joined the defense, Huggins by chance and O'Neill courtesy of the prosecution. Salzman also had ambled along very late in the game.

One had to wonder what kind of case Fahringer was planning when he gave his serenely confident opening statement. Locksmith Salzman and dowager Brown to fight back the phalanxes of family, servants, doctors, technicians—even the defendant's lover— who had built the case against him.

But then Fahringer had told the jury the defense was under no obligation to say anything at all.

A noteworthy omission from the defense was the lack of a witness to substantiate the frequent claim that Von Bülow was a prized right hand to Paul Getty. Many remained at the oil company who had worked there when Claus had. It would have been a small matter for this free-spending defense to fly someone from London or Los Angeles to validate this claim, which was surely as important as Mrs. Brown's assertion that Claus was a good husband and father.

Of course, the biggest gap in the defense was testimony from the defendant himself. From the start the prosecution was quite sure the defense would not put Von Bülow on the stand in his own defense. His haughtiness and foreignness were not the considerations they once were—the Free Claus sentiment indicated Americans were not put off by the man—but more cogent considerations would make such a move extremely risky. On cross-examination, Famiglietti could bring up many things he was forbidden to introduce on his own.

Famiglietti could ask him probing questions about his background, his precise duties for Getty, and his familiarity with the Barlow murder case in London. He could air Von Bülow's own use of drugs, his denial that the black-bag substances were his, despite the labels on every prescription, his use of needles and syringes. He could cause him great embarrassment before the jury by asking him why he had not visited Sunny once in the hospital since January 1982 (he had been in New York a number of times) and had visited her almost never before his indictment in July of 1981 but frequently after the indictment.

Morris Gurley had been prepared to testify that Von Bülow had come to him in May of 1981 to find out what Alexander and Ala wanted to call off their investigation of him. Famiglietti could have asked Von Bülow about this. He could also bring out that Von Bülow, having long told Sunny that he wanted no money or "allowance" independent from her money, early in 1980 pushed for the creation of the inter vivos trust that paid him over $100,000 a year. Famiglietti would point out that this was *after* the start of the affair with Alexandra Isles when Von Bülow, probably for the first time since marrying Sunny, needed money of his own.

Famiglietti considered most of Von Bülow's statement to Lieutenant Reise when he came to Clarendon Court the night of April 21, 1981, to be exculpatory and self-serving. Several remarks, however, locked him into positions he would have a difficult time explaining on the stand. For example, he had told Reise that he had taken "drugs" from Sunny (barbiturates and tranquilizers was the implication) as well as "a needle." When Dr. Meier, after the second coma, had urged Von Bülow for information about Sunny, specifically asking if his wife had a problem with barbiturates or narcotics, Von Bülow had said she did not. (His quickness to dub her an alcoholic removes the face-saving possibility.)

Famiglietti said that his cross-examination would have depended heavily on what Von Bülow said on direct examination. If he altered the version he gave to Reise in his statement, Famiglietti could then chip away at the inconsistencies. If he gave the precise version, he could ask Von Bülow about those aspects of his story which make little sense held up against other facts. "Why didn't you tell the police about the black bag? Why did you lock the closet? Why didn't you tell Dr. Meier or Dr. Stock about 'Sunny's' black bag, her needles, and her drug abuse?"

"One of the worst things a lawyer can do on cross-examination," Famiglietti said after the trial, "is to ask a defendant 'why.' It gives him a chance to say something totally self-serving that might confuse or convince the jury. Instead you put the question 'Isn't it a fact that . . .' which limits his answer. I thought long and hard about these inconsistencies in Von Bülow's story and I had decided I was going to take the chance and ask him 'why?' "

Famiglietti was confident he could have pinned Von Bülow down on his charge that Sunny was a drinker, his statement to Reise that he had never seen insulin in Sunny's possession (which would further refute Joy O'Neill)—and again going back to that infinite source of controversy, the black bag. Why, if the bag was Sunny's, and Von Bülow said she did not use drugs after the '79 coma, was it found in his possession one year later and with one of the several prescriptions inside (all made out to Claus Von Bülow) dated December 18, 1980, the day before they left New York for Newport for the final Christmas?

Famiglietti said he could have asked him about his relationship with Alexandra Isles, getting him either to corroborate her damaging testimony or to refute it, putting him in the position of calling his beloved a liar. Famiglietti said he could have repeated this process "lining Von Bülow up against all my witnesses" forcing him to call not just Maria, Alexander, and Ala liars, but the other thirty-six witnesses who did him harm.

"I could have had him on the stand for days," Famiglietti said wistfully.

Fahringer, on the other hand, had a different explanation for why he did not put his client on the stand. "I felt it wasn't necessary; their case against him was too thin."

XXVI

JOY O'Neill had come into the Von Bülow case by approaching the prosecution. When Reise and Famiglietti found out her testimony was helpful to Von Bülow, they turned her over to the defense, as the law required, but set out in a frantic quest for information that might discredit her. She had impressed them as so neurotic and unbelievable, they doubted the defense would put her on the witness stand. If they should, they wanted to be ready.

The weekend following her emergence, which was about two weeks before her testimony on March 3, Jack Reise and Susan McGuirl headed to New York to visit the Manya Kahn studios. Arriving there, they found it had gone out of business; the studio was closed down with no sign of a new address.

Reise could see that its closing was recent. A Dempsy Dumpster in the street outside was full of fresh-looking gym detritus. Jack and Susan climbed into the Dumpster looking for a scrap of paper that might tell them Manya Kahn's new location. They found nothing.

On first coming to New York that day, Jack had phoned the directory listing for the Kahn studio, but got no answer. Finding nothing in the trash, he figured his only hope was that Manya's old business phone number—for which he had obtained a ring—had been transferred to her residence, which was not listed.

From a sidewalk pay phone he dialed the number again. After many rings he got an answer. Yes, this was Miss Kahn's. His troubles were not over. The voice on the other end was a woman —very old, very foreign. Standing in the freezing cold, he shouted his name twenty times, getting angrier and angrier while Susan found the spectacle funnier and funnier.

Finally he got an appointment to see Manya the following weekend. They found her a fragile woman, over eighty, and in dubious health. In two senses, her recollections of Joy O'Neill were sharp. Joy was not a person of good character; she had, in fact, been fired. Reise told Manya that Joy claimed to have instructed Sunny Von Bülow on a regular basis for years.

"That's totally untrue!" Manya snapped.

Jack and Susan now felt comfortable that Joy was not a creditable witness—but proving it was something else. Reise asked if there were records to refute Joy if they should need to. Manya thought there were, but her studio was closed, everything was in storage, she was not sure in what shape . . .

With the defense announcement ten days later that they would be calling Joy O'Neill to the stand, Reise resolved to go to New York at the first opportunity and find the records.

His years of police experience told Reise that in celebrated trials such as this one, oddball witnesses invariably appear out of the woodwork to upset the most meticulous and airtight cases. He recalled a Mafia trial in Providence that hinged on whether or not the accused had been at a particular meeting. The case was going well when suddenly a priest appeared in the courtroom to testify that *he* had been at the meeting and the defendant had *not* been present. Checking, the police found that on the afternoon in question the priest had three christenings on the other side of town. Police aren't always that lucky.

So, for a Joy O'Neill "bombshell" to be announced was no surprise, but Reise was too involved in this case, had given too much of himself to it, to permit watching an ex-ballerina send it down the drain.

A bit of lucky timing fortified Reise's determination. When the prosecution rested that Thursday, February 25, Judge Needham responded to coaxing by Fahringer and declared a recess till the following Tuesday, March 2. This double-sized weekend gave

Reise some extra time to find the records of the Manya Kahn Body Rhythm Exercise Studio.

As soon as court recessed, Reise and Miranda set out for New York. Reise was exhausted. If errands like the present one didn't keep him from bed, his obsession and worry about the case kept him awake once he got there.

By this time Joe Miranda was as deeply involved in the case as Reise. At the beginning of the investigation the previous summer, it was considered a good idea for the authorities working on the case to visit Sunny in her hospital room. Miranda had been devastated by the experience and said later to a friend, "I have pulled bodies out of Narragansett Bay, I've handled corpses that can only be carried in a plastic bag. You get tough. But seeing her like that, so pathetic, so helpless, not alive or dead—it was the first time in my police work I've become emotionally involved with the victim."

Miranda had been Reise's partner for eight years; he was with him every step of the way on the Von Bülow case. In his mid-thirties, Joe had been born in the Azores and come to Rhode Island with his family as a small boy. He seemed too soft-spoken and gentle to be an effective up-against-the-wall cop, but what he lacked in palpable toughness was made up for by his loyalty and seriousness about his work.

A back problem that had plagued him for years (with Famiglietti's that made two for the prosecution) had been exacerbated by the unaccustomed hours of courtroom sitting. As he and Reise drove to New York, the pain was at its worst. He should have spent the long weekend prone; instead, he was giving it up to debunk a gym teacher.

The good luck of the long weekend was followed by bad: Manya Kahn had been taken to the hospital.

Reise and Miranda spent all day Friday learning the location of the warehouse where the records were stored and, far more difficult, obtaining authorization to enter it. With the help of Manya's lawyer they found the storage contract and got the needed permission. The lawyer told them that even if they found the records they would not be able to interpret them without the help of Miss Kahn's assistant, Jill Sanders.

They were unable to reach Sanders by phone. As far as the

lawyer knew, however, she was in town. Friday evening, Jack Reise and Joe Miranda went to Jill Sanders's address, a small apartment building on East 80th Street, buzzed, but got no answer. After an hour waiting on the street in subfreezing cold they were taken pity on by some returning tenants, who admitted them to the corridor, where they could at least keep warm.

They became friendly with the super's wife, a Mrs. Flynn, from Boston, who told them she had seen Jill that day; she was sure to return eventually. Another two hours brought no sign of her. Exhausted and discouraged, they left Jill a note explaining their mission and urging her to phone them at the Edison Hotel no matter what time she came in. They went back to the hotel and collapsed. Around two o'clock the phone rang. Yes, she would meet them the next day and take them to the warehouse, which was in Yonkers.

The following morning they picked up Jill and drove up to Yonkers, presenting themselves just after noon at the Mini-Yellow Storage Company, a vast space with cagelike compartments. What optimism they felt on locating Jill and getting her cooperation was squelched when they saw the Kahn storage area—an enormous cube, so stuffed with furniture, files, and boxes that, as Miranda said, "Even a cat couldn't have gotten through."

For about an hour and a half the three moved furniture and trunks, finally coming upon some large canvas sacks which Jill identified as containing the records. She opened one; the ledgers had come apart and were totally disordered. She broke the news to the two policemen, who were now used to such setbacks. Jill showed them how to read the records, then they headed back to Manhattan and dropped Jill at her apartment.

When Jack and Joe arrived at the Hotel Edison with their unwieldy sacks of paper, two buses had just disgorged a hundred tourists into the lobby. Miranda recalls it taking a good half hour just to get their sacks into an elevator. Once in the room, they emptied the bags on the floor and began the sorting process.

"I've got March, 1975," Miranda would call out.

"Nineteen seventy-five is on the bureau," Reise would reply.

For two grueling hours they sorted the random sheets, finally assembling them in their original order. It took an additional three hours to go through them checking Joy's claim. They discovered that in the three years for which they had records, she had taught Martha Von Bülow exactly five times—a far cry from the five times *a week* she claimed.

It was now about 12:30 A.M. Their mission was complete. Both men desperately needed sleep. They went out and, as they tossed back beers, crowed about finding Joy in Manhattan.

XXVII

FAMIGLIETTI'S six rebuttal witnesses were brief but telling. First came Jill Sanders, who had worked at Manya Kahn's concurrently with Joy O'Neill and who kept the appointment records which were now being presented in court. From May 16, 1977, the date O'Neill started working at the studio, till the end of that year, the records showed that Joy had instructed Sunny five times. In 1978 and 1979 Sunny visited the studio 210 times and had not been taught once by Joy O'Neill.

Nancy Raether, a pretty brunette, was flown in from a job in Kansas City to testify that she had instructed Sunny in 1979 and 1980—255 times compared with Joy O'Neill's five. Sunny and Raether had been fond of each other, Sunny giving Nancy Christmas presents in 1978 and 1979. Famiglietti asked his witness for her impressions of Sunny. She was, Raether said, a woman of great dignity, very intelligent, refined, with a strong interest in culture and the arts. Raether also found her consistently gracious and genuine.

When she mentioned Sunny's soft, mellow voice and her articulateness, Famiglietti, in reference to Huggins's testimony, asked, "Would she ever have said, 'Yeah, sure'?"

"No," she replied firmly, adding that Sunny never seemed depressed either.

Had they discussed sweets and dieting? Yes, but there was no mention of injections or insulin. After more questions about

Raether's friendship with Sunny, Famiglietti asked the witness if she knew Joy O'Neill. Yes. What was her reputation for telling the truth?

Raether, who had already come across as a pleasant, unaffected woman, looked pained, lowered her head and said, softly, "I'm afraid it wasn't very good."

One doesn't have to have instruction from a judge to know a witness's demeanor should not determine judgments as to his or her veracity, but any spectator of the Von Bülow trial had to be aware of the likable, natural, believable nature of the prosecution witness. Being required to discredit Joy O'Neill's honesty seemed to make her unhappy.

O'Neill, on the other hand, had sent out nonstop signals of a different sort of mental distress; she had attacked with gusto not only her former employer, but a woman she had worked with twenty years earlier, Nora Kaye. Other defense witnesses had revealed similar off-putting qualities. As Robert Huggins was preparing to announce Sunny's suicide statement, his mouth twitched into a funny little grimace. The psychiatrist, John Carr, was constantly moistening his lips. Margaret Neilly responded to routine questions with an inappropriate vehemence. Dr. Hamolsky never once looked at the jury before whom he testified for hours.

What did it mean? Probably nothing, but there was an unmistakable pattern of ticks and quirks on the part of the defense witnesses and an opposing naturalness and, in most cases, an appealling quality to the prosecution witnesses that greatly bolstered their credibility.

The few prosecution witnesses who had made no attempt to ingratiate themselves with the jury—Dr. Stock and Alexander, for example—had good reason to be tense and unbending. About the only defense witnesses who didn't reveal off-putting quirks were Mark Millard and Mrs. John Nicholas Brown—but just being that old and that rich qualified them for statutory eccentricity.

Famiglietti next presented two doctors—Sunny's plastic surgeon and the chiropractor she had often visited after fracturing her hip. Both doctors had their offices on Central Park South, where Charlie, the chauffeur, had testified taking Sunny; this had been Fahringer's "evidence" that Sunny was getting prescription drugs beyond those Claus was getting for them both from Dr.

Stock. The two doctors said they never prescribed for her the kind of drugs the defense was talking about.

The only aspect of Charlie Roberts's testimony not wiped out by the two doctors was his claim to have made visits to the area *after* 1979, the last year either doctor saw Mrs. Von Bülow. Roberts, however, had already shown confusion on other dates and frequencies.

John Reise was called back to the stand to affirm that when he had interviewed Dr. Carr during his investigation Reise had been alert to the possibility that Sunny had attempted suicide and if she had the case was a waste of the state police's time. Carr had told Reise in a brief statement that at worst Sunny might be a closet drinker and a user of barbiturates, but had said nothing about suicidal tendencies.

When Richard Kuh was called to the stand, Famiglietti tried to establish that Kuh had once been District Attorney of New York, and was immediately stopped by an objection. Famiglietti tried to rephrase the question and was again shouted down by Fahringer. Remarkably, Judge Needham shot his finger toward Famiglietti and bellowed, "Don't try me, young man! We made a side-bar agreement, and you abide by it!"

As the trial neared its end, Judge Needham had finally revealed the public lawyer-bullying which tempered the respect most of his profession felt for him. Famiglietti was a particularly exasperating naughty child and the judge had had enough. It was a strange moment.

Kuh testified that the chauffeur had told him in a forty-five-minute interview that Mrs. Von Bülow generally ordered prescriptions by phone, but sometimes sent Maria out for them. Her automobile stops at the drugstores were usually for cosmetics, never for prescriptions.

Dr. Chernow from Newport Hospital reported that he tested the blood sample Huggins had drawn from Sunny at 8:06 A.M. on the morning of December 31; that Huggins came to work at 7 A.M. Therefore, the conversation between Sunny and Huggins must have occurred between seven and eight in the morning of the thirty-first, not the thirtieth, as Huggins testified. This made little difference except to discredit Huggins's accuracy.

The next witness, Helen Behan, had been Sunny's private nurse the morning in question. She remembered many conversational exchanges with Sunny, indeed had written some in her notes of that day, but she had no recollection of Sunny ever saying she tried to kill herself—either to her or anyone else. Behan said she remained in the room at all times, as her patient had just emerged from a serious coma; if she had left to go to the bathroom she would have gotten another nurse to sit in for her. Since she was obliged to leave the room when the family and doctors visited, she had no recollection of getting someone to stand duty for her, even for a few moments.

Famiglietti read from her record how Sunny had been in good spirits, that on January 1 she was in a talkative mood, chatting with Behan about things she wanted to do in the future.

If Helen Behan hadn't destroyed Huggins's testimony altogether, she at least had substantially raised the possibility he was lying. The prosecution's locating her on short notice could be credited to Jack Reise, who didn't believe Huggins's testimony and combed his memory for a way to refute him.

When he thought to search out a nurse who might have been present, both Famiglietti and McGuirl discouraged him, saying too much time had gone by, a nurse might not have been in the room at all times. Undaunted, Reise phoned the Newport Hospital and learned that hospital nurses had not been used for Sunny; her twenty-four-hour crew had been obtained from a nursing agency in Providence.

Reise drove to Providence, dug into the records, and found the name of Sunny's nurse that day, Helen Behan. When he called Behan his persistence was justified by her strong recollection of that particular job and of her certainty that she had not left her coma patient alone.

At ten minutes to three on Monday, March 8, the state rested its case. Judge Needham said he would allow each lawyer two hours for rebuttal the next day. Jurors would be sequestered and should bring overnight bags. The four alternate jurors were dismissed.

The prosecution team, for the most part satisfied with its case, was smarting under two of Judge Needham's rulings. Famiglietti had been anxious to introduce testimony of Von Bülow's efforts to cut off Sunny's life-support systems when she arrived at the Boston hospital; Needham ruled that this might prejudice the jury against Von Bülow without saying anything about his guilt or innocence of the crimes under adjudication.

The prosecution also had another witness Needham disallowed —an eighth doctor to rebut a specific of Hamolsky's testimony. Hamolsky had cited several articles to substantiate his view that low body temperature could cause coma. The prosecution's doctor could testify that Hamolsky had misread the articles; their conclusions were quite opposed to Hamolsky's interpretation.

This would reinforce Famiglietti's campaign to reveal Hamolsky's biased distortions. In addition, this rebuttal witness intended to add yet another medical opinion that exogenous insulin was the only possible explanation for Sunny Von Bülow's coma.

Judge Needham would not allow this additional doctor to testify on the grounds that Dr. Hamolsky had been sufficiently refuted earlier by Dr. Cahill's testimony. The barring of this final witness might not have worried the prosecution too much except for one of the dismissed jurors telling a reporter that, while he had leaned toward Von Bülow's guilt, he had been troubled by Hamolsky's testimony. This was a rare glimpse of juror thinking. If it was representative, it conjured up a prosecution nightmare of losing the case—now tallying forty-four witnesses—for the barring of one rebuttal witness.

XXVIII

AUTHOR'S note: Like all other journalists at the trial, I had been turned down in my requests for an interview with Von Bülow. I was surprised, therefore, on returning one Sunday evening to the apartment I had rented in Newport, to hear Claus on my answering machine saying that since Judge Needham had declared a day of recess at the conclusion of defense testimony two days hence would I like to meet for a talk?

I phoned Von Bülow's hotel room and suggested lunch. Lunch would be fine, he said, but since the entire day was free, why didn't we start earlier? Did I work with a tape recorder? I said I preferred it if the subject did not object.

That Tuesday at nine in the morning I presented myself at Von Bülow's room. He greeted me in a turtleneck sweater of lightweight gray wool; after the seven weeks of dark suits and neckties, it had the raucous impact of a Free Claus T-shirt. His home for the past two months was at the northern extremity of the Sheraton-Islander. A smallish sitting room had a wall of glass that overlooked the hotel tennis courts, now wet and bleak in the gray March morning. A staircase rose to a sleeping balcony; a bar had been set up on a chest of drawers recessed under the stairs.

For our conversation we sat at opposite ends of a hard sofa, the tape recorder between us. Von Bulow chain-smoked throughout the four hours we spoke.

A ground rule for our talk was to limit it to his background and avoid subjects that related to the trial. Reaching for some books on the coffee table (alongside one of mine), he said he wanted first to clear up a matter that had been upsetting him: the press's saying he was not really a "Von."

By way of putting the insult to rest once and for all, he showed me Von Bülow entries in the *Almanach de Gotha* and other frayed genealogies. I wondered what difficulties he had faced in order to have these volumes on hand in his Sheraton room. I wondered even more what they proved. Placing his finger on a sixteenth-century Eric von Bülow in no way established a connection to Claus. He might as convincingly have claimed Plantagenet kinship.

My feeling was that the matter was frivolous when held against the crimes Von Bülow stood accused of. In addition, I was prepared to believe his assertion that once a member of a family is a "Von," all subsequent members of that family may adopt the "Von" if they choose. His grandfather chose to drop it and he, at Sunny's prodding he said, put it back.

I was relieved when we left his pedigree and began exploring his early life. Almost immediately another idiosyncrasy appeared, one that I felt threatened the interview. Von Bülow would seize any opportunity to depart from his own experience and elaborate upon an impersonal subject. A question from me about the first years of Nazi occupation in Denmark brought forth a twenty-minute discourse on the history of Danish-German relations. I quickly learned not to invite such digressions.

As the information about his early years emerged (most of it is in Chapter Four of this book), he began breaking his prohibition of trial-related matters. He did this with increasing frequency and with only one subject: the failings of Sunny. Since his wife's personality defects were a major part of the defense and in fierce dispute in court, I considered this out of bounds. But it wasn't his rule-breaking I found interesting; it was his constant returning to this theme. Whenever we reached the end of a line of thought, he would launch himself into yet another of Sunny's shortcomings.

It was as though I had announced at the outset that I was most anxious to learn the reason their marriage was failing, or was urging him to list the aspects of Sunny that drove him to desperation. But no such curiosity was ever expressed (or felt), no such questions asked.

His leitmotiv would have been more relevant to his trial if it had pointed to the possibility of Sunny's having taken her own life, but his anecdotes had a different thrust: the impossibility of Claus's situation. He was portraying a man trapped in a torturous marriage and who lived in a realm where divorce didn't exist.

"From the earliest days of our marriage, Sunny was a voracious reader of the most esoteric subjects—comparative religion, anthropology, the development of the human brain from the aboriginal. I often tried to get her to discipline this interest by taking one of the auditor courses at Columbia or The New School, but of course, *that was people.* . . .

"Nothing one could do could make her feel better about herself. Not even the love of a man—and we did love each other—not even in the small ways, saying 'You look terrific in that dress,' but she would say 'You didn't like the one I had on yesterday?' A book came out in the early days of our marriage called *How to Be a Jewish Mother.* We joked about how like Sunny it was. A compliment was always taken in relation to something negative about her.

"Look, we have all known couples where one or the other had certain proclivities before marriage—I'm not talking about sexual things—they might have certain habits, whatever—and you always think your love will be the curing factor.

"Look, this is all so tragic and so on—of course she had a drinking problem, and of course Alexander and Ala would not be aware of it, they were too small. You can speak to any expert on alcoholism. You have three categories: the chronic drunk who is drunk every day, the acute drunk who only drinks in certain circumstances—in society, the pressure of going out, on the rare occasions, while I knew her, of emotional upset. I'm not suggesting (Sunny had) an unhappy life, but be it your mother, your husband, your adolescent children, we all have moments when we are upset, and those are the only moments, in my time, when Sunny would drink something.

"And then you have this category invented for the purposes of this trial: that she got inebriated on two drinks. That is what would happen to my fourteen-year-old daughter. It is not what happens to an adult. It is baloney.

"What happened quite clearly and should have been dealt with much earlier, as I don't think it was purely psychological, was if Sunny had two drinks, she had to have ten. The next day she wouldn't touch it, and the next three weeks she wouldn't touch it. But once she started, she had to go on. . . . Her last year, she got the message and didn't drink."

Not only was Von Bülow talking at length about a major issue of the trial, he was insisting on a point that had been disproved to most people's satisfaction by court testimony: that Sunny had a drinking problem of any sort. Alexander and Ala's being "too small" only works if the problem is confined to a period at least fifteen years back. His arguing the incompetence of their testimony was ignoring the parade of household servants, two of whom were defense witnesses, who created a picture of a woman who not only had no problem with alcohol but who drank far less than the average American.

As gently as possible I suggested it would have been an easy matter for his lawyers to produce at least one witness to corroborate what Von Bülow had just said. He froze and changed the subject. I could see that any appearance of arguing his trial-related points would drive us back into the agreed-on areas, so I let him wander freely through Sunny's imperfections as a wife and as a person.

"There was this defensive trait in her character," he said. "I don't want to mention specific sums of money now, but for the last two years she became tantamount to a recluse. It was her money and she was entitled to do with it what she wanted, but she would continue ordering the big evening dresses for what amounted to gigantic sums of money. She wouldn't admit she wasn't going to wear them. They'd just be hung in the closet. . . .

"If someone would call up to invite us to dinner, three weeks before Sunny would say, 'Oh, Claus, do you mind speaking to them?' I'd say I'd call them back. She'd say, 'Oh, let's go.' As we got to within three or four days of the event, she'd say, 'Can't you say you've got a business thing or you've got someone coming in for a visit?' And she would cancel. It was consistent.

"If I had to summarize, being married consists of a compromise between the two parties on her territorial imperatives and yours. Certain things Sunny considered her territorial imperative were very unimportant and one would quickly adjust to them. No one, not even her children, could use Sunny's bathroom. It didn't matter if you had to walk through four other rooms, you did not go into Sunny's bathroom.

"On trips, there would be quite a substantial bag of reading matter. You did not read Sunny's books before she read them. You might treat them as nicely as possible, and you would not tell her what the book was about. It wasn't a sanitary, germ thing either. She just—I don't know—I'm deliberately telling you things that you will say 'So what?' These things were easy to adjust to. . . .

"Before we married, I'd led a very social life. I'd hoped to go on. But at this price, I was prepared to give it up." (Despite the ironic ambiguity, it was clear Von Bülow, by "the price," meant the pain socializing caused Sunny.)

"It was a problem I had hoped to solve. When I was unable to solve it—all right—we'll give up going out. That's relatively easy.

"My life had included a great deal of classical music, either going to the opera, listening to the hi-fi. Sunny, who had apparently been a remarkable amateur pianist at school and was asked to give a recital at her graduation, gave it up completely from 1966 when we were married to roughly 1977 or '78. Not only did we never go to opera or concerts, I couldn't have [music] on in the house. . . . I got a tape deck and would listen in my room with earphones.

"Suddenly she changed and we went a great deal to opera and concerts. I would quickly add that she took my tape deck and was constantly playing it to herself. But for eleven years I could not have music on.

"I was brought up with church every Sunday. I always went to church the fifteen years I lived in England. Sunny refused. We went four times in the time we were married: when we were married at the Brick Church in Manhattan, Tom Hagemann's memorial service [Hagemann was the decorator of Clarendon Court], Cosima's christening at St. Peter's in Eaton Square, perhaps one or two other memorial services.

"I felt strongly that the children should have religion. It's like learning languages. If you don't do it as a child, you haven't got the option later in life. You need an alphabet before you can read a book. But even times like Christmas Eve, Sunny just wouldn't go. You see, it meant *people*.

"The choice of Newport was all wrong. Sunny wanted to live on Fifth Avenue, but she didn't want to live the life of Fifth Avenue. All the connotations of Newport were very wrong. Now, take someone I'm fond of and who's been loyal to me all through this, Doris Duke. She lives in a house that is five times the size of Sunny's. Her idea of living in Newport is to phone four or five friends and say 'There's a good film in Middletown, let's go.' And then have the group for supper.

"The only thing that makes you realize this is Doris Duke and not . . . somebody quite different . . . is that the wine is a museum piece—whether she laid it down or her mother or father. With that simple scenario—you might not wear a tie—the evening is simplicity itself and civilization itself. That's the way one should live.

"Nin Ryan, she was the salt of the earth, for years she would bring interesting house parties to Newport. One could have led a wonderful life here importing attractive friends. Once or twice a season, Sunny would have a mammoth dinner party—getting rid of what she was supposed to do. The idea of having six people around is more attractive for me. You get to meet your guests and talk with them. We didn't do it often enough.

"As for Sunny's money, you take your average trust officer, their whole game is security. If you are Paul Getty or Gianni Agnelli or Henry Ford II, you may be rich, but you own your own shop, you know what you're going to do, you have people you're responsible to, you fit in. I think it is very hard to live with owning a little bit of everything and nothing of anything, the balanced portfolio. You don't have an interest.

"Happy Van Buren [a Campbell Soup heiress who lives in Newport] has inherited a great deal more money than Sunny ever saw. She's opened a dress shop. She's doing this, she's doing that. I always tried . . . I mean that exercise teacher who will be the undoing of me now . . . do you think I would have fallen for that? There have been so many crank calls—do you think I would have fallen for that if I hadn't known she existed? I mean, if someone said 'Joy O'Neill' to me, I would have said, 'Who that?' But if you said 'Joy at Manya Kahn's,' I would have said 'Oh, yes' because Sunny was always talking about her. I think it is just the years that are wrong. It may have been 1976.

"Sunny would talk about Miss Susan, her hairdresser. She was always striking up these friendships. Two reasons I knew the business about Joy was true. Sunny disliked the idea of going to the salon with all those fat women around—you know, *other people*. When Cosima moved to Ala's room, Sunny talked about installing Joy in the nursery so she would have her own resident exercise teacher. I certainly remember Sunny saying, because I might have been directly involved, she might like to back Joy—not alone, some other names were mentioned.

"I talked at length to Sunny about opening an antique shop in the Brick Market which John Nicholas Brown restored and gave to Newport. Isabel and Price Glover could think about spending their summers in Newport [to run it]. I told Sunny she might like to buy for the shop in Europe. Something for her to do.

"Since she was seeking exercise, I said, 'You know, lots of people in England do their own gardening. Why don't you try that?' Our inside staff was in some ways absurd. For six years we had this perfectly fabulous chef who'd been at the Elysée Palace, meaning with de Gaulle. And of course, Sunny wouldn't eat his meals. She'd go refrigerator raiding, in the middle of the day or around 11:30 at night. In the end the chef simply got bored—there were no dinner parties, so he left.

"Sunny overstaffed on the principle that someone might walk out. She had someone to fall back on. The amount of times Sunny wanted to fire Maria! I always said to Sunny, look, you don't need a butler, you don't need a chef, you don't need a chauffeur because you can call up Fugazy—all these things you can do without, but you cannot do without a personal maid. And Maria is a damned good personal maid. Thanks a lot!

"The Germans are either at your throat or at your feet. Maria has a very nervous temperament. She would suddenly go into rages. I can remember in June of 1979 when Cosima returned from the hospital after having her tonsils out. We were bringing Cosima into the house with Sunny under one arm and me under the other.

Maria came flying out at us. 'You wicked child!' she screamed, 'I don't want you in this house! You can go right back to the hospital!'

"Sunny and I tried to calm Maria. It seems that Cosima had tied up the phone line she and Maria shared and Maria missed an invitation to dinner. There were endless other occasions. Maria is somewhat hysterical.

"In New York, Sunny was dissatisfied because her bedroom wasn't big enough. She felt she wanted something better. I said, 'Sunny, there's nothing to prevent you from converting the 33-by-20-foot living room into your bedroom. Then you'll have five windows on Fifth Avenue. You can convert the library into your bathroom; then you'll have what you want.' Why did we need a living room? We weren't receiving *anybody*!" His voice cracked with exasperation.

"I think we are getting in on the essential. I mean, once I didn't take the stand—yes, it was my choice not to . . . well, it was *a* choice—Sunny and I—as far as unsolvable confrontations—it was only the work. I mean, Maria was lying through her teeth when she said"—he parodied her voice—" 'Oh, Madam wanted to be married to a successful businessman.'

"Baloney! Sunny *had* married a successful businessman!"

I was struck by his challenging this one mild slur from Maria while leaving uncontested her catalogue of the most devastating accusations against him.

"In 1968, Sunny said no more Getty or divorce. When we married, it was part of my conceit, I thought I had what it took to work it out [her wanting to live in New York]. It was apparent that to work for Getty, there were only two places—London or Los Angeles. Sunny wanted to raise her kids in the U.S., but refused to live in Los Angeles.

"Had I stayed in England, I would have been given . . . I mean there was a very big Getty operation in the North Sea. There would have been plenty left for me. Even in 1973 Getty commissioned me to do a very big transaction which he'd worked on for two years, an antitrust. I had to fly to England to see Mr. Getty and the president of one of the biggest U.S. oil companies. Sunny said, 'If you're going to do that sort of thing, we'll have to get a divorce.' She didn't say it nastily.

"When Ala testified that Sunny wouldn't have minded my having a nine-to-five job, she should have been asked, 'What about three and a half months off in the summer?' You find me the job with a three-and-a-half-month summer vacation, another month and a half for traveling in Europe just for the heck of it, and where you leave every Friday at one o'clock because you're picking up your child at 1:30—well, you find me the job.

"So I had missed the boat, so to speak, when I left Getty. I then found it was very difficult. I had reached an age when fitting into the corporate picture of existing companies was not that easy. With Mark Millard and American Express, it was starting all over again. I wasn't going to say no to my second big chance.

"My greatest strength in business is as a front man. You don't go to Texas and tell them how to find oil. You must offer what the other fellow doesn't have. I'm good at meeting people, getting them to relax and confer easily. Now, of course, all that is finished for me."

Around noon, Von Bülow, rather than showing signs of wanting to end the interview, produced a half-full bottle of red Bordeaux and offered me a glass. I told him that, to my palate, it was a "museum piece."

"The owner of Annabel's—a good friend of mine—sent me a case. I don't want to say anything against the Sheraton. They have been wonderful, but their wine cellar is not their strong point. It was a most thoughtful present. At a time like this, one appreciates such gestures."

I offered Von Bülow lunch. Since the day was cold and rainy, he opted for the hotel dining room. On the way he picked up a batch of mail at the desk. Everyone in the Sheraton dining room watched as Claus Von Bülow chose a booth and sat down.

After asking if I minded his opening his mail, he glanced at each then handed it to me without comment. They were fan letters, pathetic offers of friendship and support, all from women. Some enclosed a photo. None of the middle-aged women in the pictures aimed at sexiness, but rather likability. In a typical note, the writer said she was a widow in her late fifties living in a small house in New Jersey; if Claus ever felt the need to talk, he would find in her a sympathetic ear.

Von Bülow placed the letters and the torn envelopes in a pile at the edge of the table. When the waitress was removing our soup bowls, she gestured toward the letters.

"Is this garbage?" she asked.

"Yes," Von Bülow said pointedly, "it's garbage."

In the weeks following my interview with Von Bülow, much of what he told me was contradicted by others. Some of the discrepancies were innocuous, like Maria's insistence that the French chef, still a good friend of hers, never worked at the Elysée Palace for Charles de Gaulle. Others who knew Sunny well scoffed at the idea that anyone as private and family-bound would consider ensconcing Joy O'Neill in her house. (There *was* an economy attempt in this area. When Manya Kahn wrote Von Bülow a condolence note after Sunny's final coma, he responded with a request for a refund of Sunny's unused fee, some two-hundred dollars.)

As for his adding the "Von" to please his wife, it came out that Claus had often used the "Von" in his pre-Sunny past—at school in Switzerland, at Cambridge; *The New York Times* article on his wedding to Sunny refers to him as "Von Bülow."

Of more significance perhaps was a story told by Ruth Flood before she knew of Claus's lament about being unable to interest Sunny in any activity. Shortly before Sunny's second coma, Ruth had a house party at her Connecticut house that included Sunny and Claus and Isabel and Price Glover. In conversation with her two oldest and best women friends, Sunny said that now that Cosima was almost grown, she was eager for a project to occupy her time. Ruth and Isabel felt the same way, so they came up with a scheme to start a business together—a catalogue company for expensive gifts.

"All three of us were wild about the idea," Ruth Flood said, "but particularly Sunny. Claus spent the rest of the weekend throwing cold water on the plan. He said it was harebrained, the field was overcrowded, we would lose our shirts . . ."

If he indulged Sunny's throwing away a small fortune on unused ball dresses, his panic at her risking a relatively small amount of money on a business enterprise is hard to understand.

I ruminated about Von Bülow's boldness in presenting to me as fact disparagements about his wife that were at best disputable but in some cases easily refuted. My wonder diminished when I considered the widespread success he had in the media with his portrayal of Sunny. I came to realize that this said less about press gullibility—although reporters, I think, are more prone to listen for distortion than for outright lies—than about the reluctance of those closest to Sunny to engage in a public debate about their most private friend with a man they considered a scoundrel.

With all Sunny had suffered, she was also to suffer, it seemed, from the discretion of her friends.

XXIX

FAHRINGER started his summation with praise for the jury and gratitude for their lengthy attention, then launched into a catalogue of points he considered exculpatory. No one saw any sign Von Bülow wanted to harm his wife; Mrs. Brown testified to his concern for Sunny; hadn't he called the doctor for her fractured hip against her wishes? Von Bülow loved his daughter, Cosima. How could he try to murder this girl's mother? (This was risky as it was possible no juror had made this connection until now.)

Mark Millard had testified to the defendant's earning capacity. Von Bülow wanted to work; he did not want to live off his wife's money. Fahringer took a bold shot: "Is there any question in anyone's mind in this courtroom that Martha Von Bülow had a drinking problem?"

Since the defense had not brought forth one witness to attest to a drinking problem and the prosecution had shown that these stories all originated with Von Bülow, Fahringer might have been forgiven for sidestepping this issue, which was dangerously suggestive of Von Bülow's "unhusbandly" behavior. But Fahringer added, "Her own children testified that *two drinks* had an effect on her," blithely subverting the accepted meaning of "drinking problem."

The first coma in all likelihood happened "instantaneously" when Dr. Gailitis arrived, he said, not when Maria first saw her.

Huggins heard her say that she had tried to kill herself. Why would he lie? Dr. Carr confirmed she had suicidal tendencies. Fahringer underscored the suicide notion by quoting the Edwin Arlington Robinson poem about Richard Cory, a man who had everything in life and still "went home and put a bullet through his head."

With one of his strongest points, Fahringer asked the jury if Mrs. Von Bülow, after her first coma, wouldn't have been more curious about how it happened. She wasn't curious, he said, because *she knew* how it had happened. She'd done it to herself. Likewise, wouldn't she have complained about feeling unwell? She didn't, for the same reason.

He hit hard at the discrepency between Maria's grand jury testimony and her trial testimony about Sunny's reason for wanting a divorce. "If a witness has lied," Fahringer said, "you can reject all of his testimony. If you order Irish stew and you find one piece of spoiled meat, you don't fish around for a good piece; you tell the waiter to take it away."

Fahringer jeered at Alexander's admitting going out for a drink after his mother had shown symptoms and "after one year of suspecting insulin injections." As for the black bag, Maria saw insulin in it, but the bag was Mrs. Von Bülow's. Alexander and Ala knew these things were hers; that's why they didn't go to their mother when Maria told them about the bag. And why had Sunny put her needles and things in a bag in her husband's closet? She wanted to hide them from Maria.

If the jury had not been confused before, they certainly were now. Out of the swirl of dust he had kicked up, however, Fahringer delivered a body punch. In the second coma, *when did Von Bülow have an opportunity to inject her*? The family all had dinner together, went to the movies together, came back and had a nightcap together. When could she have been injected? The prosecution never even offered a hypothesis.

It was amazing that at the end of a trial as long and detailed as this one, an important area still existed about which there had been no testimony. Not one of the many medical people had said anything conclusive about the time needed for insulin to take effect in the human body.

Fahringer settled into the always confusing medical testimony and claimed that the prosecution's entire case "boils down to the blood sugar and insulin tests being done on the same sample." With blithe disregard for days of expert testimony, he added, "All evidence is pretty much agreed that other factors could have caused the coma."

Fahringer said that Salzman's testimony established that the black bag was not found in the metal box but "someplace else, someplace not incriminating." The bag had no fingerprints taken. No one ever saw Von Bülow with the bag. If it was his, why would he have left it around to incriminate him?

The prosecutor will hit hard at Alexandra Isles as a motive, Fahringer told the jury, but Martha Von Bülow had agreed to a divorce. "Mr. Von Bülow had no motive to kill his wife." He wanted to earn his living; he had no desire to be idle.

For some reason, Fahringer concluded his recapitulation with the weakest and most damaging parts of his defense. He reminded the jury of the chauffeur who drove Sunny often to Central Park South, a street Fahringer seemed to have fixed in his mind as dedicated to dispensing drugs. "Is the chauffeur a liar?"

Having resurrected the weakest witness Fahringer then reminded the jury about his most damaging one, Joy O'Neill. Would anyone give flowers and wine to a gym instructor if they'd only been taught by her five times?

When Judge Needham interrupted to tell him he had ten more minutes, Fahringer shifted to an elaborate peroration stressing his obligation only to create reasonable doubt. He sympathized with the terrible decision facing the jurors, the burden to their consciences of an unjust guilty verdict, the assault the system would suffer if they convicted on such "paltry evidence."

Famiglietti started his summation with a challenge to the jury: if they thought that Alexander and Lambert had planted the black bag in Von Bülow's closet as a deliberate frame-up, they should not waste the state's time but rush back with a verdict of not guilty. But would Lambert, a twenty-five-year police veteran, bring a third party if he were embarked on a criminal expedition?

Alexander had no reason to accuse Von Bülow falsely; the young man is well fixed and would not realize any more money for twenty-one years if Von Bülow was eliminated from the will. Even if the jurors suspected Alexander of a conspiracy, "would the Rhode Island police become a party to it? Would I?"

Jurors must ask who started the investigation. Not Alexander, not Kuh, but Maria, who became highly suspicious when she watched Von Bülow ignoring his wife's serious condition at the first coma. When her life was saved, it was not by Von Bülow but by Maria.

Maria spotted the black bag among Von Bülow's possessions, saw it again several times over the year, saw insulin in it. Where did Alexander and Lambert find it? In Von Bülow's closet. The defense claim that it was planted in Von Bülow's closet is a red herring, a typical defense strategy to confuse, to create a mystery.

Eight weeks ago Mr. Fahringer stated what he would prove— although the law puts him under no obligation to prove anything. Here are some things he said he would prove, but never did: that the defendant was Getty's right-hand man; that the trouble in the marriage was about his wanting to work, not other women; that Mrs. Von Bülow lost interest in sex and that he was allowed sexual freedom; Von Bülow's capacity to earn ("He never earned more than $25,000 with Mark Millard; the rest is pie in the sky"); that Sunny took Valium and barbiturates constantly ("We know she took them, but there is no evidence she took them *constantly*"); that the black bag was hers.

Other servants, not just Maria, contradicted his version of the 1979 coma. Mr. Fahringer said Maria wondered why insulin was in her *mistress's* bag. Is that the jurors' recollection?

Then Famiglietti revealed his contempt for the defense's case. The jurors might find it interesting, he said, to note the change in the defense strategy from the trial's beginning to the present, as evidence destroyed their theories. They shifted to a multiple choice in the hopes you would buy one of them. They gave you the hypoglycemic-reaction-to-eggnog choice; they gave you the Joy O'Neill weight-loss theory. If you didn't like A or B they gave you the deliberate attempt to commit suicide, not making it clear if the eggnog was a suicide attempt. . . .

Famiglietti was bristling at his opponent's audacity. "Or perhaps it was none of the above. Perhaps she was hit by a meteorite from outer space."

Famiglietti reminded the jury of yet another choice: that Von Bülow administered insulin to his wife in an attempt to kill her.

Subsiding from his burst of sarcasm, Famiglietti said that witnesses from both sides all portrayed Von Bülow in the same way: as an intelligent, sophisticated man. "So are his crimes. He was ingenious enough to paint himself as a loving husband while in love with Alexandra Isles, to establish that his wife was an abuser of alcohol and drugs." The defense has attempted to switch her alcohol problem from constant drinking to low tolerance. The problems are opposite. The one and only source of the alcoholism charge was Claus Von Bülow.

Mr. Fahringer kept asking if witnesses saw evidence Mr. Von Bülow was trying to harm his wife. Would he advertise it in the newspapers?

Why did Von Bülow ask Dr. Gailitis for a letter in writing affirming Von Bülow had acted properly? If all he wanted was reassurance, wouldn't a phone call have done just as well? Gailitis wrote that Von Bülow's call to him had saved his wife's life. But we know what prompted the phone call: Maria. The phone calls with Neilly were a deliberate attempt at an alibi. Also, the call she forgot to mention was after the coma, but she said she learned of the coma in a *later* phone call. Either he hadn't mentioned it to her in the first or she fabricated the second call when she said he had been weeping.

Returning to Von Bülow's intelligence, Famiglietti said no one is above making a mistake. The defendant's neglecting to destroy one needle showed he was "intrinsically arrogant." Also, he underestimated Maria. Still further, he probably didn't realize that exogenous insulin has recently become detectable in the human body.

When Von Bülow's first attempt failed and the doctors diagnosed the cause as reactive hypoglycemia, this fell into his plan and made him bold enough to try again. Once it was on her record that she had a blood sugar problem, he was even safer trying the insulin method.

Then Famiglietti became philosophical. "Mr. Von Bülow is not the first person charged with trying to kill his wife. Don't be naïve. It happens in all levels of society."

Simple as this admonition was, it may have had more of an effect on the jury than anything else he said. Beyond a knowledge of human nature, Famiglietti had no way of knowing that this remark addressed itself to what was later learned to be the jurors' biggest problem: a difficulty in believing that anyone could do what Von Bülow was accused of doing, and particularly the nice-looking gentleman with whom they had been sitting for two months.

The defense portrays Mr. Von Bülow as a wealthy man, Famiglietti continued, yet they showed he had to sell works of art to pay for his defense. The salary he might earn with Mark Millard would be a far cry from the income from $75 million he had grown accustomed to enjoying. He was not willing to give it up. His wife's agreeing to a divorce does not remove the motive, it strengthens it; she could change her will at any moment. If she died, he could live lavishly with the woman he loved; it was an irresistible combination.

Then Famiglietti moved into a particularly devastating area, one that had not been pointed out before. He traced the testimony ("uncontradicted") of Alexandra Isles and showed that the two crises between her and Von Bülow, her first deadline and the Watergate love scene, both occurred a month before a coma. Everything shows, he said, that with her Von Bülow wasn't out for sex, he was in love with her; he wanted money for a complete and permanent relationship with her. The two comas occurred at times when Von Bülow was most in danger of losing Alexandra.

After such a dramatic point, it was almost anticlimactic when Famiglietti plunged into a review of the medical testimony, emphasizing the validity of the tests and the conclusions all the doctors he presented could not escape. He pointed out that the doctors and technicians he presented who did the insulin test were not even cross-examined by Fahringer, yet his opponent argued that their tests were inaccurate.

The reason Mrs. Von Bülow did not show slurred speech and other symptoms when tests were run in the hospital in April of 1980 was that those symptoms resulted from her being drugged, and not from the insulin. That she is still alive now has enabled us, through Dr. Holub, who treats her, to ascertain that she has no hypoglycemia, her metabolism is normal.

Famiglietti then reviewed the testimony of the specialists who all arrived independently at the conclusion of exogenous insulin, placing emphasis on Cahill's worldwide preeminence in the blood sugar field and Hamolsky's total lack of expertise in the same field. He reminded the jury of Hamolsky's "extracting misleading and isolated facts to prove Mrs. Von Bülow was not a healthy woman." Even he could not exclude exogenous insulin.

All the other doctors arrived at exogenous insulin without relying on the fact that Maria saw insulin in the Von Bülow's bag and that the needle was found to have traces of insulin on it. "If these facts are unrelated, it is the most incredible coincidence in the history of mankind. . . . On December 19, Maria saw insulin in the bag," Famiglietti said, then added another of his intriguing juxtapositions of dates. "In January, when Alexander got the bag, it was gone. Someone had used it."

Famiglietti went back to Joy O'Neill, finding yet new aspects of her testimony that were unbelievable, then proceeded to Huggins, who had remained silent for two years only to come forward with a highly personal confidence made to him by this woman who was so private she cleared people from her *bedroom* when she used the bathroom. "Huggins is a liar," Famiglietti said with finality. "He wanted to sound interesting and never thought he would have to back it up in court."

Von Bülow, who had sat with his usual impassivity throughout Famiglietti's summary, had reddened several times, but with this denunciation of Huggins he turned bright red.

Famiglietti was equally contemptuous of Dr. Carr's coming forward after two years with detailed recollections of questions and answers he never recorded and that he never told the police investigators who were seeking exactly that kind of information. Based on those few questions, the psychiatrist made a complete diagnosis of a patient he'd never seen before. "It's ridiculous!"

If she committed suicide with insulin, Famiglietti asked, why was no vial found? No one commits suicide in a secret fashion. Would a depressed, suicidal woman go to exercise class every day? And continue to do so after the first coma?

Charlie the chauffeur now keeps the Von Bülows' Mercedes; he must be loyal to Von Bülow; Mrs. Von Bülow can't do anything for him anymore. He tried to create the impression she was going to doctors for drugs. I brought in the doctors she *was* going to. "We can try this case till October and I'll bring in every doctor in midtown Manhattan to testify they never treated Martha Von Bülow!" During the chauffeur's testimony, Mr. Von Bülow knew that the doctors she was visiting on Central Park South were the chiropractor and the plastic surgeon, but he said nothing. It was another attempt to mislead.

Famiglietti admitted that there were still a number of questions the jurors might ask about the evidence, questions Mr. Fahringer didn't raise. When was the insulin given? How much? "Some we'll never know," Famiglietti said; "for others I can give you guesses."

Why leave the needle in the black bag? It was possibly one of several and was carelessly left behind. Why insulin? He thought it hard to detect and it was available. Why both attempts in Newport? He may have thought Rhode Island's hospitals less competent than New York's. Why no needle marks? The black-bag needle has a fine gauge. Also, the absence of a mark is consistent with someone else's giving the shot.

Famiglietti didn't add a point brought out elsewhere. Why were both attempts done on a Sunday? This might have been what some call "the Pearl Harbor strategy": the assumption that manned facilities such as defense installations and hospitals will be operating at partial capacity.

Famiglietti then lumped various Von Bülow actions. His lying to Dr. Gailitis on the phone and at the hospital, his going off to Florida with another woman while his wife was in a coma, his rarely visiting his wife in the hospital—these are all the actions of a guilty man. Why did he ask Maria not to come to Newport for Christmas in 1980? She got in the way the first time.

Von Bülow first learned of the investigation in April 1981, then showed up at Clarendon Court four days later and went right to the closet and to the metal box. When the police came he went back to lock the closet, later saying a shotgun was kept there, which is illegal. It is *not* illegal. All his actions are those of a guilty man.

The key to the case is the black bag and its contents, Famiglietti said. Once you reach the conclusion that exogenous insulin was the cause of the comas, all you must do is determine who owned the black bag. Famiglietti listed the evidence tying the black bag to Von Bülow and added there "was not one iota of evidence to tie Martha Von Bülow to that bag."

One bottle marked Seconal was actually amobarbitol. Why would she change the labels? It would have been easy for him to anesthetize his wife prior to injecting her. It would have been easy for him to give her powdered amobarbitol in a glass of anything.

Famiglietti then made a generalization that could be taken as a motto for the entire case: "You are more vulnerable to people you love and trust than you are to the most vicious murderer." As Famiglietti warmed to the various ways Von Bülow could have gotten barbiturates into his wife, Judge Needham interrupted him and said, "Don't go too far, Mr. Famiglietti."

Famiglietti moved to his conclusion. At the beginning of this trial the jurors had promised him they would find the defendant guilty with circumstantial evidence if it was strong enough. The prosecution had given overwhelming evidence of this man's guilt. If we had an eyewitness, Mr. Fahringer would have said he was mistaken or lying. Some crimes have no eyewitnesses. Jurors have a way of separating the wheat from the chaff. It is not easy in this case—or in any case—but if you examine the evidence carefully, there is only one conclusion: guilty.

In Fahringer's summation he had raised two questions that had not been emphasized heretofore: what opportunity did Von Bülow have to inject on the second coma and why would Sunny not have been more curious about the cause of her first coma? On the first question, Famiglietti dealt with it honestly: he didn't know when he did it, or how. Privately he said that his personal belief was that Sunny's symptoms while talking with Alexander—the slurred speech and the loss of energy—resulted from the barbiturates, which were merely a prelude to the insulin shot administered *after* she went to bed.

One could also hypothesize that when she went to the bathroom she encountered her husband, who was in his study (off her bedroom) making phone calls. He might have suggested a shot to make her sleep well that night, to soothe her nerves, or whatever their routine may have been.

As for her lack of concern about the first coma's cause, Famiglietti felt this was covered by the retrograde amnesia Dr. Funkenstein said was common to all coma victims. He also had two witnesses he could have brought forward, Sunny's hairdresser and Isabel Glover, who would have testified Sunny *was* worried about the coma's cause.

Other damaging points were not brought out either during the trial or in summation, according to Jack Reise. If, as the defense argued, the black bag was Sunny's and she was injecting herself with insulin, surely Von Bülow knew about it. Why, then, when he briefed first Dr. Stock and later Dr. Gailitis on matters that might relate to her condition—her "alcoholism," etc.—did he not mention the bag full of drugs and needles?

Or when Reise came to Clarendon Court to accuse him, why didn't he say "This has gone too far. My wife has this black bag with drugs and needles . . . " But there was no mention of it. And why was the bag, which seemed to travel with him wherever he went, left behind in Newport after Sunny entered her final coma? Famiglietti might have argued that Von Bülow had no further need for it—had lost interest in it, in fact—until he learned there was an investigation, at which time he traveled two hundred miles to get it.

All in all it had been a meticulous and exhaustive prosecution and a brilliant summation by Famiglietti. Of all the "neutral" people who had been in the courtroom from the trial's beginning, such as journalists and courtroom personnel, most had, by the trial's end, become certain of Von Bülow's guilt. By no means all of them felt he would be convicted.

Reporters, more than most, grow cynical about the system. Several of those who felt Von Bülow would escape conviction quoted the opinions of lawyer friends who pointed to the circumstantial nature of the evidence. This opinion implies that all you must do to commit murder with impunity is make sure you have no eyewitnesses. You can leave behind all the poisoned brownies, used needles, and smoking guns you want—as long as you remember to close the door. No husband or wife in the country would be safe.

When Judge Needham dismissed the four alternate jurors, the press pounced on them for a reading on juror thinking. Predictably, the four alternates would say nothing about how the others felt, but one of them, Paul Otis, gave a tribute to his colleagues in citing Von Bülow's good fortune. "That guy has got a very good jury," he said. "There's a lot of intelligent people in there, a lot of nice people."

Judge Needham started his charge to the jury by telling them not to seek out hints in what he was about to say regarding the facts of the case. "I am the authority on the law; you are the sole judge of the facts."

Neither were they to consider anything the lawyers said as evidence. The presumption of innocence was still in effect. It would only be overturned if the jurors brought in a unanimous guilty verdict. Only the state must prove anything regarding the two separate charges. The jury may not make unfavorable inferences because the defendant chose not to testify.

The state need not prove that the victim was seriously injured by the injections of insulin they allege the defendant injected, only that he intended to take her life. There has been no direct evidence to support the state's assertion. No one saw on either occasion the action the state accuses him of. Indirect or circumstantial evidence must prove beyond a reasonable doubt. The jurors may draw reasonable inferences from what they have heard. They have heard testimony about what happened in 1979 and 1980. They have heard doctors with personal knowledge of the victim and consultants who testified on her records.

Whether Martha Von Bülow was injected with insulin or not is an issue in this case. The *effect* on her is only an issue if the jury finds the intent was to take her life. The crime takes place at the time of the injection. If the jurors find conflict between the testimony of experts like doctors, they must resolve the conflict. They may not resolve it by weighing the number of witnesses.

They must determine if the evidence points to the defendant. They must determine if the defendant had the opportunity to inject his wife. They must determine if he did inject his wife.

Circumstantial evidence is as good as direct evidence. Information relating to motive may not be used in any way unless it establishes motive. The state need not convince them of motive.

If the state proves motive, but not that the defendant performed the act, that would not justify a verdict of guilty.

How do they decide if the state has proved its case? It must be a judgment on their part. He urged them to use their "God-given common sense." Weigh the probability or improbability of testimony. Has a witness been impeached? Were the statements of a witness consistent with prior statements to the police or to the grand jury? Some witnesses do not tell the truth. The jury can reject their entire testimony if a witness is proven untruthful about one point.

There are areas where the jury may not speculate. With a sustained objection, they may not speculate on what the answer to the question would have been. They may not speculate on the contents of the eighty-four-page statements of Claus Von Bülow. They may not speculate on what the defendant would have said if he'd taken the stand.

They may not let their personal likes or dislikes of counsel or the defendant influence their decision.

Proof beyond reasonable doubt does not mean proof beyond all doubt. A doubt must not be fanciful or imaginative. It must not be a doubt conjured up to avoid making a judgment. Doubt must rest in the evidence.

If after studying the evidence the jurors fail to arrive at a moral certainty, then the state has failed to prove its case beyond a reasonable doubt. Their judgments must be unanimous. There are four possible verdicts of the two events. The defendant may be guilty or not guilty of both. He may be guilty of one and not the other.

He told them to keep an open mind, but not to yield a point of view to reach unanimity. They are to yield a point of view only if fellow jurors convince them the evidence demands it. They are not to let the personality of their fellow jurors sway them—only the evidence.

If after weighing all the evidence they believe that Claus Von Bülow on December 26, 1979, injected his wife with insulin with the intention of killing her, they are duty-bound to convict him. If they do not, they must acquit him. And he repeated this for December 21, 1980.

* * *

At 11:30 in the morning, after roughly one hour, Judge Needham finished his charge indicating that just he and all the participants in the case of Rhode Island versus Claus Von Bülow had completed their job—investigators, lawyers, witnesses—except the twelve jurors; theirs was about to begin.

XXX

THE Von Bülow jurors were housed in an attractive motel on a windswept hill overlooking the sea in Middletown. The first day, Thursday, March 11, they deliberated for five hours, then asked to be excused.

The morning of the second day of deliberation started with the manager of the Opera House, one of the two movie theaters on the square facing the courthouse, arriving at his theater at 8 A.M. to find someone had taken down the name of the film he was showing, *Making Love,* and replaced it with *Free Claus.* Without waiting for one of his workers to come in, the manager scrambled up a ladder to correct his marquee; he was worried that if jurors saw it from their windows it could cause a mistrial.

Later the same day a well-built young woman appeared outside the courthouse modeling a FREE CLAUS T-shirt, which nearby vendors started selling briskly at ten dollars apiece. A day or two earlier people had appeared carrying FREE CLAUS placards and had stood listlessly among the crowd. Because of the sudden emergence of these pro-Claus manifestations, Dick Kuh said he "smelled the fine hand of a public relations firm."

During the trial, the streets outside the courthouse had been the scene of a number of small demonstrations, straggly groups carrying NO NUKES or anti-abortion signs. Straggly or not, these people were smart enough to get themselves and their causes on national television, filmed by cameramen desperate for some footage other than the top of Von Bulow's head getting into a taxi. It is doubtful if the potential for publicity was lost on Von Bulow's lawyers.

After being closeted for another seven hours, the jurors sent Judge Needham a note: they would like to hear again the portions of Maria Schrallhammer's testimony that related to events of December 27, 1979.

Judge Needham, in collaboration with lawyers from both sides and the court stenographer, worked frantically for two hours combing Maria's two-and-a-half days of testimony for the relevant portions. Finally, the jury entered the quickly filled courtroom, Judge Needham took the bench, and the stenographer read the portions.

The effect was strong on all assembled; the river of information that had flowed through this room in the intervening five weeks had blurred Maria's horrifying picture of Von Bülow's obstruction of efforts to save his dying wife. If the prosecution had chosen an excerpt from their case for reprise at the finale, they could not have asked for anything more damaging to the defendant.

Saturday, the town of Newport celebrated St. Patrick's Day, a major holiday in the heavily Irish town, by sending a parade down Broadway, past the courthouse, into Washington Square. The satin-and-gold-braided high school bands provided a bizarre accompaniment for the aristocratic, chain-smoking European gazing down on them from a courthouse window.

When by the end of Saturday the jurors had still not reached a verdict, Judge Needham gave them the option of skipping Sunday. Since they would have to remain sequestered, they chose to return to the courthouse and continue their deliberations. Optimism ran high that their zeal suggested a verdict was near, but Sunday ended with no word. Nor did Monday bring a hint of progress. After lunch, Judge Needham sent them a note with two questions. Would they reach a verdict today? Would they reach a verdict if given sufficient time?

The answers came back: no to the first question, yes to the second.

The Von Bülow trial was already the longest in Rhode Island history; by Tuesday the record had been broken for duration of a jury's deliberation as well. At 10:45 Barbara Connett came out of the jury room and gave a sheriff a note for Judge Needham. Needham then summoned the lawyers to his chambers, an action trial veterans said was not customary if a verdict had been reached. Everyone was summoned back into the courtroom, expecting more testimony to be reread. As the crowd filled the room, Famiglietti shook hands with Jack Reise; the small action said that the moment had arrived.

As the jury filed in from the rear of the courtroom, not one of them glanced at Von Bülow as they passed his table. This is another portent to trial veterans, this one of a guilty verdict. Von Bülow, seemingly serene and imperturbable as on the trial's first day, sat leaning forward, his elbows resting lightly on the table, his fingertips intertwined.

As the clerk began to read, "At 10:40 A.M. on the sixteenth of March, 1982, the jury reached a verdict . . ." Von Bülow was immobile except for the small action of pressing his thumbs together, arching them away from his fingers, then back. When the clerk asked foreman Barbara Connett how the jury found the accused on the first count, and she stood and said "guilty," Von Bülow's thumbs stopped, but only briefly, then resumed their in-and-out motion.

There were gasps in the courtroom when he was pronounced guilty on the first count, even more when the word "guilty" followed immediately for the second count. Someone said, "My God!" Otherwise the packed room remained calm. Fahringer and Sheehan kept their heads down and looked at the table in front of them. Mary McGann, Sheehan's secretary, started to cry.

At the adjacent table, Famiglietti squeezed Susan McGuirl's hand under their table and she in turn clutched Jack Reise's, who grabbed Joe Miranda's. Famiglietti was heard to say, "My God, we've done it!" Reise tried to lessen his broad smile by closing his eyes.

The jury was polled, each of the twelve rising in turn to tell the court how he or she responded to each of the two charges. As the word "guilty" rang through the courtroom twenty-four times, the manner of each juror suggested the pain of his or her decision.

Constance Jennrette, who had cleaned Mrs. Slocum's mansion, gave her verdict in a loud, firm voice. The nursing-home kitchen worker, Aldina Paiva, chewed gum and glanced quickly at Von Bülow as she spoke the words. Arthur Hull glowered fixedly at Von Bülow throughout the clerk's questions and his answers, registering more hostility than had Alexander von Auersperg.

Judge Needham thanked the jury for their time and effort and told them they were now free to return to their homes. As they filed out, again passing within three feet of Von Bülow, not one glanced down at him as they often had in the past weeks.

Famiglietti argued briefly for jailing Von Bülow immediately, on the grounds that he might flee. Fahringer countered that there was no need for such harsh action; his client had "always appeared," has "deep roots in this country," and has a daughter who "is his whole universe." Judge Needham continued the $100,000 bail on which Von Bülow had been free since his arraignment, and set April 2 as the hearing for the new-trial motion at which time the judge could exercise his power to overturn the jury's decision.

As Von Bülow and his lawyers rose and started to exit through a door to the left of the bench—a door hitherto unused by them, which symbolized his new status—Famiglietti alone in the courtroom rose to his feet.

When court was recessed, pandemonium broke out. The prosecutors hugged each other and received the crowd's congratulations; reporters rushed out to intercept jurors. An English reporter asked Famiglietti his theory on why the case had attracted so much attention. Was the reason its being "a real-life who-done-it"?

With a broad smile Famiglietti said, "It's not a who-done-it any longer."

When the prosecutors—Famiglietti, Reise, and McGuirl—emerged from the courthouse's main entrance into the cool sunshine, they encountered a crowd of some three hundred spearheaded by camera- and microphone-wielding news people. As Famiglietti made a measured statement, there were shouts of "Claus was innocent" from the crowd and snide jeers like, "You going to run for governor, Steve?" The crowd's displeasure did little to dampen the spirits at the prosecution's victory dinner that night at Providence's Blue Point restaurant.

Immediately following the verdict, three of the jurors agreed to a press conference in the Colony House. Although foreman Barbara Connett was present, the ponytailed computer analyst, David Taffs, was designated their spokesman, in all likelihood because his colleagues felt he would be most adept at adhering to the jurors' pledge to say nothing about the substance of their six-day deliberation. (Eventually there would be breaks in this resolve.)

Fahringer and Sheehan also came to the Colony House to speak briefly to the press. Von Bülow remained in the defense room and phoned his daughter, who was in Palm Beach, for the first time breaking down as he told her the news. Back at his hotel, as he checked out of his suite of two months, sympathy for him ran high among the Sheraton staff, one housekeeper rushing up and tearfully kissing him in the lobby. A tray of four glasses and a bottle of Moët et Chandon was left behind in his suite. He and Fahringer said little on their drive to New York.

The six-day ordeal of the Von Bülow jurors is a revealing and affecting saga of twelve people whose emotions, which told them no one could commit such a crime, battled their intellect, which told them the incriminating evidence was overwhelming. Most jurors tend to strain toward acquittal if only from the dread of convicting an innocent man. This jury seems to have been plagued by an almost metaphysical sense that Von Bülow's guilt would affect them all; their perception of humankind and therefore of themselves would be permanently altered.

Without taking a vote on guilt or innocence at the outset, Barbara Connett threw them into an examination of the evidence. An intriguing scheme was devised for systematically weighing each bit of testimony. They sketched a chart—like an upside-down tree with the the the trunk representing a guilty verdict. The trunk was split into two main "branches": one, that the comas were caused by injected insulin; the other that Von Bülow had injected the insulin with the intention of causing death.

Taking the first of these two suppositions, the jurors went over every bit of medical evidence presented by the prosecution's doctors, measuring it against Hamolsky's opposing testimony. As they discussed this aspect of the case, they would take a consensus; did everyone agree that injections caused the comas? Anyone who was unconvinced was asked to state his or her reservations. Whichever juror recalled testimony that answered the particular concern would volunteer it. When everyone was agreed on a point, they would proceed to the next.

When they got to the more difficult question of *who* had injected Mrs. Von Bülow, they considered every possibility, starting with the most farfetched. (When the aged maid, Mrs. Sullivan, was suggested as a possible culprit, one juror exploded with laughter.) "The only ones we didn't suspect were the dogs," one juror said. Actually, the dogs were considered, but as accessories. One of the group hypothesized a reason for insulin's presence in the house: One of the labradors had diabetes.

They worked their way through every person who had access to Mrs. Von Bülow, examining the possibility that each might have either injected her or made it appear that Von Bülow had done it. After laborious hypothesizing of the guilt of Alexander and Maria, they finally eliminated all but two possibilities, Von Bülow or his wife.

In weighing the scenario that had Sunny injecting herself, the suggestion made by Joy O'Neill and Huggins, the jurors had great difficulty believing that anyone could take the witness stand and, under oath, deliberately lie; yet they eventually concluded that both O'Neill and Huggins had done precisely that. Juror Donald Zuercher said, "When Joy O'Neill testified, I was elated. I believed her 100 percent. When the prosecution shot her down, I was very depressed."

When they had eliminated all possibilities except Von Bülow himself, the testimony of Alexandra Isles became important to them and, for the same reason of motive, the testimony of Morris Gurley about Von Bülow's share of the will.

The most surprising aspect of the jury's deliberation was the major importance they gave to Von Bülow's letter to Dr. Gailitis in which he reconstructs the events leading to the first coma. Jurors' concern over conflicts between his version and Maria's prompted their request to hear again the maid's testimony about this day. They were also bothered by Von Bülow's seeking from the doctor written documentation of this exoneration.

On Saturday, with the St. Patrick's parade rollicking outside, they polled the table for a general consensus; it became clear they were approaching a guilty verdict. Emotion ran high. One woman, on concluding he was guilty, broke down so badly she had to be taken to the rest room to recover. Women were not the only ones to cry on arriving at the grim conclusion.

On Monday, when they received Judge Needham's note, only two jurors remained unconvinced; one of them capitulated, finally satisfied the others were unwavering in their decision (his only reason for holding out, he said). The last juror to decide Von Bülow was guilty was Arthur Hull. Later, in an interview with the *Newport Daily News*'s Catherine Callahan, Hull said he was so anxious to find Von Bülow innocent ("I kept thinking Cosima has no mother; if we find him guilty, she'll have no father") that he clung to the testimony of Joy O'Neill.

His colleagues' rejection of O'Neill angered him into threatening to hang the jury and cause a mistrial. After making this stand, he told Callahan, he sat back and said to himself, "You damn fool. You *know* he's guilty." The next morning, Tuesday, Hull admitted as much to his colleagues and Connett called for a vote, the jury's first, which was unanimous. She sent Judge Needham the note.

Jurors were stunned to learn, on emerging into the world again, that the man they had just convicted had become a hero. A number of jurors were castigated by both friends and strangers, particularly Donald Zuercher when he returned to his job at the Sheraton Islander, where Claus's long tenancy had made him beloved by the staff. "I told them unless they sat in that courtroom everyday for six weeks listening to every bit of the evidence, they had no right to question our decision."

Other comments from jurors: Aldina Paiva: "I'm exhausted and just want to forget the whole thing." Winifred Shaw: "We gave Mr. Von Bülow the benefit of every doubt. We did not have a vengeful attitude. No one ever said anything against him personally." Robert Kirkwood: "This was one of the most emotional experiences I've ever had." David Taffs: "We were all trying to prove that he was innocent." Constance Jennrette: "There are no more question marks. I'm at ease with my decision."

Jurors were not only harassed by their fellow Newporters, they found themselves visited by another of Herald Fahringer's research squads, this time two detectives hoping to discover aspects of the defense's case jurors considered weaknesses. ("They had no case," one juror responded.) Because of some questions asked, a number of the jurors suspected the investigators were trying to make them admit such causes for mistrial as newspapers in the jury room, conversations with nonjurors about the case, or other improper influences. The exhausted and emotionally spent jurors were outraged by this new defense tactic.

In considering the Von Bülow jury's agony in arriving at a guilty verdict, it becomes more difficult to understand the ease with which so much of the public pronounced him innocent. The rationales were as varied as they were illogical. Women picketed for acquittal because of Von Bülow's beautiful eyes and lustrous skin tones; an Italian intellectual living in New York snapped, "Americans are always out to get Europeans!"

Supporters of Von Bülow based their sympathy on several different personas invented for him. They saw him as the underdog despite a defense only a small elite could afford; as the plot victim despite proof no one had a motive to plot his downfall; as the friendless foreigner despite the efforts of powerful friends like Mrs. Brown and Mark Millard.

The one snap defense that made any sense—that an intelligent man couldn't have bungled the crime so—could be answered in many ways, most promptly by pointing to how close he came to getting away with it, his nemesis being one tiny needle and an unusually vigilant maid. In addition, Von Bülow had no reason to think he was (or would be) under suspicion, or that insulin could be detected in the human body as coming from outside. The crime was not bungled; he had rotten luck.

As for trying the same way twice, this was all but mandated by the doctor's conclusion, after the first coma, that Sunny was hypoglycemic. The diagnosis provided the perfect setup for a second attempt with insulin.

The people who point to Von Bülow's intelligence as exoneration are the same ones who say conviction should not result from circumstantial evidence; they see nothing circumstantial in their assumptions of Von Bülow's error-proof intelligence on one side and stupidity in a gone-awry crime on the other. The only apparent consistency in this double view is a determination to find him innocent. No matter how strong the refutations of the pro-Claus rationales, they rarely weakened a belief in his innocence; the most that could be achieved was driving the supporter to a *different* rationale.

Some persist in pointing to the German maid as the true culprit, insisting that she plotted to destroy Von Bülow out of jealousy for her beloved mistress. Maria firmly denied there was any bad feeling between her and Von Bülow prior to the first coma and no evidence was presented to the contrary. But even allowing for animosity, given the two motives—fifteen million dollars and marriage to Alexandra Isles against a maid's fifteen-year-old jealousy—it doesn't seem possible that anyone could consider Maria a more plausible suspect. Yet some did.

If pinned down, those holding the strained rationales for Von Bülow's innocence usually nurture a belief that *no one* could coolly and calmly commit such a crime. This is a pretty defense, but one finally that says much about the person who espouses it and nothing about Von Bülow.

The trial also attracted a small group of theorists who were driven to alternative conclusions, not so much by a belief in Claus's innocence as from a repugnance to the banality of attempting murder for love and greed. They whispered that Claus's fondness for inert forms caused him to inject Sunny for purposes of erotic sport. It did no good to point out to these fantasists that, should a husband want to render his wife unconscious for a period, insulin would not just be far down on the list of means, it wouldn't be on the list at all. It rarely causes prolonged coma; it is either assimilated or it kills. "That's just the point," they say. "The danger was part of the game."

Of all the many theories that flourished from time to time, perhaps the most bizarre was the one that had Sunny a knowing collaborator to her own murder. Indeed, her oblivion to what was going on under her nose tends to nudge the speculator in this direction—as does the ease with which surreptitious actions can be committed against a trusting spouse. This strained plot falls apart from the lack of evidence that Sunny wanted either to end her life or to do harm to Claus.

With or without such fanciful alternatives to the jury's decision, large numbers of people still believe that an innocent man was convicted. As difficult to explain as the outpouring of clichés of support was the absence of the clichés of condemnation. Where were the complaints that a rich man can get away with anything? Where was the disdain for the silky, poor foreigner marrying the innocent American worth millions? Was there a snort at the man who lived off his wife's money? Who had a lover while doing so? While such derogations are probably as unfair as the Von Bülow apologies, the hard thing to explain is that one set of prejudices was present and the other seemed totally absent—or at least totally silent.

Was there lurking in the Von Bülow aura a Jesse James aspect? An undercurrent of brash loner taking on powerful interests? Or maybe he was perceived as a suave Lothario who romances silly rich women and steals their jewels? Or was he given one of the other legendary personas that throughout history have served as lightning rods for grounding public hostility toward the rich? Perhaps his supporters recognized his guilt and were excited by it, turning Von Bülow into a 1982 amalgam of Bluebeard and *Dallas*'s J.R.

While there is no doubt Von Bülow represented each of these things to at least some of his following, many more who took his side gave the whole business even less thought. For such snap verdicts the place to look is perhaps the medium that is most used by the public for its snap impressions, television. Television was a prime suspect in the Free Claus phenomenon as it was a strong, new element in the trial. Having created widespread Von Bülow interest, television was obliging that interest with a fullness of coverage that gave it a controlling voice in public perceptions of the case.

Did it somehow benefit Von Bülow that six hours of complex testimony was reduced each day to two minutes of network time? That the reduction of the day's disclosures to brief headlines had an overall exculpatory effect? It is unlikely. While one day's headline might be "Joy Said Sunny Injected Self With Insulin," another day's headline would counter with "Maid Says Von Bülow Watched Wife Die." On a score-keeping basis, the latter-type headlines won by far (forty-eight prosecution to twelve defense witnesses).

Television appears to have benefited Von Bülow in a more subtle way. It is much easier to impute heinous crimes to anonymous names in the newspapers than to people known personally. To an extent, someone seen regularly on television becomes "known." This would be particularly true of one seen—not glowering for a mug shot or dashing into court with a coat over his head—but turning up calmly in court each day, reserved, well dressed. With each decorous appearance, the defendant becomes less and less capable of committing brutal crimes.

The Von Bülow jury said they had trouble reaching a guilty verdict, not because they considered the prosecution's case insufficient, but because they resisted believing such a crime could be committed by anyone. Perhaps what they meant, if their interior reasonings could be uncovered, was that they had trouble believing such a crime could be committed by anyone *they knew.* The jurors were under the judge's orders to put aside such reasoning; the public was not.

In his *Newport Daily News* interview, in reference to the jury's daily parade past Von Bülow, juror Arthur Hull said, "When you walk by the man every day, this isn't just a figure, this is someone you start to get to know." To a lesser degree, the same psychological mechanism was at work on watchers of the evening news.

Television made Von Bülow the beneficiary of a further helpful impression. With a battery of people haranguing him day after day he remained throughout silent, reserved, dignified. Because the most exposed man was also the only one in the bitter proceeding who remained silent, this may have caused him a daily deposit of sympathy that, by the trial's end, had become an accumulation of heroic proportions. For an American public woozy from the effusions of celebrities trying to talk themselves into a personality, Von Bülow's spectacle of silence was impressive and winning.

Von Bülow once complained to a reporter that everyone involved in his trial had a function but him; lawyers, witnesses, the judge, the press—all the courtroom regulars had jobs to do. He could do nothing but sit. If the above theory is valid, his sitting mute was the best ploy of his defense.

While the carnival fervor of the pro-Clausers had a bewildering newness about it, the underlying sentiment—sympathy for the criminal rather than for the victim—has become an increasingly frequent phenomenon. Russell Baker in a *New York Times* column on the acquittal of John Hinckley alludes to it: "The old principle followed by criminal lawyers with difficult murder cases to defend was to 'try the victim.' As a reporter, I covered a few such cases. It was fascinating to see how the dead party, long in his grave, lost the sympathy of the courtroom as the terrible plight of the murderer engaged everyone's attention."

In the celebrated murder trial of Jean Harris, Dr. Herman Tarnower—to the extent he was remembered at all—was depicted as a ruthless exploiter of women and a posturing social climber. But that mattered little; the title of Diana Trilling's book on the case, *Mrs. Harris,* leaves no doubt where our interest should focus.

In no recent crime was sympathy for the criminal so apparent as in the 1977 murder of a Yale student, Bonnie Garland, by her boyfriend, Richard Herrin, who had just graduated from Yale. When Bonnie told Richard Herrin she wanted freedom to see other men, he took a hammer to her head and killed her. The facts of the case were not in dispute; Richard freely admitted the crime and its reason. This clarity, however, did nothing to stem an outpouring of sympathy and support for Richard, the most tangible from Yale and his church, both of which raised money for his defense and steadfastly stood by him, to the outrage of Bonnie's parents.

It was perhaps this aspect of the case—sympathy for the killer rather than the victim—that caused psychiatrist Willard Gaylin to write a book on the subject, *The Killing of Bonnie Garland* (Simon and Schuster, 1982), in which he advances a theory on the phenomenon's psychological underpinnings:

When one person kills another, there is immediate revulsion at the nature of the crime. But in a time so short as to seem indecent to the members of the victim's family, the dead person ceases to exist as an identifiable figure. To those individuals in the community of good will and empathy, warmth and compassion, only one of the key actors in the drama remains with whom to commiserate—and that is always the criminal. The dead person ceases to be a part of everyday reality, ceases to exist. She is only a figure in a historic event. We inevitably turn away from the past, toward the ongoing reality. And the ongoing reality is the criminal—trapped, anxious, now helpless, isolated, often badgered and bewildered. He usurps the compassion that is justly his victim's due. He will steal his victim's moral constituency along with her life.

Gaylin's subtle and imaginative analysis applies as well to the Von Bülow case; if ever a victim was a nonperson during a trial, it was Sunny Von Bülow. The trial was perceived by everyone as it was billed: Von Bülow versus the state of Rhode Island, never Claus versus Sunny.

Anyone subjected to casual discussions about the Von Bülow case and similar crimes detects an attitude toward the victims that passes beyond mere indifference or forgetfulness into the area of hostility. People who know almost nothing about the victims are heard making harsh angry judgments about them. Painfully aware of this phenomenon are rape victims who have found themselves harassed and hounded by the authorities, who are supposed to be pursuing their assailants.

Of course, it was in Von Bülow's interest to vilify his wife, but the disparagements were adopted with curious speed by a public all too eager to believe ill of the victim.

If we can believe the criminal was driven to his act by failings of the victim, we feel better about him and bring within manageable limits our vision of evil. Bonnie Garland was portrayed as spoiled, unfeeling, promiscuous. Sunny Von Bülow was portrayed as neurotic, idle, self-centered. With each pejorative the criminal's criminality is lessened, as is the damage done our view of humankind by the villainy of one human. In rejecting such wanton criminality for a base motive such as greed or lust, the mind races to seek out provocation.

If it is any consolation to the rape victim, the hostility she feels from her "protectors" may well be a reflection of their horror at the crime rather than their indifference to it.

XXXI

ON the way back to his hotel after the conviction, Von Bülow told his bodyguard he felt no animosity toward the judge, the jury, the prosecutor—only toward Lieutenant Reise, who he claimed had not given him his rights and had tricked him into saying things when he came to Clarendon Court in April and took a statement.

Putting his chagrin ironically to a friend, Von Bülow said, "Instead of telling me anything I say *might* be held against me, he should have said: anything I say *will* be held against me."

These two versions are not nearly as opposite as Von Bülow seems to think; both are warnings to be cautious about what he says, something Von Bülow clearly did not want to appear to be doing, so in fact did not do.

His focusing on Lieutenant Reise suggests the weight Von Bülow, and perhaps his lawyers, gave to the statement to Reise of April 21, in all likelihood the principal obstacle in their minds to Von Bülow's taking the witness stand in his own defense.

Famiglietti was well aware that Von Bülow's two statements were rich veins of inconsistencies which he planned to mine relentlessly if Von Bülow should brave the stand. His emergence from the trial angry at only one person—Jack Reise—suggests Von Bülow was aware of this as well. Reise would make no comment.

Von Bülow's summation also showed an interesting evolution from his first characterizing the action against him as a von Auersperg money-making scheme* he now made the sizable leap to police trickery. Either he envisioned the family conspiracy as having expanded to incorporate the Rhode Island State Police or he was no longer protesting his innocence, merely the methods used to catch him.

His recruitment of Harvard Law professor Alan Dershowitz shortly after his conviction would tend to reinforce the latter view. Dershowitz enjoys a wide reputation as a last resort for convicted criminals, being especially keen at finding legal loopholes that render his clients' convictions unconstitutional. An article about him in *Time* magazine said Dershowitz readily concedes that few of his clients are innocent—a concession that probably pleased few of his clients.

Fahringer's reaction to losing the case was curious. He immediately grabbed headlines from the winning team by announcing the morning following the verdict that he had discovered a "mystery witness" who could upset the verdict. Stealing the spotlight from the victors was not difficult, as the Rhode Island Attorney General's Office forbids their prosecutors from going on television.

Similarly, Von Bülow's accusers—Alexander, Ala, and Maria —were invited on every major talk show, but declined them all; they felt appearances by them would be improper and seem like gloating. The defense may have lost in the courtroom, but they had a clear field with the media.

Fahringer accepted invitations from *Good Morning America* and the *CBS Morning News* the day following the verdict and riveted the nation's attention with an announcement that a woman had come forward during the jury's deliberation with evidence that Mrs. Von Bülow had injected herself with insulin, the same claim made in court by Joy O'Neill.

The witness's reason for not coming forward sooner, Fahringer said, was that she had been convinced Von Bülow would be acquitted and chose to spare herself the inconvenience of appearing at the trial; guilt-ridden at the possible outcome, she had presented herself to Fahringer while the jury was in deliberation.

---

*During a recess Von Bülow approached me and said "I have a perfect title for your book —*The Second War of Austrian Succession.*"

So while the entire country was absorbing the jury's decision, Fahringer shook this growing certainty of Von Bülow's guilt back to the possibility his client was the victim of his wife's idiosyncracies. Reporters who had followed the case from the start and who were familiar with Fahringer's resourcefulness were taking bets that the "mystery witness" would disappear into the mists in a day or two, having served her diversionary function.

They didn't have to wait that long. She lost any credibility she had when, that same day, reporters went to John Sheehan in his Providence office for details about the mystery witness.

"What mystery witness?" Sheehan said with likable candor, then did a good job of backing and filling when reporters told him of the morning's television revelations by his legal partner.

The trouble with the story was that Fahringer had her coming forward during deliberations, a period when he, Sheehan, and Von Bülow were closeted together in the Newport courthouse for long, empty days of waiting. The Rhode Island reporters found it impossible to believe that had a bombshell witness come to the defense in those hours together when anxiety ran high and conversational topics ran low, Fahringer wouldn't turn to Sheehan and say, "By the way, I just heard from a witness who can get Claus off in the event the jury convicts."

Later that day, Herald did another national interview, this one on Cable News Network. In this he neatly set up the mystery woman's mysterious disappearance; the woman had not given her name or phone number, he said, but had assured Herald she would be getting in touch. (Would it be his fault if she never called?)

Herald had more tricks up his sleeve in that pre-sentencing period, when he was still smarting from his defeat. Having lost his case in Rhode Island's Superior Court, he took it to a higher court: the national celebrity tribunal, Justice Barbara Walters officiating. Herald arranged for Von Bülow to go on ABC's popular magazine show 20/20. One had to think long and hard to find a precedent for a convicted would-be wife-murderer being so graciously received into American living rooms.

With Herald sitting just off camera, Barbara Walters allowed Von Bülow to claim a number of things that had been laboriously disproved in court. As an example, Walters asked if the black bag had been his. "It probably belonged to me at one point," Von

Bülow replied airily. Anyone who had followed the trial would have pounced. What of the recent prescriptions inside made out to you? What of its being found in your closet, a closet you slipped off to lock when the police came?

Instead of asking any of these questions, Barbara nodded and went on to another subject.

Another head-slapper was Von Bülow's asking rhetorically why only one needle was tested for insulin when the bag contained three others. Newspaper readers across the country could have answered: because only one needle had been used—the others were still sealed in their plastic cases. On 20/20, Von Bülow's "mystery" was allowed to remain a mystery.

At the end of this public-relations bonanza, Barbara fixed Von Bülow with her eyes and said, "I have just one final question, Mr. Von Bülow. Did you try to murder your wife?"

"No," he replied. "I did not."

A surge of relief flooded the land that this nice-looking man was not a murderer. There was also relief that this highly regarded journalist could still ask the tough, rude question.

The hostess of another talk show invited Von Bülow to be a guest and was told by Fahringer that he would accept on condition that the questions were screened in advance. ABC would not comment on whether they had agreed to such a one-sided deal for 20/20.

By not taking the witness stand, Von Bülow had exercised his constitutional right. But by going on national television he could have his say without the risks. This is particularly true if ground rules protected him from embarrassing questions; with or without that comforting assurance, he would be in far less peril facing a busy television personality than facing a feisty prosecutor who has lived with the case for six months.

When Rhode Island allowed TV cameras in the courtroom, observers worried about a number of potential problems, all of which happily proved groundless. Even the jury, in posttrial discussions with state representatives, said the cameras had not bothered them. One problem not considered was that the two-month TV exposure would turn the defendant into a star, with all that implies today in terms of power. Few convicted criminals are granted such a nationwide forum.

Television audiences do not decide the fate of convicted felons. Still, there are dangers. Judges, many of whom are elected, could be influenced by the media's transformation of the man they must judge into a popular cause. Happily, in this case, word came down that the Rhode Island Supreme Court did not look with favor on Von Bülow's public appearances, thus ending with a shot his talk show career.

A more worrying aspect of ABC's collaboration in converting Von Bülow into a martyr is the contempt it shows not only for the jury system but for those twelve jurors in particular. With the network's one-sided hearing presenting Von Bülow as the persecuted innocent, it can only incite public criticism for the twelve men and women who underwent agonies of conscience and great personal hardship to do their civic duty.

Fahringer had yet another rabbit in his hat. The night before the sentencing he went on television with film footage of author Truman Capote telling of a weekend house party at which he and Sunny Von Bülow were guests. At the time, and at subsequent lunches, Sunny, he claimed, had shown Truman how to inject himself with vitamin B-12.

On the television show Fahringer called this information new and "impressive." As for its newness, testimony during the trial had established that injections were part of the lives of Mr. and Mrs. Von Bülow. As for its being impressive, Capote is well known among his friends for having an inflammable fictional sense. A poll of Sunny's close friends from the period Capote was talking about (twenty-five years earlier!) suggests Sunny did indeed meet Capote when he was staying at the Winston Guests (his claim) but took a strong dislike to him and never saw him again. With his needle story, Capote seemed to be injecting himself into the Von Bülow business.

In this pre-sentencing limbo, Fahringer gave an extraordinary interview to Marian Christy of the *Boston Globe*, in which he rambled on to a worrying degree about winning and losing. In seven paragraphs of the interview he made the following references: "Winning is very important to me, I cannot stand to lose. ... When I was growing up, I would not play games unless I could win. ... The problem with not winning was that I had a feeling of utter desolation. ... You realize that losing is sometimes part of winning. . . . You huddle with the football team and say to them, 'We've got to do something to win. Winning is everything. . . .' I'm a workaholic. It's all related to winning."

And then in a lyrical paroxysm of self-blame he said, "I worked myself to death and I didn't win. *Why? Why?* I'm not religious. Oh, sometimes I say to myself—and I know it sounds foolish— that it must not have been in the cards. It almost gets mystical. . . . Maybe there is a strong force deciding this case. Maybe it was not meant to be."

Maybe his client was guilty. Curiously, that doesn't enter into Fahringer's formula for winning or losing. Naturally, he cannot suggest that Von Bülow was guilty, but neither does he refer once in the entire eighteen paragraphs to Von Bülow's being innocent. In Fahringer's vision of the courtroom as a gladiator fight to the death between two lawyers, the merits of his case are absent from his postmortem analysis.

But even stranger is the absence in this lament of Von Bülow himself. Fahringer says his client was devastated by the defeat, but brushes this aside as the single major catastrophe in Von Bülow's life. The real suffering is not Von Bülow's but Fahringer's; he depicts Von Bülow off with friends trying to drive the experience from his mind, partying while Herald agonizes alone. Von Bülow didn't lose; Herald did.

John Sheehan had less trouble with the verdict. When asked by the Reuters correspondent why he felt they had lost, he replied, "They had overwhelming evidence against us." Whatever pain both lawyers suffered through Claus Von Bülow, they were well compensated. The word was that Fahringer's fee was $250,000, Sheehan's $150,000.

April 2 was another bad day for the Von Bülow team, not only because Judge Needham denied the request for a new trial—this was expected—but because he reviewed the case and endorsed in detail the prosecution's evidence. It was an hour-long recapitulation of the complex and exhaustive proceedings.

The prosecution had presented convincing evidence, in Needham's view, that Von Bülow had the opportunity to inject his wife and that he possessed the black bag containing drugs later found in her system. Needham accorded the testimony of Dr. Hamolsky "no weight at all," as the doctor was unable to provide an opinion on how the comas were caused. The two defense witnesses who claimed Mrs. Von Bülow had done this to herself, Joy O'Neill and Robert Huggins, "were not believable." The testimony of Maria Schrallhammer "stood on the record uncontradicted." Needham raised Von Bülow's bail from $100,000 to $500,000. John Sheehan promptly handed over five certificates of deposit for $10,000 each to meet the 10 percent required.

The day of the sentencing, May 7, the town of Newport, having been abruptly abandoned, was once again a swarm of reporters, photographers, television cameramen, crowd-corralling sheriffs, and pro-Claus groupies, now dubbed "Clausettes." It was a Brigadoon that after a long sleep had sprung back to life, full of the same bustle and self-importance that had vanished on March 16.

The courtroom was a precise re-creation of the January 11 to March 16 scene, with one major exception: the presence of Von Bülow's daughter, Cosima. Of all the principals in the case she alone had never been seen either in court or in photographs. In a family with more than its share of good looks, she had been dismissed as a gawky teenager. These reports proved inaccurate. She was tall and lovely, with a womanliness that belied her fourteen years. She was well on her way to maintaining, if not topping, the family reputation for physical beauty.

Famiglietti made his arguments for the maximum sentence of twenty years on both counts, arguing that although the victim was alive, her life was finished, that Von Bülow's motivation was simple greed, and that there was no argument between the victim and her assailant, no passion—the crime was coldblooded, deliberate, premeditated. Fahringer responded that Von Bülow needs no rehabilitation, has an unblemished record, and is no threat to the community. Before Fahringer got into a lengthy rehash of the issues in the case, he once again referred to Cosima as the "center of Von Bülow's universe."

When Famiglietti rose to speak again he startled the court by attacking Cosima's presence. Since the beginning of this trial, he said, everyone involved has shown compassion for the plight of this young woman, even the press, who could have waited outside her school to photograph her but resisted doing so out of a feeling for the harm the scandal has already done to her life. Now this man brings her to court, exposing her to the fullest publicity "in a blatant attempt to evoke compassion and pity for himself."

Sheehan rose to protest that Cosima was there because *she* wanted to show the world the love and support she felt for her father and implied that Von Bülow had nothing to say about it. The next morning Cosima's picture was on the front page of *The New York Times* and newspapers across the country in addition to being shown on most television news shows. Her anonymity was destroyed forever.

Judge Needham asked Von Bülow if he chose to say anything. He stood and said, "Thank you, your honor, I will not avail myself of that right."

Needham made the point that because the victim had recovered from the first attempt to murder her, he was sentencing Von Bülow to ten years on that count, but to the maximum of twenty years on the second count. Needham would allow Von Bülow to remain free pending his appeal but fixed bail at one million dollars, one tenth in cash, the rest in Rhode Island assets Von Bülow could prove were his.

After several months of rumors that the appeal might not be heard for two or three years, it was set for October of 1983, the unusal speed suggesting that Rhode Island was eager to dispose of the notorious case. After hearing the appeal, the state Supreme Court could take from one to five months to hand down a decision. Denial of the appeal would not preclude other ploys, but Von Bülow would probably have to engineer them from jail.

In passing sentence, Judge Needham said he had "no respect for Von Bülow." Later, Needham was publicly rapped on the knuckles by the Rhode Island Supreme Court for showing such "negativism." This was a bizarre capping of Needham's exemplary role in the affair from people trading in justice. Needham had been obliged by law to concur with or overturn the jury's decision, and so was on record as believing the jury had been correct. It seems odd that a judge should be required to show respect for a man who had been legally proven to have tried to kill his daughter's mother for money.

Before making the remark in open court, Needham had given Von Bülow and his lawyers in chambers detailed reasons why he had no respect for the man he was about to sentence. He had refrained from spelling out the catalogue of villainy in court out of a concern for Cosima, who he knew would be present and who he knew was under a psychiatrist's care. This was the reason the remark appeared to be gratuitous.

Elsewhere in his sentencing remarks Needham had said, "The trial of Claus Von Bülow is over and the trial of the trial justice is about to begin." He later wrote to a friend, "In the rapport which exists between the trial bench and the appellate bench, I treat the 'negativism' comment as the opening salvo, and secondarily harbor the wish that the remaining salvos may be the same kind, i.e., they hurt a little, but they don't result in a reversal."

Cosima, who had indeed been kept offstage throughout the long drama, was now being pushed to the front by her father. Either under advice of lawyers or on his own inspiration, Von Bülow began to use her as the hook with which to retain a hold on Sunny's luxury. He hired attorney Roy Cohn to represent Cosima and shortly began a campaign to advance "her" interests.

Through the trial, Alexander and Ala had maintained, to their surprise and relief, friendly relations with their younger sister. Frequently during the two-month ordeal Cosima had dropped down to her sister's apartment, never to talk about the trial but merely to chat in the routine manner of fond sisters not embroiled in a tragedy. Always sensitive to Cosima's plight, Ala and the others stood ready to discuss with her the torment she surely was undergoing, but waited for her to introduce the subject. Cosima never did.

On one occasion shortly before the start of the trial, Cosima showed up at Ala's door and was told by Maria that Ala was not home. Cosima looked strangely at Maria for a moment, then asked if she might talk with her instead. Maria, thinking that at last Cosima wanted to confide in someone, said that by all means they could talk and went to fix tea.

When she returned with the tray and settled in the living room, the girl she had helped rear broke into tears. Without waiting for Cosima to speak, Maria said that since the affair began she had wanted to talk with Cosima about it and she was very glad they were finally going to open up with each other.

"I don't want to talk about *that*," Cosima said still sobbing.

Maria was surprised when the girl told her that the cause of her grief was that her boyfriend had gone away, maybe for weeks. "Like me," she said, "he comes from a broken home. He must fly to Florida to visit one parent, then somewhere else to visit the other. I don't know when I'll see him."

Her reference to a "broken" home was as close as Cosima came to acknowledging, at least to her family, that their life together was different from anyone else's.

Months later, at the time of the verdict, Ala had flown off to Bermuda to get rid of a bad cold. When Alexander phoned her the jury's decision, which he heard over the radio in his Providence apartment (he had returned to college), Ala immediately phoned Cosima, who was staying with a friend's family in Florida. Cosima had already heard the verdict from her father, but was nonetheless touched by Ala's call—and even more touched by Ala's offer to fly to Florida to be with her.

On Cosima's birthday, April 4—scarcely three weeks after the verdict—Alexander and Ala gave a dinner party for her at Manhattan's River Club. It turned out to be a happy occasion, with Cosima warm to everyone and in good spirits. Several weeks later, on May 2, five days before Von Bülow's sentencing, Maria ran into Cosima in the entrance to the Fifth Avenue building they shared. Seeing Maria, Cosima ran over and threw her arms around her. Shortly *after* the sentencing, Cosima again encountered Maria in the building lobby; this time she walked by without answering Maria's greeting. Maria was stunned by the sudden change.

A bit less abruptly, Alexander and Ala began receiving the same coolness from Cosima. One or the other of them would phone her from Rhode Island to announce a visit to New York. Could they have lunch? Cosima would be friendly, but always unavailable, usually with a vague excuse.

A reason for this belated estrangement suggested itself when Morris Gurley at the Chemical Bank received a letter from Cosima requesting Clarendon Court for the month of August.

Alexander and Ala were dumbfounded. Immediately, Ala wrote her sister a letter saying how thrilled she and Alexander were that Cosima wanted to come to Clarendon Court, adding how much they loved her and how happy it would make them to be reunited. Ala added that Cosima should of course come whenever she wanted and to bring any of her friends.

Gurley then got a letter from Roy Cohn more formally demanding Clarendon Court for his client. Gurley replied that it had never been Sunny's policy to exclude any of her children from the house; Cosima could come, but Alexander and Ala would remain.

A friend of Ala's, hearing about her note to Cosima, said to her, "You were inviting Cosima to Clarendon Court?"

"I wasn't *inviting* her," Ala snapped. "It's her house as much as mine. I was just telling her how happy Alexander and I would be if she came."

Between the lines the note also was telling Roy Cohn, as Gurley had, that the two von Auerspergs had no intention of getting out of the house. One of the Rhode Island newspapers, perhaps on information from Von Bülow's side, printed that Cosima had been banned from Clarendon Court by her brother and sister. The family began receiving long, typed letters from Cosima, legalistic and complaining, that did not reflect the young woman's style as either a writer or a person.

There was a strong possibility that the change in Cosima toward those closest to her was a legal maneuver imposed on her by lawyers or by her father. Mulling over this possibility, Maria said, "She's living alone with him up there. Who knows what he's telling her?"

Alexander, who because of his closeness to Cosima perhaps felt the schism even more than the others, expressed his outrage that the disaffection of Cosima might be "strategy." "We're the only family she's got!" he said bitterly. His dismissal of Von Bülow as "family" reflected the von Auerspergs' and Aitkens' belief that Claus would eventually go to jail.

Even if Von Bülow did not share this belief, the slightest chance of his eventual removal as a father would seem to make reckless any attempt on his part to isolate his daughter from those most disposed to look after her. That the new stategy involved Cosima cutting herself off from her grandmother as well would mean that Von Bülow, if he indeed was behind the girl's sudden change toward the others, was flirting with losing for her a massive inheritance she had every reason to expect.

For whatever reasons, Cosima finally broke completely with her brother and sister just before the sentencing of Von Bülow and her appearance in the Newport courtroom.

Other changes appeared in Cosima, changes that lacked any apparent exterior impetus. A wild side emerged that had not been present before; she would party relentlessly and stay out at discos until dawn. She also began spending money in a wanton manner that had never characterized any of Sunny's children. They all had incomes to meet their routine needs. If they needed money for something extraordinary, they had only to ask the bank; if the request was deemed reasonable, it was usually granted.

Bills now arrived at the bank from Cosima that no one deemed reasonable for a fourteen-year-old—such as a bill for a ball gown she bought in London so she could fly to Italy for a party. None of her requests was refused. Some argued that the flamboyant, defiant reaction was better than a cowering, broken one. Still, some who knew her and who had been impressed by her months of equanimity in the face of superhuman strain were now fearful for her future. Others among those concerned, including her stepbrother and sister, felt that the vigorous socializing was normal behavior in any teenager left unsupervised.

As for Von Bülow, with all his efforts to retain the Fifth Avenue apartment he seemed to be spending little time there. Columnists mentioned him frequently as dining with friends in fashionable restaurants, attending parties (some in his honor), and on one occasion boogying at the month's disco. One socialite insisted he was the most sought-after extra man on the Manhattan dinner-party circuit. Eventually, he threw a number of parties in Sunny's apartment.

At a cocktail party of good friends he encountered a woman friend he had not seen for some time. Noticing her hand was bandaged, he said, "What's the matter, darling? Did you have trouble with your syringe?"

Without smiling, the lady said she thought his remark in questionable taste. Not to be squelched, Von Bülow called others over. "Look here, everyone," he said merrily. "Vi's had trouble with her syringe."

As fall approached, forces were marshaled for civil litigation. Action was set in motion to obtain a court-appointed conservator for Sunny's property, a first step in altering arrangements frozen in place by her being technically alive but unable to function. One such changed arrangement could be Von Bülow's living on indefi-

358 / WILLAM WRIGHT

nitely at 960 Fifth Avenue (which now seemed inappropriate to most everyone but him).

But ultimately there is a much bigger issue: that of Von Bülow's being the fifteen-million-dollar beneficiary of Sunny's will. Two laws come into play, and perhaps into conflict, here, according to lawyers involved in the matter. One is a statute that prevents anyone from profiting from a crime; the other makes it legally difficult to connect a result, Sunny's death for instance, with a crime committed more than a year before. Morris Gurley and others think it will be a relatively simple matter to remove Von Bülow from Sunny's will at the time of probate; still others believe it will require civil litigation that could stretch over years. Both views agree that if no legal move is made, Claus would still inherit fifteen million dollars with Sunny's death.

Judge Needham had given Von Bülow several weeks to establish possession of the assets needed to cover the bail. After an embarrassing few weeks of Von Bülow's presenting lists of furnishings from Clarendon Court and Fifth Avenue—one valuable desk he claimed was his was clearly visible in a 1950s photograph taken in Sunny's Kitzbühel house—Von Bülow finally gave up and got a friend to put up the remainder of the million dollars on his behalf. (Judge Needham felt sure Von Bülow would not flee —if only to prove Needham wrong in his mistrust.)

So Von Bulow's freedom until the appeal was assured provided he did not try to leave the country. Those outraged that a man convicted of such a crime should be free tend to forget that in this case the victim is still alive. While this says more about the convicted man's competence than about his morality, United States law holds in vastly different lights murder and attempted murder. In addition, the law doesn't allow for gradations within these two categories; it regards Sunny as alive.

In the bar of San Francisco's Fairmont Hotel a handsome middle-aged couple were having martinis on a mild August evening in 1982. A man sitting alone an empty bar stool away was eyeing the woman's Givenchy suit of crisp beige linen and, in particular, a lapel pin which only the sharpest connoisseur's eye would recognize as a museum-quality object of great value.

The two people were taken aback at being addressed by the man but were quickly charmed by him and fell into conversation. It seems he was waiting for his daughter, whom he was taking to a tennis camp in the Carmel Valley the next day. Claus's new friends, as it turned out, were one of the richest couples in the United States.

Back in New York, Alexander, Maria, and Ala (now several months pregnant) celebrated Sunny's birthday in September by visiting her hospital room, taking a cake and presents, including a new nightgown.

In newspapers across the country, a syndicated columnist told her readers that Claus had a new girlfriend and promised to divulge the lady's name shortly.

Index

A

Adams, Norton, 51
Adams, Peggy, 51
Aggarwal, Dr. V. J.:
    testimony given by, 259;
    recalled by prosecution,
    277–78
Aitken, Annie Laurie
    Crawford, 4, 5, 12, 14, 17,
    26, 40, 43, 51, 54, 57–58, 59,
    69, 75, 78, 86, 87, 91, 92,
    94–95, 99, 109, 112, 129, 191,
    212, 226, 230, 272, 273;
    marriage to George
    Crawford, 8–10; birth of
    daughter Sunny, 9;
    overprotection of daughter,
    11, 13; holds family meeting
    after daughter's second
    coma, 124–25
Aitken, Russell, 14, 40, 51,
    154, 162
Almanach de Gotha, 310
Aspinall, John, 41–42
Azevedo, Debra:
    and Newport Hospital
    blood samples, 119–22;
    testifies for the prosecution,
    238–39

B

Baker, Russell, 343
Bancroft, Tommy, 12
Barlow, Kenneth:
    tried in England for
    murder of wife by insulin
    injection, 269–70, 290
Barry, Philip, 53
Baxter, Leslie, 90, 226, 277
    interviewed by Lt. John
    Reise, 139–40
Bedford, Peggy, 23, 45–46
    early friendship with
    Sunny Von Bülow, 11–12
Behan, Helen:
    testifies as rebuttal
    witness, 306–307
Berdy, John (Von Bülow
    houseman), 113, 147, 151;
    testifies for prosecution, 234
Bernhard (prince of
    Lippe-Biesterfeld), 15
Biastre, Robert (Von Bülow
    butler), 78, 88, 116, 151;

Biastre (cont'd.)
  testifies for the defense,
  281–82
Bismarck, Anna Marie, 36
Blood and Money
  (Thompson), 270n
Borberg, Svend, 27
  tried in Denmark for
  collaboration, 28–30
Brady rule, 190
Brown, John Nicholas, 292
Brown, Mrs. John Nicholas
  [Ann], 51, 55, 57, 58, 162,
  295, 320, 340; testifies as
  defense witness, 292–94
Bruce, Lenny, 127
Brucker, Mary Beth, 120
  testifies for prosecution,
  240
Bülow, Eric von, 310
Bülow, Fritz, 27
Bülow, Jonna, 27
  raises son Claus in
  England, 29–31

C

Cahill, Dr. George, 158, 290,
  308, 326; offers important
  medical opinion to Lt.
  Reise, 155–56; as witness for
  prosecution, 268–69
Callahan, Catherine, 339
Capote, Truman, 227, 350
Carlyle, Thomas, 211
Carnegie, Andrew, 180
Carr, Dr. John, 212, 305, 306,
  321, 326; interview with
  Sunny Von Bülow after

first coma, 84; testifies as
  defense witness, 294–95
Chanel, Coco, 15
Charles, Oatsie, 55
Chernow, Dr. Marvin:
  testimony given by, 244;
  called as rebuttal witness,
  306
Christy, Marian, 350
Clarendon Court: Von Bülows
  move to, 48–59; history of,
  52–53; jury's tour of,
  205–208
Clark, Sir Kenneth, 58
Cohn, Roy, 354, 356
Connett, Barbara (jury
  foreman), 180, 185, 334, 335,
  336–37, 339
Crawford, George:
  accumulation of wealth
  by, 7–9; marriage to Annie
  Laurie Warmack, 8–10;
  birth of daughter Sunny, 9;
  death of, 9
Crosby, Bing, 16, 53
Curran, William, 155

D

d'Arenberg, Prince Charles,
  12, 23
Dark Shadows (TV series),
  64
Death Trap (Levin), 92
de Gaulle, Charles, 315, 318
Dershowitz, Alan, 347
Diplock, Kenneth, 269
Donahue, Jessie, 16
Douglas, Barclay, 55, 58

Duke, Doris, 314
d'Uzès, Duc, 12

E

Edwards, Cheryl:
  and Newport Hospital
  blood samples, 119–22;
  testifies for the prosecution,
  238–39
Eisenstaedt, Alfred, 59
Eve of New York
  (hairdresser), 137

F

Fahnestock, William, 49
Fahringer, Herald, 1, 169, 172,
  182–83, 184, 191–93, 196,
  199–200, 203, 207, 229–33,
  237–39, 240, 241, 243–44,
  246–47, 248, 249–50, 263–5,
  267, 268–69, 276–77, 279,
  282, 284, 287, 288, 289–90,
  293, 295–96, 298, 300,
  336–37, 339, 352; enters the
  case for the defense, 159–61;
  opinion on television
  coverage of trials, 166–67;
  and jury selection, 176–81;
  moves to bar press from
  pretrial hearings, 188–90;
  opening statement by,
  209–15; final summation to
  jury, 320–22; reactions to
  losing case, 347–52
Famiglietti, Angela, 156, 157
Famiglietti, Rocco, 156, 288
Famiglietti, Stephen, 1–2,
  93–94, 133, 138, 139, 172,

174, 182–83, 190, 194, 196,
  199–200, 207, 210, 214,
  216–20, 225–28, 229, 233,
  235, 236–37, 238–39, 242,
  243, 244, 246, 247, 248,
  249, 252, 254–59, 261–63,
  267, 268, 270n, 277–78,
  279–80, 282, 284–85, 286,
  287, 288–89, 290–91, 293,
  294–95, 298, 304–308, 335,
  336, 346, 352; brief
  biography of, 156–57; and
  jury selection, 176–79;
  opening statement by,
  208–209; press interview by,
  240–41; final summation to
  jury, 322–28
Famous British Trials, 270n
Famous Criminal Cases, 270n
Farouk (king of Egypt), 23
Farr, Sims, 93, 125
Feller, Dr. Marc, 236
Fish, Mrs. Stuyvesant, 55
Flood, Ruth Dunbar, 11,
  45–46, 90–91, 153–54, 155,
  318
Flynt, Larry, 160
Ford, Henry II, 247
Funkenstein, Dr. Harris, 125,
  139, 328; as witness for
  prosecution, 248–51

G

Gafgen, Pierce (juror), 186
Gailitis, Dr. Janis, 75, 109, 118,
  138, 212, 226, 247, 294, 295,
  320, 324, 327, 329, 338; and
  Sunny Von Bülow's first

Gailitis (cont'd.)
coma (December 1979), 77–79; interview with Claus Von Bülow following first coma, 82–83; letter from Claus Von Bülow, 86–89; as witness for prosecution, 240, 241–44

Gamberdella, Dr. Ronald, 131, 259
testimony of, 251

Garland, Bonnie, 344, 345

Gaylin, Willard, 344–45

George III (king of England), 53

Gertler, Gayle, 189

Getty, J. Paul, 27, 39–40, 81, 274, 285–86, 296, 316, 323; Claus Von Bülow as assistant to, 33–35

Glover, Isabel Hinkley, 11, 46, 103, 109, 112, 154, 159, 315, 318, 329

Glover, Price, 315, 318

Goldstein, Al, 160

Goulet, Robert, 51

Gurley, Morris, 6, 92, 93–94, 124–25, 153, 217, 276, 338, 355–56; as witness for prosecution, 271–74

H

Hackett, Walter, 58–59

Hagemann, Tom, 313

Hailsham, Lord, 31, 269

Hamolsky, Dr. Milton, 291, 305, 308, 326, 337, 351; testifies as defense witness, 288–90

Harris, Mrs. Jean, 160, 166, 172, 344

Haywood, Maysie, 52

Hearst, Patty, 166

Herrin, Richard, 344

High Society (film), 52–53

Himmler, Heinrich, 15

Hinckley, John, 344

Hohenlohe, Prince Alexander, 15, 21

Hohenlohe, Princess Honeychile, 15–16, 21, 25, 46, 65; friendship with Sunny von Auersperg, 22–24

Holub, Dr. Donald, 325
testimony for prosecution, 267–68

Hope, Bob, 15, 16, 23

How to Be a Jewish Mother, 311

Huggins, Robert, 82, 295, 304–305, 321, 326, 338, 352; testifies as witness for the defense, 290–91; testimony discredited by rebuttal witnesses, 306–307

Hull, Arthur (juror), 185–86, 336, 339, 343

Hypoglycemia, 96–97

I

Insulin:
"exogenous" and "endogenous," 138

Isles, Adam, 64, 111

Isles, Alexandra, 60, 68, 81–82, 111, 132, 192, 217, 228, 296, 297, 322, 324, 325, 338;

begins affair with Claus
Von Bülow, 64–66; doubts
Von Bülow's ability to
divorce Sunny, 71–72;
resumes affair with Von
Bülow, 98, 102–105; trip to
Nassau, 133–34, 141; pretrial
interview by prosecution,
251–54; as witness for
prosecution, 255–59
Isles, Philip Henry, 64

J

Jablonski, Walter (juror), 185
Jane Pickens Theatre, 113, 171
Jennrette, Constance (juror),
187, 335, 339
Jimmy (Crawford family
chauffeur), 11, 13, 14
Ju, Dr. (plastic surgeon), 61
Juliana (queen of the
Netherlands), 15

K

Kahn, Manya, 284–85, 300,
301, 318
Karajan, Herbert von, 37
Kaye, Nora, 305
Keeler, Christine, 37
Kelly, Grace, 53
Kennedy, John F., 50
*Killing of Bonnie Garland,
The* (Gaylin), 344
Kirkwood, Robert (juror),
185, 339
Kneissl, Ala von Auersperg,
5, 6, 44, 45, 46–47, 60, 63,
67, 69, 73, 77, 86, 90–91,
103, 109, 123, 133, 136, 139,
141, 160, 164, 191, 217, 221,
227, 229, 249, 262, 273–74,
296, 298, 311, 312, 315, 317,
321, 347, 354, 355–56, 359;
debut ball for, 59; marriage
to Franz Kneissl, 98–100;
first visit to Richard Kuh,
126–27; pretrial relationship
with half-sister Cosima,
158–59; as witness for
prosecution, 274–77;
cross-examined by defense,
276–77
Kneissl, Franz, 133, 277
  marriage to Ala von
  Auersperg, 98–100
Knight, Clara, 52
Knight, Edwin, 52
Krupp, Arndt, 23, 35
Kuh (Manhattan doctor), 131
Kuh, Richard H., 3, 5, 113,
133, 136, 139, 141–42, 153,
193, 194–95, 196, 199, 203,
209, 219, 220, 224, 262, 333;
first meeting with Ala and
Alexander, 125, 126–27;
organizes search for Von
Bülow's black bag, 127–32;
takes Von Bülow "case" to
Rhode Island authorities,
132–33; testifies as pretrial
witness, 190–92; testimony
as rebuttal witness, 306

L

Lambert, Edwin, 151, 162,
192–93, 194, 195, 207, 219,
279, 280, 322, 323; and
search for Von Bülow's

Lambert, Edwin (cont'd.)
  black leather bag, 128–30;
  testifies for prosecution, 223
Lanin, Lester, 12
Larisch, Countess, 16–17
Lehr, Harry, 55
Linslay, Lady, 31
Liszt, Franz, 43
Lucan, Lord, 38
Ludwig II (king of Bavaria),
  43
Lund, Robina, 34

M

Manya Kahn Rhythm
  Exercise Studio, 283
  See also Kahn, Manya
McGann, Mary, 169, 335
McGuirl, Susan, 1, 172,
  201–203, 248, 278, 284, 299,
  335, 336, pretrial interview
  of Alexandra Isles, 252–54
Meier, Dr. Gerhard, 117–18,
  120–22, 139, 239, 297;
  testifies as witness for
  prosecution, 235–38
Mendl, Lady, 15
Metternich, Prince Klemens,
  36
Millard, Mark, 92, 93, 154,
  211, 317, 320, 323, 325, 340;
  hires Claus Von Bülow,
  66–67; as witness for the
  defense, 285–86
Mini-Yellow Storage
  Company, 302
Miranda, Detective Joseph,
  133, 136, 139, 142, 145, 146,

148, 150, 156, 198, 199, 216,
  251, 254, 301–303, 335
Miss Susan (hairdresser), 315
Moltke, Count Bobby, 64, 65
Moltke, Mab, 64
Moore, Grace, 16
Morgenthau, Robert, 127
Mrs. Harris (Trilling), 344
Murphy, Alan, 13, 14, 39–40,
  45–46, 69–70, 154–155

N

Needham, Judge Thomas H.,
  2, 166, 168, 171, 172, 173–75,
  177–78, 181, 182–84, 185,
  189–90, 195, 199–204, 206,
  207–208, 214–15, 217, 219,
  231, 233, 244, 248, 254, 258,
  259, 260, 262, 270, 276,
  277, 290, 295, 300, 309,
  322, 328, 329, 334, 335, 336,
  339, 351–52, 353, 358;
  in-chambers conference on
  Famiglietti interview,
  240–41; disallows two
  prosecution witnesses,
  307–308; charges the jury,
  330–32
Needham, Ursula, 2
Neilly, Margaret, 115–16, 213,
  305; as witness for the
  defense, 286
Newport, Rhode Island:
  history of, 48–51
9 to 5 (film), 113
Nitis, George:
  testimony of, 259
Nussbaum, Fred (juror), 186

O

Oelrichs, Mrs. Hermann, 49
Onassis, Jacqueline Kennedy,
  50, 135
O'Neill, Joy, 291, 295, 297,
  315, 318, 322, 323, 326, 338,
  339, 347, 352; as witness for
  the defense, 283–85;
  investigated by Lt. John
  Reise, 299–303; testimony
  discredited by rebuttal
  witnesses, 304–305
Onyenokoproh, Chukwemaka,
  244
Orsini-Rosenberg, Prince, 16
Otis, Paul (alternate juror),
  330

P

Pacia, Shalla (juror), 186
Paiva, Aldina (juror), 186–87,
  336, 339
Pare, Capt. Edward, 133,
  136
Passanante, Sheila Anne:
  testifies as defense
  witness, 291
Pell, Senator Claiborne, 59,
  155, 222
Philadelphia Story, The
  (Barry), 53
Pines, Dr. Kermit:
  testimony for
  prosecution, 266, 267
Porter, Cole, 15, 53
Pound, Ezra, 29
Profumo, John, 37

R

Raether, Nancy:
  testimony as prosecution
  rebuttal witness, 304–05
Reise, Lt. John, 1–2, 133,
  159–60, 172, 190, 195, 200,
  204, 216, 239, 247, 248, 251,
  281, 291, 294–95, 307, 329,
  335, 336; begins
  investigation of Von Bülow
  case, 135–45; and
  discrepancies in Sunny Von
  Bülow's "drug/alcohol
  problem," 137–39;
  interviews Leslie Baxter,
  139–40; first confrontation
  with Von Bülow, 141–45;
  interviews Von Bülow at
  Clarendon Court, 146–52;
  and Dr. George Cahill,
  155–56; testifies as pretrial
  witness, 195–99;
  investigation of Joy O'Neill,
  299–303; testimony on Dr.
  Carr, 306; Von Bülow's
  anger at, 346
Reise, Susan Sullivan, 135, 138
"Richard Cory" (Robinson),
  321
Ripa, Lt. Paul, 117
  testimony for
  prosecution, 235
Roberts, Charlie (Von Bülow
  chauffeur), 305–306,
  326–27; testifies as defense
  witness, 282–83
Robinson, Edwin Arlington,
  321

Rosenberg (doctor prescribing Valium to Leslie Baxter), 139

Rothschild, Edmund de, 36

Rothschild, Pauline de, 292

Russell, Rosalind, 39

Ryan, Nin, 314

S

Salzman, Marshall (locksmith), 295, 322; engaged in search for Von Bülow's black leather bag, 129–30; testifies as defense witness, 279–81

Sanders, Jill, 301–302, 304

Schloss Mittersell: history of, 14–18

Schrallhammer, Maria, 2, 22, 23, 40, 56, 69, 80, 86, 88, 94–95, 97, 106, 107, 112, 123–24, 128, 132, 136, 138, 139, 141, 153, 156, 195, 209, 212, 216, 217, 218, 243–44, 250, 266–67, 275, 280, 281, 298, 306, 315–16, 318, 320, 321, 323, 324, 327, 334, 338, 341, 347, 352, 354, 355, 356, 359; devotion to Sunny Von Bülow, 20–21; and Sunny's first coma (1979), 74–79; finds black leather bag in Von Bülow's closet, 89–91; discovers insulin in Von Bülow's bag, 106; writes letter of distress to friend, 109–11; second letter to friend, 134; as witness for prosecution, 223–29; cross-examined by defense, 229–33

Seddens, Elizabeth, 270n

Shaw, Winifred (juror), 186

Sheehan, John, 1, 147, 148, 158, 159, 160–61, 169, 177, 183, 196–98, 200–203, 238–39, 248, 260, 284, 290, 293, 337, 348, 351, 353; hired by Claus Von Bülow, 155

Silvia, Barbara (juror), 187

Silvia, Irene (Von Bülow cook), 113, 234

Sinatra, Frank, 53

Slocum, Mrs. John, 180

Stanley, Oliver, 29

Stock, Dr. Richard, 67, 76, 85–86, 87, 90, 91, 94, 95–96, 131–32, 139, 150, 212–13, 219, 227, 237, 275, 282, 297, 329; treats Sunny Von Bülow's head wound and asprin toxicity, 107–109; as witness for prosecution, 261–67; cross-examined by defense, 263–65

Sullivan, Mrs. (Von Bülow maid), 74, 88, 338; testimony for the prosecution, 234–35

Szápáry, Countess, 50

T

Taffs, David (juror), 186, 337, 339

Taracani, Jim (TV cameraman):

interview with Claus Von
Bülow, 170–71
Tarnower, Dr. Herman, 344
Television coverage of trial
proceedings, 166–67, 342–43
Thaw, Eugene:
testifies as defense
witness, 286–87
Thompson, Thomas, 270n
Trial proceedings:
grand jury indictment,
157–58; arraignment, 161;
postponement of trial to
January 1982, 165; attempt
to move location of trial,
166; television coverage of,
166–67, 342–43; pretrial
motions, 167–68; first day of
trial (January 11, 1982),
171–75; selection of jury
(voir dire), 176–82; first
week of trial, 182–84; profile
of the jury, 185–87; motion
to bar press from pretrial
hearings, 188–90; three
principal pretrial defense
motions, 190–204; jury tours
Clarendon Court, 205–208;
prosecution's opening
statement, 208–209;
defense's opening statement,
209–15; case for the
prosecution, 216–33, 234–44,
248–60, 261–69, 271–78; case
for the defense, 279–95;
author's analysis and
questions about, 295–98;
rebuttal witnesses called by
prosecution, 304–308; final
summation by defense,
320–22; final summation by
prosecution, 322–28; Judge
Needham's charge to the
jury, 330–32; jury
deliberation, 1–6, 333–35;
jury brings in guilty verdict,
335–36; author on jury
deliberations, 337–40;
author on public sympathy
for criminal rather than
victim, 343–45
Trilling, Diana, 344
Trotta, Liz, 3
Trumbauer, Horace, 52

V

Van Alen, Jimmy, 63–64
Van Buren, Happy, 314
Vanderbilt, Cornelius II, 50
Vanderbilt, George
Washington II, 48
von Auersperg, Alexander,
4–5, 45, 46–47, 59, 63, 69,
73–74, 75, 78–79, 80–81, 86,
90–91, 105, 106, 109, 112, 123,
132, 133, 136, 141–42, 150,
151, 153, 160, 162, 163–64,
191, 192, 199, 207, 209,
213–14, 216, 227, 229, 250,
261, 262, 273–74, 279–81,
296, 298, 311, 312, 321,
322–23, 328, 338, 347,
355–56, 359; relationship
with half-sister Cosima,
43–44; informed by mother
of her intention to divorce
Von Bülow, 72, 105;

von Auersperg (cont'd.)
coming-of-age party for,
101–102; and mother's
second coma (December
1980), 113–17; first visit to
Richard Kuh, 126–27; finds
bag with insulin, 127–32;
pretrial relationship with
Cosima, 158–59; testifies as
pretrial witness, 193–95; as
witness for prosecution,
217–20; cross-examined by
defense, 220–23
von Auersperg, Hetty, 17, 23
von Auersperg, Prince Alfred
"Alfie," 74, 83, 92, 210, 229;
courtship and marriage to
Sunny Crawford, 16–18;
married life in Kitzbühel,
19–26; attitude toward
marriage, 22; divorced from
Sunny, 26; relationship with
Sunny as ex-husband, 59,
100
von Pantz, Baron Hubert,
15–16
von Pantz, Terry McConnell,
16, 24, 25
Von Bülow, Claus:
childhood of, 27–30;
educated at Cambridge, 30;
changes name from Borberg
to Bülow, 32; social life as
bachelor, 31–33; as assistant
to J. Paul Getty, 33–35;
various reactions to
personality of, 35–38;
rumors about, 38; London
friends of, 37–38; meets

Sunny von Auersperg, 25;
marriage to Sunny von
Auersperg, 26; first years of
marriage, 39–47; leaves
Getty organization, 42;
adds "Von" to name, 43;
birth of daughter Cosima,
43–44; coldness to Sunny's
old friends, 45–46; moves to
Clarendon Court, 48–59;
need to impress others with
wealth, 57–58; differences
from Sunny in attitudes
toward money, 62–64;
begins affair with
Alexandra Isles, 64–66;
begins working for Mark
Millard, 66–67; informs
friends of Sunny's
"drinking problem," 67–69;
becomes
"economy-minded," 70–71;
addiction to Valium, 76;
and wife's first coma
(December 1979), 73–84;
interview with Dr. Gailitis
after first coma, 82–83;
letter to Dr. Gailitis, 86–89;
Sunny establishes trust fund
for, 91–94; and Ala's
marriage to Franz Kneissl,
98–100; and Alexandra
Isles, 102–105; wife enters
second coma (December
1980), 111–18; urges family to
remove wife's life-support
systems, 125–26; insulin
found in black bag of,
127–32; trip to Nassau with

Alexandra, 132, 133–34, 141; first confrontation with Lt. John Reise, 141–45; interviewed by Reise at Clarendon Court, 146–52; reactions to family's investigation, 153–54; hires lawyer John Sheehan, 155; indicted by grand jury, 157–58; indignities at arraignment of, 161; post-arraignment reactions of family and friends, 162–64; dress and demeanor in courtroom, 169–70; cooperation with TV cameraman, 170–71; first day of trial, 171–75; behavior in courtroom and at recesses, 183–84; exchanges with press, 245–46; interviewed by author, 309–19; found guilty on both counts, 335–36; public support for, 340–43; anger at Lt. John Reise, 346; TV interview with Barbara Walters, 348–50; day of sentencing, 352–54; post-trial behavior of, 357–59. See also Trial proceedings

Von Bülow, Cosima, 6, 20, 45, 83, 105, 111, 113, 114, 116, 123, 124, 128, 132, 141, 153, 162, 164, 211, 213, 221, 273, 313, 315–16, 320, 339, 352–53; birth of, 43–44; relationship with half-brother Alexander, 43–44; pretrial relationship with siblings, 158–59; post-trial portrait of, 354–57

Von Bülow Hans, 43

Von Bülow, Martha "Sunny": birth of, 9; childhood of, 9–12; appearance as "less than bright," 10–11; overprotected by mother and grandmother, 11, 13; early friendships, 11–12; friendship with Peggy Bedford, 11–12; debut season of, 12–13; self-consciousness about education, 13–14; reading habits of, 13; romance with Georgi Wasilichicoff, 14; sent off to Schloss Mittersell, 14–18; courtship and marriage to Prince Alfred von Auersperg, 16–18; married life in Kitzbühel, 19–26; devotion of maid Maria Schrallhammer, 20–21; friendship with Honeychile Hohenlohe, 22–24; meets Claus Von Bülow, 25; marriage to Von Bülow, 26; first years of marriage, 39–47; birth of daughter Cosima, 43–44; husband's coldness to old friends of, 45–46; moves to Clarendon Court, 48–59; painfulness of social life for, 58–59; relationship with ex-husband Alfie, 59, 100;

Von Bülow (cont'd.)
affection for her dogs,
60–61; sense of humor of,
61; has plastic surgery on
face and neck, 61;
differences from husband in
attitudes toward money,
62–64; alleged "drinking
problem" of, 67–69; tells
son Alexander of intention
to divorce Von Bülow, 72,
105; enters first coma
(December 1979), 73–84;
emergency-room tests,
79–80; interviewed by
psychiatrist John Carr
following coma, 84; settles
trust fund on husband,
91–94; diagnosed as
hypoglycemic, 94–97; and
Ala's marriage to Franz
Kneissl, 98–100; and
Alexander's coming-of-age
party, 101–102; learns of
husband's Manhattan
apartment, 103; suffers
aspirin toxicity and
resulting head wound,
107–109; enters second
coma (December 1980),
111–18

W

Wagner, Cosima, 43
Wagner, Richard, 43
Wallace, Helen, 11
Walters, Barbara:
television interview with
Claus Von Bülow, 348–50
Ward, Stephen, 37
Warmack, Robert, 8, 9,
Warmack, Mrs. Robert, 8, 9,
11
Wasilichicoff, Georgi:
romance with Sunny
Crawford, 14, 83
Weymouth, Lally, 169
Wilhelmina (queen of the
Netherlands), 15
Williams, Wayne, 166
Wilson, Theo, 3, 188–89
Winslow, John, 55
Wodehouse, P. G., 29
Woodward, Ann, 163
Woodward, Elsie, 163
Wright, William:
interview with Claus Von
Bülow, 309–19

Z

Zuercher, Donald W. (juror),
177–78, 186, 338, 339